W9-CJN-183

WITHDRAWN

Also by Lucy Sprague Mitchell

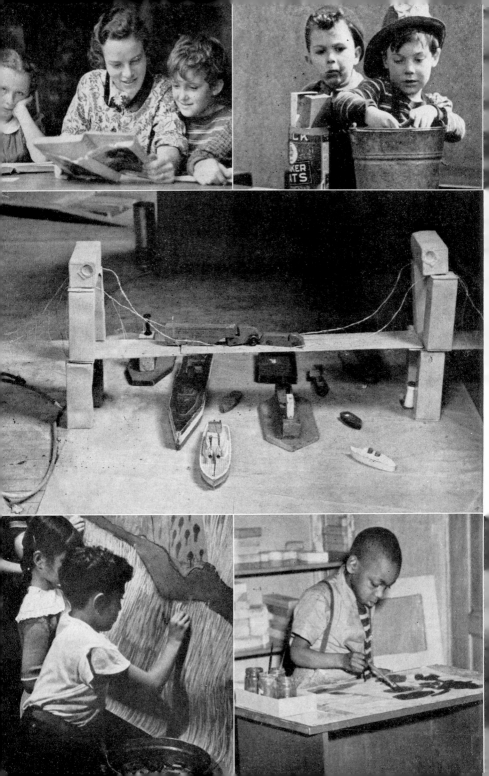

OUR CHILDREN
AND OUR SCHOOLS

*A Picture and Analysis of How Today's Public School Teachers Are
Meeting the Challenge of New Knowledge and New Cultural Needs*

By LUCY SPRAGUE MITCHELL

Chairman of the Bank Street Schools

SIMON AND SCHUSTER · NEW YORK · 1950

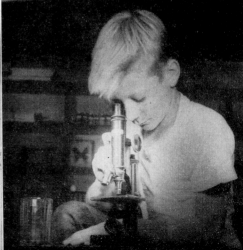

The photographs on the title page and jacket are reproduced with the kind permission of: Bank Street School for Teachers; Florence Ellsworth, courtesy of Parents Magazine *and City and Country School; Ethel Tyrrell, courtesy of the Board of Education of the City of New York; and the Pragan Studios.*

MANUFACTURED IN THE UNITED STATES OF AMERICA
BY KINGSPORT PRESS, INC., KINGSPORT, TENN.

To Harriet Johnson

WHO STILL LIVES IN THE HEARTS

AND THE WORK OF MANY

Foreword

HOW can modern methods in education be made to apply effectively in large city public schools? It was this question, which perplexes many, that set the Bank Street staff off on a series of experiences in co-operation with the New York City Board of Education.

Within this book, a documentation of these experiences is presented. In addition, the book focuses on the extensive work of a group of professionals who have bound themselves together for research, teaching of children, teacher education, and professional improvement. This group we have come to know as Bank Street.

Many public schools have undertaken programs of improvement. Only a few have had the resources to document the processes by which reorientation and improvement were achieved. Teachers and supervisors are so busy carrying out their assignments that they have little time to record, much less to communicate to others, the results of their work and thinking. The process of curriculum development itself is so time-consuming and exacting, and the resources for research and writing are so limited, that some of the best work done is never known outside of the group participating in it.

This project is set in the matrix of a city school system of approximately one million pupils and forty thousand teachers. This school system is seeking to make operative the ways of working outlined in this report. Such concepts as the following are basic to this program.

Effective curriculum work is a peer operation. Teachers, supervisors, parents, specialists, and research workers all participate at the point where each has something to show. Children, too, are active members of this team. It is recognized that the experiences of everyone are important. This principle also applies to the work of the teacher in the classroom.

The school plant and the community are important resources for curriculum development. They are used as the basis for many of the experiences in the classroom. They provide firsthand content, out of which experiences are forged.

The Workshop is recognized as one of the best ways of launching a program of curriculum improvement. The informal atmosphere in which it is conducted provides a setting where real problems may be considered in a sympathetic manner. By showing "how," it helps teachers to organize themselves to operate classrooms on a permissive, rather than an autocratic, basis.

When one understands children one has a much better basis for working with them and for them. Because of intensive work which the Bank Street staff has done in combining teaching of children with research studies on how children mature, they have been able to inject into the curriculum a more realistic understanding of children—what is important to them, how they learn and develop.

Action or co-operative research can be a rewarding experience for both teacher and research worker. Teachers participating gain materially in their insight as to growth processes. Since action research combines the practical and the theoretical, the result is much more readily understood and can be applied more quickly in a classroom situation.

In carrying through the project which is described in this book, the Bank Street group has brought to bear what we know about child growth and development. They have applied group processes to the training of teachers, both as persons and as professional workers. They have developed and applied practical techniques of using resources which help teachers carry forward their instructional programs. These resources are both human and material. Printed materials and visual materials have a place as resources, as do the situations which children face at school, at home, and in the community; these situations are being recognized as important curriculum material.

It is significant that this whole project was launched as an inservice program. Out of that inservice program it was possible to determine more effectively the needs of teachers—both expressed and unexpressed. Building on the premise that a program of improvement must start where teachers now are, the work has progressed to the point where it has significance for all schools concerned with the democratic process and with better ways of working with teachers and children and parents. It is a living example of extending the American heritage through good education.

WILLIAM H. BRISTOW

Acknowledgments

PARTS of this book have long been in the making and my indebtedness extends to many more people than I can thank. Here in this book is the impress of the twelve early experimental schools in which I worked. In particular, there are pages that bear evidence of the influence of two early colleagues with whom I worked for over twenty years, both charter members of the Bureau of Educational Experiments: Harriet Johnson, one of the first scientist-teachers of young children, first director of our Nursery School which now bears her name; and Elisabeth Irwin, daring experimenter with a broad social vision, founder of the Little Red School House.

To the present staff of the Bank Street Schools I also owe much. If I were to acknowledge my debt to all the colleagues who have clarified my thinking about children and schools, the list would indeed be long. I can mention only a few who, in their several ways, have helped me to wider perspectives: Dr. Barbara Biber, whose scientific approach to the study of children has never lessened her human warmth; Dr. Agnes Snyder, whose critical powers combined with social vision have been a stimulus and support ever since we collaborated on a Social Studies Series for children; and Jessie Stanton, who for long years has generously let me use her insight into the way young children think and feel as a testing ground for my own work and thinking.

Part II of this book describes six years of the work of the Bank Street Workshops, of which I was chairman for the first three years.

Since then, the chairman has been Charlotte Biber Winsor, a teacher of children and adults who raises her profession to both a science and an art. Though I held the pen, this part of the book, in a very real sense, is a joint product of the Bank Street Workshop staff. The planning and thinking is theirs. The records used are theirs. It would be inappropriate for me to thank them, for this book has been written for them and with them. Rather, I here acknowledge their contributions both to the active work and to this book. First, the contributions of the two Bank Street staff members who, with myself, planned our first Workshop and for the first year carried on the actual work in addition to our full-time jobs at Bank Street: Eleanor Hogan, Chairman of the Executive Committee of the Bank Street School for Teachers, who manages to hold primary issues steady in the midst of administrative problems, and whose devotion, skill, and energy have made it possible for us to continue our Workshops; and Dr. Barbara Biber, Director of the Bank Street Division of Studies and Publications, who has remained an active member of the Workshop staff. During the six years of our Workshop story covered in this book, the following people have been Workshop staff members, some consecutively, others for a brief time, and most of them on part time: Barbara Biber, Eleanor Hogan, Charlotte Biber Winsor, Claudia Lewis, Agnes Sailer, Dorothy Stall, Virginia Schonborg; and as Board of Education appointments, Tillie S. Pine, Annette Frank, Vivienne Hochman, Salina Cypres. Each has made her contribution. Particular acknowledgments are due to Mrs. Winsor, who wrote Chapter 14, and to Dr. Snyder, who wrote Chapter 19.

I and my colleagues gratefully recognize our indebtedness to many officials in the Public School System of New York City for help in formulating our first Bank Street Workshop and for advice and sustained support in carrying out its developments. In particular we wish to thank: Dr. John E. Wade, formerly Superintendent of Schools; Dr. William Jansen, Superintendent of Schools; Miss Regina C. M. Burke, Associate Superintendent; Miss Ethel F. Huggard, Associate Superintendent; Dr. Steven F. Bayne, Associate Superintendent, now retired; Dr. Jacob Greenberg, Associate Superintendent; Dr. John F. Conroy, Assistant Superintendent, Assigned to Superintendent; Dr. George Zuckerman, Assistant Superintendent; Dr. John J. Loftus, Assistant Superintendent; Dr. Edward J. Bernath, Assistant Superintendent; and Dr. William H. Bristow, Director, Bureau of Curriculum Research, who has placed us still further in his debt by writing a Foreword to this book.

Our thanks reach out to those schools where we came as strangers and were soon accepted as members of the school family. We wish we could name each one of you, for without your understanding help, we could have accomplished nothing. To the principals and assistants to the principals in the schools disguised as Schools I, II, and III, we render individual and sincere thanks. We remember, too, all of the teachers too numerous to mention by name who helped to work out a realistic approach to the problem of inservice education. And if we do not thank you, it is because we think of you as colleagues to whom thanks seem inappropriate. These feelings of ours explain why we have used that word "our" so freely in speaking of the schools in which we conducted Workshops.

Another group we wish to thank—those whose financial help has made it possible for Bank Street to conduct Workshops in public schools. The funds we have received have covered about half the Workshop expenses. The other half has been contributed by Bank Street itself largely through unpaid, overtime work on the part of the staff, which indicates how seriously Bank Street believes in public education. We thank the following, from whom, in different years and in varying amounts, we have received financial support for the Bank Street Workshops: The Field Foundation, New York Fund for Children, Independent Aid, Inc., New Land Foundation, and several individuals. For a number of years the Board of Education through its appointments of teachers on the staff has made it possible for our work to be effective.

Of the Bank Street staff members who worked on the manuscript, I owe very special thanks to Dr. Snyder, who helped to organize and edit the entire manuscript, and Dr. Biber and Mrs. Winsor, helpful critics throughout the writing and editing periods. I thank also the secretaries for their valiant work, in particular Roselyn Sherman and Marian Weber.

LUCY SPRAGUE MITCHELL

69 Bank Street
New York 14, New York
May 19, 1950

Contents

PART II

Our Public Schools in Action: Stages of Workshop Growth

PART III

Broad Learnings and Implications of Workshop Experience

PART IV

What Next?

Introducing
the Problem, the Book, and the Authors

CRITICAL times are questioning times. We feel confused and without direction when our old ways do not work. We feel something has gone wrong somewhere in our basic cultural patterns and attitudes that we were not able to prevent a new crisis or are not better able to handle it when it comes. And we wonder what we should do about it. It is so today in these critical worrying times. One of the questions many people are asking is, "How can our schools be improved—how can they develop people equal to the problems that their own lives and the times bring to them?" This question is asked wishfully, perhaps, in the hope that if we find an answer, we may get nearer to the solution of some of our social problems.

We are writing this book not to answer this question dogmatically but to express what kind of thinking about children and teachers our schools are leaving and toward what kind of thinking they are moving. The times have brought forth a deepened interest in children and in education which warrants an attempt to state what today's schools are beginning to consider their job, and in what practical ways their new job has changed the curriculum and the school's atmosphere. It seems both important and timely to set down the results of comparatively new research and experimentation which tell us what children are like, their ways of learning and feeling, their ways of growing; to express something, too, of what teachers are like and how they grow. Our children and our schools are beginning to be studied with a scientific attitude and scientific methods. To us this seems a momentous cultural advance. This book is our attempt not only to state some of the scientific findings but to show "applied science"—children and teachers in action.

We believe that in these critical times, many groups of people, both lay and professional, want to know more about the direction in which our schools are moving and why. So we are addressing this book both to the lay public and to school people—in particular to those whose jobs concern children of elementary school ages. This approach to lay and professional groups in one book is intentional. Both the public and school folk have a large stake in our children's schools. This common concern must develop a common basis of understanding and a common goal for our schools. The hope for our schools rests ultimately upon active working together of the public and professional school people.

Happily, an increasing proportion of the lay public—parents and citizens at large—feel a responsibility for what happens to our children in our schools. Today's schools want a "good life" for children while they are children; they also want children to develop in ways that will give them an intelligent, interested and responsible approach to whatever problems lie ahead for our country. Happily, an increasing number of people want for our children what our schools are trying to accomplish. For these people we shall try to show, not by philosophical statements but by concrete illustrations, how their schools are approaching their job and what children and teachers need in order to make it possible for schools to accomplish this job.

We are also addressing this book to professional people whose jobs concern schools and teachers—school systems, school administrators, teacher education organizations, people who are conducting Workshops for teachers who are already teaching. And finally, and quite definitely, we are addressing this book to teachers.

The plan of this book needs a word of explanation. We feel that there is a need not only for general discussion of what today's education is aiming at but also a need for detailed accounts, with reports of both failures and successes, of how special educational problems or situations have been attacked. This book, therefore, attempts not merely to tell the directions in which modern education is moving but to tell in some detail the story of one current educational experiment which we, the authors, are conducting.

Who are we? We are a group that back in 1916 asked the question that many people are asking now, "How can our schools be improved—how can they develop people equal to the problems that their own lives and the times bring to them?" The original group started an organization, the Bureau of Educational Experiments (now generally known as the Bank Street Schools), to work toward an answer to this question. They believed the question could be approached with a scientific attitude; that the ultimate answer must be based, as is all science, on careful observation and experimentation, checked and rechecked. They believed such an undertaking demanded a close give-and-take relationship between research and education—the interaction between the study of children and how they grow and the working out of a good life within the school for children in progressive stages of development. To accomplish such a program the staff was composed of a group of specialists—doctor, psychologists, teachers, social worker—who together determined the problems to be studied, shared their findings and made a joint study of implications in terms of children and teachers and their school experiences—their curriculum. After thirty-four years we, the present group, still hold these beliefs and still function as a co-operative, experimental group of school people and research workers.

We grew, one undertaking leading to another. In 1919 we started what was in those days a pioneer experiment, the Bureau Nursery School, at 144 West Thirteenth Street, now the Harriet Johnson Nursery School. There the give-and-take between research and school was very close. Harriet Johnson, our Nursery's first director, and the teachers developed behavior records of young children along with an experimental curriculum, first for two- and three-year-olds, later expanding through four- and five-year-olds. From these behavior records combined with family histories, the records made by physician, psychologists, and teachers came our first formulation of maturity levels for young children. Maturity levels included stages of growth in physical development, interests or drives, the kind of relationships the children could understand, their ways of learning, their growing independence of adults, and their emotional stability.

During this same period we were working with children of elementary school ages and their teachers, first in the City and Country School, and later as educational advisers to a number of schools. This led us directly into teacher education. Directors and teachers of schools who were experimenting with curriculum based on the study of children met at our library for discussions of children and curriculum. Always came the question, "Where can we get teachers who understand what we are trying to do?" In 1930 in answer to this pressing question we started the Cooperative (now the Bank Street) School for Teachers, so called because "co-operating schools" worked with us on an experimental curriculum in teacher education and took our students into their classrooms for practical experience with children.

From the beginning, our curriculum for our students was built on the conviction that a teacher of children must be far more than a good technician, though, of course, he must be that. A good teacher must have a scientific approach; he must have zest for his work; he must enjoy living with children; he must enter into a broader, larger life than that of the classroom. In attempting to develop such teachers we organized our curriculum around experiences planned to give understanding of children, understanding of the modern world, experimental experience with the arts, acquisition of classroom skills, and insight into curriculum building.

Though there have been many changes, this basic framework has not been fundamentally altered during the years. Nor has the basic means for carrying out our aims been changed. That is, we are still as in the beginning having students spend the major part of their time—four full days a week—in the classroom, and the rest of the week—about a day and a half—in classes, seminar, studio and laboratory work supplementing and interpreting the work with children in the classrooms.

Gradually, too, publications became an important part of our work. We combined this with research as a Division of Studies and Publications. Within this Division developed the Writers' Laboratory—a group of writers writing for and about children. Books for children were now added to the growing list of publications which our research staff produced. Through this threefold organization it has been possible to maintain that relationship between study of children, education of teachers, and research that we believe to be essential to a vital educational program.

Our teaching, both of children in the Harriet Johnson Nursery School and of students in the Bank Street School for Teachers, has absorbed the implications of our research findings and, in time, our research program has taken its direction from the continuously evolving problems of our educational activities; our findings and the materials we have developed have resulted in publications. We have tried out procedures, made systematic observations and analyses, in the "natural" laboratory of the classroom as well as under controlled laboratory conditions, and reported results so that they might be given wider scrutiny and use.

Now our Nursery School, our Bank Street School for Teachers, and our Division of Studies and Publications, still one organization, housed at 69 Bank Street, are commonly known as the Bank Street Schools or just Bank Street.

Our early work with children and teachers required small-scale, fluid situations where experimental work could be carried on and full records kept. But such work we always regarded as preliminary laboratory work. Public schools always held our deepest interest, and our ultimate aim was to make our experiences a contribution to public education. In 1943 we were asked to co-operate with a committee of the Board of Education composed of modern-minded men and women who were engaged in revising the curriculum for New York City schools. This meant much to us from two points of view. From the personal point of view, it gave us a real working relationship with public education—which had been our goal from the beginning. From a broader point of view, it meant that public education was reorganizing its school curricula along lines we had worked on and believed in for so many years. Soon the Bank Street School for Teachers was launched on the experiment of conducting Workshops for teachers in public schools.

In Part II, which is addressed to professional school folk more than the rest of the book, we shall tell rather fully the story of these Bank Street Workshops. It is only one of many experiments in one of today's many school problems. It will, however, illustrate how our convictions about children and teacher education work out realistically in city public schools. It will illustrate also a give-and-take relationship between those who are studying children and teachers who are teaching them—the interaction of research and school. Of necessity, any single experiment is local. Yet we believe the problems that Bank Street and the New York City public school administration and the teachers and the children faced in this experiment are typical of those found in most of our schools. We all learned much in working together on these problems. Our hope is that what we learned may be of use to others—both to the lay public and to professional school people—who want our schools to catch up with the times.

PART I

What Our Schools Are Leaving; Moving Toward

1. A GOOD LIFE: FOR CHILDREN; FOR TEACHERS
2. THE SCHOOL'S JOB
3. WHAT SCHOOLS ARE DOING TO CARRY OUT THEIR JOB
4. SCHOOLS MUST FACE THE TIMES

1

A Good Life: For Children; For Teachers

MOST people, in a hazy, good-natured way, would like everyone to have a good life—at least if it wouldn't interfere with their own pleasures and prospects. Fewer feel it their job to see that this comes about. Most people would like children, in particular, to have a good life. Parents commonly feel it is their job to help this to come about—at least for their own children while they are children. And many parents feel that they have failed in a measure if their children are not able to make a good life for themselves in the world which they later live in as adults. What about schools? A large part of children's lives is lived in schools. Do schools feel that it is their job to see that children have a good life there? Do schools feel in a measure responsible if their children fail to develop ways that will give them a good life as adults?

Yes, today's schools are beginning to take on this twofold job—to give children a good life while they are children and to give each child opportunities, within his potentiality, to develop ways that will lead toward a good life as an adult. Schools are beginning to feel, as parents do, that their twofold job is really one—that the best chance to have a good life as an adult lies in having had a sound childhood. Schools are beginning to feel that it is their job to see that teachers, too, have a good life, both for the sake of teachers themselves and for the children they teach. Children and teachers live side by side in one room for many hours a day. Neither

3

children nor teachers can have a truly good life unless both have it. Indeed, the essence of a good life for either children or teachers is that they live it together.

WHAT IS A GOOD LIFE?

In its essentials it is the same for both teachers and children. For both are human beings. No matter what their age, healthy human beings have certain qualities or characteristics with corresponding needs which demand satisfactions for a good life. Every person, young or old, is *sensitive to the attitude of other people towards himself.* In maturity, it is obvious that the degree of his sensitivity and the expression it takes depend upon the individual and what has happened to him. There are some lonely souls who seem able to walk through adult life without human companionship. But their very loneliness indicates that they are not completely indifferent to human relationships. Only a Buddha can attain to an existence without awareness of his fellow men, and who among us has ever met a Buddha? The old Greeks considered the severest punishment that could be meted out to a human being was to ostracize him. William James said that no person could keep his sanity if all his fellow creatures ignored him. We all need attention, at least at times. Adults have their own ways of "getting attention" as well as children!

We all need to be thought well of, too. We adults know that we work more efficiently in an atmosphere of approval than in an atmosphere of hostility or indifference where we don't count. We may plod on in such an atmosphere if for any reason we feel that we must. But we are not satisfied, not happy, nor is our work as good as in situations where our efforts arouse interest or support from others. And this holds true for teachers both in their personal and in their professional lives.

As for children, psychologists now tell us that from babyhood up, they are extremely sensitive to the attitudes of people around them. Babies and young children get this needed sense of approval

Taken together, these two human characteristics—the urge to
find out and the urge to do something about what has been found
out—make real education possible. Together, they form the basis of
thinking, of learning, which is essentially the same process in children and adults. Learning is essentially taking in something and
then giving out something that makes what we have taken in a part
of ourselves. Children and adults alike need what we can call "intake" and "outgo" in order really to learn. It is by this twofold
process that we see relationships between isolated facts or experiences. And seeing relationships is a distinguishing characteristic of
human learning.

Take an adult reading a book or listening to a lecture or exposed
to any other situation from which he may "take in" factual information. He may intellectually comprehend the fact before him and
yet be left entirely unmoved if he sees no connection between this
information and something that he has already experienced and
which really interests him. In this case, the information will probably not stay with him. He will forget it. If, however, this information fits into some interest, some drive of his, it may "give
him a new idea." A new idea means seeing a new relationship,
putting an old 2 with another old 2 and forming a 4 which is
quite distinct from either 2. No one gets a new idea without active
exertion. A genuinely new idea causes an inner excitement: it is
like an explosion inside one. It starts a series of new activities because of the human urge to do something about anything that
arouses interest. A new idea may lead to mental turmoil in trying
to follow out the relationship of this new idea to the old ones; it
may also lead to a plan of action to test out the idea; and if the
inner excitement has sufficient driving force and circumstances permit, it may lead to physical activities which are in some way related
to this new idea. All of these are active responses. Thinking and
planning are "doing something about it" as genuinely as physical
expressions. If an individual responds actively to some new information or experience, then, and then only, it becomes a genuine

part of him. He will have digested or have begun to digest this new information or experience and to that extent he will have grown. Unless he completes the learning process and makes this idea his own by doing something about it, the idea will fade. He can hardly be said to have learned. The situation is fundamentally the same whatever the form his activity takes—an art expression, an intellectual working out of the consequences of the new idea, a practical application in his work whether his work lies in the home, the school, or anywhere else.

Growing children whose lives are crowded with new impressions and new experiences have a tremendous urge to get into action in some way. Small children get into action through their play. Play to them is really their work. Their play is based on some interest aroused in their experiences. Through their play they digest their experiences and grow. Older children have this same urge to do something about anything that interests them. Their interests gradually expand to include more complicated behavior in the physical world around them and finally to the social world. They cannot really learn new facts or experiences passively. Digestion is an active, not a passive process. The forms their active expression may take are manifold and may not be the same for all children. But the need to translate information and experience into their own terms is common to all. To accumulate facts with no digestion of those facts in terms of using them in active thinking or some active form of expression is a parody of learning—an empty form which is not conducive to growth. To go through the motions of expression and thinking with no intellectual curiosity as the driving force is equally an empty form and not conducive to growth. A good life is a learning life.

One more all-important characteristic of young or old human beings is that they *react to situations as a whole*—not piecemeal. They are organisms—not machines. What happens to any part affects the whole. Bodily, mental, and emotional satisfactions are all interactive in complicated organic ways. A good life is one in which the whole person—child or adult—is functioning fully.

What, then, is a good life? As human beings, children and teachers together need for their good life an atmosphere of approval, not of hostility; of belonging, not of being left out; an opportunity to find out about things that interest them; and an opportunity to express or to do something about what they have found out. The whole child or the whole adult is involved in the achievement of a good life.

A GOOD LIFE FOR CHILDREN; WHAT CHILDREN ARE LIKE

Children are human beings, yes. But *they are not diminutive adults.* Not any more than an egg is a chicken or, worse still, an old hen or rooster. That children are immature is one of the obvious facts not always thoroughly incorporated into our thinking about them. Physical immaturity is, of course, universally accepted. Yet so anxious are many parents and teachers to have their children "beat the usual" in performance that they tend to wish their children to be more advanced in muscular co-ordination than they are. A parent, for instance, often tries to make a small child walk before the child himself takes on walking because his muscles are ready. A teacher often expects a kindergarten or first-grade child to handle fine brushes and small pieces of paper when the child may still be in the "large muscle stage." Even more common among parents and teachers is the attempt to make him use words and general ideas which are beyond his mental maturity to understand. He may still be using his senses and muscles as both tools of learning and expression, rather than words which are symbols, and generalizations based on many experiences. The picture is worst of all in emotional and social maturity. Adults still try to shame a child out of his immaturity—"Only babies cry, not big boys." Or to make a child take on adult social techniques on moral grounds—"Shake hands with the lady like a good girl." Children are immature in every way—not only in their bodies, but in their concepts, their ability

to function independently, in their ways of expression, in their sense
of social values.

Boys and girls are far more complicated in their make-up than
the neatly parceled out ingredients of the old nursery rhyme—
"snips and snails and puppy dog tails" for boys, and "sugar and
spice and everything nice" for girls. From the moment they are
born, boys and girls react and behave organically; that is, with all
their interrelated and interacting parts. They have bodies and minds
and emotions that make them behave in definite ways. Children
respond to living, actively. Their bodies demand activity—children
respond to life through their legs, their hands, and their whole
muscular setup. Their minds demand activity—children respond to
life by constant inquiry and investigations. Their emotions demand
activity—children are swept by a succession of feelings: fear, confidence, love, hatred, pleasure, anger. Their bodies, minds, emotions
will grow—nothing can stop them. But *how* they will grow, what
their bodies, minds, and emotions will be like as they are growing
and when they are grown, depends to an appreciable extent on how
they are exercised.

A body that is bound or hampered in free muscular activity will
grow, but in distorted ways. It will not attain a healthy development
any more than did the feet of Chinese women in the days when
they were bound. A mind that is bound or hampered in its free
questionings and investigations will grow, but in distorted ways.
It will not attain a healthy development. Children's questionings,
their intellectual curiosities, their urge to investigate will abate
unless they are kept in action. Minds need exercise as much as
bodies. Emotions that are suppressed or hampered in their free expression will grow but in distorted ways. They will not attain
healthy development. Children's relations to other human beings
will become warped or twisted. And such is the complex interaction within a child's organism that an unhealthy condition in one
part may spread to another part. An unhealthy body may produce
unhealthy emotions or a sluggish mind, and vice versa. A child

will not be made up of "everything nice" unless he is healthy
everywhere.

Ages and Stages: Maturity Levels

As children add years to the time they have been living and
experiencing, they gradually add new powers in their ways of
handling their bodies, their minds, their emotions, and their relations to other people. But ages are not the same as stages. Our
children are not equally endowed, nor have they been given equal
opportunities for healthy growth. Children do not "grow up" at
the same rate. There is no exact measuring stick against which
teachers can place a particular first-grade, fifth-grade, or any other
child and know just how satisfied or worried they should be.

Nevertheless, there are growth stages through which every child
passes at his own speed. And a teacher can be satisfied if an individual child or a group of children is growing from one stage to
the next. That is, growth, not any particular performance, is the
significant thing to keep track of.

Though in schools we mark children off chronologically in
grades, every teacher knows that children at each age, in each grade,
cover a wide gamut of stages in their development. The best we
can do is to plan a school life in each grade to fit the development
that most children of that age reach, then modify the school life
to a higher or lower stage of development to fit a particular child
or often a whole group.

Obviously, if we are to help children have a good life it becomes
all-important to pay attention to stages in maturity. At each stage
we must know what gives most children a sense of security, toward
what kinds of things and activities they have the combination of the
urge to learn and the desire "to do something about it," and we
must remember the organic interaction between security and interest drives. Growing up is, at best, a difficult performance. A
school cannot do away with all the difficulties of adjustments which
growing up demands. But surely, a school should reduce the agony

of the process by planning experiences for its children consistent with what we know about the stages of their development, or what is often called "maturity levels."

Psychologists today generally distinguish maturity levels by placing children through two in the "infancy" period; from two through four in the nursery period; five-, six-, and seven-year-olds in a transition to the "middle years"; eight- and nine-year-olds in the "middle years"; ten- and eleven-year-olds in the "preadolescent" period. None of the terms "infancy," "nursery," and "middle years" as used by psychologists seems very happy to laymen. They have more meaning if we think of "infancy" as suggesting that children through the second year are still in a stage of extreme dependence upon adults; that in the succeeding nursery years, from two to five, they become more aware of the world around them and are beginning the process of feeling and asserting individuality as well as gradually moving out of the orbit of home and family into wider group living. The five-, six-, and seven-year-olds are making the transition toward the "middle years," which also include the eight- and nine-year-olds. During this period children take on more realistic, objective patterns of thinking and feeling and are busily preoccupied in learning the skills and absorbing the mores of adults. In the subsequent years of preadolescence (ten- and eleven-year-olds) and adolescence, they begin to work out their roles as independent personalities and members of the adult community. In a general way, elementary schools use these same groupings for their children. They group together kindergarten, first and second grades; third and fourth grades; fifth and sixth grades.

All five-, six-, and seven-year-old children still live largely in the here-and-now world around them, the world both of things and of human beings. They learn about things largely through firsthand experiences where they can find answers to their curiosities through exercising their own senses and muscles. Telling them about experiences of other people, in words, has comparatively little meaning for them. They have little power to "identify" with people with whom they have no personal contacts. The spontaneous play of these young five-, six-, and seven-year-olds not only shows that they live in the here-and-now; it also shows what kinds of things in the world around them interest them and have meaning for them. Play is an essential part of a young child's way of learning.

Gradually children's curiosities extend beyond the here-and-now to the faraway and long-ago. Eight- and nine-year-olds are more capable than younger children of learning through words. But they still need to translate these words into action in their own ways to make them have real meaning. They begin to make a distinction for themselves between play and work, by the latter meaning grown-up work. They learn through both a play and a work approach. Ten- and eleven-year-olds are the preadolescents and are beginning to think about human relations—themselves in relation to others and how people behave toward one another. They are beginning to care about whether or not other people have a good life, to think in terms of values. They can take in more through words than younger children. Also words become a genuine tool for learning. Discussions of their own ideas become extremely important to them. Yet they, too, need direct experiences and to translate words into their own action in their own ways to make words have much meaning to them.

For all the broad characteristics these children have in common in these maturity level groupings, within each grouping there are distinct stages of growth. In the following chapters when we come to planning a good life for children in their schools we must discuss in more detail the characteristics of children from kindergarten through sixth grade. At every stage we must watch what interests them and in what ways they make their investigations in the world they live in. We must watch what experiences help them to grow in healthy ways.

Though in many areas we are still fumbling in our understanding of child development, there are certain patterns of attitudes and interests and activities and expressions that appear with marked regularity in children who have a chance to grow in healthy ways. It is these relatively "free" children whom we must watch first. From them we can learn the potentialities of children in the various maturity levels. Also when it comes to planning for specific children, we have to know to what extent and in what ways their healthy growth has been hampered by their actual life experiences and plan accordingly. For it should go without saying that we have to accept children as they are, and that may be tragically far from what they might have been if they had grown up under different influences or conditions.

What, then, is a good life for children? An active, a full, a rich life of meaningful experiences at each stage of their development. It is a sound humanitarian impulse to give children such lives. But it is more than that. A good life is a life in which one keeps growing in interests, in breadth of emotions and powers of expression, in depth and extent of human relations. Growth in all one's powers, step by step up through the early stages toward maturity, leads on to an adulthood which is not static, completed, but still retains the capacity and the eagerness to grow. Adults, for good or bad, retain in their very fiber the results of their childhood experiences. Children's best chance to be learners, doers, creative, constructive members in the society they live in as adults is to have lived lives which gave these qualities a chance to grow steadily from a child level to an adult level. A good life for children is, above all, a chance to keep growing as "whole children."

A GOOD LIFE FOR TEACHERS; ADULT SATISFACTIONS

A good life for teachers is essentially the same as for children, but on an adult level. What, in particular, are the adult satisfactions which teachers must have? What opportunities for growth?

In Their Personal Lives

It should go without saying that teachers, like other adults, need a full, rich personal life. They need the approval of others, the assurance that they count as human beings, that others value them. They need this in their personal lives as do all human beings—in family life, in personal friends. They need to feel that they are a genuine part of the larger society in which they live, that what they are doing is important.

Teachers need to have active, live, intellectual curiosities which they pursue with eagerness. Adults, like children, can be eager learners unless they have been reduced to mental inertia by lives that gave them little or no opportunity for following up their natural curiosities. Witness the crowds of adults who gather to watch the excavation for a large city building. Witness the flood of newspaper and magazine articles and books on atomic energy that followed the dropping of the first atomic bombs. These, in a large measure, were a response to the desire of adults to learn something that was new. In adults the urge to find out about things which begins with the baby's investigations of his immediate environment should have spread to remote happenings everywhere. The environment which adults should want to explore should have become the world and its people.

Adults, too, need and are capable of inner excitement and active expression of it. Intense emotional excitement may make adults behave in ways which surprise them greatly. Under the stimulus of the announcement of the end of the war, for instance, practically every adult in this country exploded into some physical action, mild or violent. This for adults is, of course, an extreme and very obvious case.

In their personal lives all adults need satisfactions which come from these interest drives—the urge to find out and the urge to get into action. Yet these needs have not always been recognized for teachers. Often they have been set apart as people who do not need personal satisfactions. Women teachers lost their jobs if they married. They were expected to hold aloof from politics and were slightly suspect if they indulged in any art expression. They were supposed to get their satisfactions primarily from the respect of their children and the community. A curious denial that teachers are human beings!

In Their Professional Lives

In their professional lives, too, teachers need the common human satisfactions which make a good life. Here again come the complicated organic interactions within the human being. Only in an atmosphere of approval, not of hostility, only when they feel a success—that they belong to something bigger than themselves—can teachers carry on their work with full efficiency. Teachers must feel they count in their own classrooms in relation to their children. They must feel they count in their own schools in relation to other teachers and to the principal. They must feel they have some share in determining the larger aspects of education, in their school system, in teacher organizations. They must feel they are respected members of their profession, making a contribution. They must get satisfactions by living as whole, fully functioning professional people.

For a good life teachers, again like children, need opportunities to keep growing, to keep learning, to find out something they didn't know before and to make it their own through some active expression or thinking. Their profession should and can bring them great opportunities for growth. Within their own job the closest urges are to find out more about what children are like and what the world in which they live is like, and to put whatever they have found out into action in their lives with children. The more the conception of their job broadens to other children, to other teachers, to schools everywhere, to education in the widest sense, the fuller will be their satisfactions.

Teachers can have the satisfactions of both scientists and artists in their professional lives. They can have the scientific approach to teaching: careful observations of their children, which is gathering evidence; experimental attitude in planning programs for their children, which is testing their data; flexibility in changing plan according to their findings. Teachers can function as artists in building a curriculum. They can be creative, not slavishly bound to a pattern in thinking and planning for and with their children. Yes, the job of teaching affords exciting opportunities for satisfactions and for growth. Teachers have a good life when they are given such opportunities to grow professionally.

The teacher-child and the child-teacher relationship is a close one in a more significant way than spending hours each day together in the same room. There must be a sharing of interest, a sharing of planning, a sharing of putting interests into action. The teacher remains an adult though she becomes a member of the group. Her role is different from the role of the children. But it remains true that teacher and children must have a good life *together,* or neither will have a good life.

2

The School's Job

SCHOOLS are always in transition, or should be. Static education is certainly undesirable if not a contradiction in terms.
Times change. Always new discoveries, new ideas, new problems
are appearing, which give schools new orientation and direction.
At all times we, school and lay folk, should be asking: What are
our schools leaving behind? Toward what are they moving? These
are not easy questions to answer today in our big complicated
United States. Our schools are spread over wide lands which differ
greatly one from the other in natural physical and in man-made
characteristics which have brought about different kinds of work—
agriculture, mining, industry—and in a measure different kinds of
thinking and attitudes. We live in rural areas, in cities, in suburbs,
each bringing about a special way of living. And everywhere are
"our" schools—the products of differing conditions and resultant
thinking.

We are trying not to be black or white in our statements about
today's schools. Can one be dogmatic when we have so many kinds
of schools, so many kinds of worlds in our country? Then, too,
progress is never even, and certainly not in schools. Even within one
city system, we find schools in very different stages of transition:
some that are fairly content with the school thinking and procedures
of forty or so years ago; and some that are questioning this past
thinking in the light which has been thrown upon child development in fairly recent research and experiments in schools and in the

varying pressure of the times, and have moved far in their thinking and procedures.

THE SCHOOL'S JOB: AS IT CONCERNS CHILDREN

To prepare children for adult life has always been a fundamental aim of the school. It still is. The shift in the concept of the school's job is primarily in the kind of life children should live while they are children in order to grow up into well-rounded, fully function- ing adults, equal to meeting their life situations. Schools are moving away from the concept that the best preparation for a good adult life is to train children to take on adult forms of thinking and be- havior as early as possible. Schools once bent their energies on get- ting children to become adults fast. John Dewey once said that peo- ple seemed to think "a promising child" was one who outgrew childhood quickly. Adult manifestations in children were taken to mean growth. Though we believe we are leaving this attitude, it nevertheless persists. Today, in and out of schools, we see many adults expressing this attitude of pushing children toward adult- hood.

Adults who have this attitude toward children are not looking at children objectively. This is a difficult thing for grownups to do. The child-adult relationship is apt to be charged with emotion. In many—perhaps in most—people, small children arouse a warm, protective attitude just as do most helpless small animals. A certain type of person calls children "the poor innocents." Babies and little children are called "cunning," "cute," "sweet"—all indulgent terms of endearment as well as abuse of accurate English! This attitude sometimes degenerates into using children as decorations satisfying to adults. Many little children are dressed not for their own comfort in their own activities but to provide pretty pictures, entertainment for their parents' guests. This parental pride may go deeper than dressing children to look "cute." Parents are proverbially blind about their offspring. They project themselves into their children and are sensitive to any adverse criticism of their children's behavior as well as their looks. This attitude is by no means confined to parents or the family circle. Many teachers, too, particularly teachers of the younger ones, fail to see children objectively as little persons because they are sidetracked by children's picture quality—their sheer beauty and grace—or because of affectionate overidentification with them.

The exact opposite emotional attitude toward children is perhaps as common. To many adults children are profoundly irritating intruders into their adult world. Children's incessant activity, their endless questions, their lack of inhibitions, their self-centered interests certainly do get in the way of orderly adult life. When this happens, many adults are inclined to blame or cajole the interrupting child. Here the adult is interpreting the child's behavior in terms of his own mature standards, unconsciously attributing to the child the same antisocial impulses and motives that would lead an adult to behave in this "childish" way. Discipline, punishment, "training," "breaking his will" result, with the primary aim of protecting the adult's life and making the child fit for adult society. Parents and teachers often evince this attitude at times if not continuously. This impatient, irritable attitude, too, fails to look at children objectively.

Still a third attitude toward children is common. It is based on a sense of responsibility for doing the "right thing" for children. And the "right thing" is sometimes interpreted to mean making a child do something just *because* it is disagreeable. A school director, not many years ago, said he didn't care what his boys studied so long as they didn't like it. This interpretation of the "right thing" for children has waned. Yet the responsibility for children still weighs heavily on conscientious grownups. Many young mothers are so overwhelmed by their sense of responsibility that they are actually afraid of their children and lose spontaneity and pleasure in their relationships with them. Many teachers, too, are afraid to be themselves with their school children, afraid their children will get "out of hand" if they, their teachers, give away the fact that

they are fallible or warmhearted human beings. This attitude may
breed a certain grimness within the home or the classroom. The
grimness may spring from conscientiousness but it is none the less
grim because of its righteous intent. The adult, here, has his eye on
the future "good of the child" and often fails to see the child himself. He is like the person who looks at a window and fails to see
the gorgeous view but notes that the window is covered with fly-
specks. This attitude of attending to the future and ignoring the
present also fails to see children objectively.

Indulgence to the point of sentimentality, irritability to the point
of protective punishment, moral conscientiousness to the point of
grimness—all these and many other common adult attitudes toward
children tell us more what adults are like than what children are
like. They tell us that many adults do not respect children as young
human beings with personalities of their own and ways of their
own. The emotions, varied but intense, which children arouse in
nearly all adults may be one reason why objective study of children
has come so late in the history of science.

In the history of education there are a few people who made a
valiant effort to study children objectively—Pestalozzi, Pryor, Hall,
Stern, Sully. Yet as a science, the objective study of children, except
for sporadic studies, is only forty or so years old. It was then that research organizations in child development and experimental school
curricula for children began in any broad, serious way. About the
same time came intensive study of adult psychology, particularly of
adults who had difficulties in adjusting to their life situations. The
findings of these new studies of human beings, as children and as
adults, produced a veritable wave of new thinking which has affected, to a greater or lesser extent, most of us in our country. From
the objective study of children, in and out of schools, came our
present conception of how children grow and what they are like
in their progressive stages of growth or what we have called maturity levels.

From the study of adults came the realization that maladjustments in adults are commonly rooted in childhood experiences. Insecure children are likely to grow into insecure adults. And it is a major undertaking to make an insecure adult secure enough to handle his life adequately. Children whose eagerness to find out about things has been thwarted rather than fostered are likely to grow into apathetic adults who drift or who simply endure an uninteresting life. Children whose impulse to do something about situations has been thwarted are likely to explode in antisocial action or to grow into inexpressive, inactive adults who are afraid to "give themselves away" through creative effort, who are sideliners, critics rather than doers, and who feel little responsibility for taking an active part in the world they live in. Happily, we believe the reverse is also true—that a happy, secure, fulfilled childhood is commonly an assurance of a satisfying adulthood.

The findings of these objective studies have profoundly changed the concept of how to prepare children for adult life, both inside and outside schools. These findings have shown adults that children at all ages need for healthy all-round growth a life suited to them, not to adults. They have moved schools toward new thinking about *how* to prepare children for adulthood. Children are now regarded as persons (young, but still persons) with individual personalities, and their full quota of emotional impulses and natural intellectual curiosities which adults should respect. Instead of trying to train children to accept adult thinking and behavior on an adult level before they understand what it is all about, schools are trying to help children to live full lives as children, with a chance to learn *how,* not *what,* to think, to learn from direct experiences, through finding satisfaction for their interest drives, and to take on responsibilities which have meaning to them in their own stage of maturity; and thus to help them grow gradually from one stage to another toward mature thinking, mature drives, mature responsibilities. This attitude is based on the conviction that growth is a process proceeding from within, not a conforming to patterns of behavior and thinking imposed from without; that only as children live each stage fully can the next stage be fully lived all the way up to adult-hood. Hence the school's great concern for maturity levels. Another conviction is that children get their humanity through living with human beings. Hence the school's great concern for group living within the classroom.

In brief, this means the schools are moving toward the conception that their job is to give children a good, a full, a rich all-round life at whatever stage of development they have reached, and full opportunities to keep growing at their own rate in their own way in bodies, minds, emotions, and social standards. Put still more briefly, the school's aim is to be a place for children to grow in all-around healthy ways.

How, more specifically, can schools be a place for healthy growth for children of elementary school ages? What needs and impulses of children can be at least partially fulfilled in their school lives? At kindergarten, first and second grades? At third and fourth grades? At fifth and sixth grades? A suggested answer to these questions was drawn up for the teachers in our Bank Street Workshops by our Bank Street psychologist. We believe it will suggest ideas to other teachers and schools who are trying to provide for healthy growth of their children.

SOME NEEDS AND IMPULSES OF CHILDREN THAT CAN BE PARTIALLY FULFILLED IN THEIR SCHOOL LIVES

All children need
> To:
>> feel safe and unafraid;
>> feel that people care about them and are interested in them;
>> feel understood as children and accepted as people;
>> trust people;
>> think well of themselves and develop confidence;
>> get a sense that it's only human to make mistakes—everyone does.
> To:
>> realize rules are needed to make things run smoothly;
>> accept authority without cringing before it;

believe that they are being treated fairly and justly;

form a close group relation among themselves;

have a right to a few secrets of their own;

have a chance to enjoy co-operation more than competition;

live democratically in order to believe in democracy.

To:

play;

be active;

relax;

express their feelings;

make some of their own choices;

have plenty of opportunity to imagine and create;

try out their talents and inclinations.

To:

become skilled and capable;

be entrusted with responsibility;

take some real part in adult affairs;

feel that what they are learning is important and interesting;

have heroes and ideals;

understand the world in which they live;

identify with the miracles of modern life and the adventure of
human progress;

realize that people everywhere are trying to work out the same
problems.

FRAGMENTS OF A GOOD LIFE FOR KINDERGARTEN,
FIRST AND SECOND GRADE

These are the years of growing out of babyhood into childhood, so—
children still need a good deal of mothering from grownups—good
healthy mothering that will let them be quite babyish at times and
take great pleasure in helping them grow up at other times.

They are still really very young in body and spirit, so—

they will get restless if they have to sit still too long,

they may cry if their feelings are hurt,

they get angry quickly and get over it quickly,

they can call names and even strike someone without being "bad"
children.

They should have space and time to use their bodies freely and vigor-
ously and get tired in healthy ways.

They should have warm and hearty people around them, who can laugh with them and never at them.

They will want to talk and will not mind the noise their voices make.

But they are beginning to grow up, so—
   the boys may strut a little,
   and games with rules, simple rules, will be fun to learn,
   and they don't want to be talked down to,
   and they can understand that there are times and places when they must be quiet,
   and they need to be reminded often of many things they mean to do but somehow don't,
   and they get interested, very interested, in finding out the ways of the world around them, and even a budding interest in faraway worlds.

Give them a chance—a few dolls, some cloths, blocks, boxes, a little open space—and they'll play—a wonderful kind of playing in which they rescue people from fires, deliver bread from a bakery, dress the children for school, blow up the airport, kill giants by trampling their images in the wastebasket—and in their playing they will be thinking and learning and wishing and letting off steam.

They need each other when they play—a store clerk has to have a customer, an engineer needs passengers in his train, the farmer needs horses and a baby colt and a wife—and so each gains a kind of importance that comes to people from being needed.

FOR THIRD AND FOURTH GRADE

These are big children who can only patronizingly recall they were once babies.

Teacher doesn't need to be a mother kind of person any more—not obviously, anyway.

She needs to know how to do some things and find out about others.

Here is the time when children develop an urge to do things as they should be done.

That's one way of feeling grown up, and that's a feeling they cherish.

Jobs around the school, real jobs, are important.

From adults they need guidance, direction, information, arbitration.

Give them a chance and they will form a social group that will be almost a world of their own; they will tend to develop customs, verbal expressions, mannerisms that will be very important to them; they will care more for each other's approval than for that of teacher or parent; this is an important chance for children of this age to have because it gives them freedom to find happiness and security among their contemporaries instead of from their elders.

This is probably the worst age for a child *not* to be liked by other children. Moral for the teacher: to make favorites of certain children may ostracize them.

No sarcasm is a good rule—the child still needs a deep feeling that adults are his friends; sarcasm usually hurts a child at a spot that is sore, anyway.

Can absorb a great deal of information if properly motivated. It is safe to count on interest in people, adventure, anything exciting and dramatic.

Just beginning to form opinions and attitudes—can't get these abstractly—should have rich contact with lives of great people—also be introduced to the qualities of greatness in just ordinary people —history can give them a sense of the great potentialities of human beings if presented this way.

This is important to personal development as much as to attitudes, especially for children who may have to find their identifications— the people they want to be like—outside the family circle.

Play must not be forgotten—physical exercise should involve games with rules and team arrangements—dramatic play is still important but they don't want to reveal themselves as much as do younger children so it needs to be a little more formal—a plot, a planned sequence of what to say and do, content that connects them with other worlds than their own—all these make a fine framework for expression. The role a child takes still leaves room for personal expression but with limits—which is what he wants.

FOR FIFTH AND SIXTH GRADE

These children have their sights set on what it will be like to be a grownup and are beginning to chafe about their position as children.

Boys tend to cluster in their "man's world" of athletic prowess, mechanical-constructive interests, greater freedom to stray and roam, the taste of paid-for jobs like paper selling or store deliveries, maintaining in most cases considerable indifference for the girls, whose feelings may be a mixture of relief and chagrin at not being included.

In this stage on the road to adultness, children are intent on becoming as capable, as knowing, as adequate as possible. Interest in appearance wanes but blossoms again later, when, in adolescence, attractiveness to members of the opposite sex becomes an important drive.

Although friendships between individuals are more lasting than they were in earlier years, there is still a strong tendency to form clubs, cliques, or gangs whose interests and activities are strongly subject to environmental influences.

Greatly increased ability to think abstractly makes it possible for these children to comprehend complex relationships. Still, if they are really to absorb these ideas, their curriculum should continue to provide for direct experiences, experimentation, and dramatization.

Interests are expanding from how things work and the people who do the work to evaluating the position of the worker and the life he lives in connection with the nature and conditions of his work. This is an example of the spurt toward developing a system of values which often characterizes this period.

On a more personal plane, they are constructing a code of values which is deeply influenced by the codes of their families and teachers. Many a child's growth as a stable person is thwarted at this period because of the poverty of values or the conflicts associated with contradictory values. This is where the all-around, well-developed teacher becomes, in himself, a salient educational factor.

THE SCHOOL'S JOB: AS IT CONCERNS TEACHERS

Inevitably a shift in the conception of the kind of lives children should have in school means a shift in the conception of the kind of teachers they should have. Teachers today have a genuinely new job. Schools have always asked that teachers know their subject matter and see to it that children learn a desirable body of information and acquire skills in the three R's. Schools still ask this of their teachers. It is the shift in school thinking in *what* is considered desirable information and in *how* children learn it that has changed the teacher's job. Schools are moving away from the conception that the best source of information is in well-organized textbooks containing information which will be useful to children when they are grown; toward the conception that information should be immediately useful to children; that teachers should know children and what information children can use in the world in which they are living; that teachers should know subject matter not merely from books but from direct experiences in living situations. Schools are leaving the conception that children learn largely by memorizing and that, consequently, teachers should drill their children until their answers are correct or their skills approach those of adults; moving toward the conception that children learn primarily through direct experiences, activities, and thinking out things for themselves on their own level, and that consequently a teacher should provide children with developmental experiences. Schools used to regard a good teacher as one who could keep her children attentive, receptive, quiet, and discipline them when they weren't. Schools are moving towards regarding a good teacher as one who keeps children's interests alive, actively doing, actively thinking, actively learning self-discipline, actively a member of the school group. Schools are leaving the idea that the teacher's role is to stand apart from her children, to appear infallible as a person whose statements and standards should never be questioned; they are moving toward the idea that a teacher should be a member of his group, a guide rather than a supreme authority, entering into children's interests and pursuing investigation and activities with them in a warm human relationship.

Schools and communities are leaving the attitude that teachers are somehow set apart from other human beings in their personal lives; that they should see all sides of a question but have no convictions; should refrain from entering into politics; that they should always be serious, dignified; be respectful to superior officers and follow their instructions unquestioningly; that women teachers should not marry; that teachers should find their satisfactions only through the respect of the community and devotion to the job even if personal sacrifices are involved. Schools and communities are far more than formerly thinking of teachers as normal human beings who need adult satisfactions both in their professional and in their personal lives. Communities and schools are more and more realizing that the more teachers have rich, satisfying personal lives the more they have to give to children of what children need and the greater their capacity to take from children what children need to give—in short, that well-rounded human beings are the most likely to build a well-rounded rich group life with children. Schools are more and more realizing that professional satisfactions for teachers come only from carrying genuine professional responsibilities—responsibilities not merely for following out instructions but responsibilities for planning, for thinking, for experimenting within their classrooms, also for sharing in the responsibility of planning within their schools, even for sharing in the responsibility of planning within the school system of which their school is a part.

So, more and more the school's job as it concerns teachers becomes one of changing their status from docile followers to constructive creative initiators and thinkers. How schools and school systems can and should provide opportunities to keep their teachers growing professionally on the job will develop as we discuss the curriculum. Suffice it to say here, once again, that the school cannot genuinely accomplish its job with children unless it also accomplishes its job with teachers. Children *and* teachers, together living an interesting, yes, even an exciting, life, together exploring the world of things and people, together finding ways of expressing what they have found out about the world, together building up standards, values—that is the concept of their job toward which schools are moving.

3

What Schools Are Doing
to Carry Out Their Job

WHAT IS A CURRICULUM BUILT OUT OF?

CURRICULUM is a formidable word. And it may be a formidable thing in a child's life—in a teacher's life, too. Curriculum is what schools do to accomplish what they consider to be their job. We have just taken a look at the concepts of their job that schools are leaving and moving toward. Now we look at the curriculum—the attitudes towards children, experiences planned for them, the specifics of materials and practices, or what can be called the "know-how" of the school—which obviously changes as the school's aims change.

To many people curriculum means merely subject matter, neatly arranged in compartments—arithmetic, history, civics, music, geography, art—organized according to the logic of each subject, neatly chopped into lengths labeled kindergarten, first grade, second grade, and so on up through high school—all to be followed in detail for all children, everywhere. For children, this means that if they do not acquire information and skills at the prescribed rate, they will not be promoted. They will be "repeaters" until they meet the requirements laid down in the curriculum. For teachers this means that they are rated successful in so far as they succeed in keeping their children up to the prescribed rate of acquiring subject matter and skills. Indeed this is what curriculum meant in most schools until comparatively recently. Curriculum had no meaning below the elementary school ages—that is, below the ages when subject matter in compartments was doled out to the "pupils" in the definite length apportioned for each half year. A curriculum for younger children seemed an absurdity if not a contradiction in terms. This curriculum consisted of training children to give back accurately a body of information which they imbibed through textbooks and teachers' statements, to acquire skills and patterns of social behavior acceptable to adults. This conception of a curriculum fitted schools that considered their job was to make children into adults as fast as possible, and believed that learning was primarily passive absorption.

Today curriculum breathes in a wider and more friendly atmosphere. Our very vocabulary in curriculum discussions has changed. We speak of "flexibility," of "building" a curriculum. Instead of "pupils" we commonly say "children" or "boys and girls." We talk about "environment," "experiences," "activities," about "child investigations" and "research," "emotions," "art expressions," "social thinking," "social studies." These are not new words or new expressions. All of them were freely used when talk ran on human beings in the world outside the school; but they seldom found their way into the old subject matter and skills curriculum. These words, now so commonly found even in fairly formal curricula, indicate a new attitude toward children and their education. They suggest both the conception of their job toward which schools are moving and what they are doing to fulfill their aims. These words mean that today schools are thinking in terms of a curriculum which contains much more than subject matter and training in adult ways, though subject matter and acquiring habits are still and always must be there. They mean that a curriculum is built out of more than skills in the three R's, more than content materials taken from various fields of learning, and that a curriculum when built has to fit more than the logical development of these various fields, more than behavior acceptable to adults. *What, then, is the curriculum toward which schools are moving? What is it built out of besides systematized subject matter? What is it designed to fit?*

GROWING BOYS AND GIRLS AND THE WORLD
THEY LIVE IN

Boys and girls—that is the first answer. The curriculum is designed to fit growing boys and girls, those immature human beings endowed with emotions and the urge to learn which produces such incessant activity of bodies, minds, and emotions. If the curriculum is to fit growing boys and girls, it must provide them with developmental active experiences at every stage of their growth. And these experiences must have meaning for the children themselves. They must deal with the *world in which children live.* For children do not live and grow in a vacuum.

From one point of view children live in an adult's world, a world dominated by adults and in a large measure made by them. Babies are born into what James called this "big, buzzing, booming confusion." Part of this bewildering confusion which impinges upon children's senses is the natural world—the warm sunshine, movement and noises of animals, the smell of green growing things, the feel of slippery water and hard rock. Part of the booming confusion is man-made. Modern children are born into a mechanized world, where human voices boom out of a small box, where water from nowhere gushes out of a faucet, where people move and talk on a screen, where swift-moving autos honk and airplanes hum high in the sky. Even the simplest home nowadays is full of gadgets, of mechanisms produced by unknown scientists and engineers and the work of unseen workers. Elaborate patterns of work surround every school child.

Children are born, too, into a world of complex human relations where grownups love and hate, help and fight one another, where people live and work in groups. Children are plunged at once into relations with "the other fellow," giants upon whom they are dependent, who meet or do not meet their needs.

CHILDREN LIVE IN AN ADULT WORLD

How do children react to the adult world? How do they learn about the things and people in the world around them? A baby starts with a very narrow world in which he is so much the center that it is some time before he grasps that there is a world of things and people outside of himself. He has to learn everything, even that his own toes belong to his own body. He acquires factual information about things by incessant and firsthand exploration of the world which impinges upon him through his senses and his muscle experiences. In this early stage of learning, he is exercising both his body and his mind. He also acquires attitudes toward people at this early stage according to the way the people in his immediate environment treat him. His emotional mechanisms of fear, security, love, hate, pleasure, pain, and anger are actively at work from the very beginnings of his life. The baby's world is the home—things and people that he experiences directly. That is why psychologists and psychiatrists nowadays place such emphasis upon the home and family relationships. Here is the world which conditions babies' and small children's bodily and mental and emotional growth. From this narrow home world, a child "takes in" and grows. Whether his growth of body, mind, and emotions will be healthy or distorted depends upon how appropriate his experiences are to his stage of development and how adequately he can adapt to the experiences which life brings to him.

What from the unstable world where adults control human relationships do children select for their own world? What has meaning to them in terms of "the other fellow" as they progress from babyhood to the preadolescence of eleven-year-olds?

Little children live in a narrow personal world dominated by powerful giants. They live in houses planned primarily for these giants' precious possessions that must not be touched. Even in the most indulgent homes, a small child's life must of necessity be filled with many "don'ts." Perhaps that is one reason that little children nearly always learn the word "no" before they do "yes." These giants not only determine what eager small hands may touch: they determine when small bodies are to sleep, when and what they are to eat. These giants, moreover, set a form of behavior for a child in regard to the other fellow who must be greeted, smiled at, thanked, regardless of the child's own feelings. Few children escape the pressure of "manners" long before these adult social forms have meaning to them.

How do little children react to this adult-dominated world? From the first they react in two opposite ways. They accept; and they protest. They accept not merely because, perforce, they have to since they are genuinely dependent physically; but also because they are dependent emotionally. They need attention from grownups not merely to attend to physical needs of food, dry clothes, to hand them things and carry them places. They need attention from grownups to give them the inner security of individual affection. They need to feel they share in the life around them. Children brought up in institutions or in grim homes may have their physical requirements adequately met. But if they do not have affectionate personal attention and a sense that they help the group life as well, they are unhappy, inhibited little persons or unhappy, aggressive little persons. The implications here concern the attitude of adults toward children within both homes and schools. And attitudes of teachers are now considered a part of a school's curriculum.

Yet babies, even in the early stage of extreme dependence, begin to resist adult domination. It is not a reasoned resistance, of course, when a baby yells as he is being dressed, yet it is a genuine spark of independence. Fluctuating dependence and independence is the human pattern in relation to the other fellow, from babyhood to the grave, modified in each individual according to his personality and his maturity, and also according to his life experiences with the giants who have dominated his world. We sometimes think of babies as being completely dependent upon others. And so they are in the sense that they cannot meet their physical needs without help.

Yet everyone knows that an unsatisfied baby can express his desires lustily, aggressively, which shows "a will of his own," a demand that *his* will prevail, not the other fellow's. We think of adults as completely independent. And so they usually are in the sense that they can run through daily physical life by themselves. Yet every honest adult knows that in certain areas or at certain times of his or her life, he needs attention, emotional support, from someone even to the point of accepting the other fellow's judgment against his own.

Our school children from kindergarten through sixth grade lie between the baby and the adult. It is easy to see their growth in control of their own bodies and in what we often call "self-help," a kind of growth we definitely plan for. This kind of physical growth in muscle co-ordination is often confused with emotional growth in human relations. Many mothers and teachers assume that if a child can put on his rubbers, for instance, he has outgrown the stage of needing affectionate attention. But emotional independence is not so easily or quickly achieved as a new muscle technique. He continues to need the security of feeling wanted, of having his own appreciated place in his world. If he doesn't get this assurance from the powerful giants in his life, he will protest, but often in subterranean ways. He may pretend he cannot put on his rubbers. He may rush around the room hitting other children. He may retire into himself and not take part in activities he would enjoy if he were not so absorbed in his own unhappiness at being ignored. He will probably not be consistent in his behavior but will waver back and forth between feeling more grown-up and independent than he is and feeling more of a baby and dependent than he is.

A school should therefore expect and accommodate to a child's fluctuations between the desire to be helped and the desire to be left alone. The younger the child, the more extreme and obvious are such emotional fluctuations. But they persist to a lesser extent up and into adulthood.

Nevertheless, children who are growing healthily in their emotional life do advance, though in spurts and relapses, in their ability to adjust to new human relationships. Just as the physical environment in which children feel at home widens in size and complexity as they mature, so the world of human beings with whom children feel at home widens in numbers, size of group, and kinds of relationships. We call this social growth. Here the point is that a child's social growth is intimately tied up with his emotional growth; that his emotional life is dominated by adults who control his human relationships; and that upon these human relationships depends whether or not the world which he builds for himself from his life experiences is full of satisfactions or anxieties.

Schools are moving toward the meeting of a child's emotional needs as a part of curriculum. A school should have a warm human atmosphere for children of all ages. Schools are leaving the attitude that it is unimportant whether or not children enjoy their school life; that enjoyment of school work weakens a child's moral fiber; that since doing unpleasant things develops an ability to endure, a school contributes most to a child's future by making his present school life unpleasant and one in which he has no choices. Schools are accepting the attitude that children learn best in a friendly co-operative atmosphere; that a school contributes most to a child's future by giving him satisfactions in his school life with a share in determining what it shall be and thus help him to build deep interests and a desire to participate in the living problems around him.

Before children reach kindergarten or first grade, their world has been tremendously widened from the baby's world though his home is still the center of his deepest experiences and the most potent conditioning factor in his growth. Already, however, he has been exposed to the world of things and people immediately outside his home and has selected, taken in, from this complex environment and built himself a world of new and more complex relationships. His world may now include animals and machines and work and workers on the farm, the moon, growing plants, a brook, if these lie within his immediate environment. His world may now include city streets with their variety of moving things, people doing all kinds of work. It may even include the movies, if his parents have no place to leave him when they seek this modern diversion for themselves. Whatever lies around him, whatever he experiences at first hand is raw material from which he selects or takes in according to the interests and the understandings of his stage of development. The older he grows, the wider the world he has built both in the variety of things he can understand and in the variety of people he knows. By the time boys and girls reach sixth grade, for better or for worse the experiences in the community have entered thoroughly into their thinking and their attitudes towards people. They bring to the school what they have learned about things and people in their homes and communities outside the school.

The elementary school is moving away from the idea that it can or should expect the same development in children of the same age or that it should provide the same curriculum for all. The school is moving toward the idea that it must understand what children bring to school with them from past experiences; that a school should begin where children are and build a curriculum for their growth from that point.

CHILDREN BUILD THEIR OWN WORLD

Thus, from another point of view, children live in a world of their creation. This child's world is a changing and expanding world, but it is not an adult's world until he himself is an adult. Children select for their own those things that have meaning for them in this buzzing confusion around them, this mysterious natural and man-made world where powerful grownups live. On what basis do children make their selection? Out of what do they build their child's world?

This a school must know in order to build a curriculum for children which will have meaning for them, will bring them satisfactions and opportunities to learn at their own rate, in their own ways.

Take, first, the physical world. What in the natural and man-made world has meaning to our elementary school children as they pass through the growth levels from kindergarten to seventh grade? What do they wonder about? What do they want to find out about?

This a school must know if it would have its children eager to learn about how natural things behave—which is the basis of science—and about how people use the natural world which is the basis of work and inventions.

The younger the child, the more his selection from the physical world, both natural and man-made, is on the basis of what gives him strong sense and muscle experiences. But with children of all ages, as indeed with human beings of all ages, the world which registers directly through senses and muscles has a kind of smiting power, an immediacy utterly unlike tales of other people's experiences. Young children, up to nearly eight years of age, live and learn largely through direct, firsthand experiences. This is what we mean when we say they live in the here-and-now world. What vicarious or secondhand experiences do get through to them through words are largely recalls of their own experiences directly or by way of obvious and concrete contrasts. Children from eight through eleven years can more and more give meaning to vicarious experiences gained through words, can incorporate them into their expanding sense of "the real." But all through the elementary school ages, direct experiences have a significance, an interest, and carry a conviction for which no "telling about" other people's experiences is a substitute.

The school is moving away from the conception that the chief emphasis in a school's curriculum should be on information through words; toward the idea that a school's curriculum should grow out of direct experiences for the children.

Young children's senses are more alert than adults'. They love to explore through the tactile sense, to finger soft and hard things, to feel and splash water, even, experimentally and cautiously, to touch edges that they know are too sharp for comfort. They are notoriously fond of exploring with their tongues—probably a combination of taste and touch. They sniff everything with pleasure, not merely flowers or other smells which jaded adults still enjoy, but also smoke and clothes.

They respond to almost anything they hear. They love sound, per se, even when it becomes mere noise to adult ears. Babies laugh —that is, respond to—the rattling of a piece of paper. Kindergarten children respond to a boat's whistle, to the whispering snow on the windows. Response to sound quality in words precedes any understanding of the meaning of words. Two-year-olds repeat words with lovely or amusing sound over and over with rhythmic cadence:

> Jane isn't wake up,
> Mary Anne isn't wake up,
> Judy isn't wake up,
> Mollie is!

Somewhere around six, children almost always develop a mania for rhyming, that is, matching sounds in real or nonsense words. Nine-, ten-, and eleven-year-old children whose pleasure in sound has been respected and kept alive often select, from words of like meaning, those that have a sound quality they like, often a quality that most exactly fits the thing described. Here is a poem by a nine-year-old and his own correction.

THE RAIN

> The rain is falling very hard.
> The streets are wet and the gutters are full.
> The toys are out and all over the floor.
> I play all day till bedtime comes.

The boy read his verse out loud. Then he said, " 'Full' sounds wrong. Barrels are 'full' but gutters are 'running.' "

A school from kindergarten through sixth grade should keep alive children's sensitivity to sounds and sound quality. In the early years when children learn through play, a schoolroom should be full of sound experiences, sound expressions. For this sensitivity to sound quality cannot be preserved—and it is one of the bases of literature—unless children feel free to use sounds spontaneously as a play medium.

This nine-year-old's verse illustrates how children relive their experiences through images and through this reliving extend their experiences. It also illustrates another characteristic of children's language found in great literature. Their language is direct. It gives the direct image of what is experienced—reports evidence, not merely interpretation, which is so often characteristic of an adult's language. Here is another example. A three-year-old moved to a new house where he played for the first time on the sunny play space on the roof. After supper when he returned to the roof, he found a big change. Most adults would have said, "The sun has set"—an intellectual, memory description. But the child reported what he saw in direct language: "The big shadow is all around." Again we feel the quality in this directness which characterizes the best adult literature.

All the natural experimentation of children in rhythm, sound quality, and pattern or design is really a kind of play with language. Moreover, it is experimentation with the same elements that heighten language to literature in adult poetry or prose.

A school should encourage this natural art expression of children in their spontaneous language. A teacher should not always use language to convey information, should not always be intent on clarity and standardization in children's language, always feel that correctness in adult language forms—grammar, punctuation, etc.— is more important than this art use of language.

Her encouragement will be greater if she can sometimes bring herself to play with language herself without feeling undignified or even operatic. The reading of good poetry and good prose to children, though good in itself, is no substitute for children's own play use of language.

Children early notice and show preferences for certain qualities in the things they see. Strong clear colors please them. That is probably why so many toys are painted red. In children's own paintings pleasant things are nearly always painted gay colors. For children are not cramped by "reality," are not under any compulsion to repeat in their paintings the drabness of an actual object. Look at a six-year-old painting a dirty, dun-colored ferry she has enjoyed. She splashes on her paints until there appears a gay boat such as never plowed a real harbor. And as she makes a bold wiggly white line behind the bright ferry, she whispers gentle noises such as she heard the real water make as it churned against the real moving ferry. Yes, her ferry is based on her actual sense and muscle experience. But in her recall she creates her own ferry, heightened by her pleasure in color.

With paints and clay as with other art media a school should encourage children to creative expression on their own young level so long as these expressions satisfy them. When children begin to feel frustrated, impatient of their own techniques, then is the time to help them with adult techniques. But free experimentation is an earlier stage, satisfying to children if adults neither set them a model nor reject their products.

John Muir said that you saw a bird in a bush only if you had one in your heart. That is true of more things than birds! A walk down a city street with a seven- or eight-year-old child will convince you that he has many things in his heart which yours does not hold. The water hydrant, the license number on the passing automobile, the open manhole in the street with the sign "Men working," the clang of a distant fire engine, the coal clattering down the chute from the tipped-up truck—these things hardly enter your consciousness unless they are irritating obstacles to your progress. But the child's heart, the child's world, is full of such things. And if a teacher is to answer his gush of questions, or, far better, give him experiences which will let him answer them himself, her heart will have to expand to hold such things, too. Her atrophied senses will have to wake up and register the sights and sounds and smells, the tactile and muscle impressions with which the world, everywhere, is bombarding her.

All of children's senses are vividly taking in the world around them. They are building a child's world far more rich in sensuous qualities than an adult's world. They prove what they have taken out of the world by their spontaneous play in which they give back memories of sense experiences. Take two five-year-olds playing auto. One honked around the room; the silent follower said he was "the smell."

Grownups have let many of their senses atrophy until now most of them use only their eyes efficiently and, to a lesser extent, their ears. To most grownups a "description" suggests only something seen. A part of adult insensibility is a kind of protection technique. City folk learn not to hear the constant noise around them. An adult "lost in thought" means one who is not admitting the sounds and sights and smells of the world around him. Touching objects has become largely "taboo" in the adult world, though women shoppers surreptitiously use their fingers to supplement the observations of their eyes. And licking objects has practically passed from among adult enjoyments. We may well ask ourselves why grownups, excepting the rare artist, have become so insensitive to sense and muscle experiences which mean so much to children. How far have their past school experiences contributed to this atrophy of their senses? Certainly, the kind of schools we are leaving, the kind most adults went to, gave them little opportunity to enjoy sense experiences, little opportunity to explore the world through their senses. Indeed, the schools actively inhibited such sense pleasure, such exploration. The schools considered it their job to get children out of this "childish" pleasure as quickly as possible to train them in the "adult" way of taking in pleasure and information through their minds, not their bodies. Yes, we may well question whether our schools have not been in a large measure responsible for the typical unresponsive adults most of us have become, and whether it has been a contribution to us as individuals or to our culture to be able to take in the world around us very seldom through our senses.

The kinesthetic sense—muscle tensions and balance—is an active pleasure to children, a way of taking in the world. Watch them on a rocking subway train. They love having their balance disturbed and then righted by their own muscular efforts. One sees no such pleasure registered on the faces of their adult, strap-clutching neighbors!

Here again, children's memories of happenings show how important to them are muscle experiences. A four-year-old had been up a hill on a walk with a grownup. Later the adult tried to make the child recall this walk. She spoke of the houses and trees passed, the view from the top, which were her adult memories. No response from the four-year-old. Then suddenly she smiled. "Oh!" she said. "You mean the place where the legs ache!"

Action is natural for children. They enjoy movement for itself. Before they can sit up, babies laugh as they kick their legs and toss their arms. When they first learn to balance on unsteady legs, they have a real "drive" to walk, then to run. Kindergarten and first-grade children will run, not walk, to get anything unless they are prevented. They, and much older children, will squirm in their seats even when interested in a story that is being read aloud or a discussion they are taking part in. Recess is often referred to as a necessary time for children "to let off steam." This same "steam" can make children attack all kinds of constructive activities—carpentry, dramatization, art and crafts—with zest.

A school should not merely permit but also utilize expressions of this urge to bodily action through classroom activities.

Full-body activity is a natural response of young children to pleasure, anger, or any other gripping emotion. Every baby and every young child in the world enjoys throwing things. With a fine sweep of his big arm muscles a baby throws his toy or his spoon from his high chair. If it lands with a bang, he has achieved two of his most excruciating pleasures—muscular action and noise. Kindergarten children who have never before built with blocks can hardly resist knocking down their first buildings. Again muscle and noise enjoyment. Outdoor games of older children are based on the pleasure of using big muscles, legs, back and arms. And they usually add the noise for good measure. Little children dance up and down with rage, even throw themselves on the floor. They laugh with waving arms, and actually shrink, "cower," with fear. They talk the muscle language of gestures more eloquently than that of words.

Little by little children learn to inhibit these full-body responses. Yet even "free" eleven-year-old children do not wear the masks by which adults conceal their emotions except when a mild smile or frown momentarily cracks the mask. If a child does sit passive with a concealing mask, we know that something has happened inside him, that he has worked up a protective technique to conceal emotions which, when expressed, are unwelcome, are "taboo" in the world of grownups.

Closely allied to the pleasure in movement is the pleasure in rhythm. Children seem peculiarly responsive to rhythm, to have a definite urge to express themselves rhythmically. It shoots through nearly everything they do from the time they repeat meaningless sounds endlessly and rock themselves endlessly on knees and hands, to the time they write poetry or music or invent dance steps. Repetition is, of course, a simple form of rhythm, and poetry, music, and the dance are elaborated forms. No adult has "outgrown" rhythm. But most adults have inhibited many of their native rhythmic responses. Here, the point is that children are naturally motor and rhythmic. They enjoy muscle activity for itself, particularly if heightened by rhythm. They express themselves in muscle, motor ways. The body expression of the young child becomes more and more localized as his control of his fine muscles develops. But all our children in the elementary school have more need of muscle activity, muscle expression, than all adults, except those who keep "young." Again we may ask how much the fear that most adults have of using their bodies expressively is due to the attitudes of the schools to which they went as children. There, activity was sternly suppressed. Screwed-down desks, rules that prohibited leaving them or even squirming in their seats, approval for passive attention, certainly helped to build up masklike faces and inhibited bodies. Certainly these things meant suffering as children. We may also doubt that they were a contribution to adult life.

A child's world is an active world. A school should see to it that its children's school life is full of motor activities.

What does a creature with strong motor impulses take out of his physical environment? What has meaning to him? Things that have movement, things that he can understand and enjoy, can "identify" with because they are doing something, which is the way he himself wants to behave.

In the natural world this means animals above all other things. The behavior of animals seems altogether natural to children. Every child responds to animals unless some unfortunate accident has brought about fear of an animal, or unless a grownup has communicated his own fear of animals. Small children identify readily with animals, as is shown in their spontaneous play. In their dramatic play, they become animals. They may just romp around like animals with heightened pleasure in muscular activity. Or they may put animals through their own child programs—feed them what they themselves eat, put them to bed and cover them up as they themselves are put to bed. Spontaneous dramatization of animals is close to "personification" of animals, in which animals are endowed with the human characteristics of talk, of emotions and of behavior in general. But long after children have ceased to endow animals with human speech, they treat animals much as they treat human beings. Indeed, many adults talk to their pets for companionship.

A school, if possible, should have live animals for children to love and care for. It should take children to see animals. It should provide opportunities for children to express their identification with animals in dramatic play and in the dance.

Other things in the natural world—plants, moon and stars—do not make any such motor appeal as do animals. They may make a strong sense appeal through the smell and color of flowers, the brightness of the moon. But, by and large, a sustained interest in slow-moving natural phenomena comes at a later maturity stage. It is tied up with wonder, and wonder is the basis of science. Wonder about how natural things behave certainly appears before kindergarten age. By five, children are full of genuine science questions but their questions often reach far beyond their understanding of the answers. They are interested, however, to observe what happens when snow is brought into a warm room, when water in a glass or bottle freezes, when wet clothes are put on a radiator. They are interested to observe that plants die without water, that flowers bloom and trees grow new leaves in the spring. They watch these and many other changes in the natural world with the absorption of scientists. Close observation is the beginning of scientific inquiry. By nine, even by eight, children have a veritable urge for such inquiry and can carry out real experiments to answer their questions. By ten and eleven, most children have more eager wonder about the natural world than most of the adults who teach them.

The natural world can easily become an elementary school child's laboratory. But he cannot explore it to his own satisfaction without help and, in the older grades, without tools for experimentation.

A curriculum built to fit children should include explorations of the natural world from kindergarten through sixth grade through observation and experiments.

CHILDREN'S INTEREST IN HOW THINGS AND PEOPLE WORK

In the man-made world, the moving quality of things also dominates children's selection from the big, buzzing, booming confusion around them. From the egg beater in the kitchen, to the engine on the tracks, to the complicated machinery in a factory, movement interests children. Young children—kindergarten five-year-olds—are interested and content with movement and accompanying noise per se. First and second grade—six- and seven-year-olds—are beginning to add maturer intellectual curiosities: wonder about *how* these things behave, which leads to the *function* of things. What is the train carrying? Where is it going? Where did it come from? Where does the water in the kitchen sink come from? They are, in other words, beginning to think in more mature relationships. The functional aspect of the man-made mechanized world is beginning to interest them. And it continues to interest older children in more and more elaborate relationships. Their child's world is expanding in ways that bit by bit include new areas of the adult's world.

Through trips to see their community at work, city eight- and nine-year-old children learn a great deal about the way railroads, or boats, or docks, or market and store function together in relation to their own lives. And country children get a great deal about the way farms or trucks or busses or neighboring reservoirs or any other fairly simple work situations function in their own lives. They get some appreciation of the work relationships of their home town with faraway places, wherever they live. For there are few homes, nowadays, that are not closely linked with other places. Through direct experiences, these third- and fourth-grade children can also get an appreciation of the way people lived and worked long ago. Eight- and nine-year-olds are intrigued by what happened long ago on the very spot where they now live. Few places have not some traces of the early environment left which they can explore. These children have expanded their interests beyond the here-and-now world around them. They are ready to take on new and strange environments and new and strange people, whether far away or long ago, in a dramatic, half-play way. Eight-year-olds really feel like Plains Indians if they can get information about these Indians into action on their own level—make some of the things these Indians made and play out Indian ways of working and living. The Great Plains with their grass and buffaloes become important, become real.

Fourth-grade children also need a dramatic approach to the unknown. But, far more than third grade children, they are interested in origins—how and why things began. They ask real scientific "hows" and "whys," why some people are nomads, some farmers. Why have deserts so little rain? Why are some places mountainous, some flat, some places hot, some cold? Were the mountains always here? Were living things always here? The regions of the globe, their plants and animals, and the peoples who live there can become a part of a nine-year-old's world if he can play out these peoples' ways of working and living, and find out how and why their environments are so different from his own through science experiments.

Fifth- and sixth-grade children add still more mature relationships as to how the world's work is done to those already learned. When they visit a clothing factory, for instance, they not only enjoy the movement of machinery, which remains a pleasure never to be ignored, not only are aware of *how* things are made; they get, also, a sense of the complex teamwork of human workers and work. They can get the planned sequence, the interrelationships of the faraway herder with his sheep, the many processes from shearing, through textile mills, the clothing factory he has seen, through store, to his own coat, and understand that all these processes depend upon roads of some sort and that all begins with raw material which in turn depends upon the earth. These ten- and eleven-year-old children get a great deal from words. But words alone are not enough. Actual observation of some part of the complicated process of turning sheep's wool into a coat will make the interrelationships that they read about seem more important, more convincingly real. The world of fifth- and sixth-grade children is not yet an adult's world. But it holds the beginnings of most adult interests.

A school should utilize opportunities for children of all ages to explore how work is done in the modern world; to use simple tools and basic machines with which to make simple things with their own hands; to see how our complicated machines have developed through inventions from such simple beginnings.

What particular direct experiences school children can have will depend, obviously, upon their community, and upon their environment in the larger sense. But everywhere people are working. Everywhere they are using the patch of earth which they live on for some special work or pleasure. This is true of farms, cities, villages, and suburbs. The earth is there—the sun, the rain, the warmth and coldness, the moving air we call the wind, the soil, plants and animals—all the things that people find on earth but do not make. Everywhere, too, are people using the earth, near or far away, in their daily lives. Children everywhere are eating food which came from the earth forces of sun and rain and soil, plants or animals somewhere. They are wearing clothes which, like food, workers somewhere have made through their work from some living things. They are living in houses built of earth materials, using machines made from underground deposits, moving over the surface of the earth on some kind of road, and using some method of communicating with other people, near or far away. These are basic patterns of our culture and of the culture of any people. The "hows" that lie behind these patterns of work interest children of all ages and stages. This is essentially human geography—what the earth does to people and what people do to the earth.

A school should recognize that the important relationship between human work and earth conditions begins when kindergarten children play putting a man-made boat into earth-made water and that it extends through the study of peoples living and working anywhere, in the present or in the past.

No matter what the specific experiences are, they should proceed from the familiar to the unfamiliar. Each step must be built on the experiences that have gone before. Children, like adults, carry around with them what they have learned—really learned—by living and experiencing. And the major, uniquely human characteristic of learning, as we have said before, is seeing new relationships. Children interpret new situations in the light of their old experiences— the relationships already learned.

To illustrate: A school group of city six-year-olds had experienced buying eggs with their mothers and their teacher in an A & P store. They were taken to the country where they first saw a hen sitting on eggs. They were completely unaware of the relation of hen to egg. One child turned to the farmer and asked, "Did you get those eggs for the hen at the A & P store?"

The reverse would probably have been true of a farm child, who might have looked around the A & P for hens. Another of these city six-year-olds saw minnows swimming in a pond and called out with excitement, "Look at the live sardines!"

Hens and eggs—eggs being transported by truck or train—eggs in a store—are separate steps in relationship thinking, any one of which may come first in a child's actual experience according to his environment. They are all parts of the big, buzzing, booming confusion of the adult world of work. When they get related, the confusion disappears in time. The synthesis of this particular set of work relationships—farm, hen, egg, transportation, store, city—will lead to a more complicated synthesis involving still other relationships: farms feed city people; eventually, people everywhere depend upon the products of soil; preservation of soil is a national concern. But any of these wide syntheses comes only after many experiences, many learned relationships hooked on to one another until they have built a generalization which is utterly unlike the separate relationships out of which it has been built.

The school should consciously plan experiences for all its children —explorations of the natural and man-made physical world (trips and experiments), follow-up discussions, and art expressions— through which children become aware of the fundamental relationships which are understandable at whatever stage of development they have reached. Children's experiences should cover a wide range, but they are not to be chosen in a haphazard way. A teacher should plan a program which gradually leads her children toward the understanding of a few basic relationships in the world of natural phenomena and in human work—people's use of the natural earth forces. These general relationships the teacher should have constantly in mind but should not express verbally to the children until they themselves are beginning to sense them and express them.

CHILDREN'S INTEREST IN HUMAN RELATIONS

Upon a child's emotional satisfactions in his personal human relationships rests, to a large extent, the development of his later attitude toward "the other fellow," what we have called his social growth. His acceptance of other people, his ability to identify with them, to feel a part of ever-widening groups is, like everything else, a matter of growth. Young children should not be expected to identify closely with people outside their own personal groups— people they can know only through words. Eight- and nine-year-old children can identify with far wider groups of people provided they can live the lives of these people dramatically—their lives as related to their work far more than in relation to other people. But ten- and eleven-year-old children in fifth and sixth grades have entered the preadolescent stage of maturity. Human relations in their own lives take on a different tone. They become more conscious, often verbal, about their own position in the family, their family's position in the community, sometimes their country's position in the world. And this interest in human relationships within their own lives now extends to human relationships everywhere. They now approach their own culture and that of differing cultures with interest in people as human beings like themselves added to the younger interests of how things and people work. At a factory (to use the same situation used to illustrate the maturity level of fifth- and sixth-grade children in the work relationships they could understand) these children identify with workers *as people,* not merely as links in the work process. They wonder if these factory workers are having a good life. Even more significant, if the identification is close, they *care* whether these workers are having a good life. That is, fifth- and sixth-grade children have achieved the level of thinking in standards of people's relationships to people—in values. They are interested to know about family structure in cultural situations different from their own, to know about our own jury system and courts and how justice is mediated by faraway or long-ago people; about the human qualities which command most respect and admiration in differing cultures—now and long ago—who are considered "successful," who are the "wise men."

Children grow from the simple to the more complex in their thinking and feeling about the relationships of people to people just as they do in thinking about relationships in the natural and man-made physical world. Each relationship understood can be thought of as a hook that reaches out and grabs a new relationship. The kindergarten child comes to school with a scant set of understood relationships both in the physical world and among groups of people, learned in his home and on the streets. So that is where we begin. Bit by bit, his explorations of the physical environment and how people are using it widens in extent of actual area and in complexities of work and science. It widens steadily if he has experiences from which to learn new relationships until at last, ideally, it includes the whole physical world. In the same way, bit by bit, a child's interests and experiences gradually widen from his own narrow personal home group to school, to club, to church groups, to work group, to neighborhood, to country, until at last, ideally, he includes all the peoples of the world as members of his group.

A school should consciously plan experiences for its children for social growth. Learning at first hand about relationships in work and workers is a young stage in social experiences. When children reach the stage of maturity (in fifth and sixth grades) in which their interests extend to relationships among people not known personally, it is of utmost importance that a program of experiences be planned which lead them gradually toward the building of stand-

ards in the relationship of people to people—or social values. Values cannot be built by words alone, though discussions of current problems of living should supplement direct experiences. Exploration and, whenever possible, participation in social situations in the neighborhood and the larger environment accessible to fifth- and sixth-grade children are basic in such a program of experiences. Social situations—problems of living—vary with the special environment. They may range from play space, housing conditions, nursery schools to children's courts, techniques of becoming a United States citizen, or soil conservation and irrigation projects. Direct exploration of such social situations gives a common background for discussion of how social situations are handled among faraway and long-ago peoples. It helps to build up values in people's relationship to people.

Here, then, we have a kind of bird's-eye view of the kind of world children live in. They live in an adult world filled with mysterious natural and man-made physical objects which they both accept and wonder about, and filled with mysterious giants who waver between affection and rejection of them, between indulgence and complete control, and who can make them conform arbitrarily to mysterious adult standards of behavior and standards of right and wrong or can help them gradually to build up such standards within themselves as they mature.

Out of this manifold world which surrounds them, children select those things that have meaning to them and live in *a child's world* which they have thus built. This world is filled with vivid sense and muscle impressions and expressions. It is an active world—filled with activities of bodies and minds and emotions. Through these active experiences, little by little, children bring order into the puzzling confusion into which they are born. Through their experiences, physical, mental, social, emotional, proceeding from the familiar (already known relationships) to the unfamiliar, they gradually learn more complicated or mature relationships in the physical world and in the world of human relations. Their world is a changing and ever-widening world. That is, it is if their life experiences bring them opportunities for healthy growth.

The children, themselves, as we have watched them behaving and growing, have given us cues for building a curriculum which will give them a good life and make the school a place for them to grow in. These same cues suggest curriculum materials and school techniques. These curriculum materials and teaching techniques are not ends in themselves. They are the means by which schools can give children active learning experiences in living situations, from kindergarten through sixth grade. These experiences will be both "intake" experiences—finding out about something that interests them—and "outgo" experiences—doing something about what they have found out. A school can give such interrelated experiences through which children learn.

We have talked largely about the conception of the school's job, the curriculum, and the teaching techniques toward which schools are moving. They are in striking contrast to the school's job, curriculum, and techniques that we believe schools are leaving. To make clearer the contrast in what schools are leaving and what they are moving toward in the conception of their job, the curriculum, and teaching techniques, we have drawn up a chart. Like any other chart, it merely highlights the chief points. We have chosen the extremes to make the contrast clear.

TRENDS IN SCHOOL THINKING ABOUT CHILDREN AND TEACHERS

The School's Job

Children as Individuals and Group Members

What Schools Are Leaving	What Schools Are Moving Toward
POINT OF VIEW	
The school's job is to prepare children for adult life by training them to take on adult	Each stage of growth has its own needs and potentialities. Adult development is dependent upon how well the needs

Children as Individuals and Group Members (*cont'd*)

What Schools Are Leaving   What Schools Are Moving Toward

POINT OF VIEW

forms of thinking and be-having as soon as possible.

and potentialities of each stage have been considered. Hence it is the school's job to meet the needs and develop the potentialities of each stage of development and thus help children to grow gradually into adulthood.

A child's success should be measured by his achievements in terms of adult standards.

A child's growth is more significant than his specific achievements; it should be measured in terms of progress through successive growth stages and with consideration of his own individual pace and patterns of growth.

The school should develop citizens who will carry on the best traditions of the culture. But the schools must keep within the *status quo.*

The school should develop citizens who will identify themselves with constructive forces operating in its improvement.

IMPLICATIONS

Train a child to accept adult thinking and to conform to adult standards; have him accept adult statements without questioning.

Encourage a child's native interests and his own expression of these interests; help him to think out solutions of problems through free discussion.

Stimulate a child to success by fastening his attention on promotion, rewards, and punishment.

So provide for meeting the needs of children that interest in the activity itself will develop with little need for rewards or punishments.

Controversial social and political questions should have little place in the classroom;

The problems of living as they manifest themselves in current society form an increasingly significant part of the

Children as Individuals and Group Members *(cont'd)*

What Schools Are Leaving   What Schools Are Moving Toward

IMPLICATIONS

a strict neutrality must be maintained.

curriculum as children advance in years. Controversial issues are increasingly handled and the scientific approach to problem solution is developed.

Attention is fastened on individual achievement with little attention to the give-and-take of group living.

Gradually from the earliest years children become aware of their membership in the group with rights and responsibilities; as they grow older they become increasingly active participants in class, school, home and community life and thus learn the rights and privileges of democratic living.

Teachers as Individuals and Group Members

POINT OF VIEW

A teacher should know her subject matter and be able to impart it to children. This is the chief qualification of a good teacher.

A teacher should know children and the world in which they are living. She should know subject matter not merely from books but from direct experience in living situations.

A teacher should be devoted to her work, if necessary to the exclusion of normal human interests.

A teacher needs first of all to be a good human being leading a normal life and finding both within and without her profession satisfying life activities.

Teachers should see all sides of a question but not be drawn into the stream of controversy.

Teachers are citizens. Only as they themselves participate in public affairs can they develop in their children a feeling for the rights and responsibilities of citizenship in a democracy.

Teachers as Individuals and Group Members (*cont'd*)

What Schools Are Leaving	What Schools Are Moving Toward

IMPLICATIONS

A teacher's preparation should consist mainly in the mastery of the subject matter she is to teach and in methods of teaching it.	A teacher's preparation, even for teaching the youngest children, should be built upon a broad general education encompassing the major fields of knowledge. Specific professional preparation should include thorough study of child development, the physical and social environment, and the application of these to teaching.
Teachers should conform to the mores of the community.	Every teacher has the right to her own personal life. She should have as much latitude in conforming to mores as is granted to any other normally adjusted member of the community.
Teachers should keep out of politics and current problems, whether local or national.	Teachers in exercising their responsibilities as citizens should take a courageous stand on all matters of public interest; they should never, however, use their classrooms to propagandize their views.

The Curriculum

Children: Their Intake and Outgo

POINT OF VIEW

A curriculum is a course of study prepared by a central authority and given to teachers to be followed in any classroom of a given grade in any school within the school system.	A curriculum is a body of learning experiences planned to satisfy and stimulate children's interests and impulses, through which, as they mature, they may progressively develop vital relationships to the real world around them.
A curriculum consists of a body of separate syllabi in	A curriculum is a closely integrated body of experiences built around life

Children: Their Intake and Outgo (cont'd)

What Schools Are Leaving   What Schools Are Moving Toward

POINT OF VIEW

arithmetic, geography, history, spelling, etc.

situations with subject matter related to these.

Learning is largely a matter of drill and memorization and absorption of what other people have found out.

Learning means absorption of experiences. Other people's experience is not so significant as one's own active participation and discovery.

Children should take in a body of desirable information, completely organized and interpreted for them by adults. They should give out such information in the same terms and forms in which they have taken it in.

Children should take in the world about them; they should give out their impressions freely and in terms of their own ideas and feelings. Intake and outgo are the bases of learning.

The best sources of information are well-organized textbooks which contain essential facts to be memorized.

Information should be gathered by children from a variety of books and source materials, through experiments, and through exploration of the environment in which they live.

Some subject matter, though not in itself useful, has a certain disciplinary value in that it develops attention, memory, and reasoning.

There is no need to draw upon subject matter which is not of itself useful. When the curriculum is concerned with life situations there is need for abundant subject matter, and attention, memory and reasoning are developed in its use.

Children should be drilled in all subjects until facility and correctness are acquired.

Drill should be incorporated in a program as a means and not an end and should take its place as part of a process through which a definite goal can be accomplished.

Children: Their Intake and Outgo (cont'd)

What Schools Are Leaving	What Schools Are Moving Toward

POINT OF VIEW

The techniques of art must first be learned before children can be expected to express themselves competently in any art medium.

Free expression should precede attention to techniques. There should be abundant time for exploration with materials. Children's natural expression should be improved by teaching them the techniques when needed for the better expression of their ideas and feelings.

Play is necessary as a way of releasing energy and resting from the real job of school learning. To want to play is part of being young and immature. The appropriate school time for play is recess. Inside the classroom children should concentrate on learning facts and becoming skilled in techniques, etc.

Play enters into the child's way of learning. In the younger grades, play and work are synonymous and only gradually become separate. They are never, however, completely divorced in a satisfying life.

IMPLICATIONS

Programs are organized on a subject matter basis—so many minutes for geography, history, etc.

Programs are organized around activities, projects, problems, trips, etc., and subject matter is related as it is used for a purpose.

The schedule is planned to include many short periods, and it is generally rigidly adhered to.

The schedule is planned in large blocks of time and is flexible to meet the needs of the program.

Drill periods are separated sharply from other periods.

The content of drill grows out of other activities.

Children: Their Intake and Outgo (cont'd)

What Schools Are Leaving	What Schools Are Moving Toward

IMPLICATIONS

All children in a class have the same textbooks.	Children use libraries and other sources of materials freely.
Learning is largely a classroom matter.	Children use all resources available in the community—libraries, museums, docks, stores, fire engine houses, farms, and the people connected with them.
Emphasis is placed upon acquisition of knowledge.	Emphasis is placed upon the development of scientific thinking—defining a problem, collecting and organizing data, drawing conclusions and testing them in action.
Adult pictures are copied and traced. Art principles, color charts, music scales, grammatical forms are emphasized as fundamentals.	Spontaneous language, singing, drawing, and modeling are encouraged, and materials provided for their exercise. Techniques are so used as not to interfere with the freedom of the child's expression.
Play is confined to recess periods, where, in general, children dash about a school yard while the teacher welcomes the time as a brief period of rest from the children.	The younger the group the more difficult it is to distinguish between work and play. Children earnestly engage in playing house, Indians, knights, etc., while the teacher uses this activity as a means for important learning.

Teachers: Their Intake and Outgo

POINT OF VIEW

Teachers make up the rank and file of the profession. As such, they must carry out directions from above.	Teachers are active participants in all that pertains to their work: development of curricula, selection of equipment and instructional materials.

Teachers: Their Intake and Outgo (cont'd)

What Schools Are Leaving | What Schools Are Moving Toward

POINT OF VIEW

Teachers must continuously study to increase their professional information and skills.

Teachers must not only continually study to increase their professional knowledge and skill but must live broadly and richly in the world of today.

Art is a matter of special talent, but there is nothing much one can do about it if one happens not to have it.

Art is a matter of sensitivity and responsiveness to the qualitative aspects of all experience. The full development of a teacher includes growth in original, creative perception and expression which permeates all the functions and relationships of daily living.

The play spirit is not generally associated with teachers. They should be serious and dignified.

The play spirit is an essential part of a teacher's life. It makes it possible for her to enter into the play life of children through which so much of their learning takes place.

A teacher's professional life is largely confined to her classroom.

Teachers are members of committees working actively in the curriculum and other aspects of their profession.

IMPLICATIONS

A teacher's immediate preparation consists of making daily lesson plans in conformity with the course of study given her.

A teacher's preparation consists of studying the children and the community; planning a program and developing materials as needed.

A teacher generally feels inadequate in the arts and welcomes opportunities to be relieved from teaching the arts.

A teacher finds herself developing her own creative life as she lives creatively with children. The arts play a large part in her professional preparation.

Any playful style in the classroom is inappropriate and

A teacher enters into the play life of children and, at the same time, de-

Teachers: Their Intake and Outgo *(cont'd)*

IMPLICATIONS

not consistent with a teacher's role.

velops the play spirit on her own adult
level.

School Atmosphere
Children: Their Role

POINT OF VIEW

Training in acceptable manners will develop good social
attitudes.

Social attitudes are built from direct
experience in human relations. Good
manners should be encouraged, but as
an expression of good social feeling,
not as a mere form.

Character is built through discipline. Expression of feeling
and emotion should be well
controlled. A child is never
too young to control himself
and to adapt his childish impulses to the requirements
and mores of adult life. Too
much affection will spoil a
child.

Control should be arrived at gradually. The child should grow up in an
atmosphere at school as well as at
home that permits expression of feeling and understands its roots. School
should provide experiences for emotional development—expressive materials, free social relations, warm human beings.

The teacher must first establish herself as an authority.
She must not let children win
any battles over her.

Teachers need to know how much and
when to limit children's freedom. Too
much is as bad as too little. But the
teacher does not wish to symbolize absolute or harsh authority.

Competition is a sound way
to stimulate children since
thus they are prepared for
real life in a competitive
world.

Co-operation should be developed in
the classroom as a step toward building a more co-operative world. Children enjoy group effort and successes
as much as individual and competitive
ones.

Bad behavior means a bad
child. But a good child is one

A child is not inferior to an adult. A
cowed, docile child is not a good child

Children: Their Role (*cont'd*)

What Schools Are Leaving	What Schools Are Moving Toward

POINT OF VIEW

who accepts adult superiority in all things, follows directions and commands, does not give vent to ugly feelings or ideas, finds his happiness in adult approval.

or a happy one. Secure children are not self-centered or spoiled. They carry responsibility for themselves and others, have confidence in their ability to meet life's demands and problems. They have not been emotionally used up in premature competition.

IMPLICATIONS

Insistence on adult forms of courtesy along with unquestioning obedience.

Emphasis on co-operative forms of behavior, on sharing, on waiting turn, on playing and working together, with consideration of each other's rights—children's and adults'.

Classrooms set up with rows of screwed-down desks that make ordinary social intercourse impossible.

Classrooms arranged to suit the activities going on—tables, chairs, workbench, library corner.

Children not allowed to talk to each other or to move about the room.

Children encouraged to work and play in groups, talking and moving freely as needed to carry out the job on hand.

Children always reminded that they are in school—laughter suppressed, excitement kept down, normal emotional expression suppressed.

Through spontaneous language, music, painting, modeling, dance, children's real emotional life is revealed. This the teacher takes into account and, instead of suppressing it, tries to guide it into constructive channels.

The teacher is the supreme authority. She metes out rewards and punishments and is the arbiter in all disputes.

The classroom is a community in which each member has his rights and responsibilities. Discipline grows out of the needs of the situation. Rules are developed rationally as needed. Intelligent self-control is the aim.

4

Schools Must Face the Times

BEFORE the war the changes in school thinking and attitudes summed up in the chart at the end of the last chapter had been taking place to a greater or lesser extent in our schools. Then came the war. The war struck at the children in our schools. Fathers overseas, mothers at work in war industries, food rations, were not merely practical experiences in the homes: they were deep emotional disturbances. Broken homes and parental anxieties touch children of all ages where they are most sensitive. The war made our school children insecure and excited. From violent war play in the kindergarten to helpless but genuine worry over the future of their families and their country in the sixth grade, our children showed varying degrees and kinds of jitters.

The war struck at the teachers in our schools, too, both practically and emotionally. They, of course, in common with all adults in a country at war, felt the impact of the war in their personal lives. They felt it, too, in their professional lives in practical ways. They eagerly took on the many war jobs asked of them, from distributing ration books in school buildings after school hours to helping the children in *their* war jobs of gathering paper, selling war stamps, and doing countless other things large or small. They also felt the war vicariously through their jittered children. Few were the teachers who did not try to help the children through this shattering experience. Few were the teachers who did not worry lest they were not doing the most they could for their children. With all its anxieties and difficulties the war brought some good things into many classrooms—a new atmosphere in teacher-child relationships, and new thinking in curriculum subject matter. Many teachers thought more about the children as persons who were going through an emotional experience; teachers and children shared a common interest and a common job. Also, many teachers turned to the present—not to textbooks—for actual subject matter close to the children's interest. This was most evident in geography where war areas were studied through the newspaper war maps. But it spilled over into social thinking about other people in other lands, even into the new world problems in which all were involved.

The war ended. Reaction set in. The new problems brought by the war shifted to no less critical postwar problems. Schools and teachers felt the impact of the problems brought by critical times both directly and indirectly. Indirectly, schools and teachers were a part of a new surge of national and world thinking and feeling. The terror and futility of a war that involved practically all the people of the world brought active thinking about how to prevent another such war. This active thinking about how to attain a stable peace was swept to an exalted plane by the splitting of the atom. The success or failure of the United Nations became a matter of personal concern to millions of people who had hitherto left such concern to others—particularly to the government. Social thinking on a global scale sprang up within new groups of people. The One-World concept became a credo. The startling possibilities of atomic energy for civilian use roused hitherto apathetic people to a pitch of unprecedented excitement. People clamored for action.

Schools and teachers felt a great impulse toward making over the school curriculum to include these national and world problems of the "atomic age"; some felt that these problems should determine the curriculum. That was the schools' way of wishing to get into action. The reaction was correspondingly depressing when dissension that threatened failure arose in the United Nations and when atomic energy seemed likely to be exploited for war purposes only or, like other of the world's resources, for individual gains rather than for public good. These and other problems of our times have a profound even if an indirect influence on our schools— teachers and children.

What problems concerning administration, teachers, and children does the public now face? We say "the public" advisedly, for in the long run the public is responsible for our schools. Only the public through informed opinion can get our schools out of the national dilemma they are in.

OUR NATIONAL SCHOOL DILEMMA

In many ways, notably in curriculum revision, our schools have gone forward even during this period of national disturbance. In other ways they have been like Alice, who by running as fast as she could managed to stand still, and in still other ways some of them have gone backwards, though most of them have been trying to catch up with the times.

One study [1] of certain aspects of our schools covering many areas in our country reveals many needs, of which only a few can be mentioned here. First is the obvious need for better school buildings and equipment. From a national point of view, our children have always had very uneven opportunities to get an adequate education. Poor states spend far less on each child than do rich states, though it must always be remembered that many poor states spend a larger proportion of their income on their schools than do rich states. Of eleven states lowest in expenditures for schools, nine are highest in the percentage of total income spent on schools. The extremes in expenditures per pupil (in 1947) are Mississippi, with an expenditure of $25 for each white child, and New York, spending $125 per child.

[1] For fuller details see Benjamin Fine, *Our Children Are Cheated* (New York, Henry Holt and Company, 1947).

A further well-known inequality in opportunity to get an adequate education lies in the separate schools for Negroes in the South. President Mordecai W. Johnson of Howard University has drawn a dramatic contrast between the inequality of educational opportunity for white and Negro children: "If the American primary and secondary school system were a sixty-story skyscraper, on the top floor would be 20,000 New York school children, receiving an education which cost $6000 per classroom per year. Sixty stories down would be 38,000 Negro children in schools of Arkansas, Georgia, and Tennessee receiving financial support of less than $100 per classroom."

In the North, of course, colored and white children are not legally segregated in schools, though practically they often are because of segregation in housing. For colored and white children—North, South, East, and West—bad aspects of the school situation have been aggravated during and since the war.

School buildings have not been adequately maintained and fewer new schools have been built. At the same time, the number of children has increased. The result is obvious—greater overcrowding of classrooms and many thousands of children not going to school at all! Remember, too, that this piles up hardships on the teachers as well as children.

As for new equipment—libraries, laboratories, supplies and books for classrooms—it has not been added even at the old rate, which was never adequate. And all this in a rapidly changing world which demands more new equipment rather than less. In some schools, for instance, the maps being used are pre-World War I. And textbooks and supplementary reading also date back in many cases to the 1920's. Is it surprising that teachers sometimes feel it is impossible to carry out a new curriculum handed down to them from some high board without the tools to implement what is actually prescribed?

Another aspect of our school dilemma is that teachers' salaries have not risen with increased prices at a rate comparable to increase

in income in other professions or in fields such as industry, and
white-collar and domestic services. Again, the schools for colored
children have the worst record, salaries for their teachers touching
the low level of $232 per year.[2]

It is true that salaries have increased, though the actual pur-
chasing power has fallen. The average salary for 1947 was $2,026
(about $40 a week); that of 1948, $2,424. But these are national
averages, and many salaries fall far below these. In 1948, more than
half the teachers in our country got less than $40 a week. Two
hundred ten thousand got $25 weekly or less and ten thousand of
these got less than $12 a week.[3] Inequalities in salary for teachers
mean inequalities of opportunities for children.

In an article in the New York *Times,* January 4, 1948, Benjamin
Fine characterized the staffing of schools with good teachers as the
number one problem of 1948. Some of the facts he presents indicate the extreme gravity of the situation: 110,000 substandard
emergency teachers employed; 10,000 children on waiting lists unable to enter kindergarten; in addition to 110,000 qualified teachers
needed to replace substandard teachers, 110,000 more needed to
reduce class size to what it was before the war; within the next six
years 2,000,000 to 4,000,000 more children will be in school than
were expected; the number of graduates of teachers' colleges does
not meet replacement needs; an annual deficiency of 40,000
teachers is anticipated; 3,000,000 children received seriously substandard education in 1947–48.

The plight of the teacher, though always serious, reached a new
high at the close of the war. Is it surprising that as one response to
the general situation teachers' unions have grown apace? They have
even used the strike as a method of getting increase in salaries.
Strikes are a new phenomenon among teachers, shocking to many
people and to many of the teachers themselves.

These are by no means the only factors which have led to the

[2] Fine, *op. cit.,* p. 153.
[3] Fine, *op. cit.,* p. 43.

wholesale *teacher shortage* felt in every state, in city, suburban, and rural schools. Teachers have been and are continuing to leave the profession by tens of thousands. Moreover, the yearly supply of new teachers has dropped—registration in teacher education centers has fallen 55 per cent during the past five years.[4] What has been the result? New and often completely untrained teachers are replacing experienced teachers in overcrowded classrooms, in run-down school buildings with archaic equipment. The need for better-trained teachers, always great, has become the outstanding imperative in our schools. Students in teacher education centers need a curriculum fitted to the modern world. Teachers who are already teaching need organized ways of keeping themselves up-to-date professionally through inservice education. Here, again, our schools have not even stood still in this postwar period. Our average teacher comes to his job today less ready for his job than ever. Yet the atomic age is upon us, demanding, from any sane point of view, teachers with background in our new science world and in sound thinking in our new world of international relationships and responsibilities.

Against this wide picture of how our nation is facing—or rather *not* facing—the need for greater educational opportunities for our children, and the need for making teaching a genuine profession with economic and social standing, we should put the picture of the "new job" which most schools, to a lesser or greater extent, before and even during the war were trying to do. Glance back at the chart of what our schools are leaving and what they are moving toward, at the end of Chapter 3. It is a common historic experience that during the excitement and drama of a common danger people work together. It is also a common and a tragic experience that when the emergency is over, people fall back into the old grooves of separate interests and work—often further back than before the emergency aroused them. This kind of reaction has happened to our schools in the postwar period. The aroused interest in our children

[4] Fine, *op. cit.*, p. 106.

and our schools has waned if the reluctance to appropriate funds for them is a measure of public interest.

Moreover, there has been a wave of reactionary thinking which repudiates almost any change in schools as "newfangled" or "fancy." The scientific attitude toward children and their education has lost prestige. The hard work of child psychologists, of school experiments, has been under ruthless attack. These attacks, coinciding with our general school dilemma, have made still more difficult the task of those schools that continue to try to catch up with the rapidly changing times, to do what they conceive as their new job. The real crux of the situation is what we have allowed to happen to the teaching profession in the welter of postwar confusion. Many of our experienced teachers—those who are sticking it out—were trained in traditional thinking and techniques. Yet many of them are reaching out, genuinely wishing their profession to catch up with the times. Many of our new teachers, who are filling the places left by the tens of thousands of teachers who have abandoned the profession, have had inadequate or in some cases no education at all in teaching techniques, child development, or curriculum building. And *teaching is a genuine profession requiring genuine professional preparation* just as does any other profession. It is a crazy picture in our wealthy, powerful nation where a good education has long been regarded as the essential right of every child, and also as a sound investment for the preservation and development of democratic thinking and ways of living. It is a crazy picture—but it is a true picture of today's school problem.

IN NEW YORK CITY

Now we narrow the picture to one spot in the national scene— New York City—with a realization that what is happening here is also happening elsewhere. New York is a big "spot." It has some 830,000 students and 35,000 teachers in its public schools. In the elementary schools alone are nearly half a million children and

18,000 teachers. New York contains a great variety of environments —the neighborhood and homes of the school children. There are environments with people of mixed national, religious, and racial background and environments with distinctive ones—Italians, Negroes, Chinese, Jewish, most of whom have been in the United States for several generations and are citizens, and some who have recently arrived (largely Puerto Ricans). There are crowded, low-income neighborhoods with comfortless, dark tenement homes and neighborhoods with higher incomes where the homes have more comforts and more rooms with more light. (The children of the really high-income neighborhoods seldom go to the public schools in New York.) These city school children play in the occasional playgrounds or parks but mostly on the busy streets.

The elementary school buildings where these New York children go to school range from modern up-to-date buildings with auditoriums, spacious light lunchrooms, libraries, some cooking facilities for the children, big playgrounds, teachers' rooms, to old-type buildings with none of these modern improvements, a few still having outdoor toilets. In the war and postwar period the normal rate of new building has not been kept up. The result has been overcrowding in certain sections even to the point of limiting children to one morning or one afternoon session. Nor have the new school equipment and books increased as rapidly as they would have without budget curtailment. Yet in New York City as elsewhere, children of school ages have been increasing.

New York City schools, like those of the rest of the country, have felt the teacher shortage. It began during the war when many men teachers left. It rose to an acute stage after the war when many men did not return to their teaching jobs and many women began leaving them. Substitute teachers, some of whom had been on the waiting list for twelve or more years, now received regular appointments. But this did little to relieve the shortage as many of these substitutes had for years been carrying work of regular teachers though without the same standing and without being eligible for pensions. The percentage of new, inexperienced teachers rose in New York as elsewhere.

New York City teachers have been among the higher-paid ones in our country. But living expenses have also been high in New York and recently rents have soared in spite of rent ceilings. Many teachers, particularly the married ones, have had to take on extra jobs to meet family expenses. This is particularly hard on the married women, many of whom have children who need attention after their schools let out. It has also made it hard for these teachers to take after-school courses to keep themselves up-to-date professionally.

Where do these 18,000 elementary school teachers live? Most of them choose to live at a distance from the schools in which they teach, particularly if these schools are in low-income neighborhoods. In many schools, particularly in the low-income neighborhoods, the yearly turnover among the teachers is high. Frequent transfers, as well as not living near their schools, means that many teachers do not know the resources and problems of their school neighborhood well and have little to do with the life of the community outside the school walls.

What about the curriculum within the school walls? Beginning about 1922, a curriculum revision program in New York City was outlined with twenty or more courses of study in as many fields, stating the level of skill in the three R's to be taught and the subject matter to be covered in each semester in each grade. Before the war this curriculum was undergoing revision. The revision, which a committee had been working on for a number of years, was being drafted along the lines of what we have said the schools are moving toward. Several steps had already been taken before the war to introduce the new kind of curriculum to the children and teachers. The "activity program" had been in process for a number of years. This was a move away from the old passive recitation and memory kind of learning toward active learning through direct ex-

perience. Also several excellent bulletins had been issued by the
Board of Education. They discussed fundamental principles, a
child's day in school, and other general points of view but gave no
detailed curriculum for the various grades such as the teachers were
used to following. In 1946 came the bulletin, *Development of
Curriculum in the Elementary Schools,* which was prepared as a
step toward the new curriculum. Within the school, the teachers
were encouraged not to follow the old courses of study slavishly but
to try out in their classrooms the principles and the subject matter
suggested in the recent Board of Education bulletins. In brief, before and during the war, the official curriculum was in a stage of
transition, from traditional to newer thinking and attitudes. Thus,
naturally, among the teachers there was a wide range of thinking
and attitudes about children and subject matter and teaching techniques. This, in turn, led to confusion as to what the new curriculum actually meant. The confusion continues. For thinking and
attitudes do not change automatically with the decision to follow a
new curriculum. The Board of Superintendents recognized the problem of inservice training of teachers as a major one. Long before
the present teacher shortage, with the consequent influx of teachers
with little training, official inservice training courses had been begun, which teachers were required to take until they had acquired
a certain number of credits.

Such were the problems of schools on a national scale and in one
big city in 1944 when we at Bank Street had offered to us a chance
to work on one of these problems in public schools. The problem
seemed to be that of inservice training of teachers in a New York
public school. It was during the war in this period of transition in
curriculum and in the conception of a teacher's job and the consequent teacher confusion that Bank Street began its first Workshop.

In Part II we shall tell rather fully the story of our Workshops
because we believe that a single experiment illustrates the problems that schools everywhere face. We believe that the concrete

details of what happened in our Workshops, the stages of growth of teachers, administrators, and our Bank Street staff in six years will show far better than do the generalized statements we have thus far made what thinking and attitudes schools are leaving and what they are moving toward.

PART II

Our Public Schools in Action:
Stages of Workshop Growth

5

Preview and Stage Set in First Stage of Growth

PREVIEW OF OUR FIRST WORKSHOP

IN JUNE, 1946, we were all in a ferment of work at a big public school in New York City. There was the usual speeding up of work that the approaching end of the year always brings to a school. The 6B children were soon to graduate. Fifteen hundred more children were to move on to new teachers, many to other schools. Children monitors moved in and out of the fifty-eight classrooms gathering teachers' records and leaving more to be filled out. The three clerks in the big office were clicking typewriters, completing countless records for the files. The offices of the principal and two assistant principals were fuller than ever of questioning parents, children, and teachers, and their desks were heaped with documents, luncheon lists, promotion sheets, milk lists, inventory sheets for books, and maps, health cards—all the usual administrative work plus the end-of-the-year records and interviews, order lists for books and supplies, and countless other preparations for the following year.

This spring there was an additional element in the end-of-the-year speed-up. These were the last weeks at the school of the principal who had been at this school for five years. The air was charged with the preliminary jitters which sweep any school when an unknown person is to take charge. In this case, there was special agitation: no one wanted an administrative change. For the principal had established relationships with his fifty and more teachers which were founded on a genuine human respect for them as persons, a searching for (and finding) their strong points as well as their weak, a sharing with them of the problems of a big school in a "tension area," problems which concerned the needs of the children as much as, perhaps more than, the subject matter of the curriculum. Now he was leaving them. All the teachers, from the newest substitute to the teacher longest in service, knew that whoever sat in the principal's office next year could raise their jobs to the level of an interesting, significant profession or lower them to the level of underlings whose attitude must be to follow and never "to question why."

Yet in this atmosphere of normal congested end-of-the-year work, of uncertainties concerning the following years, about half the teachers were carrying on another piece of work—voluntary, after-school work. They were the teachers who were taking part in the first Bank Street Workshop in Curriculum and Child Development, to use its impressively long official title as published in the Inservice Bulletin of the Board of Superintendents. For three years, the Bank Street Workshop staff had worked in the classrooms with about half the teachers in the school, and had held weekly after-school meetings with these teachers and the three administrative officers at which nearly every kind of school problem had been discussed. Our early nervousness in this school had disappeared. The teachers with whom we had worked, spontaneously and eagerly shared with us any new happenings in the classrooms. At the same time, a number of teachers had developed who not only were able to carry fine programs independently but were also leaders capable, we felt, of helping other teachers. On the street and in the halls the children greeted us—"When are you coming to us next?" "Can't you come to see our mural?" "Will you see our play in next assembly?" We felt accepted. We now spoke of "our school" and "our children," and teachers and administration spoke of "our Workshop."

Our special work, that spring, was a second revision of curriculum materials and methods in social studies for the whole school. This writing of a social studies curriculum, stimulated by a preliminary official bulletin revising the entire curriculum in the New York public schools, had been an unexpected development in the second year, as will appear as we tell the chronological story of our first experimental Workshop. Our curriculum materials (which involved the exploration and use of our particular school neighborhood, maturity levels of children, classroom techniques, as well as subject matter) were developed by the Bank Street Workshop members, tried out in classrooms by the teachers, revised on the basis of what had and had not worked, tried out again, and a second time revised in the spring of 1946 in the congestion of the end-of-the-year work and agitation of impending changes in administration. This second revision involved all Workshop members. It was no light task for the Bank Street members—but it was their job. It was no light work for the teacher members—but *they considered it their job,* too. For the Workshop had become *our* Workshop— the joint undertaking of teachers and Bank Street staff. The teachers' professional attitude, their broadened conception of their job as teachers, *that*—not the written curriculum materials—was what all of us, teachers and Bank Street staff alike, counted as the real result of our three-year experimental Workshop. How this came about is the story of the *first stage in our Workshop growth,* when a staff composed entirely of Bank Street members worked for three years in one school with one principal.

WHAT IS A WORKSHOP?

What is a Workshop? It may be almost anything in the way of laboratory or studio work, or demonstration teaching, or background material on children or subject matter, or just discussion of school problems which is offered to teachers who are already on the teaching job. It is a word which has recently increased in popularity as "Inservice Training" for teachers has decreased in popularity. Why?

Largely because "Workshop" suggests that learning is an active process, whereas "training" suggests that learning is the passive acceptance of instructions as to how to behave. The contrast in connotation becomes evident when applied to another field. Who ever heard of a Workshop for animals? But training of animals is the ordinary expression for making them obediently behave according to an imposed pattern. Not that all Workshops for teachers live up to the connotation of active learning, nor that all training centers follow the pattern of mere instructions and drill as to how to behave in a classroom! Yet the change in vocabulary is significant as indicating the genuine change in school thinking and attitudes described in Part I.

Our Workshop story is of one local experiment. To us, and we believe to others also, this experiment is significant because through it we hope to throw some light on techniques through which teachers can keep growing professionally in the big public school system in New York City. That is, we regarded our work as a laboratory experiment *for* the school system which we hoped would take over and use such of our findings and techniques as they found sound and could make use of in their problem of inservice training of teachers. We believed that the Board of Education committee who asked us to conduct a Workshop also regarded it as a laboratory experiment for them. Why else should they have asked us? Why else should they have helped us plan the work before we started? Have stood behind us throughout the years of the experiment, ready to give not only advice and consideration of what we felt to be the next steps in our growth, but practical help in making these steps become real? Their role in the Workshop was not merely reading the long reports we made to them each year. It was an active role. They, too, felt this was their Workshop.

We had also a broader aim than being of use to the New York school system. We hoped through our experiment to throw some light on the much bigger problem of attitudes and techniques in teacher education everywhere, whether that of teachers already in schools or of people preparing to be teachers.

We began our Workshop in one school and stayed there three years before expanding to three schools under conditions so different as to amount to a new experiment. So our Workshop story is divided into two stages of growth and will be told that way. We begin our story in the first school where we conducted a Workshop and where we worked three years with one principal.

STAGE SET OF OUR FIRST WORKSHOP

Locally, our Workshop job, as we saw it, was to work with these teachers in *their* school, with *their* children, in *their* physical and social neighborhood, and in that concrete situation to work with them realistically to build a curriculum suited to children in modern-day United States. To do our job this way, we had to know this one school well. That meant we had to know the practical setup of the school particularly as it affected the teachers' job; the administrative system, not only its structure but how this structure affected the teachers; the children and their neighborhood; and above all, the teachers themselves, their psychological slants toward children and toward their job as well as their teaching skills and practices.

The practical setup was fairly easy to learn, though it took time. We give a brief summary of it in our first school:

Setup in the School

"Our" school, as we came to call it, was an elementary school with classes ranging from kindergarten through sixth grade. It was housed in an old-type building, classrooms with screwed-down desks, some rooms with sliding doors which when opened made the auditorium, a rather small paved courtyard as the only play space for seventeen hundred children (including kindergarten classes) except the big dark entry hall which was also used as a passage by classes or by children going to the toilets, a children's library, no laboratory of any sort, no carpentry benches except in two rooms for special classes, in one of which was also a cooking stove and running water. The equipment in the regular classrooms consisted of books, textbooks, many of them out-of-date, with some supplemental reading largely of the informational type except in kindergarten; maps, almost exclusively political with a few physiographic maps where elevation was shown in colors, two fine large globes that could be chalked on, no atlas in the school, only old-fashioned geographies; a small quantity of paints, no plasticine except when supplied by the teacher; no science equipment of any sort and no electric outlets for use in classrooms; no tools or wood except as supplied by a teacher. In the supply room were some other supplies of materials for painting, clay for modeling or map making, papers, etc., which were seldom used in the classrooms. New supplies and new books not on the authorized list were ordered by an assistant principal on requisition slips and usually took about a year to get through.

The school record of each child contained the ordinary factual information about parents, past schools attended, school record in academic subjects, brief health record (the school had a school nurse), I.Q. or other mental record if for any reason the child had been examined, and any outstanding facts about the family or the child. The teachers kept attendance records, health cards, lists for morning milk or free luncheon at school, promotion sheets, inventory sheets for books and maps. For the most part the teachers kept no other records of the children. Their records were made during teaching hours. Classroom interruptions were frequent as child monitors collected various lists, delivered and collected milk bottles, or brought around a variety of papers to be read or signed. In addition, the principal asked each teacher to write a case history of one child each year.

Since we have already described the official curriculum in Part I, here it is necessary merely to recall that it was in a stage of radical revision. In this period of transition, some teachers still followed the old courses of study in detail. Others were trying to put into practice the principles and attitudes stated in already-issued official bulletins but not yet embodied in detail in an authoritative curriculum bulletin—an effort which our principal supported.

How the Workshop Functioned

Our Workshop, of course, had to be fitted into the complicated administrative school system of a big city. Details of how this was done will probably interest only readers who are working along similar lines in other schools or other school systems. We have therefore put the statement of how we functioned within the system in Appendix 1.

Our working relations with the administration in the school where we worked were, of course, of prime importance to our experiment. Suffice it to say here that in our first school, the principal considered the Workshop an experiment for the school administration as well as for Bank Street. The various practical ways by which he and his assistant principals helped to make the Workshop a joint school and Bank Street experiment will appear as our story unfolds. Even more important than these practical ways was the psychological atmosphere within this school. The relationship between the principal and teachers was extraordinarily free. The principal wished the experience and thinking of the teachers to function in school policies, school curriculum thinking, and school practices. And it is something to note that in this tension area, there was practically no tension within the school caused by the presence of colored and white children, either between teachers and children or among the children themselves.

Our Children and Their Neighborhood

Now, a word about the children and the neighborhood of our first school.

In our school were 1700 or more children from kindergarten through sixth grade, with 58 teachers. There were 9 special classes, which included 1 health class; 1 of foreign-speaking children (largely Puerto Ricans); 2 CRMD classes (mentally retarded children); 4 Grade Op classes (disturbed children, academically but not necessarily mentally retarded); 1 OpD class (boys, mentally retarded and problem children). The number of children in an OpD class was officially limited to 20; in Grade Op to 25; the number of children in regular classes was from 32 to 40. We came to know the children in all types of classes as, from time to time, we had teachers from the special classes in the Workshop and worked with them and their children in their classrooms.

Before we began our Workshop, we explored the externals of the school neighborhood—the buildings which contained the homes of our children and the streets on which they played. The school was in a typical city, low-income neighborhood. When we first came, the 1700 children were about evenly divided between colored and white, with about 15 per cent Puerto Ricans. Later, the percentage of colored children rose to nearly 80. Most of the children lived in crowded apartment houses over small stores, with fire escapes zigzagging down the front, dark inside halls, hall toilets, lines of wash from the back windows flapping over back yards often filled with trash. Some children lived in a small area of single houses with neat front yards. The streets where the children played were flanked by many kinds of small stores—groceries, hardware, etc., with a larger five- and ten-cent store; small shops with work going on, such as shoe repairing, printing, laundries, but no big industries; garages, a post office, fire station, public library, two public playgrounds; many cheap hotels, movie houses; many churches. The neighborhood was linked to the rest of New York by surface electric cars, busses, and two subways. It was linked to the rest of the country by the near-by Hudson River with ferries, barges, and war boats on its waters, and by the George Washington Bridge, with the old lighthouse at its base, spanning the river farther north; and on the riverbank, by the automobile highway and railroad tracks with freight cars from all over the United States.

The neighborhood was linked to the past—to the Indians of Inwood, to Henry Hudson and Robert Fulton, to the Dutch who gave the section its name, to the early postmen galloping up the Albany Post Road, to George Washington, who commanded his army from the near-by heights, to Alexander Hamilton, who planted in front of his house thirteen trees symbolic of the colonies, some of which are still standing.

Like all city neighborhoods, ours held much for curriculum building. Modern city housekeeping pervades them all. Everywhere trucks are delivering food to the stores, coal to the houses and schools; street cleaners are at work; water is running into city sewers; and under the streets, pipes are bringing light and power to radios and telephones; postmen are delivering mail, policemen stand at street intersections and firemen near their fire engines.

The faraway and the long-ago as well as the present pervade all neighborhoods. Part of our job was to find the local situations where our young children could study at first hand enough of the present to give meaning to the here-and-now world around them, and where our older children could study at first hand more complex present-day situations and enough of the past and the distant to give meaning to the lands and lives of people who lived long ago or far away. For to help teachers to use the school environment to widen their children's experiences and interests and to give meaning to the study of the world they live in was an essential part of helping teachers to understand and enjoy their job.

The social environment was less easily read. To be sure, the five movie theaters in our school district showed their importance in our children's lives in many of the school discussions as well as in their free play on the streets. The neighborhood supported many churches, and most of the children attended some of them. Organized religion—churches—seemed to be the strongest cohesive force in the neighborhood. We ourselves had little direct contact with the parents. At their request, we did conduct a number of meetings where child psychology was discussed. But lack of time prevented our following this important aspect of our children's environment—their homes and their parents.

From the children themselves we gathered that in their homes the outward conventions of society were greatly valued. For instance, practically all the children came to school in shirts and ties, which was the parents' wish, not a school requirement. We saw that our children felt more secure when they conformed to such external mores of society. Also the children's attitudes showed that obedience was expected of them. In general, the parent seemed a symbol of authority in the home and the teacher the symbol in the school.

The school records showed a high percentage of broken homes. Such homes furnished most of our "difficult" children. The records also showed that many children did not get enough or the right kind of food at home. School lunches and midmorning milk (free when needed) were a part of the school's regular program. The records also showed a rapidly shifting neighborhood population. Negroes were moving in rapidly. Since most of them had lower incomes than the people who moved out, neighborhood people in the stores and the movie houses, the policeman and others, often said the neighborhood was "going down." But from the point of view of our children, this neighborhood meant "going up," for most of them had come from even lower rent areas.[5] Further discussion of these and other environmental factors will appear in later chapters.

We came to know well large numbers of the children in our school. We found many brilliant children among them. We also found many who showed the lack of cultural opportunities characteristic of low-income groups everywhere. Many children showed the effect of past repressive discipline probably both in their homes and in former schools. Many of them, particular those recently

[5] Some of the facts and the analysis of the social environment of our school neighborhood are taken from a study made by a group of students from our Bank Street School for Teachers, who were placed for practice teaching in this school.

come from the South, had had an inadequate number of years in any school—some even eleven years old had had no schooling at all. The percentage of slow or non-readers was naturally high, as was the number of special classes. Yet we found the response of these children to new experiences and new content just like that of "privileged" children in some of the schools where we had taught. In spite of their slender opportunities in the past, their ability to think, to express themselves in all kinds of art media was, in the regular classes, up to their age level.

Our Working Program

Our real work was with the teachers, and our working program revolved around them. Above all we had to know the teachers, both as a group and as individuals. All our long experiences with our Bank Street student teachers and with teachers in a wide variety of schools had taught us that general group seminars or courses must meet the group needs of the moment. In addition, we were convinced that each individual's personality and what he considered his problems must also receive consideration through individual conferences and practical help. We resolved to try out a working program which would include these two major techniques: (1) work with individual teachers in their classrooms on any problem connected with their curriculum programs or their children; and (2) weekly after-school meetings with the whole group of teachers or with teachers divided into grade groupings. Three Bank Street staff members undertook the actual work, adding it to their already crowded programs. The total time they were able to give amounted to less than the time of one full-time worker. Such was the program we had in mind when we began our meetings with the teachers.

6

Cues from Teachers Determine Our
First Workshop Approach

GETTING STARTED

WHAT did we want to know about the teachers to make a Workshop worth while for them, both as a group and as individuals? First, we had to know their attitude toward a Workshop in the school. We conceived of our role not as that of "experts" from the outside, people coming in to make a demonstration of how things should be done. On the contrary, we wanted our role to be that of other teachers who were ready to become intimately involved in the specifics of their daily jobs and to make these daily jobs and problems growing out of their own situations the basis upon which to discuss with them any questions which troubled them about children and the new curriculum that they were being asked to put into practice. We believed that if the teachers once experienced directly what the newer attitudes and thinking meant in terms of growth of the children, they themselves would take them over and become independent of us—which was our ideal. Growth of the teachers was the criterion by which we measured the success or failure of any of our Workshop techniques. Whether or not we and our Workshop would be accepted on this basis was a troubling first question as we began our work. Most important of all, we had to know the teachers' attitudes toward their own job. This attitude, whatever it was, would condition all our own work in the school.

We got the quality of these teachers in our first contact with a group of seven of them called together by the principal for a preliminary discussion of the Workshop plan, a group that continued to act as a Planning Committee throughout the year. They knew what the teachers wanted, what approaches would interest them, far better than we and better than the principal, too. They thought the Workshop should be thrown open to all teachers in the school and that no fee should be asked. They agreed with us that participation in the Workshop should be voluntary, though a considerable proportion of the higher officials with whom we talked felt that few teachers would be willing to spend a weekly hour and a half after school unless attendance was made compulsory. It was interest, however, rather than numbers that we wanted. We did not want the atmosphere of "must" in the Workshop. We felt sure that such an atmosphere would delay even if it did not permanently undercut the establishment of sound human relationships between our staff and the teachers. We knew that confidence on both sides had to be established before we could be useful.

As a matter of fact, on a voluntary basis, about half the teachers in a faculty of fifty-eight were Workshop members each of the first three years that we worked in this school. The Workshop members were not always the same teachers. In a public school there are always a number of transfers each year. Each year some teachers new to the school, and some who had originally held off, joined the group. About the same number each year dropped out. More surprising was the number who stayed with the Workshop for three consecutive years. Most of the teachers were married and many had children. Home duties made it difficult to stay after school one day a week in addition to the day a month on which the principal met his faculty. Many of our teachers had to earn money to supplement their teacher salary—a situation which was aggravated in those war years when the cost of living had risen without corresponding increase in salaries. We were pleased when at the close of the first meeting where the principal put the Workshop plan before the whole faculty twenty-six members enrolled in the Workshop. We were off to a good start!

WHAT THE TEACHERS WANTED
FROM THE WORKSHOP

Then came our first meeting with these enrolled Workshop members. We discussed details of our plan, saying that we had not planned a course of lectures as we wished the teachers themselves to determine what should be discussed at our meetings, and we expressed our readiness to work in the classrooms with those teachers who wished us, perhaps with each of the three Bank Street members working with teachers divided into three grade groups. We then suggested that we begin with informal questions on their part which would give us a background for planning the program.

We got a very definite expression from the teachers in response to our question, "What do you wish to get from a Workshop?" They stated their problems in the form of questions which they hoped we might answer. The following questions are excerpts from the minutes of our first meeting with the teachers who had signed up for the first Workshop:

What is an activity program?

How would a teacher approach an activity program for the first time?

Having got an activity program started, how can you keep interest alive?

What part does the teacher play? Does she introduce the program and does she have some part in it?

When a committee has chosen the activity program, how can you stimulate the children and keep them at work on what the committee has chosen?

How are the tool subjects integrated with an activity program?

How far can you let a child with special interests go on his own?

How can you do research with children who have language difficulty?

At other early meetings these questions were asked:

How can you maintain order and discipline if you let children move about the room?

How can children learn in a room where there is noise, such as talking as they plan and execute a mural or do carpentry?

How do you divide children into committees?

How do you conduct a discussion? Just hand it over to the children?

How long should a unit be?

How can you cover the prescribed subject matter unless all the children are using the same textbook?

How can you teach history and geography together when our courses of study and our textbooks are not written that way?

As we listened to the teachers in our early meetings with them, we became convinced that those who joined the Workshop—and the attendance was always voluntary—were not so much resisting the newer psychological and educational thinking as they were puzzled as to *how* to carry it out. The above questions showed that their interest centered in classroom techniques. Indeed, they constantly said they wanted "no more theory," that it was of no practical use to them.

We asked ourselves why all the questions the teachers asked had to do with teaching techniques—all rather *how* than *why*. Their questions indicated that what they wanted to get out of a Workshop was skill in carrying out the new curriculum instructions in methods. The questions also told us something about their attitude toward their own job. For obviously they would wish to get out of a Workshop what they thought would help them in their job as they conceived it. The teachers' initial attitude toward their job was that they were responsible for carrying out official instructions —not for planning or initiating programs and experiences which fitted their children.

These initial attitudes toward the Workshop and their job gave us our cue as to where to begin in a practical working program. The teachers' early attitudes made us feel that we should place the major emphasis upon working out teaching techniques with individual teachers with their children in their classrooms; and that our early weekly after-school meetings should be discussions, with teachers divided into grade groupings, of the techniques they had tried out

with their children and what their children got out of them. So
that is the way we started.

FIRST WORKSHOP APPROACH THROUGH
CURRICULUM EXPERIENCES

The various new teaching techniques which within the last few
years the teachers had been asked to follow out were trips, discussions, committee organization among the children, child research, free art, constructive play—all in their minds more or less
centered around units. So we began on those techniques which in
our minds were curriculum experiences which would eventually
lead to real curriculum building. Each of the three Bank Street
members worked with the teachers in one of the three grade groupings—kindergarten, first, second grades; third and fourth grades;
fifth and sixth grades—in the classrooms as soon as teachers wanted
us to, and each held weekly after-school discussion with the teachers in her group, the three small groups meeting simultaneously,
with occasional meetings of all Workshop members.

Thus, following the leads of the teachers, the first Workshop
approach was necessarily limited largely to isolated curriculum experiences revolving more or less around units. In the first exploratory discussions, in each of the grade groupings, the teachers told
about current or past units they had tried—the subject matter and
techniques used. Those early discussions revealed not only what
part units played in their total programs but also something about
what the teachers considered their chief job with children; how,
practically, they planned their programs; to what extent they based
their programs on the children's interests. As illustrations we give
brief excerpts or summaries of three early discussions, one in each
of the three groupings. The quotations are condensed from full
records of these discussions taken at the meetings by a Bank Street
secretary.

CUES FROM KINDERGARTEN, FIRST- AND SECOND-GRADE
TEACHERS

At the first meeting the Bank Street member opened the discussion: "I suppose our big question is: What do you wish to accomplish with your children? To understand your situation, I'd like to ask two other questions first: How much do you have to follow a syllabus? Do you have to make the children read? And at what age?"

Teachers: "We have to cover a syllabus—according to the Board of Education. They haven't told us not to follow it." . . . "I don't stick to the old syllabus. I have freedom. But I do teach reading in the first grade." . . . "The kids are not ready for reading." . . . "Maybe they're not ready for reading but the teacher following you complains if the children can't read." . . . "Children have language difficulty all the way from kindergarten to third grade." . . . "I have a class of 1B–2B slow children. We use charts and hope they will learn. We also began our own reader. I found that the children had memorized their readers." . . . "I teach my children that they *must not* interrupt while I am teaching reading."

Bank Street: "What can we give the children who are not interested in reading? What could first-grade children do that would be a developing experience?"

Teachers: "Trips—classroom experiences" . . . "Coloring pictures— we have books for this." . . . "Clay" . . . "Pre-reading games" . . . "Activity program" . . . "Singing" . . . "I give my morning to formal work." . . . "Looking for pictures; getting acquainted; learning how to work together" . . . "Conference—which is a free period. In it we decide what each child will do—sew or read or paint. Then we talk about things—we call it the Show and Tell. My conference is about fifteen minutes."

Bank Street: "Do you have a program in your own minds?"

Teachers gave their schedules (not their programs) of different periods for different subjects.

Bank Street: "How many opportunities are there for the children to do things together? Working in clay, for instance, isn't social."

Teachers: "Play" . . . "Play with dolls." . . . "Play with blocks."

Bank Street: *"Play!* Where could you put in play so children could do something together?"

Teachers: "Through art" . . . "My children played they had a fruit store." . . . "Let the insecure child play with blocks." . . . "Not mine, he's helter-skelter. Has no ideas. Knocks the blocks down."

Bank Street: "Do you have 'people' or characters to play with? For instance, a mother, a policeman, tradespeople?"

Teachers: "We make dolls. We have them in books and poke them out." . . . "We have to have more substantial toys than those book dolls."

Bank Street: "When do you see a time in your day when there could be free dramatic play? In playing, children learn about the world. What are your first-grade children interested in?"

Teachers: "Airplanes" . . . "Comic books" . . . "Parties."

Bank Street: "Do your children know the neighborhood? Do you take them on trips and help them to see it? If they have a chance to play, will they bring out what they have seen? What do you read? Couldn't you bring in books that tie up with the trip?"

Teacher: "I took my children to see the autumn leaves. They didn't like the leaves but they liked the trains they saw—so I am going on from there."

Bank Street: "How can we get the children's play developed so that they are really learning something? For children must learn in school. How about domestic play? Where's the father going? To work? That's teaching a child indirectly—to have him play out what he knows about. Going back to group play. Take a family, father going to work—group or one child might be playing the family; another group might be building a station. Try to connect children's play, especially in the first and second grades. Mustn't get play too elaborate for kindergarten children. Then, in your next conference group, you might talk about father's work; the station, selling tickets. Play isn't all individual. You could bring in a story about trains."

Teacher: "With a large group, how can you follow the children? How do you know what's coming up?"

Bank Street: "It is hard to manage in a big group—but out of group play and follow-up discussion, with some information brought in by you, comes learning. There is a time when maybe you need to be formal. If there's lots of free play then they'll like the times of formal teaching. You ought to get an activity going so strong that they'll want to read about it. We have to get down to concrete cases. Perhaps you'd bring in some actual situations with your children which we could discuss in our conferences?

"The core of our problem is: How to keep a program going with children at different levels of interests and skills? How keep something that's good for all going? How to manage formal and informal work, so that there will be learning? I want to go over the syllabus and see where we can relax."

Teachers: "This was made an 'activity' school and it was one for eight years. Then a state examiner sat for five hours in the school. Handed us the fundamental words the children must know; the phonetics they must know. Where did the 'activity' come in?" . . . "Another thing is all the clerical work we have to do. It's against the rules to take roll or record books home. You can imagine where we do them."

Bank Street: "Our problem is how to keep the program going. What kinds of interests between kindergarten and third grade can we develop?"

The discussion at this first meeting with kindergarten, first- and second-grade teachers brought out the common problem that these teachers had: that of teaching reading at the age prescribed in the old syllabus. It showed the degree to which these teachers felt under compulsion to follow the old syllabi in detail—only one teacher "felt free." Though recent official bulletins had given them much leeway in choosing subject matter, none had yet given anything nearly as concrete to follow as the old syllabus. This discussion also gave leads for curriculum experiences which might be developed for the children: in the use of the neighborhood as a laboratory; in developing play as a learning situation as distinguished from busy work or play as an interlude for relaxation; in developing subject matter and teaching techniques and classroom atmosphere in keeping with young children's interests and needs; in finding and using a variety of source materials.

CUES FROM THIRD- AND FOURTH-GRADE TEACHERS

These teachers were chiefly troubled about units, which were largely about faraway and long-ago people. At the first meeting with one Bank Street member the teachers reported on their units. One teacher had tried a unit on food. She said, "I gave it up—not enough interest. Children didn't even know their own neighborhood. I took the class on a walk to see Hamilton's house." When asked, "Do they know Manhattan is an island?" she replied, "Yes, they know that. We studied about Peter Stuyvesant." Three teachers had units on China; two on children of all lands. One explained, "The class has made an igloo; now they are making a Congo home; I plan eventually to make an American home. They work from pictures." The other asked in connection with the study of Holland that the Workshop teach her how to make a windmill for her children that "wouldn't fall to pieces."

None of these teachers used the neighborhood work and workers as a laboratory for her unit. When they did use the neighborhood, it was to see historic places; none made any special effort to give children experiences or source material from which to think out relationships of the work of the Chinese to the lands they lived in. The maps they used gave the children no images of the land. The only maps in the school were political maps or maps in which elevation was expressed in color symbols. The school had three large globes with continental outlines, which could be marked on with chalk; they were not used by any of these teachers. Instead, they used maps of the world with the Mercator projection in which northern and southern regions are distorted in size and the Pacific Ocean is split in two. There were no science experiments. Dramatic expression was largely limited to assembly programs. They used some storybooks on Chinese life. One teacher had the children make individual books, which were illustrated by making tracings of the pictures in the storybooks, then cutting out and pasting the tracings into the individual books. The children had taken no trips in connection with their units. In short, the teachers counted on words and adult art rather than firsthand experiences as the children's source of information.

These reports led to discussions. When the Bank Street member suggested that trips could be explorations for the children through which they could discover, for instance, that Manhattan was an island, one teacher said, "Trips are impossible with large groups. Beautiful idea, however!" A Bank Street member suggested how many kinds of source materials there are besides reading material which can give children a sense of people in other lands—pictures, posters, a book of Chinese proverbs, movies about China, phonograph records of Chinese music, maps that look like land and water, folk songs of all lands, science experiments, meeting people from other lands. She said she could bring much of this source material to the classrooms if they wished it. For the children who were studying China she suggested that she arrange to have a Chinese woman from the Bank Street Nursery School come in her Chinese clothes and talk about her country and answer children's questions. She suggested that we have some Workshop meetings on science related to their units. The teacher studying Holland could help her children make a windmill that would be turned by a current of air from the radiator and explain what makes winds.

Thus, this discussion with teachers of third- and fourth-grade children gave the same leads for curriculum experiences suggested in the discussion with the kindergarten, first- and second-grade teachers, with additional leads: in the study of faraway and long-ago lands and people through some direct experiences; in the use of maps for thinking out relationships; in simple science experiments.

CUES FROM FIFTH- AND SIXTH-GRADE TEACHERS

The early meetings with teachers of the fifth and sixth grades showed much the same attitudes toward units but an even greater concern about covering the required subject matter. The teachers

were all following the old separate and unrelated courses of study
for history, geography, and civics, and seldom had units which were
closely related to the subject matter of these fields. They all used
political maps or maps showing elevation in color symbols; the
school had no others. Science experiments were unknown. In English, the emphasis was overwhelmingly on grammar, punctuation,
and other formal techniques. Trips—the few that were taken—
were largely to museums. All felt that one of the biggest problems
was the "slow readers" in their classes. These children could not
enter into classwork but remained a group apart. The teachers felt
that someone to help on remedial reading was, perhaps, their greatest need. Though these teachers were not at all opposed to an integrated program, they saw no way to accomplish it and at the
same time cover the required subject matter.

WHAT WE LEARNED FROM EARLY MEETINGS

As the three Bank Street members discussed the early meetings
with their several groups and their early work with individual
teachers, certain common elements emerged. The teachers in all
three groups were trying, with a few exceptions, to fit new techniques into the old framework of separate courses of study. Many,
perhaps most of them, were confused and worried because these
new techniques seemed "extras"; they didn't seem to fit the old
curriculum—as, indeed, they didn't. Yet, the teachers were trying
their best to follow both new techniques and the old curriculum.
To us, the advantage of approaching our Workshop first through
the unit was that the teachers thought of it as an *experience* for
the children in which they might draw upon any of the content
from the many courses of study. The disadvantage was that most
of the teachers thought of the unit as an episode, an "extra" added
to the real work which was outlined in the courses of study.

All three of the Bank Street workers felt that our early discussions in small group meetings had established good working
relations between Bank Street and teacher members. We all talked

freely and with less self-consciousness than in the beginning. The teachers' questions continued to revolve largely around *how* rather than *why*. We sympathized profoundly with the teachers' impatience of theory divorced from practical situations. Concrete help to individual teachers with their own classroom problems was the basis of our working program. Yet, more and more, we felt that all these teaching techniques in what they interchangeably called the "activity program" or the "new curriculum," of which the unit was the symbol, were mere empty forms of little value to the children and hard on the teachers unless they understood the purpose and goals of the new curriculum. Teaching techniques are tools, not ends in themselves.

The problem was fundamentally to think in terms of children—under what conditions children best learn, what opportunities for true learning came through these new techniques which the old techniques did not provide. In our own thinking, curriculum and child development are so closely related as to be inseparable in practice. So, while continuing to work with individual teachers on practical techniques, we began to organize our group Workshop meetings on a broader basis which would lead toward the interpretation of these techniques in terms of child development.

SOCIAL STUDIES AS AN OPPORTUNITY TO THINK IN TERMS OF CHILDREN

From the beginning we concentrated on social studies rather than on the academic tool subjects. Social studies gave the best opportunity to think in terms of children. In social studies we had constantly to think of what interests, drives, understandings, children have in the various stages of their development; of what experiences had meaning to them, would be learning experiences in the world around them, and lead them to the next developmental stage.

All this was recognized in the new official curriculum and gave official sanction to the kind of programs we hoped would develop. In the official bulletin, social studies were treated as an integration of the old separate studies of history, geography, and civics, to which we added science. The bulletin of Curriculum Design gave *themes* for children in three stages of development (kindergarten, first and second grades; third and fourth; fifth and sixth grades) around which programs of activities and subject matter in social studies should be organized. The theme for kindergarten, first and second grades was: *Living and Working in Home, School, and Neighborhood.* This theme made it logical to begin with what was familiar to the children and gradually widen their experiences. It made use of the neighborhood, its work and workers, as a laboratory, the logical basis for subject matter in social studies. The theme in social studies for third and fourth grades was: *Living and Working Together in New York City and in Different Kinds of Communities.* We quote the bulletin interpretation of this theme: "The emphasis during these years should be on human geography, on how people live, how they adapt themselves to their environment, and how they change the environment to meet their needs." Thus, again, there was official support for what we hoped would develop. The theme for fifth and sixth grades was: *Living and Working Together in the United States of America and in the World*—a further widening of the study of people and their lands.

In all of these themes the emphasis is placed squarely on people, but people in a specific environment—how they live and work, beginning with the home and ending with the world. Our job in the Workshop was to work out practical experiences, practical techniques, through which our children from kindergarten through sixth grade in our school and neighborhood could learn about the life and work of people and the lands they lived in through active exploring, expressing, and thinking.

PRACTICAL NEXT STEPS IN OUR WORKING PROGRAM

Individual teachers wanted different things from us. For several months some teachers did not wish us to visit in their classrooms—

we went only after a definite invitation—but wanted to talk over their programs. Most of them wished us to begin at once with what they called "demonstration teaching." Practically, this meant preliminary visits to the classroom and talks with the teacher about her unit, then planning with her some appropriate curriculum experience such as a trip, going with her and her children on the trip, and leading the follow-up discussion; helping to develop classroom activities such as dramatizations, art, creative language, crafts, science, map making. From the beginning, all of us brought a wide variety of source materials to the classrooms, both for actual use by the children and as background content for the teachers.

Each of the Bank Street members, at the request of any of the teachers she was working with, met with her to discuss any troubling problem. Of necessity the out-of-classroom time was limited —often to the lunch hour. So as time went on, we developed other techniques. We found that the teachers liked us to leave with them written suggestions for the next step in their programs. This technique proved valuable also in keeping the principal in close touch with our work in the classrooms. We gave him copies of all written suggestions we gave to the teachers; also minutes of our after-school meetings, though he nearly always came to the meetings.

Our after-school discussions, at both the small meetings and the combined meetings, covered a wide range. In a general way, they followed the leads of the teachers. At the early meetings, the teachers often reported on some work with their children—a trip, dramatic play, painting, or anything else. Sometimes we discussed in detail the teacher's role, for instance, on a trip or in the follow-up discussion with the children. In time these discussions led at the teachers' requests to talks on various kinds of background content for the teachers themselves, such as the work patterns of New York and how they are conditioned by the geographic earth conditions, or the meaning of play in children's lives. Our Workshop meetings were not, by any means, all talk. At some after-school sessions the teachers went on trips themselves to explore at first hand such a work process as the distribution of food from the A & P distribution plant. We had several science meetings where a specialist brought simple, largely homemade apparatus and showed the teachers how to conduct simple science experiments on matters related to their programs. The teachers themselves modeled maps of the countries their children were studying. Other discussions led directly into a consideration of child psychology and maturity levels.

In all the work, either with individual teachers or in group discussions, curriculum and child development were combined. When we discussed curriculum and teaching techniques, it was in terms of what had meaning to children. When we discussed child development, the implications for curriculum were always stressed. Nevertheless, for clarity, we shall have to talk about curriculum experiences and child development separately as we continue the story of the Workshop in the following chapters.

7

Thinking about the Development of Children

CONSIDERATION of the development of children permeated all our thinking in the Workshop and should not, by rights, be plucked out of context and treated in a separate chapter. Yet, for clarity, as we have already said, we are doing just this. However, it should always be remembered that this work in developing the concept of child development, here told separated from the total work, grew out of problems of teaching children in the classrooms and was fed back into the teaching. Attitudes of the teachers, questions they asked, led from time to time to full Workshop meetings with the psychologist on our staff; a few of these meetings are reported on in this chapter. They span about two years and are only roughly chronological.

INITIAL INTEREST IN "DIFFICULT" CHILDREN

The interest of the teachers in child development was in the beginning largely centered around the practical and very real problem in their classrooms of what to do with "problem" children. Most of the teachers had one or two of these difficult children; some special classes (OpD) were composed entirely of such children. Over and over again in our early meetings the remarks of teachers revealed how disturbing these children were to them. We have referred to the kindergarten teacher who said "her" maladjusted child was "helter-skelter—had no ideas—knocked down the blocks." [6] Teachers of older children said "slow readers" created disturbances—even to fighting in the classrooms. The teachers had different attitudes toward these disturbing children. "They shouldn't be in school." . . . "We should have more OpD classes—they don't belong with normal children." . . . "They just disturb the work." . . . "We should know about the family—we can't do anything for a child with a bad home."

This attitude of the teachers presented a dilemma and a challenge in more than one sense. They were thinking of the disturbance caused by difficult children, not the disturbance children feel. Problem children were more real to them than children's problems— the difficulties all children encounter in the course of growing up. This distinction was not too surprising, since in their classrooms they often did have deeply disturbed children with serious problems for whom therapy was needed and for whom it was not available. Yet this contrast between normal children and problem children interferes with understanding of the drives and needs common to all children, fulfilled for some and woefully denied to others. It also leads to concentration on behavior rather than on the motives which are the springs to behavior.

Fairly early, the teachers asked for Workshop meetings with the psychologist on the Bank Street staff on what they usually called "mental hygiene." At first, she tried discussing needs and impulses of children in various stages of their development as a basis for planning children's school life.[7] The teachers' response was almost always in terms of the difficult child. With notable exceptions, they felt they understood children who "behaved themselves," conformed—or at least they felt they could handle such children and were not particularly interested in discussing what they were like. Such discussion of "good" children seemed "theory," and here, as elsewhere, they wanted only "practical help."

[6] Chapter 6, p. 94.
[7] See Chapter 2, pp. 23 ff., for the statement she later gave the teachers— "Some Needs and Impulses of Children That Can Be Partially Fulfilled in Their School Lives."

So our psychologist suggested that she come to the classrooms to observe some of these troublesome children in their relations with other children, in their relations with their teachers, in their attitudes to the work going on. This she did. We give as illustration the notes she took with her to the Workshop discussion, following a morning of brief visits in the classrooms.

Notes	*Questions for Discussion*
Walter—who is clean, good boy. Described as child who fights back when he is attacked. (Teacher approves)	Why study a child who isn't a problem? Doesn't every child have problems that deserve to be understood?
Marie—observed in class; report by teacher. No relation to work. Flits and stamps around. I.Q.—80	
Cried bitterly when Miss Y. visited home—although was careful not to antagonize. Separated from mother who is down South —living with married sister.	Child needs to bring her two lives together—needs help in accepting separation from mother— how is it dealt with at home?
Child sang French song (New Orleans) while teacher and psychologist are chatting.	Why not have her teach this song to group or part of group?
Facial expression changed from set belligerence to calm, benign look of longing as she sings.	
Psychologist asked if she had seen boats in New Orleans—learned she had lived on a houseboat— never mentioned it when class was studying houseboats on the Yangtze River.	How could she have a chance to bring this experience to the group?
Jack—observed in class; report by teacher. Incessant talking—not loud, just talkative.	What is motive behind incessant talking? Why doesn't he stop when he is told?

Notes	*Questions for Discussion*
Obeys orders only when he wishes.	
Last to obey commands to stop work.	
Talking reported to mother.	What do you want to see mother for? What is goal in talking to mother about child? Must be adapted to teacher's knowledge of mother-child relations.
Mother accuses teacher of picking on Jack.	
Reported for hitching on truck, fighting in yard.	
Denies fighting.	
Uses decalcomanias though told not to use them.	
General, nonconforming, disturbing behavior; constantly reported for disobedience.	What is he fighting against inside himself?
Objects to being talked to about his wrongdoing.	Why? Would you like it better if he listened and did the same thing over again, a minute later?
Hits—even when accidentally hurt or slightly so.	This is pattern of young anxious child.
Pushed a girl because she didn't return a dictionary fast enough for him.	What does teacher do or say when this happens?
Not stupid.	
"Not bad today—had something interesting to tell class."	
Improved since he brought in puppet—helping other children make puppets.	
During "Show and Tell"—got up to talk instead of keeping his seat.	Did teacher tell him to sit down—what does she undo when she does that?
Keeps left hand cupped around writing hand—test—prevent copying? Head low over paper.	What is this child's primary need? How can you get him to want to conform?
Mouth active, quiet singing to himself.	

At these discussions with the psychologist the teachers showed genuine eagerness. These were their children, their problems.

Though these discussions began with "problem" children, they involved the school life of the class as a whole—all the human relations and also the program or curriculum. This experience strongly suggested that *all discussion about child development should spring from concrete situations within the school*—at least at first. Our psychologist developed this idea along several lines. Her approach, which was sometimes direct, sometimes indirect, led gradually toward a broadening of the teachers' interests to include *all* their children and ultimately to their thinking of the needs and interests of their children as the basis for planning a curriculum for them. We give a few excerpts from discussions in our after-school meetings with our psychologist to illustrate some of the lines of her approach.

ARE AWARDS THE BEST REWARD? [8]

The giving of awards to the children was another practical situation in our school which concerned all the teachers. "Gold stars" were not given but "praise cards" were. The school had developed an interesting and unusual point of view about the "praise cards." This situation seemed a good approach to a discussion of emotional aspects of a child's life through the whole question of what rewards and punishments did to *all* the children in a class. The following excerpts are from the minutes of a meeting with all the Workshop teachers led by the Bank Street psychologist. The principal and two other Bank Street members were present.

The psychologist on our staff led this first of a group of three meetings that we had planned for, to take up some of the mental hygiene or emotional aspects of the child's life in school. She announced that for this meeting she would like to approach the subject through the school's praise cards, gold stars, and perhaps even the whole question of rewards.

It became apparent at once that praise cards are not universally liked

[8] This question was also discussed separately by the principal and two assistant principals and the Bank Street staff. The principal changed his point of view and the school policy in regard to praise cards after these discussions.

by the teachers in our group, nor even used with regularity. One teacher told us about her little scheme, which she felt would overcome the inherent punishment or rejection that children suffer who never receive a praise card. She has a chart in her room on which the children enter their own achievements, after discussion with her as to the legitimacy of a given achievement going on the chart. Achievements are not by any means entirely in terms of academic accomplishment. A good report on a unit, a good picture, a good contribution to the arts and crafts end of a unit, even some special behavior achievement, are all possible entries. Then at the end of the year, this teacher, although she is a little hesitant about this, gives a prize to the child who has the most entries. She tries to surround the prize giving with a party, refreshments, and some recognition of the others.

There was certainly general agreement with the proposition that one or two praise cards given each week must of necessity mean that some children can never get praise cards throughout the whole year. The idea seems to be that the praise card is a token of improvement in a given situation: an habitual late-comer comes early, spelling score shows decided improvement, fighting child stops fighting. The question was rightly raised as to the child whose behavior is pretty acceptable from the outset. Are we really penalizing him?

The discussion then became more theoretical. One teacher made the point that rewards in essence represent an exchange of values or efforts and that this is only natural in any code of behavior. Another teacher made the point that theoretically there should be no need for any reward. The good work or behavior should produce its own satisfaction in the individual.

The discussion leader (our psychologist) made the point that we seemed ready to accept the premise that some kind of award was almost a necessary culmination for all of us—young and old—so that our discussion really becomes, "What kinds of awards serve the purposes of child development best?"

Teacher: "Then anything in the program that a child does can be made the reward of the moment."

Another teacher: "The most meaningful and wholesome reward is the immediate approval of the teacher. The whole program should offer spots for such rewards. An awareness on the part of the teacher of a child's good performance and approval at the moment has more weight in terms of development than a formal report."

A Bank Street member developed the point that all teachers in all schools, almost because of the very fact that they are teachers and attempting to lead children onward, tend to watch carefully the negative aspects of children's accomplishments. Therefore, teachers need constantly to be on the lookout for whatever there is that is positive to comment upon and to show the children their positive reactions.

Psychologist: "What are some possible activities in which children engage that are reward-producing by their very nature? What about a play that children give? What satisfaction is there? What rewards?"

A teacher: "I feel my children were more deeply rewarded by the reception their play had in the assembly than they would have been by anything I could have done for them."

Psychologist: "Could we say then that in this situation, a group co-operative undertaking was more rewarding than competition within the group?"

Teacher: "Children feel the applause of their friends as the most important kind of reward."

Psychologist: "That brings us right to a point of basic importance in the emotional aspects of the children's lives, namely—the relationship of acceptance from one's peers. Now, what about praise cards again? Do they help or hinder the children in accepting each other?"

Two teachers explained that in their rooms they have the children choose the candidates, yet they are not satisfied because they feel that the children seem to be taking their values from the teacher and at best are mimicking standards laid down by the adults rather than expressing the feelings and values of the children themselves. Another teacher felt that by the sixth year, there was little interest left in the whole business of praise cards—that the children who had had praise cards before came to accept them as their due and others felt in a resigned way that it was a goal impossible of achievement.

The discussion then went on to what follows concretely for the children who get praise cards and for those who don't.

One teacher commented that the best outcome of the whole situation consisted of the few minutes that the children had talking to the principal when they had received the praise cards, that he had a way of highlighting the meaning of the cards without making it all too solemn. The principal commented here that from his point of view he liked the praise cards because it gave him an opportunity for positive relationships with some of the children in the school.

Psychologist then asked the question: "Is there some value that the praise card has for the child that spontaneous praise does not have?"

This led to considerable discussion on the value of the praise card as a symbol. The point was made that we must not neglect the possible values for these children who in so many cases suffer from minimum home standards and a real paucity of home attention. Taking a praise card home gives the child a positive situation for his parents to react to, so for the child himself there is some ego-building value in this kind of commendation.

Psychologist: "I will try to sum up briefly the points we have touched on in this discussion. We need first to find as many additional ways as possible to build up children. When we use the mechanism of a praise card for one child we cannot slight the responsibility for the injured feelings which this implies for all the others. In every child, there is something good—something positive which the teacher can find and bring to the surface—a spontaneous praising remark may have much deeper value than the more formal praise cards. One of the dangers in the use of formal rewards has to do with the fact that they tend to set the children against each other, whereas all teachers have had the experience of seeing their children enjoy and feel rewarded by success of co-operative enterprises such as giving a play in assembly. We realize that there are these undesirable aspects in use of praise cards but nevertheless are aware of certain positive values such as the contact for a few children with the principal who likes to know them. Further than that, there is the question of the child having a concrete symbol of his positive achievement. For children whose families and home situations may be relatively barren with respect to ego building it could be very important that they can show themselves to their parents in these concrete positive lights. As responsible teachers, however, we cannot use this method or any other method of singling out certain children for praise without being sure that we have taken care of the dangers implied of hurt and injury to the other children."

THE STUDY OF ONE CHILD

Still another practical situation in the school which all the teachers faced concerned case studies. The principal each year asked each teacher to write a case study of one child. He asked the Bank Street psychologist to discuss with the teachers what to look for in the children they were studying. The first year, she read the case studies the teachers had already written and made full notes on them before they were given back to the writers. As far as possible, she discussed their case studies with the teachers. The second year she changed her plan of work to meet with the teachers' requests for more guidance in writing up case studies. She drew up the following Case Study Guide.

This guide is not intended to be used as an outline for what you wish to say about the child. It is really a reference sheet to be read over from time to time which may help you to observe the child in greater detail and to organize the information you have.

If you write a report, use any form or style of writing you prefer. Just try to present to the reader as clear and graphic a picture of the child as you have yourself. The more you can use real instances and examples of his behavior to illustrate your general remarks, the better.

Don't be surprised or disappointed if you cannot answer all the questions in this guide. They are only meant to suggest to you the kind of thinking about children that you may find valuable and practical in your teaching. You may want to begin by collecting specific anecdotes which will help you, in the long run, to answer some of the questions raised.

What general impression does he make?
Think of his characteristic facial expression, the way he walks, the build of his body, his comparative size, his tempo, the clothes he wears and the way he wears them, his own attitude toward his appearance. Any special defects or advantages? Mannerisms? How healthy does he seem to be? Is he generally active or passive? How does he approach new situations? Does he live up to your first impressions?

Describe his level of achievement with respect to what you are trying to teach him.

What important information, ideas, attitudes, has he acquired as a result of the program of studies in your class? Where does he stand in reading, writing, and arithmetic? Is he able to express his ideas in speaking? In writing? In free play? What about his vocabulary? Does he have a lot of ideas? Can he do things with his hands?

What is he curious about? Does he seem confused to you? Does he show signs of developing mechanical ability? Scientific interest? Athletic prowess?

Does he tend to imitate others? Would you say he is a creative child? How does it show? In craft activities? Rhythms? Use of language? Ideas for dramatic play? Does he have any special talents?

Do you think he is living up to his ability? If not, what do you think is hindering him? Is he falling behind? In what?

What appeals to him most and holds his interest? Why?

Skill subjects like reading and arithmetic? Activities like drawing or crafts or being chairman of a committtee? Activities involving physical energies? Quiet or exciting things to do? Show and Tell periods? Yard or gym? Listening to stories? Movies or comics? War games or stories? Does he have any special dislikes? Does he have goals for himself?

How does he approach his work?

Does he carry through on what he undertakes? Or do you have to prod? Can he concentrate? On some things more than others? Is he worried about how well he is doing? Does he really get interested in what he is doing? Is he proud of what he does? Does he care about neatness or messiness? Thoroughness or superficiality? Is he efficient or fumbling? Is he a plodder? Is he easily bored or distracted?

In what ways does he seem original or independent?

Does he enjoy free activities in which the specific directions are at a minimum? Such as painting where there is no model or assigned subject, free dramatic play when the children develop the plot as they play, spontaneous rhythms to music, writing an original story? How much opportunity is there in your program for activity in which the children follow through on their own ideas? Do you think this child needs more of this kind of opportunity? Or is he a child who is dependent on being told just what to do at every step? Has he had a full share of play?

What is his position with the other children in the class?

Is he isolated or does he have friends? Any particular friends? How does he try to make friends? Does he need to be the center of attraction? Is he content to be a wallflower? Does he act humble?

Can he work or play successfully with other children? Does he have a ready sympathy with other children's misfortunes? Does he like to be the one who protects? Does he have rivals? Enemies? Does he tease, bait, or bully the children? How does he act toward the girls? Toward the boys?

Is he likely to be the center of fights, quarrels, etc.? Is he usually the victim? Does he refuse to fight? Or fight at the drop of a hat? Is there a lot boiling under the surface?

Would he rather be liked by the children or praised by you?

Can you describe his feelings?

Is he moody? Cry easily? Giggle readily? Get enraged when frustrated? Does he insist on his rights? Does he seem generally tense or relaxed? Predominantly happy or unhappy? Is he easily irritated? Does he seem to have any particular fears? Any special mannerisms such as thumb-sucking, nail-biting, etc.? Does he get enthusiastic?

Does he hold grudges? Does he blame others when things go wrong? Grow sullen when rebuked? Does he need a lot of praise to be content? How easily can you praise him?

Does he daydream? Does he tend to conceal his feelings? Is he ambitious? Competitive? How much confidence does he have? Do you have any idea of how he feels about himself? What his deepest wishes might be? How does he react to success or failure?

What is his relation to you as his teacher?

In what ways does he depend on you? For ideas? For directions? For affection? For encouragement? Is he more or less dependent than the other children?

How much do you have to control him or stop what he is inclined to do? Does he accept your authority? Do you have to repeat, threaten, punish? What keeps him on an even keel? Are there special times like dismissal or changing from one period to another when he gets into trouble with you? Does he accept the rules that have been made for the class?

Do you feel safe when he is out of your sight? What do you think he might do if you weren't looking? Do you trust him? Does he know whether you trust him or not?

Does he openly contradict or resist you? In what way? Does he acqui-
esce and then do as he pleases? How do you think he feels about you?

What can you say about the child's life at home?

What are the physical conditions of his home life? Is it poor? Barren?
Crowded? Has he known serious privation? What is the general atmosphere? Gay? Depressed?

What is the composition of the family? Who is the most important
person in this child's life? Who is responsible for him? To whom does
he look for care and protection? What is the relation between sisters
and brothers?

Does he talk freely about his family and his experience at home? Does
he seem to feel protected? Neglected? Abused? Is there anyone in the
family he is proud of?

Do you know the parents as people? How do they feel about the
child? What are their ideas of how a child should be controlled or
disciplined? Do they come to his defense when he is in trouble? Does
he accept the family's control?

What do you know of his developmental history or his previous school
experience?

Were there any unusual events in his life? Loss of parents? Prolonged
illness? Family moving from one part of the country to another?

How many schools has he attended? Does he have a reputation in the
school? What is it? Does he present any special problem to his
teacher?

Planning for the child on the basis of what you know.

Do you feel you really get to know him in school? Are there many
contradictions and inconsistencies in his behavior or personality? Do
you see signs of growth? Have you ever seen him on the street or with
members of his family? Does he seem different from the child you
know in school?

What would you like to be able to do for him, if you could? How
much can be done in school? What is worth trying? What advice do
you want to pass on to his next teacher?

This guide was distributed to the Workshop teachers at an after-
school meeting led by the psychologist on our staff. Two other

Bank Street members were present. Excerpts from the minutes follow.

Our staff psychologist opened the meeting with a reference to the fact that each teacher had been planning to do a case study of one child, because of help in understanding other children from having studied one child well.

"Last year, I spoke about this but I didn't want to use an outline because it might kill the real understanding the teacher has about the child by writing about the headings instead of the child. Now we have prepared a group of questions covering what it would be interesting to know about children. There are items which aren't included on this list and one wouldn't know all of this about any child. It is tentatively for use with the entire school. We will want to discuss and criticize it. The chief question is: Do you think it would be easier to write a study of a child using this guide or not—is this a help or not?"

Teacher (echoed by others): "After we write a case study, and a child is seen by a psychiatrist, and everything, will anything come of it?"

Psychologist: "You mean, what is the purpose of writing this up? Will it have any real value?"

Teacher: "Yes, what will be the effect?"

Another teacher: "One time my notes were used by the Guidance Bureau."

Teacher: "I know there is value in writing up the studies, as far as understanding the child better is concerned. I just meant what will happen as a result, practically?"

Psychologist: "Problems have taken a long time to develop—they can't be cured in a few weeks. But if we can get a child started on the right road, because we understand him better, that would help considerably."

Teacher: "In every class you don't have a case. What then? If a child is not to be referred to the Guidance Bureau, what is the purpose of doing a long study of him?"

Psychologist: "To understand the child better. Even if the child is happy and adjusted, it takes a lot of study to understand him and know the problems he faces in life."

Teacher: "How do we build up techniques of collecting materials?"

Psychologist: "Pick any child you are interested in, not necessarily maladjusted—maybe a child who functions well, who helps you a great deal —any child who interests you. Do you begin to write about the child as he is, from your impressions, or do you begin to keep notes from time to time out of which you can build a report at the end of the term? Which are you inclined to do?"

Teacher: "Do I do this at the beginning of the term or do I do it at the end of the term when I have noted things and know him better? Is this guide to be used as a summary or is this an introduction to the case study?"

Psychologist: "It can be either. If you had collected a lot of material, you could use this for a summary. This could be a help in organizing your thoughts. At the end of the term, you could take all the notes and write them up, guided by these questions. This could help too all the way along as a reminder as to what notes to take. It is a guide, not an outline."

Teacher: "If you are going to use it as a frame of reference, you would look at the child and get a first impression—an all-over pattern. Then you would use questions for detailed information. This would get the information that is in the background, that could be lost and would tie up with daily notation of child's behavior."

Teacher: "We should know something about the child's home life—it is important, and shows a lot."

Psychologist: "The sequence in putting down these questions is not accidental. I have put the questions about the family situation at the end rather than at the beginning for a definite purpose. Now that we have begun to understand the importance of the home situation in a child's life, we sometimes tend to be blocked about what we, as teachers, can do to help a child. There is a tendency toward a sense of futility about what the school can do when the home situation is inadequate. My point is that we do not sufficiently appreciate how valuable our teacher's eye is, how much we as teachers can know about children just from observing them well in school. School is a real and important part of a child's life. We can see the real people behind the classroom relationships as we train ourselves to observe carefully. Then when we have seen the child as a person and as a personality, we are ready to use facts and information about his home life constructively for his further growth and development."

Teacher: "But we can understand his school behavior so much better and not expect the wrong things of him if we understand more about the home. I had a difficult child and talked to the nurse, who had visited the family. She said the situation was hopeless. He has been impossible in school—just won't conform. The nurse says his mother doesn't conform, and his sister doesn't conform and his father doesn't conform."

Psychologist: "What do you think of her opinion?"

Teacher: "I don't think it is final. I think I should go on and study him some more."

Psychologist: "That attitude of the nurse's is just the feeling I am afraid of—that we will think there is no use."

Another teacher: "We should get a first impression of him in school, then build up further information including his home situation. The last step would be the summary—these questions."

Teacher: "If we say the home is the strongest element in conditioning the child, how can we counteract the home situation?"

Psychologist: "That point of view frightens me—teachers sometimes assume that a child's school life doesn't really affect him if he has a bad home situation. But it will really make a big difference in the course of his life. He may have come from a home that has been bad for years and will continue to be bad. But does that mean that his whole life must just be abandoned? We may be going overboard with that idea. The best spot to give them the guidance they need, to do all that can be done, is in school."

Teacher: "Well, then, we simply have to accept just what the child gives us at any time."

Psychologist: "No, sometimes through our relationships as teachers, through new ideals, through fun, through friendships, through your trust in him, through any of these things or others, we may give a child an anchorage in life."

Teacher: "Do you think that can be done in an ordinary class? If we had more opportunity classes, that would be fine, but we don't. A child needs help which we could give if we had smaller classes or more time, but as it is, how can we do much?"

Psychologist: "But you still have the child and can do some things. We can't solve everything, but we can do more than we think, sometimes."

Teacher: "Can we have a week to digest these questions and then discuss them?"

Psychologist: "We might try an experiment—we might have three teachers try out the questions and discuss a child in these terms for us next time."

Teacher: "That wouldn't help everybody. Let's everybody try it."

Psychologist: "Fine. Even if you take only three minutes in talking about your child, be ready to discuss him." [9]

FREEDOM IN THE CLASSROOM

From the beginning many teachers had been troubled about the use of the word "freedom" applied in the new curriculum to classroom activities. What did "free art" mean? A child didn't know how to draw. Didn't you have to teach him how? What did freedom in discussions mean? Children never got anywhere when they tried to take charge of a discussion—they just got bored. And then there were questions such as "How can children learn if they move around the room? If they talk? If an activity produces noise?" All these questions resolved into the fundamental question: How do children learn? Some of the teachers clung more or less to the old idea that children learn passively, by imbibing information through words, in books or from the teacher. Many thought that to give children freedom, the teacher had to keep hands off completely. Much of their confusion was not so much that they believed in a "passivity program" rather than in an "activity program," as that they did not know the techniques of being a guide, of stepping in when the situation needed them, of keeping out when the children were handling the situation well. In some cases a teacher interpreted freedom for the children as letting them do just what they wanted to, her role being to endure the chaos that inevitably followed. That is, she did not distinguish between license and freedom. Few of the teachers believed in the old repressive forms of discipline

[9] See Appendix 2: Brief Write-Ups of Individual Children and Discussion of a Teacher's Presentation of a Case.

or the old methods of punishment. We all agreed that a teacher *must not* let behavior in the classroom get out of control. Some kind of discipline was necessary. The question was, What kind? This question was often discussed in Workshop meetings. We give just one discussion at a meeting led by the psychologist on our staff whom the teachers had asked to talk on discipline. The Workshop teachers, the principal, two student teachers, and three Bank Street members besides the psychologist were present.

The teachers had talked so freely and fully about their ideas and problems at Workshop sessions that this session was used to present a considerable amount of organized material on psychological foundations for teacher-child relationships in the elementary school, leaving only a short period for discussion. It would have been meaningless if it had not been preceded by relaxed sessions in which everyone talked freely without too much concern for sequence and content covered. On the other hand, the teachers enjoyed these more structured sessions, informal lectures actually, in which they could see their own developing attitudes projected against a more organized body of information about child growth and development.

The *psychologist* spoke to the group on *control and discipline in the new program.* She said that a basic way of working with children is through curriculum and program. There is a need and a wish often to come back and think about the children more directly in terms of their social and emotional development and the needs they express, and to reevaluate what has happened to our ideas about how we shall control children in groups and how we shall expect them to begin to control themselves as they go on.

What are we trying to get to as a *way of control, both from the teachers to the children and the child to himself,* in our new kind of school? In every group there are a few special children who are problems. It is important to distinguish all the children from the few disturbed children.

It is easy enough to make children do what they are supposed to do. The problem is not can we control them, but *are we satisfied with the way in which we are controlling them and with what we think our ways of control are doing to them?* We used to be very absolute about this.

Why is it hard for us to accept certain kinds of control which we often see? We feel that children are paying too great a price for this kind of control.

We must try to understand for ourselves what are *the healthiest ways in which to have children accept control.* We are looking for a kind of school life where *the children will do what the teacher expects not because they are afraid of her but more because they like her,* that they will feel so close to her as a person that what she wants will gradually become part of what they want. What we are looking for is an acceptance of the teacher's authority, not on the old basis of fear (which worked, but has a terrible price psychologically), but on a new basis of establishing a sound, positive relationship between the teacher and the children. More broadly, we want children to accept authority because they like the people who hand it out. And we want children to accept the authority of their parents because they like them, not because they are afraid of them.

Once children are permitted to be free and are active they must also be able to hold themselves back. They have to become able as individuals to put aside some of their impulses *for the sake of*—for the sake of what? In the new school we try to develop a real motivation on the part of the children so that they will want things to go right among themselves as children.

In the early years you have a child in the stage of development where his main line of psychological relationship is with grownups. While children are so young the basic method of control is to get it through the kind of intimate, protective relation which the teacher has with the child almost person to person. As the child gets on to the middle years, seven, eight, nine, ten, he comes into a new stage of development where the teacher is still important, but what becomes more important is the children's feeling toward each other as people and as children.

The way in which the teacher can most soundly control the children in these middle years needs to take into account how the children are changing. The children want to protect the life of the group together. They begin to love what is going on in the classroom, what they are studying together, the things they are making together, etc. One of the teacher's ways of controlling them comes through her being able to protect what they are interested in. They have a vested interest in not having the classroom too upset. Once they love what they are doing they do not want anybody to get in the way of it. Once they as a group are protective of what is going right, the teacher has a resource for control.

We hope that this stage develops, as they get on into the sixth grade or junior high school, into what we call conscience. In the old school we telescoped the process of developing conscience. We expected six- and seven-year-olds to take ready-made from us a system of what they should consider right and what they should consider wrong and learn how to act on it. The price of this is that we have developed individuals who really do not have sound consciences. A good conscience cannot be something which is imitative.

What are some of the *don'ts* for teachers to apply as they approach this point of view? In the middle years, if you are trying to get the children to accept each other as children, you do not make the mistake of being *sarcastic*. Sarcasm is a technique whereby the child is being humiliated by using words and ideas which he cannot hit back with. If a teacher is concerned about having this control remain on a positive basis with the children, she cannot find it within herself to use this technique. (Perhaps none of us who were subjected to the old ways of discipline and control really outlive them completely, but many of us are trying hard.)

Another technique which cannot be used is *shame*. Where is the difference between sending a child out into the hall to get steady and standing him in the corner with the stigma of shame? There is a difference, and it is necessary to think it out. Should we single out children? Should we ever use a child in the middle years as a watchman in any form over the other children, or do we have to learn how to protect the loyalty of the children to each other above everything else? If we transgress the children's loyalty to each other, we should feel disturbed about this because this is a primary thing we want to protect.

What does *isolation* do to the child? What about the tendency of some of us as personalities to try to get control by personal *appeal,* the tendency to appeal to children not to make trouble because it hurts the teacher's feelings that they should be so mean? The teacher says she can't believe it of the child, and feigns a sort of simulated shock and surprise. How honest is this as a technique of control? And if we aren't completely honest, how much are they taken in?

In the modern school we all find ourselves saying that if there is so much disturbance we will not have much time for play period, or perhaps we won't have a play period at all. We do work with deprivations, but the deprivations have to do with the play and work program of the children.

We said that one way of control is to get children to like the teacher. *How do we get children to like the teacher?* When very young this has different ingredients than it has in, say, junior high school. For the young child there is need for direct expression of affection, warmth, praise, and just a kind of human lovingness. In the middle years this direct expression of affection has to have a little different tone to be accepted, especially by the boys from the woman teacher. If we had more men teachers we might find different problems among our girls in the middle years. At nine, ten, eleven, in their feelings and emotions boys are beginning to feel like men. They now need from the teacher a much more subtle way of expressing affection, sometimes very indirect, sometimes very quiet. They need much more directly from the teacher that sense that here is a teacher who knows something they would like to know, who knows how to do things they would like to do, who is capable in ways they would like to be capable in, and what they can get from her is that *feeling of how to be adequate and capable* in the world. That means acquiring certain skills such as being able to read and write, being able to make things with their hands, being able to make a picture.

Certainly in the new program the teacher has some new problems to meet. When you allow children to be more active and more free to express themselves, it builds up naturally to a greater amount of noise and excitement and a greater amount of shuffling around the room. If this is a new experience for a teacher, apart from the fact that she is worried about whether the principal will approve, etc., she isn't sure just how noisy she should let the children get. She may feel that if she lets them become too noisy they may get out of her control altogether. She has to develop the techniques for being able to put a stop to things when they get too noisy or too excited, etc. The children themselves, when they get into this new program, tend to act as though there are no boundaries. Every teacher has to find for herself what are her standards of acceptable behavior for children in a free program.

The *psychologist* pointed out that by "modern school" we do not mean absence of control or discipline. If children are not controlled at all they may feel very much neglected. If you do not take the responsibility of helping them control their feelings when they are young they will feel lost. The child is not ready to put the lid on himself until he has developed a conscience, and he wants the grownups to stop him once in a while. A teacher of children who gives a child complete freedom is irresponsible. If we are going to revise the way children are to live as groups, we must develop new standards for *what is acceptable noise and excitement* and what is too much noise and excitement. Sometimes it is necessary to protect the children from themselves and their own impulses.

Once we create a free atmosphere for children and make a situation lifelike it becomes gratifying to have the children become creative with paints and make things, etc. But when you get this much free thinking and reacting from children, you are going to get the seamy side too! A lot of *hostility and negativism* will come to the surface *along with the new level of being creative* and interested and capable. You not only have the pleasure of the creative free period but must face the fact that even though the children may feel wonderful with this new opportunity, they may begin to express in school feelings which they never before felt free to express. Children carry with themselves the struggles of growing up. They will express some of that feeling, which means that they may be difficult and obstreperous.

We must remember that if the school is free and the home is rigid, we are offering ourselves to the children almost as raw materials, as we offer paint and clay. If we offer them paint we want them to use it freely—we don't offer them stencils, we don't say we never saw a red cow, etc. We must realize that children are going to be freer, so we will have more negative feelings to handle. We must realize that children may displace upon us their feelings toward their parents or other adults.

Our control will come through having a human, lifelike relation in the classroom—when the children are younger, by being affectionate and warm and building up close relations; and when the children are older, through satisfying their needs to be adequate, giving them things to learn which they want to learn about, through somehow getting across to the children that when we stop them or control or punish them or deny them the right to do something they want to do, *we do not consider them essentially bad as people.* It is that we are trying to stop them from doing what we do not think we can allow them to do, but we do not reject them as bad children. Try to distinguish the fact that we are accepting them as people but we are teaching them what we think they ought to do. We are trying to get the child to believe, by the way we treat him, not that he is bad, but that he is a child liked by the teacher, who every once in a while thinks he does something bad, but come what may she will never put him outside her feelings. She will keep on repeating that she won't let him do this or that, etc., but she will do it in such a way that he will know that she is only rejecting certain ways in which he does things and is not rejecting him. If the teacher can get this idea across to the children, in the long run they will do what the teacher wants them to do because they like her sufficiently.

In the middle years children are out on the manhunt emotionally for *heroes.* Toward adolescence it is much easier to find heroes outside the family than within. The teacher whom the child really loves becomes a part of his development of his ego. A long-view way of developing control in certain children is to give them the sense that even though at the moment you cannot accept what they do, in the long run you have *confidence* that they will be able to do what you expect—confidence in the thing they are becoming.

In all honesty we do not know how to handle the really difficult and deeply disturbed children in the classroom. Those children have already been so distorted by life that they need a complete overhauling emotionally. When they do not get that the teacher must suffer along as best she can. One thing we know: that we do not take even the most terribly aggressive behavior of a child as a sign that this child inevitably had to be that way. We take it as a symptom of how wrong life has gone for that child, that this aggressive behavior is a pathological expression of how afraid of life he is already.

The Bank Street psychologist asked the group for the *kind of problems* they feel they must face more and more as they revise their curriculum.

One teacher felt that no matter what punishment is used, it seems that the teacher succeeds in humiliating the children. If you *punish a whole group* for something one child has done, that child knows it. She finds that this type of punishment shields a child in the group, however, and the group shares the punishment with the child.

The psychologist asked the group what sort of controls they have to use which bother them most, and which controls they do not mind using.

A Bank Street member said that one teacher seems to feel that she is depriving the group of the thing which she is trying to protect, their enjoyment in a group activity, when she punishes the group for the misbehavior of one child.

Another teacher said that she has used this group punishment, and she could feel the mounting resentment so much that she gave the children the rest of the period which she had planned to deprive them of. She feels that a teacher has to do something if a child openly disobeys— she has to save her face.

The psychologist pointed out that different punishments would vary from one school to another or from one class to another. The teacher has to know which of the things are so important to the children that when they are taken away the children are hurt too deeply.

The Bank Street member felt that the first teacher's question was basic. How can you bring about control or discipline without humiliation? What is within the capacity of a classroom situation?

The psychologist said that the old forms of humiliation were always so highly individual. The teacher separated the black sheep from the flock. She gave her acceptance to all the other children by separating out one child for discrimination. This is very humiliating to the individual child, and is more humiliating at some age levels than at others. Where the child wants to find himself in a group of children, it is most humiliating. The teacher is in a way exposing the child to the anger of the other children in group discipline, and less to humiliation.

Another teacher wondered why the entire group should be deprived for something one child has done. *The Bank Street member* felt that there is a big pressure on the child not to do something if he knows his group will suffer because of him and he will have the whole group discipline against him. *The teacher* remarked that usually the same child appears and reappears as the cause of disturbances.

Another teacher felt that often a teacher will use this type of control as a way out. *The psychologist* said that sometimes a teacher will make an overdrastic threat at a moment when she is most anxious about her own control. Then she lives up to the threat and feels bad afterwards because she is abusing the children!

Another teacher said that he finds it difficult to find a way of punishing an individual child, but finds it easier to punish a group. In his class if several children are disorderly and he says that the group cannot do something because of this, he feels that the children (age eleven) do not understand. He feels that it is an adult concept that if one person transgresses, society is hurt by it.

The psychologist felt that whether children can get this as a concept is an index not only of how old they are, but of how much experience they have already had in the course of those eleven years in really living a real group life. If they have had a chance to live a group life, the problem at eleven becomes not how to make each child able to understand that what he does affects the group, but is sometimes a way of keeping the children from judging each other too harshly in a group situation. Before using this group technique, the psychologist would want to feel that they had already developed a positive group life together. Otherwise they are mystified.

A teacher felt that one of the ways of building up group spirit is to remove the monitor system when the teacher is out of the room.

Another Bank Street member said that after the discipline is over, no grudge should be held. So many children do not bear a grudge, but the teacher sometimes does. *The psychologist* said that there is a sort of subtle way of letting a child know that you see when he is just about to go over the brink and didn't quite. Or take a chance and give some responsibility when you aren't sure whether or not he will be able to carry it. The child gets the point that you have faith in him ultimately.

One teacher felt that this doesn't often come out right. If it doesn't, however, she talks to the child and forgets about it. *The psychologist* felt that this is something very positive. It is very important in a case like this to make articulate to the child what your faith in him is. Children need a sense of our faith in their future, in what they are going to become.

A teacher said that sometimes you aim too high and cannot give the child another chance. A child was elected by the class (the class thought they were putting something over on her). He had eventually to be removed from the office, and the teacher said that she could not give the child another chance at this. She has now, however, given him a part in a play.

A Bank Street member said that you cannot have a situation which operates on the positive side all the time. This child has failed when he has had every opportunity not to fail. However, he is now being given an opportunity for other good things in life. *The teacher* said that she can overlook certain things in this child which she cannot overlook in others.

The psychologist said that the important thing is not just to be so simple about control that we think the questions of control and discipline solve themselves. They do not. She said that the question of introducing this quality of control from nine to three and sending the child home to another atmosphere poses a problem. Some raise the question as to whether we are not asking the children to adjust to very complicated lives. If our techniques do not always work, we must remember this. The psychologist felt that she would rather have inconsistency in a child's life and a complex set of things to adjust to, than to boil it down to a consistency which does not have a germ of growth in it.

One teacher said that sometimes a teacher gets a child on whom she has no effect. Shouldn't this child be taken out of the teacher's group and placed in another? *The psychologist* said that a teacher does have situations in which a given teacher cannot click with a given child's personality. Ideally, there should be free moving of children from group to group on this basis. *A Bank Street member* said that this could be the strength of a large school and the weakness of a small one. She felt that it would take a trained person to decide on such changes, however.

WHAT WE LEARNED AS A WORKSHOP TECHNIQUE

Out of many meetings led by the psychologist came a few general conclusions. The most important was that, in a Workshop, talks about child development should not be theoretical, not about children in general, leaving the teachers to make the application to their children. Instead, talks should spring from actual situations which the teachers face, such as what the giving of awards to children does to the child receiving the award and to the children left out; whether a co-operative group undertaking does not bring a deeper reward to the children than competition; or what makes a particular problem child behave the way he does and how the teacher can help him; or how a teacher can help her particular children to grow in self-control.

We found that such talks led directly into what kinds of program can give a particular group of children a good school life—which meant curriculum planning in the broad sense. Approaching child development through concrete school situations demanded that a trained psychologist be in close touch with what was happening in the classrooms to teachers and to children. A series of talks without this intimate firsthand contact accomplishes little.

By the end of the first year and a half of the Workshop, most of the teachers felt that it was their job to understand *all* their children—not just those who were difficult. They were really studying their children, observing and listening to the children's responses and modifying their programs accordingly. Many of them had become truly experimental in their curriculum planning. Both the Bank Street and the teacher members of the Workshop felt that we had passed through the preliminary approach and were ready to make a second approach—that of genuine curriculum building in which thinking of curriculum and thinking of child development functioned together for the whole child and the whole school.

This, however, is jumping ahead. Now we go back to the teachers' initial request to be shown *how* to conduct the new teaching techniques and tell the story of the development along this line for the first year and a half of the Workshop.

8

Learning Through Play and Experience
in the Here-and-Now World

CURRICULUM EXPERIENCES FOR KINDERGARTEN, FIRST- AND SECOND-GRADE CHILDREN

WE HAVE already stated rather fully in Part I the basic convictions about how young children learn which, from previous experimental work, we had long since come through to. Our immediate job with the teachers of kindergarten, first- and second-grade children was not to state these convictions. Rather, it was to plan with the teachers and help them carry out curriculum experiences for their young children and through follow-up discussions with these teachers bring out what the children learned through these experiences. When we began, most of the kindergarten and first-grade teachers, and, to a lesser extent, the second-grade teachers, welcomed a here-and-now approach for their young children. Yet some, perhaps most of them, regarded trips as impossible for large groups or just fun for the children; and play in the classroom as interludes for relaxation, a necessary concession to children's immaturity but not as a genuine learning situation. The techniques which they wished us to show them they regarded as "extras" tacked on to their real work in teaching academic tool subjects and "good" behavior. As already said, we had faith that if these teachers once became convinced that their children were learning and growing through firsthand experiences—gathering information themselves on neighborhood trips, playing back and discussing their trips and other experiences in the classroom—they would enter into these experiences, sharing them with the children actively and with relish.

With adults as well as with children, interests and attitudes are not built up through words but through direct experiences—in this case experiences of watching and analyzing their children's reactions to the various learning situations which the new teaching techniques afforded. So we philosophized little in the beginning but began to work actively with individual teachers in what they called "demonstration teaching" in one technique after another.

THE THEME: *LIVING IN THE HOME, SCHOOL, AND NEIGHBORHOOD*

We knew from our contacts with the Board of Education committee working on curriculum revision that the theme in social studies for kindergarten, first and second grades was to be *Living in the Home, School, and Neighborhood.* This theme placed the curriculum experiences and activities squarely in the here-and-now world in which these young children so largely live. It afforded a perfect approach to learning through firsthand experiences. It gave full opportunity to have the children follow their interest drives— to find out about things and people that interested them in the world around them, and to organize and express their thinking and feelings about what they had found out. In educational jargon, this theme could well be interpreted through interrelated "intake" and "outgo" experiences by which we believe children really learn.

We began by watching the children in their classrooms to find out what they were doing there and what leads to direct experiences this gave us. Very soon, we began going on trips with teachers and their children in these three younger classes to see work and workers in the school and neighborhood, with follow-up discussions and dramatic play in the classrooms. In the kindergarten, where the children were emotionally centered around their homes and their information was largely about things and people in their homes, we began with dramatic domestic play.

Why did we emphasize work and workers? Because work and workers are a significant part of the world in which children early show great interest.[10] Kindergarten children come to school with this interest in how things and people work already well developed. *Their homes are children's first laboratory.* There they learn about the work processes going on around them which are closely tied up with their personal lives: going to bed and getting up, getting dressed and undressed, taking baths, watching their food being cooked, perhaps seeing it delivered at the door, perhaps buying it at the store along with mother. And this work in their homes is done by the people who are intimately tied up with their emotional lives, with the people who take care of them, above all with their mothers or often with mother substitutes. In their homes, too, these children have already been living over their own experiences in dramatic play. In their play they are "identifying" with people they have known at first hand—their mothers and fathers, or the milk-man bringing the milk to them, or the groceryman selling food to their mothers.

DRAMATIC PLAY BEGINNING WITH HOME EXPERIENCES

When these young children come to school, the situation changes. Home and mother are gone. They are lost in a world of strange things and people. But does it have to change completely? How can a teacher use these deep home experiences which kindergarten children bring to school with them? By giving them a chance to play out all their home, their personal, experiences in school. That is what is meant by "dramatic domestic play." Such play is greatly furthered by equipment through which children can play back these precious memories—dolls, which to the child can be symbols of himself or symbols of these vanished grownups whom

[10] See Part I, pp. 46 ff.

he knows personally; doll beds and covers; small washtubs with real water to wash dolls' clothes in; small-sized irons to play ironing clothes; blocks with which he can build almost anything—a house, a bed, a stove, a store for the use of his doll people. This dramatic play needs floor space—chairs and tables should be movable, not screwed down. The kindergarten child, though he is in school, is still oriented in his home. He still needs a chance to express his own home experiences in his own way, to express his close identification with the people who make up his world at home.

All this, most of the kindergarten teachers sympathized with. They had some dolls and toys in their rooms but little that suggested *related group* play. Nor did they have the technique of guiding the play into constructive channels. So this is where the Bank Street member started. She worked directly in their rooms with individual teachers on equipment and techniques of getting dramatic play started.[11]

THE NEIGHBORHOOD AS A LABORATORY

But even kindergarten children's world has not been limited entirely to the home. They have been on neighborhood streets. The neighborhood is already a laboratory for them. And what has interested them in this neighborhood laboratory? Objects that move such as autos, trains, boats, and airplanes and how these objects work. With whom have they identified in this neighborhood laboratory? With workers who are doing something, making some of these objects move, building a house, selling at a store.

Again, we know that these are the interests of five-year-old children because of their spontaneous dramatic play. In their play they *become* the train, the airplane, the auto, the boat. Or they become the worker who is controlling these moving things, the worker building a house, the groceryman, the milkman. At first, they regard these workers who do something as almost a part of the work process. For instance, the milkman is someone who delivers milk—

[11] Appendix 3: Dramatic Play Suggestions.

not a man with a home and a family, who earns money through his work, and needs good working conditions. All that kind of interest in workers comes much later. The younger the child, the more his interest is centered on *how* the work is done, and the worker is a part of this *how*.

So our trips with kindergarteners were to see how work was done—work that was closely tied up with their personal lives. The trips had to be near by, for these children had not been on group trips and had no idea of the kind of behavior which is necessary in a group for safety. The first trips were within the school—to talk with the school nurse; to talk with the principal; to see the food being cooked for the lunchroom; to see the older children getting ready the little milk bottles they were later to bring to these kindergarten children; to see the pile of coal in the cellar and the custodian's helper shovel the coal into the furnace; to see the pipes that went from the furnace and along the ceiling and finally appeared connected with the radiators in their own room. Perhaps to see the coal truck and watch the driver grind up the truck, put up the chute, take the cover off the hole in the sidewalk, and let the coal rattle down to the school cellar. Perhaps a walk around the block (with no street crossing) to see what they could see. Perhaps a pause to watch the shoemaker putting new soles on shoes, or the laundryman ironing clothes, or the man with the grindstone sharpening scissors and knives, or the grocer selling vegetables, fruit, and other groceries. After each trip, the Bank Street member discussed with an individual teacher or the teachers of the three younger groups at after-school meetings what the children could do in the classrooms to express and organize the information and feelings they had experienced on the trips. Again, most of the teachers wanted to be shown *how* to follow up a trip.[12] So a Bank Street member, after a day or two had passed, led short simple talks with the children in which, as much by gestures as by words, they told what they had seen or heard or felt. In these discussions the Bank

[12] Appendix 4: How to Conduct Discussions Related to the Activity.

Street member acted as a guide, sometimes asking questions, sometimes contributing memories of her own. She did not try for any very logical or articulate expression from these young children. Then the children were turned loose to put their images and their thinking into action in dramatic play. Again, this play needed suggestive equipment. Small dolls, made of wood or pipe cleaners—the children called them "little people"; small autos, boats, trains—anything important that the children had noticed on the street—and plenty of blocks for building. Now the play expanded to "city play," not merely domestic play, though always many children built houses and carried on domestic family play there. Autos chugged down the street to stores; coal trucks delivered coal at the school; there were grocery stores, sometimes a movie house, sometimes boats moving on the Hudson River. Through teacher guidance, this play became more related, more group play. The housewives with their children went from their homes to buy food at the store; sometimes they ordered coal to be delivered; trucks delivered vegetables, fruit, and milk to the grocery store. The neighborhood work and workers, as the little children knew them, appeared in action on the kindergarten floor. All this did not happen suddenly. But it did happen.

At the same time the Bank Street member was working with teachers of the first and the second grade. The trips with first-graders, particularly if they had had trips and related play in the kindergarten, could take them farther afield in their neighborhood experiences.[13] The Hudson was familiar—only two blocks from the school. Now these children crossed Manhattan Island to see what was happening on another river, the East River. Now, too, the children took in more complicated work processes. At the request of the teachers, the Bank Street member drew up a way for first-grade children to study the neighborhood.[14] She also explored the neighborhood to find situations where the children could see various

[13] Appendix 5: Some Techniques to Use in Taking Children on Trips.
[14] Appendix 6: Neighborhood Study for First Grade.

steps in a work process more fully—such, for instance, as a trip to Harlem River, to see coal barges and the workers unloading the coal with great derricks and other workers filling their trucks with coal and driving off; or trips to different kinds of bakeries.[15]

The teachers of the second grade organized their work more definitely into units. They were more ambitious to have their children learn "subject matter" and were more concerned to have this subject matter in books in order to help the children learn to read. Whatever the unit the teacher had chosen, we found related work and workers for them to explore. These second-grade children are interested in still more elaborate work processes and in those less immediately related to their personal lives—post office work and postmen; keeping the streets clean, and street cleaners; city markets and food coming into the city by trains, trucks, and boats; traffic and policemen; pipes under the street that carry water, electric wires, and gas to their homes and stores and school, and the various workers they can see working with these pipes when the street is torn up or the cover of a manhole is removed. The play that followed such trips was more organized than that in the younger groups.[16] It was more mature dramatic play.

YOUNG CHILDREN'S ART EXPRESSIONS

We have talked only about dramatic play as a way in which young children express and organize their thinking and feelings. But, given a chance, young children will use all the art media for expression of themselves. The teachers recognized the art element in their children's dramatic play—the way the children transformed an actual experience through their imagination. They did not so readily recognize the play element in art expressions. The teachers of these younger groups in our school wanted their children, however, to have art work. Among the courses of study in the old curriculum were drawing, music, dancing (largely games), and the

[15] Appendices 7, 8, 9.
[16] Appendix 10: Suggestions for Post Office Play, Second Grade.

language arts (which, however, did not include language as an art). In drawing and painting, some of them set models of adult pictures for the children to trace or copy and judged the children's products by the faithfulness of their imitation of adult products. More of them encouraged "free" painting—that is, they let the children experiment with the media, paint or draw what they wanted to, and were satisfied with the product if the child was satisfied. Most of the teachers recognized that a child's crude painting was art on a young level. We recall the picture of a boat painted by one of our second-grade children after a trip to see boats on the Hudson. It is a gay red boat with tipsy smokestacks such as never sailed on any sea. The teachers, most of them, recognized that such a painting sprang from a deep experience of color, shapes, sounds, movements, and that these images were translated by the child's imagination into his own expression. The teachers recognized that this boat meant more to the child than the pictures made by adults which were hung in many of the classrooms.

In music and dancing, the teachers had much more the attitude of teaching the children techniques. They did not commonly try to have children express their own experiences. For instance, kindergarten children were taught steps to imitate Indians; first-grade children learned traditional singing games like Looby Loo. And language was seldom treated as an art medium for children to use themselves. Art experience in language was primarily exposing children to "literature"—episodes of reading them verse. To "cultivate children's imagination" they read them fairy tales. The teachers were far more concerned with correcting the children's incorrect use of adult forms of speech than with preserving their children's spontaneous use of rhythm, sound quality, and patterning of words —all elements in adult literature.

Here as elsewhere, the Bank Street worker kept notes of what children did and said. She also began "demonstration teaching" in all the arts. She happened to be a musician, a dancer, a writer, as well as a teacher of young chilldren. She assembled songs about things in the world around them in which the children had shown interest. She arranged the songs in ingenious books with the subjects on tabs so that a teacher could quickly find and use a song related to some play or remarks of the children. Often the children's gestures suggested a dance. On the piano, she played appropriate music and suggested that the children dance they were trains or boats or airplanes; that they were shoveling coal into the furnace (if they had had a trip to the school cellar) or were steam shovels (if they had been to Harlem River). The children under encouragement began to create their own simple songs and their own dances.

GETTING CREATIVE LANGUAGE STARTED [17]

On trips and in classroom play the Bank Street worker asked the teachers to notice the *way* children said things—not merely *what* they said. Some of them began to jot down rhythmic expressions that they heard from the children or anything that showed how the children were taking in the world through their senses—eyes, ears, noses, and muscles—and giving back these sense and muscle images in their own child language. In a discussion with one first-grade class, the Bank Street worker asked the children what they thought was "the quietest thing in the world." Here is a list of the things the children named:

horse (when asleep)	moon
sleep	sheets on a bed
snow	covers on a bed
rain	alligators
sun	reindeers are quiet when
house	they come on Christmas
clouds	fish
bulbs	seeds
	orange seeds

This list she left with the teacher. Here is some of the verse that the children later composed with this teacher.

[17] Appendix 11: How to Start Creative Language.

Cold   cold   cold
Steam steam steam
Hats   sweaters   ear muffs
        mittens coats and
                mackinaws
Cold   cold   cold

See the man on the street
He has a wagon full of concrete
Tall houses
Middle-sized houses
Little houses
Ten floors high
Four floors high
Houses on the Drive, streets and avenues
Houses all around us

I like to see the coal truck
        when it backs up
I like to see the coal slide
        down the slide
It makes such a clatter
        Bump, bump bump
        Br—br-br-br-br
        S S S S S

Pull the coal barges
Pull the train barges
Puff, puff, puff
I am a little tug.

The teacher used such creative language of her children as early reading charts.[18]

All these art expressions, in painting, modeling, music, dance, language, sprang from the children's experiences but none of them were limited to a mere rehearsal of experiences. These children were genuine artists, though young ones. Like all artists the children selected from their experiences what had meaning to them;

[18] Appendix 12: First-Grade Charts.

they transformed or heightened their reality by their imagination, through a creative use of the media.

The question of creative language came up in all the groups from kindergarten through sixth grade. It led to several talks at our meetings by a Bank Street worker on children's language and how to preserve and develop children's pleasure in the "play of language" —the use of the art elements in language—which they lose if language is treated only as a utilitarian method of communication in which correct adult forms are the goal. These talks also led to an additional supplemental "Writers' Workshop" held after school, where some teachers wrote stories for their children. (See pp. 355 ff for discussion on language in Writers' Workshop.)

These young children were also given an opportunity to find out how things in the natural world behave. This is the beginning of science.[19] However, we shall postpone a fuller discussion of science, since science experiences concerned all the teachers and were discussed in grade levels with all in our after-school meetings. (See discussion on science, pp. 286 ff, and Appendix 25.)

As these children became spatially oriented in the neighborhood their floor play began to reflect the beginnings of map thinking and human geography—the relation of work to earth situations. Here again we refer forward to the Workshop discussions on map thinking and human geography with all the teachers.

THE TEACHERS' THINKING AT THE END OF A YEAR AND A HALF OF WORK

In our small weekly meetings with the kindergarten, first- and second-grade teachers, we discussed what the children were getting out of these experiences—trips, related dramatic play, free painting, music, dance, creative language. From the beginning, they thought their children were enjoying their school life. Later they felt, or most of them did, that their children were not merely having a good time, nor were they merely gathering factual information:

[19] Appendix 13: Suggestions for Simple "Weather" Experiments.

they were *learning how to think.* They were beginning to see the relationships, and, as we have said, seeing relationships is thinking. Kindergarten and first-grade children began to see the relationship of the work around them to their own lives; of one step of a work process to another step. The five-year-old kindergarten children thought primarily in details of *how* things and people work—such as trains and engineers. By six, the children began to think of the *function* of the train—to carry people, food, and other things. And *they played out related work* in dramatic group play. The second-grade children were beginning to grasp new relationships which built on the relationships they had played out in first grade, such as: the city does work so that the city people can have water, light, telephone, gas in their houses—all the things we call "city housekeeping"; a sense that there are faraway workers whose work makes it possible for city people to have all these things and also to have food.

The teachers felt that this thinking, even on a young level, was satisfying to the children and that it laid a foundation for more mature thinking up through the grades and up to adulthood about work and workers that they could not experience directly. They felt that their children were identifying with an ever-broadening group of people and that this laid the foundation for identifying later with people they could not know personally.

All this thinking on the part of the teachers was reflected in the way they thought of their job. They began to think not in separate units or curriculum experiences, not in techniques but in related programs of experience in which children found out about things and people and expressed what they had found out in their own creative ways. They began to watch their children's play and to realize that whatever a child spontaneously plays has deep significance to him; and to listen to how their children used language as an art, not merely as communication. They began to think of these techniques of trips, related play, discussion, art expressions not as ends in themselves but as means through which they could give their children learning experiences. Some of them began exploring the neighborhood for situations that would clarify for the children some relationship their children were beginning to grasp. This, in turn, aroused their adult interest in the work pattern of New York. They began to ask to have Workshop talks on background content for themselves. They were taking on their "new" job. They found it hard work but it gave deep satisfaction.

This growth in thinking and attitudes of the teachers did not happen suddenly nor to all the teachers at the same time. But by the end of a year and a half of our Workshop, these teachers had moved far toward the conception of curriculum building as differentiated from separate curriculum experiences, and far toward the conception of their role as a guide as differentiated from a dispenser of information.

9

Extending the Range of Experiences and
Ways of Learning

*CURRICULUM EXPERIENCES FOR THIRD-,
FOURTH-, FIFTH-, AND SIXTH-GRADE CHILDREN*

THIS chapter will show the Workshop in action—Bank Street staff and teachers of the third through the sixth grade—during the first year and a half that we worked together. Behind the practical curriculum experiences for children from eight through eleven years that we developed together lay Bank Street's belief of what constitutes a good life for children of these ages described in Part I, and what the teachers of those children first wanted of a Workshop during the transition stage of the official curriculum described in Chapter 6. Stated briefly, our job, as we saw it, was to *work with the teachers on basic relationships* underlying curriculum thinking while we were working with them on the new teaching techniques around which their anxieties centered.

The themes in social studies as stated in the preliminary version of the official bulletin for the four older grades continued the study of how people live and work in special environments. They extended this study from the here-and-now world of the three younger grades to faraway and long-ago people and lands. The teachers of these older grades were concerned primarily with how to cover the required subject matter and still use the new teaching techniques. For them the official social studies themes raised two problems not raised for teachers of the younger groups, both of which they thought of in terms of subject matter to be covered. Stated in terms of the old courses of study which most of the teachers followed, the first problem was how to teach history, geography, and civics together; or, as we would put it, how to give children experiences which will help them to see interrelationships, both in the past and in the present, among people and between people and the natural earth conditions or forces which they use. The second problem was how to bring in science; or, as we would put it, how to give children experiences which will help them to see the relation of the way the earth forces behave and the inventions by which people have learned to use these natural forces in their work.

Our long-term aim was the working out of an integrated, experiential program. Integration in a program is, of course, utterly different from side-by-sideness, juxtaposition of facts. Integration in social studies rests upon discovering and developing relationships of people to people and of people to their environment. The last chapter told how children develop the beginnings of awareness of these relationships through direct personal experiences in the here-and-now world of things and people around them. It was clearer and broader awareness of these same relationships that we wished children in the four older grades to develop as they studied faraway and long-ago people and environments. The interests of these older children had not outgrown the here-and-now world but had extended beyond it. We believed these children must continue to explore the world around them but on a more mature level. This, both because the world in which one lives is all-important for anyone to understand, and because comparing their own ways of living and working at home with ways of living and working in other lands by other people helps to make faraway and long-ago people and lands real and vivid to children. The simplest way to approach the unknown is through comparison with the known.

Our practical job was to begin with teaching techniques and with units, since that is what the teachers wished from us, and through these techniques and development of units to give children direct learning experiences which would lead toward an integrated, experiential program through which children would think out basic relationships.

We began with each teacher where she wished us to begin, commonly with the development of a unit she had chosen. Sometimes the first step was help in arts or crafts in the classroom; sometimes finding books or other source materials to enrich the subject matter; sometimes, though usually a little later, help on a trip, on map making, or the development of a play.

EXPERIENCES IN WHICH CHILDREN AND TEACHERS CONDUCT INVESTIGATIONS

Children Explore the Environment and Discover Relationships through Trips

In the beginning many of the teachers were afraid of trips. Practically none of them had used trips except as they tied up with history, such as trips to historic sites or museums. They tended to think that exploring the ways in which modern New York functions was "an extra" since their subject matter in social studies dealt so largely with faraway and long-ago people. So, particularly in the three older grades, the early trips which we planned with the teachers and took with them and their children involved some history or geography content (not yet related in the thinking of many of the teachers). But we wanted these trips to show *basic relationships of the now to the long-ago, the here to the faraway.* We used these trips to bring out the contrast in how we now use New York's physical earth situation and how people long ago used the same situations, or how people in their work use physical earth situations different from New York's.

To give one illustration of approaching the past by a direct experience which also gave further understanding of the present-day world: In a trip to Inwood, at the northern tip of Manhattan, in connection with an Indian program, fourth-grade children saw not only the caves where Indians once lived, the heaps of oyster shells left over from Indian feasts, the whirlpool so dangerous to Indian canoes, but also the modern freight and highway bridges over the Harlem River, the barges bringing in coal, sand, and stone to storage yards along the river. In follow-up discussions, the children were excited to name differences in the ways we and the Indians used the same rivers, riverbanks, and the island of Manhattan. Such discussions are human geography on a young level, for they were based on people's use of natural earth conditions of New York—the rivers, with whirlpools caused by the meeting of tides sweeping around the two sides of the island, the island itself with the natural wild plants and animals. These discussions really involved comparison of the Indians' and our modern culture—how the Indians used the natural environment around them to meet their needs of food, shelter, clothes, and roads, and how we had modified this natural environment to meet these same needs in a machine age.

With the older children we also went to museums. Seeing how other people had worked, their tools, what they had made out of the things they found in their environments, is a direct contact with the faraway or long-ago peoples and their environments. These curriculum experiences—trips and follow-up discussions— whether they concerned the same earth situations used by a past and present culture (as at Inwood), or the work products of a faraway or long-ago culture (as in museums), brought out *the relationship of people's work to the earth forces they used*. Here again, ways of working in the past or by faraway people were made vivid and real by the contrast between the present and the past, the immediate and the distant.

Still another relationship emerged which helped the children to understand the world immediately around them. The children began to see how New York's present patterns of work in transportation, food, materials for buildings, etc., related New York to the rest of the country and faraway workers—a concept which we considered of primary importance.

Teachers Ask for Background Content: Trips on Adult Level

As the teachers of all grades became more and more intrigued by using New York as a laboratory with their children, they came to feel that they themselves needed more background content on New York's present ways of work and how this work is related to earth conditions. They asked that at least two sessions be given to presentation of such material by a Bank Street member. As a preliminary, we suggested that we use a few Workshop sessions to go on trips to explore certain kinds of work on our own adult level. We give excerpts from the records of our first trip with the teachers, which was in the immediate school neighborhood, and of the second trip, which was farther afield.

Before starting, we had a brief discussion as to why we were taking this trip. Teachers said: "To know our neighborhood" . . . "to use the environment." Bank Street member said to accomplish these ends we should not seek the unusual—rather try to see the familiar freshly and later interpret it. She asked the group to look at everything as naïvely as possible—as if they were seeing our houses, our roads, and other work patterns for the first time—almost as if they had just landed from Mars: to question *why* people had developed such things today and here on Manhattan: to think what other work or workers lay behind the immediate work patterns they saw.

We stood just outside school door; noted the old brick apartment houses across street, fire escapes on outside of all. Comments by teachers: Multiple dwellings are a response to congestion in the city; brick instead of wood and fire escapes (obviously added later) probably by city regulation; run-down condition of buildings suggested low-income tenants. No naïve comments on such familiar sights as windows (response to climate), electric doorbells, etc. Questions: Why is brick used? Where did it come from?

Crossed street to look in at a garage and examine air pump. Comment: Comparatively few work processes going on in immediate neighborhood where children can see workers at work. Question: Why?

Stopped for a minute at Radio Hospital opposite school. No one noticed other evidences of modern use of electricity in neighborhood.

A truck unloading coal, rushing it down chute into basement of one house. Truck labeled Premium Coal. Bank Street member asked the driver where the coal had come from. He said it had come in barges from Perth Amboy, then from a New Jersey pier on railroad cars to Premium Coal yards; said that the Burns Brothers' docks were better places for school children to visit than the docks of his company.

The group headed for Riverside Drive. Noticed manholes on the way. Some comments on their number—much city work goes on under the street. Passed subway. Discussed why subway is overhead at 125th Street. Teacher said there must be a natural valley at this point.

Arrived at elevated point on the Drive. Looked down at tracks with all kinds of freight cars. Comments: on third rail; switches; colors of cars—red, green, yellow, orange; names on cars of various railroads—Atchison, Topeka & Santa Fe, The Trunk Line, New York Central, Pennsylvania, etc. Came from all over U. S. A.

Bank Street member asked why city had given up our waterfront to railroads. She said post roads here were first answer to need on Manhattan; then franchise was given to early railroads. The city at great expense to get back a waterfront for auto road when "through traffic" had developed: the strip of land we were looking at had to be built by a fill with countless loads of rock, soil, etc.—railroads concealed in many places to protect view—all within her memory.

Across the river, we could see the Palisades. The Indians called cliff the Great Wall. Bank Street member said that the Hudson River proper stops at Haverstraw, where it deposits most of its load of silt. Where we were looking very little silt is dropped. From Haverstraw to mouth, it is really a fiord. Tide running in and out keeps the channel navigable. She pointed out how rock had broken off and fallen from Palisades. The line of vegetation is higher than when she first saw Palisades. This can be used to explain erosion and foothills. She gave a brief account of past behavior of the earth's crust in this area to explain why the rock of Palisades is so hard.

Up the river we saw the George Washington Bridge. Bank Street member asked why it was built there. Teacher replied that it spanned a narrow part of the Hudson. We noticed the little red lighthouse directly under it.

While the group had coffee, another Bank Street member pretended they were eight-year-olds and tried to get them to ask eight-year-old questions about the trip. The points brought up by the teachers were tides in the Hudson; names on freight cars from which they could judge contents; how much ice the refrigerator cars took and how long it lasted; routes to the West—the "Water-level" route needs less coal than Pennsylvania routes over mountains; how the boats anchored on the river got their fuel; the construction of the George Washington Bridge, and tunnels under the Hudson.

Our second trip with the teachers was to investigate one of the work patterns of food in New York. A large group went to the A & P distributing warehouse.

We saw the "climate room" where green bananas are hung and just the needed number of bunches is ripened each day by controlling temperature and humidity.

Our guide explained how the goods were delivered on freight cars in front of warehouse. Drivers of trucks arrived in early morning; were given their lists of goods to be delivered; assembled them on hand trucks; packed trucks; delivered to stores in time for morning shoppers.

The group walked out beyond warehouse where they could see up Long Island Sound and down narrow continuation of Sound called the East River. Discussion of river roads to Manhattan and their historic significance. Necessity for bridges and tunnels to get on and off island.

After the trips, a Bank Street member gave two talks about New York's present work patterns and how they are conditioned by to-day's needs and by the earth situations which are found in New York's environment. The minutes taken at one of these Workshop meetings are given in Appendix 14.

Working on Enriched Content: Unit on Roads in Various Programs

The teachers of all grades wished further individual practice in organizing units and in the techniques of trips and discussions. But they felt they needed as well some group discussion about something they all were working on, all had in common. We suggested that the Workshop group organize themselves as a class working together on a unit on their own adult level, and as a group appoint committees to work out any appropriate techniques—research trips, source material, discussions, and activities such as dramatizations, painting, map making. This plan was referred to the Planning Committee but it was turned down. (Several years later in this same school, the teachers themselves suggested and carried out such a plan in the Workshop.)

We then suggested that the group choose a subject in which the content and activities would be important and relevant to all their units and each teacher report to the group how she used the material in her special unit. We suggested *Weather,* beginning with *Rain,* as a possible subject. This, too, was turned down by the Planning Committee. Then we suggested *Roads,* meaning transportation in its widest sense, as being an important aspect of nearly every unit. This was agreed upon for experimentation by the whole group.

However, many of the teachers said they did not know how to launch a discussion on roads. The group asked a Bank Street member to write out some concrete suggestions.[20]

We give partial notes of a fourth-grade teacher's first discussion on roads.

Fourth-Grade Teacher   9:30   35 children

Teacher: "You said you saw many people on the street. Where were they going?"

Children: "To work or to school."

Teacher: "Where?"

Child: "Factories."

Another child: "Five-and-ten or other stores."

Teacher: "How do they go to work?"

Child: "If near, they'd walk."

Teacher: "How about fathers? Where do your fathers work?"

Child: "In a factory."

Teacher: "Whose father works in a factory?" (Many hands.)

[20] Appendix 15: Suggestions for Discussion with Children on Roads.

Teacher: "Where?"

Child: "New Jersey."

Teacher: "How does he get there?"

Child: "He has to ride."

Teacher: "Why?"

Child: "Take too long to walk."

Teacher: "How have you gone to 125th Street with your mother?"

Children: "Sometimes on trolley, sometimes on bus, sometimes on subway, sometimes in taxi—elevated train, walk, tunnel, private car." (Teacher writes these on board.)

Teacher: "These are some of the ways that people in New York do what?"

Children: "Ride. Travel."

Teacher: "Where do these things go?"

Child: "Through tunnel. On a road. On a street."

Teacher: "Why do we have so many ways of traveling?"

Child: "Because it's so far to walk."

Another child: "Because so many people live here."

Teacher: "What's important for people in this neighborhood?"

Children: "Busses, cars, tires, gas, and money."

Teacher helps them to general word, "road." Teacher shows pictures children drew yesterday. Vans, trolleycars, etc. Teacher asks if any child wants to tell a story about something that happened to him on any of these roads. Following are things mentioned by some child, which had not come out in discussion: trolley caught on fire in the snow; electricity, trolley station.

Teacher mentions short circuit. Evidently children don't understand much about electricity. Boy tells about his electric train. Something on the track got it out of order. Probably that was the matter with the trolley.

Girl: "Another trolley on fire. Aunt had to get off and go on bus. Coming back two more trolleys on fire!"

Teacher suggests story about a different way of travel.

Boy: "Coming home from hospital—trolley couldn't go in snow—it was like bombs dropping. Waited for half hour. Got a transfer and got in another trolley."

Girl: "How could the other trolley go if his trolley was stuck on tracks?"

Boy explains the first trolley was pushed away on the tracks by another trolley.

Girl: "Baby nearly fell out of taxi." (Full of gestures.)

Teacher: "When did you have fun?" (Note: Good way to stop tales of accidents.)

Boy: "On streamlined train to Plainfield, New Jersey. Central Railroad of New Jersey." (He sketches on board.)

Teacher: "Something funny happened?"

Girl: "I went down South. Conductor said we could play hide-and-seek behind the seat."

Teacher asks if this is true, if passengers didn't mind. Then lets it pass.

Jack (pointing excitedly to *Jane's* drawing): "That don't look like Crusader."

Teacher sends Jack to board. Two boys discuss trains they have drawn.

Teacher asks children to hear what boys are saying about board drawings.

Charles: "I was talking about the station. There are stations in Bayonne. I can't remember other names."

Teacher asks Charles to write a little story about trip to New Jersey on the board. He reads it. All children writing stories about experiences. They ask help in spelling. Teacher writes words on board and tells each child to put word in his dictionary. Each child has a dictionary made by himself.

Discussion of the stories children had just written:

James: "On way to school I met my friend and we were talking about snakes."

Boy: "Bridge—nice view. Went in bus with about thirty other children."

Another boy: "Park—picnic—took two trains. Almost got wrong train. Maybe you want to know who 'we' was—my brother and self. Saw two bears at zoo."

(*Margaret* wandering around sewing doll's clothes.) (Can't seem to listen.)

Janice: "1942 went to Allentown, Pennsylvania. In car. Enjoyed trip coming back more than going. Stopped car so suddenly my legs were where head should be and my head where legs should be."

Girl: "In trolleycar. Clown in trolleycar. He said, 'I'll show you some tricks.'"

Eddy: "Greyhound bus. School building. Saw boy climbing up on roof and I said to myself, 'Isn't that terrible.'"

Girl: "Trip to country. Fell on the ice."

Laura: "Took our roomer, my aunt, my grandmother, my cousin, etc. Came down with a bump."

Boy: "Trip to Virginia—two weeks. Went to Washington and saw snake in zoo 240 feet long."

In the afternoon following the morning discussion, the Bank Street member gave this fourth-grade teacher the following notes.

Planned discussion: Outline well thought out. Went very well. Right amount of guidance from you. Children were interested. It started their thinking about personal "travels" as shown by papers they wrote afterwards. These children need many personal outlets.

Questions: Where to go from here? I jotted down a number of leads which your planned discussion suggested. Would follow up something that would (a) tie up with your other subject matter (geography or history) or (b) which would lead to trip in neighborhood or (c) science experiment. That is, lead toward something *concrete.*

1. *Factories in city.* Nearly every hand went up when you asked if fathers were working in factories. Might get list from children of kinds of work their fathers do. Might have a father come to class and tell about what his factory does.

2. *What comes to city* on all these roads? (a) Building materials (on boats, largely). Might visit Harlem River where sand, stone, and

coal are kept in open yards. (b) Food—ask children to find out at stores where food comes from and how it gets here. Trip to city market in the Bronx.

Leads from children's talk and papers.

3. *Electricity.* Short circuit. Experiment with storage batteries. Get custodian to show meter box, fuses, etc., in basement. Discuss how electricity is made in city (from coal). How it gets to school. *Under the street.*

4. *China* (in written diaries). The duck in the story was traveling on a water road. Why houseboats on Yangtze and not on Hudson. Elsie told me "because China is so crowded."

5. *Bridges.* I have wonderful books (logs) published by Construction Company when George Washington Bridge was built. Take trip to see bridge.

6. *Hudson River.* What use is it to New York? Ask for observations first and then, if possible, take a trip to gather source material. Tide goes up to Albany—no falls, etc.

7. *Boats.* Great variety on Hudson and in New York Harbor.

8. *Greyhound bus. Trolley stations. Moving vans.* Where all these things stay at night, etc. *What happens to all these things in the snow?* Street cleaners and snow plows. Get a street cleaner to come to class and talk to children. Where does snow go?

9. *Workers on all these travel roads.* Charles and James were discussing workers on the train near me. Named: conductor, trainman, porter, waiter in dining room. Possibly fathers among these.

10. *Streamlined.* Many of the children used this word. Physical principles involved—boats, trains, airplanes.

11. *Suggestions about language.* Try to make them talk and write in images—what they saw, heard, smelled, etc. That they have these images is shown in their drawings—but not in their language except Janice, "Car stopped so suddenly my legs were where my head should be and my head where my legs should be."

About the children. They can't be given too much freedom all at once. Don't yet know how to use it. In their spontaneous stories the preponderance of burning trolleys and snakes and accidents and hide-and-seek on train indicates (to me) need of emotional release. I think you handled this well—just accepted stories without questioning truth of them and suggested something that was fun.

I think our psychologist might help you with James and Charles and Margaret.

I don't think Charles is a low I.Q. Any record? Not normally developed inhibition. (Note: Charles ran away from home a few weeks later.) (Margaret is child discussed by psychologist, Appendix 11.)

This is hasty. I'll bring you the record I took and these suggestions in typed form tomorrow if possible. Advise keeping routines steady with gradually longer and longer activity periods. They have to learn how to use freedom.

All this time we were carrying on discussions in after-school meetings with teachers divided into grade grouping—third and fourth, and fifth and sixth grades. There the teachers reported progress or problems in their units and discussed next steps. These discussions gave the Bank Street member an opportunity to introduce relevant background content to enrich the thin content in the textbooks, and also to bring concrete source material for the use of both teachers and children.

Working on Source Materials as Tools for Laboratory Approach

What are source materials? Source materials can be thought of as "raw materials"—isolated but relevant facts, images, experiences —from which relationships or interpretations can be worked out. Source materials give the opportunity for genuine thinking; they are a challenge to creative discoveries of relationships. As such they are sharply distinguished from textbooks, where relationships among facts are already worked out, interpretations already supplied. It should go without saying that no one—child or adult— can work out from source materials all the relationships necessary for an understanding of today's complicated world of things and people. We have a vast cultural heritage handed down from scholars who themselves worked with source materials and have already established relationships in many fields. It would be preposterous to repudiate this heritage and ask children to find out everything for themselves. But it is also true that anyone—child or adult—who depends completely upon other people's thinking, who never makes a laboratory approach to anything, never struggles to see a relationship new to himself, will not understand today's world of things and people, for he will not know how to think. Children are natural investigators, young scientists, young thinkers. In all areas they should be given the chance to tackle some source materials for themselves, though their discoveries may be new only to themselves —not to the world. The laboratory approach equips one as nothing else will to assess "evidence" in other people's thinking, and to accept or reject one's own and others' thinking on a scientific basis.

There is a wide variety of source materials available to teachers and school children. A trip to study the environment is a laboratory approach. It is gathering facts and images at first hand to be later related. The here-and-now world can be thought of as source material for the children to use directly—indeed, it is the greatest of all source materials. In the trips already described we used it primarily to study human geography—what people do to the earth and what the earth does to people, both aspects of which are involved in people's work. Trips to museums are to see collections of source materials, "raw materials" which the children can relate, can interpret in terms of how people lived, worked, and felt. Trips were supplemented by a variety of other source materials for children and teachers which make distant and past people and lands real and understandable. The faraway and long-ago cannot be experienced in the same direct way as the here-and-now by going to see and hear actual people at work and the actual lands they use. Yet, within the classroom source materials can bring a kind of learning experience with unseen, unheard people and lands which is entirely different from merely being "told about" them. Audio-visual aids are another type of source material recently come into use. The very word "aid" suggests that schools now have the concept of learning through manifold stimuli and that they substitute "aids" where direct experiences are not possible. Photographs and pictures, if accurate, can be source materials. They give uninterpreted images of lands and people—not so vivid as seeing directly but far more vivid than words. Most of the teachers had some collection of pictures which they used. We began accumulating pictures toward a school source material library.

Writings that have come down from past people are source materials. Their use is still a laboratory approach—first the gathering of evidence, then the interpretation of the evidence—which is the antithesis of memorizing facts in a text. For instance, reading the actual log of Columbus's voyage is an actual contact with the situation as Columbus and his sailors experienced it—the drifting in the Sargasso Sea, the fears and restlessness of the sailors, the evidences of approaching land. No text stating these things, no matter how well written, gives the same impact as firsthand evidence. A text in which the interpretations are already worked out by someone else does not challenge real thinking. So we began to use old diaries, stories of real explorations where the children gathered part of the information themselves and shared the real situation emotionally through identifying with past and distant people.

We also used current materials—factual articles in magazines and newspapers, folders describing work processes issued by industries, railroad timetables, maps, etc. These materials, too, we put into our growing source material library.

Children Find Out How Earth Forces Behave through Science Experiments

Another direction for firsthand exploration was finding out how earth forces behave, and this was attacked through science experiments. In science, the laboratory approach has long been recognized though not often used with children as young as ours. Some aspect of science is tied up with every program. The need to know something about earth science was felt first by the teachers in the relation of people's work to the earth forces they used. The study of earth forces was followed up in connection with special lands studied in various programs. By fourth grade the children were eager to understand what made the lands where different people lived so different —what made deserts, swamps, tropical forests, mountains, plains. Earth science played a large role in fourth, fifth, and sixth grades. In these same grades, experiments helped the children to understand applied science, from people's invention of simple tools to present-day complicated machines such as airplanes, diesel engines, and telephones; power, from early hand tools to electricity and gasoline —indeed, the whole role of inventions in transportation and industries. This led on to natural resources—first how they came into being and then their social use or conservation.

All this did not happen at once. At first the teachers were afraid of science—they felt that only "experts" could know enough to conduct even simple science experiments with children. So here, as in exploring today's work patterns, our Workshop programs followed two techniques: demonstration teaching and meetings with a specialist. The Bank Street staff conducted science experiments with the children in all grades. The response of the children proved to the teachers that children were interested in finding out how natural forces behave and could understand simple demonstrations in which they took part. In Appendix 13, we have already quoted a record of suggestions given to a second-grade teacher for simple "weather" experiments. In the older groups we began with simple experiments which both children and teachers could easily handle and which aroused the children's wonder. These experiments were usually repeated and fuller explanation given then. For instance, with a fourth-grade class, magnets were first handled almost as play material, children trying to magnetize various objects and trying them out with different materials. Next, compasses were made and used to orient children in their classroom and on their trips around New York; then they were related to explorers the children were familiar with, Columbus and Henry Hudson. Here is a memo given to the teacher by a Bank Street member.

MEMO ON MAGNETIZING NEEDLE

Rub needle on bar magnet one way over and over but not back and forth. Place magnetized needle on small cardboard disk or pan of water. Needle will point north.

North Magnetic Pole of earth is near Hudson's Bay in Canada, 71 N. latitude and 96 W. longitude.

More experiments in *Boy's Book of Magnetism;* Yates.

Magnets may be bought at: Bergwald Material Company, 359 Canal Street; Columbo Trading Corporation, 304 Canal Street; American Surplus Trading Company, 332 Canal Street: 5¢ to 15¢. (Sixth Avenue Subway downtown to Canal Street.)

Later, this experiment with magnets was one of several science experiments written into the Workshop social studies curriculum in connection with various explorers the children were following into various parts of the world.

We give excerpts from one more record by a Bank Street member working with fifth-grade children who were studying the northern regions of North America which illustrate how science materials were used.

As I went in child had just told story of Pandora's box.

I launched discussion—Greeks made up story to explain troubles in the world. Some of those troubles were storms. We will find how storms develop and move around the world. (One child had read a condensation of *Storm* by George Stewart in *Reader's Digest.*)

I told how meteorologist gets messages from all over world and plots his map. His symbols. Point and curves. Which cold and which warm?

Child: "Point—cold. We say 'a sharp wind.'"

I explain: Air masses cold and warm, wet or dry, move over earth and sea. Meet each other and fight (storm) or just remain still (stationary front).

Drew large map of U. S. on board of the day's weather map from New York *Times.* Children helped interpret symbols, fronts and arrows. Read from newspaper, predictions and developments. One storm now in Canada had come from Aleutians. Showed islands on large map of world.

The science experiments with children also aroused genuine interest in the teachers themselves. Once more they asked for background content. We give excerpts from the record of one of the first Workshop sessions on science.

A Bank Street member introduced the *leader* of today's talk on science as the science teacher at Stuyvesant High School and The Bank Street Schools.

The leader spoke of a book he had recently read about the education of a young child. In it he said there were scientific facts that exactly matched a list in a physics notebook of his high school children.

Children learn and experience and teach themselves science from the day they are born. Example: John in high chair—knocks off rattle, pleasant noise; does the same thing with his Teddy bear. Makes generalization—push to the floor anything you don't want to be bothered with. He has made a great step—he has seen certain things happen. He has generalized. Anything you push over the edge of the high chair falls to the ground. John continues scientific contact with life until he comes up against that organized conspiracy of formalized science! Thinks scientists have obnoxious odors, wear tortoise-rimmed spectacles. People seem to be frightened by "sorcery" of science or the "wizardry" of science. *Steinmetz—Wizard of Science* is what they see in the papers!

Good teachers make use of science, just as do the people who have been speaking prose all their lives. A good teacher *does* teach science, or the scientific attitude. She is teaching science when she makes experiments available—she gives the experience from which they can generalize.

Illustration: Dad crushes out cigar. Older brother puts sand on campfire. Clothes on fire, wrapped in a blanket. Teacher illustrates with a small candle on a table, lights it, puts a bottle over it. Candle goes out. No more air. Child discovers great truth—the candle goes out because there is no more air. The experiment was performed with simple materials. *Leader* asked a *Bank Street member* what the group of teachers was interested in. She said that in units on Holland, a low country, teachers had asked for science background on windmills. Winds in Holland—what are they? How can we understand how they work?

The leader illustrates with smoke. Movement of air associated with heat. Has a cigar box, two holes cut in one side. Puts in two short candles. Lights them. They are source of heat. Puts in some smoke from the end of a lighted window cord. Notice that smoke is drawn in one hole, moving out from other hole. Chimneys give a better circulation of air. Paper chimneys can be made. A box fixed with glass to show movement of air and smoke is valuable.

Another simple experiment. Have two basins, one filled with earth, one with water. Put outside in the sun. When the sun shines, land warms up, ocean doesn't. At the seashore, the wind is from the cool ocean toward the warm land. In the evening it is reversed. No equipment—a big generalization.

Mustn't generalize from one experiment. Child must have many experiments before he can generalize.

Bank Street member: "Any questions from your class?"

Teacher: "Child brought in article on sunspots, interferes with the radio. I couldn't explain it."

Leader explains that the sun is extremely hot. Fragments of metal in sun give off heat, cause interference. Icebox with motor no good—same thing. Static is interference.

Leader made clouds—little water in a bottle. Breathed in air. Lowering of air pressure. Vapor suspended, makes the clouds.

Teacher: "Why do boats stay up?"

Leader suggests: make a boat of tinfoil. It floats. Crush it—sinks to bottom. Floating begins when it weighs less than the volume of water it displaces.

Time up—group dispersed.

Interest in science grew steadily among the teachers, particularly as related to subject matter in their social studies programs. In the following chapters we shall tell of later developments in techniques both with children in the classrooms and with teachers in the Workshop meetings.

Children Use Maps as Tools for Thinking and Discovering Relationships

For a time we tried holding our small after-school meetings in the room of one of the teachers who was to report on her unit. This gave us a chance to see all the products of the children and also what books and maps and other materials the teacher was using.

The question of maps came up over and over again. The teachers recognized how inadequate were political maps to give children any idea of the characteristics of the land. They also felt that physiographic maps with color symbols for elevation were not understood by the children. A Bank Street member brought graphic relief maps, both those on the market and some she had made herself for the children to use. She suggested that the children model maps in relief. This immediately was greeted by "We don't know how to make maps ourselves. How can we do it with children?"

As a result, we had two Workshop meetings devoted to map making by the teachers. Each teacher modeled in clay on top of a large outline map, the land her children were studying. The Bank Street member brought graphic relief maps for them to follow. She told them to think of drainage all the time and to stroke the clay the way water would flow. While they were working, we discussed the land forms they were modeling in terms of the kind of life and work these land forms were suited to. Later we discussed the relationships of land forms to climate, vegetation, and the making of soil.

Projections of the maps had not been given much thought by the teachers. A map was just a map. In one of our meetings in a fifth-grade teacher's room, she reported on her unit. She began: "I think I started all wrong. My children plan to take a trip from New York to various countries. They have become newspaper reporters in order to travel." (This was wartime.) She had limited her children to ten countries but these were spread all over the world. On the wall hung a map of the world by which the children planned their travel routes. The Bank Street member remarked: "The map of the world you are using is the worst there is for your purpose. The Mercator projection completely distorts relative sizes—only a globe gives correct comparative sizes." She asked a teacher to measure the comparative sizes of Greenland and South America on the globe. From north to south, South America was about three times the size of Greenland. Another teacher measured the comparative sizes on the Mercator map. From north to south, South America was smaller than Greenland. The point was made that a map is good *for* some particular purpose. Some projections are good for one purpose; another for another purpose. At a later meeting we discussed projections in greater detail. The teachers worked out five of the chief projections on which maps are drawn, using scissors and paper, and compared the characteristic distortions that each projection made when the curving surface of the earth is projected onto a flat surface with a globe, which alone makes no distortion of the earth's surface.

Geographic thinking (as opposed to memorizing facts in locational geography) is often declared to be beyond young children. That, however, has not been our experience. The following record illustrates the ease with which fourth-grade children think geographically if they are not first confused by abstract information and maps with abstract symbols which they do not understand—political boundaries and lines showing longitude and latitude.

Teacher had one of the big globes in the room on which one can chalk or model. As children are doing global regions, we thought we might put the mountains on the globe. She had a modeling material I did not know, but we decided to use it. I brought my graphic relief map of North America. Children readily picked out mountains and rivers running down them. They said rivers carried down broken-off bits of mountains. (This was holdover from work with a Bank Street member last year.) Their questions on science were very mature. One child said, "Water runs downhill by gravity." I asked, "What is gravity?" Child answered, "The earth pulls everything down." I had a child put finger on north pole of globe and jump up and down. Then on equator and jump up and down. Finally on south pole. No difficulty. One boy (new) asked, "If earth pulls everything, why doesn't a big warship sink to bottom of ocean?" (Postponed answering this question and later did experiment to show water displacement keeps ships afloat.)

Finally four children began to put mountains on the Americas on globe. They worked in space which had been cleared by removing a few desks. I pointed to spot on outline of North America on globe and asked whether the land was high or low. Girl glanced at relief map on wall.

"High." Another point, another glance, then, "Low." Then she said, "Don't you worry, Mrs. ——, when we finish, everything on this globe will look just like that map, only it will stick up."

Now we give a series of records by a Bank Street member which show how sixth-grade children developed social thinking starting with map thinking.

October 11

This group of eleven-year-old children was studying Europe. The teacher asked me to take over the class for some discussion of geography. She said, "I really believe what you say—that the land should be a background for the lives and work of people living in Europe. When I try, the land seems lugged in." I found the class had been divided into committees who had worked on various countries, reporting their findings to the whole class. They knew more than ordinary textbook information—imports, exports, political boundaries, capitals, etc. They had read about the art, a little of the history of various countries. And they had organized this information well. I bring my big graphic relief map of Europe. Ask children to consider this a picture of land and water. Where would be good boundaries between nations for keeping peace among them? Different children chalk on map what they think would be good boundaries, some following mountains, some rivers. Lively discussion follows. Children decide that mountains are natural boundaries—barriers hard to cross—and work out that mountain divide would be best boundary line so that each nation would completely control its own rivers. On this basis, they mark off Spain, France, Italy, Greece with some hesitation; Great Britain as an island with natural water boundaries. I ask about Scandinavia. They mark off Norway from Sweden following the actual boundary, which is the mountain divide. Decide rivers are not good boundaries since each side of river would want to use river, which might cause conflicts.

Children study map for what they call "danger points" and mark them off in red circles on map: Dardanelles, Gibraltar, strait between Italy and Sicily. After discussion, children decide both sides of these danger points should belong to one country. "Or to all countries," says a child. Children become worried about northern plain of Europe where there are no good natural boundaries. Also worried about Balkans. Danube runs through natural mountain barriers. Wonder if these areas should be marked danger points.

I raise question, "What raw materials do modern nations need?" Children become quite excited. "Farmland," is first response. "Forests," second. Then, "Industries." I ask, "What raw materials does a nation need for industries?" One boy says, "Coal around the Rhine and the Ruhr. Both France and Germany and probably the Netherlands would want it. Can I put a danger point there?" A girl says, "Oil. Hitler wanted to get oil in Rumania." I ask them to look up where oil and coal are in Europe to put on our map. We discover there is no map in the school in any geography or atlas which can give them this information. I promise to bring an economic atlas next time which gives location of natural resources.

Children very responsive. Have much information; well organized. Have never worked with any children who could think better than these.

(The teacher afterwards told me that the children talked about my discussion with them. One boy said, "Do you know why it was so exciting? Did you notice she told us almost nothing herself? She made us think out everything ourselves.")

October 18

I show the children my economic atlas. Three children use it to mark coal and iron and oil on map in colored chalks. Then over mountains and rivers and natural boundaries, they drew political boundaries with my help. Children much disturbed that political and natural boundaries have so little relation. Divide class up into the nations various committees have been studying. Dramatize an international discussion of what each nation wants which it doesn't have. The nations try to work out trade agreements (instead of war) in regard to raw materials of coal, iron, oil. Talk spreads to sources of oil outside Europe and how European nations would want to get "rights to oil in Iran and Dutch East Indies." (Location of oil found in the atlas.)

Children look at Soviet Russia on the map. One child says Russia could raise wheat for trade. I ask a child to trace the Volga. Children disturbed that Volga empties into Caspian Sea with no outlet. Children say that explains Soviet Russia's need for ports which will get her products out for trade either through Mediterranean or Baltic. Further study of the map brings suggestion from one child that a canal could connect the Volga with the Black Sea. Children locate best place for canal, which is exactly where canal is being dug. Children generalize: inland nations need to use rivers of their country all the way down to some seaport. The teacher takes over and conducts the discussion extremely well.

Children's discussion is mature. Quick to catch social implications. The teacher enthusiastic. I think she could do this kind of geography alone. She wants children to make a map. I agree to help. Must first get more geographic thinking started with the children.

October 25

Bring my big Thorne-Thomsen graphic relief map of Eurasia. We discuss main land features. Child traces with his finger the high land running from Atlantic to Pacific. Wearing down of mountains has built northern and southern plains. Children discuss what places would have been easiest to live in long ago and what places would have developed early civilizations. They pick out southern valleys: Yangtze and Hwang Ho, Ganges and Indus, Mesopotamia with no help from me. (Africa not shown on map so they missed the Nile.) Discuss early life on cold northern plain. Children say early men were hunters. Children know about cavemen in Europe. I explain about the grasslands of central Asia, the need of grass for their animals; the dry periods when grass is scarce. Children work out that people would be nomads in central Asia. A big mouthful for these children in one session! About half the class understand it clearly. We decide to make map of Eurasia. I leave a big outline map of Eurasia. Children are to paint water blue (in oils) before next time. Give the teacher a Berry relief map of Asia.

A group of children gather around me as I am leaving. They are obviously trying to understand the projection of the big map of Eurasia in which Scandinavia lies horizontal (which to them means east and west).

Girl: "Mrs. ——, which way is this map situated? This way [laying her arm on Scandinavia pointing toward pole] or this way [arm pointing vertically toward pole] or this way [arm again horizontal but on eastern side of map]?"

Boy (studying map carefully): "Don't you see that that's the way it *has* to be because this map wraps halfway around the globe?"

This is as good native thinking about projections as I have ever found even in an untrained adult.

October 29

(Extra visit to hurry on the map.)

Children have done a careful job of painting in water on map. They begin making sketches of mountains on sheets of paper. Ask them to make the mountains look as if people could not get through them (not the ordinary separated tent mountains). About six or seven children make really beautiful sketches. Most of the others understand but find the technique difficult. They are to draw the mountains on map before I come again.

November 1

Children have drawn about half the mountains. Really very fine technique. We discuss symbols for map. I ask what a "symbol" means. One child says, "Stands for something that isn't really there. It makes you think of something." One girl: "A map is really a symbol. The drawings we are making of mountains are symbols of mountains." Another child: "A color can be a symbol." They work out some appropriate symbols for their map. Mountains—brown or gray. White for snow on top of high ones. Good farmland—bright green. (We again go over where good soil would be and pick out great warm valleys.) Deserts—light yellow brown. (We discover why Gobi Desert is dry. Map shows rivers cannot get out to sea. Clouds rise over oceans, are blown in, come in contact with cold mountains which ring the desert around, drop their rain. Little left to fall on other side of mountain.) North Arctic coast—dull light green.

Picture symbols: reindeer near Arctic, camel in desert, horses on central plains and plateaus, temples in India, China, and Tibet.

Children are to paint in mountains and plains, and have sketches of symbols ready for next time. They are eager to search through their books to get accurate drawings. This will be a beautiful map. They plan to give it to the school for use in other classes. The teacher as excited as the children!

November 8

Dropped in to see how map was progressing. Little work has been done on it as they had been working on an assembly program. A few sketches for symbols on map—camels, temples. Arranged to have luncheon with teacher on November 20 (holidays interfere with earlier appointment).

November 22

I worked with children on a technique to make the land look higher than the water—a heavy line or shadow on the water made by short, vertical strokes wherever one would see the edge of the land as it meets the water. I sketched on board, and children on individual papers. All the children got the technique easily. But many of them were confused as to *where* one could see the edge of the land in perspective—which is used in graphic relief map on a base map that is drawn without perspective. About five children got the idea immediately. Each was put in charge to paint edge of water of one section of the map; each had two helpers.

Map is really beautiful to look at. As the children paint in various areas—deserts, good farmland, etc.—they discuss incessantly why one area is rainy and another dry. The teacher joins in the discussion when the children get confused. If many children are confused, she reviews with the whole class the question of what makes rain, why water vapor blowing in from ocean condenses into rain or snow on cool mountaintops. Children are now working on details to get mountains to look real by shadows, to show mountain spurs running into flat plains, etc.

The map was finished without the help of the Bank Street member. At the end tiny symbols of the various cultures, drawn by the children, were pasted on the map. The map was mounted and framed and put in the school source material library for use of other classes. The finished map was not a fine piece of finger technique but showed real geographic thinking—relation of lands to people.

This and many other discussions of maps as tools for thinking in all the grades led the teachers to ask a Bank Street member to talk on map thinking and map making for children in all the grades at one of the combined after-school meetings.[21]

EXPERIENCES BY WHICH CHILDREN ARE HELPED TO EXPRESS AND ORGANIZE THEIR THINKING AND FEELINGS

Once more we must say that it is completely artificial (never to be done in practice) to separate, as we have here done, experiences in which children conduct investigations from experiences in which they express and organize their thinking and feelings. It is like separating two halves of a pair of scissors: you no longer have scissors left—just two blades. Information is not really made your own until you do something about it, either in new activity or in

[21] Appendix 16: Maps as Tools for Thinking.

new thinking, which, of course, is also an activity. Nor does expression take place in a vacuum: it needs the stimulus of a real situation already experienced. When taking in and giving out are separated, you no longer have true learning—just two episodes. They may be interesting episodes but neither alone will further a child's development in real learning very much. For instance, a trip (an intake experience) may be only an episode unless it has some follow-up such as a discussion where children organize what they have taken in, or some creative expression, both outgo experiences. In our first Workshop approach, we perforce had to begin with one experience at a time and try to have further related experiences develop. This, to repeat once more, was because the teachers' initial attitude toward the Workshop was to get help on how to carry out separate teaching techniques.

We wanted the children in the four older grades to express themselves freely both for the satisfaction that comes through self-expression and because we believe such expression is an inherent part of the learning process. Getting free expression started was a more complicated problem with the older than with the younger children as told in the last chapter. Why?

First, because the children themselves had developed a different attitude. The creative impulse, so strong in children, had been stifled by a too early insistence on correct adult forms. Many of these children had never been given the freedom to experiment with art media. Instead, they had been taught to copy adult products. This, historically, has been the approach to the arts. Children, for instance, have been taught to trace adult pictures, to draw a house in perspective, long before they have felt the need of these adult techniques. The consequence was inevitable. Not only have children turned out stereotype drawings and paintings, but they have lost the confidence to experiment, lost the pleasure of their crude but vigorous products because they did not look like the adult models set before them and, consequently, did not meet with the approval of adults. In our school, the painting in many classes was relatively "free"; in other classes, the stereotype houses, daisies, and rabbits were about the only things the children drew without tracing. When they were given paints and asked to paint whatever they wanted to, they were afraid to draw upon their own images, their own ideas. "I don't know what to paint. I don't know how to paint," was a common attitude. When asked to write about something that interested them, they turned in formal "compositions" based as nearly as possible on something they had read and almost completely without images. In preparing for assembly programs, they took it for granted that all language expression must come from someone else and that their share was to commit the words to memory. Yes, these children had been conditioned by past experiences to the point where they were afraid to express themselves in school.

A second factor that made it more difficult to get free expression started with these older children than with the younger was the attitude of some, but by no means all, of their teachers. Some of them were troubled by the use of the word "free"—free drawing and painting, free discussion and writing, free dancing. They interpreted "free" to mean that skills and techniques should never be taught. And it is true that the word came into use as a protest against making the first approach to the arts through technical skills. When, they asked, should children be taught techniques in the use of art media? Our answer was—after a period of completely free experimentation, after the children themselves felt dissatisfied with their own products and wanted to learn adult technique as a help in their own creative expression. Most of the teachers agreed that a young child is content with his own crude paintings or bench products or dramatizations unless some adult has made him feel they are inferior because they are not like adult products. Not so, an older child. An eight-year-old has developed standards of workmanship—he wishes his bench-made boat to look like a real boat, whereas a five-year-old is content with his boat if he can play with it. A ten- or eleven-year-old who has not been adult-dominated has usually developed standards of workmanship in painting, in language, in drama which give him a new impulse toward acquiring techniques. These older children want help in acquiring techniques. And such help should be given them in full measure. But given in order to let them say something *they* want to say—not in order to produce an adult-approved product. Yet all the teachers wanted their children to enjoy art experiences. All of them wanted to be shown how to free children in discussions, how to get the children to paint a mural, how to get dramatic play and creative writing started, how to develop original plays with the older children. These were among the teaching techniques they had been told to follow.

So we began "demonstration teaching," believing, as we always had, that the response of the children themselves would set at rest the doubts of the skeptical teachers.

In Dramatic Play

Most of the teachers of the older grades had the pattern of choosing a play for their children and training them to memorize the words. In assembly programs the children commonly stood in a row and said their pieces in turn. There was no chance for dramatic expression or for originality. Dramatic play in the classrooms was almost unknown even in third and fourth grade, where children commonly help out their inadequate words with spontaneous gestures. All the teachers wanted to see some demonstration teaching in getting dramatic play started with a group of children. At one of the Workshop meetings we tried keeping a group of fourth-grade children after school and invited a teacher from an experimental school to conduct a demonstration. These children, who were slow readers, had been studying early Manhattan—Indians and the coming of the Dutch.

NOTES ON A WORKSHOP MEETING ON DRAMATIC PLAY

Sixteen fourth-grade children stayed after school to participate in dramatic play. Teacher from experimental school took over the group.

She had brought a basket of possessions. Showed the children, first, some tobacco; how the Indians had smoked it; how they found clay in the streams, made pipes. She showed a little clay bowl she had made; it was a cooking pot. She had the children tell her why the pot was pointed. Then she showed them a wooden bowl the Indians had made. These children got out the wooden bowl they had exactly like it.

Visiting teacher poured Indian corn into a wooden bowl; showed children corn on the cob. Then showed them gay feathers. Children clamored for a turn to wear them.

She got the children to talk about island of Manhattan in Indian days; how they would go through the underbrush, etc.

She showed children an animal skin. They seemed greatly interested in this; tried to guess what animal it came from. Also showed them a gourd; this also interested the children.

Then she showed them a drum made like an Indian drum. Still more interest in this.

Next she showed them shells that Indians used for dishes.

She tried to get the children to talk about canoes. Children described birchbark canoes, canoes made by burning out logs.

She was now ready to begin the dramatic play. She took one aisle of children at a time. She picked out the first row: two little girls and a couple of boys (great excitement). The classroom teacher helped the children put on the feathers, tying bands of cloth around their heads and sticking in the feathers. The boys sat on top of the desks, one in the bow, one in the stern, and paddled to the beating of the drum. They landed, pulled the canoe up on the beach; the boys pretended to catch fish; the girls made a fire. The boys cut wood and dragged it to the camp. The girls fixed some corn in shell dishes.

This group's turn was over; another group given a chance. This group's task was to show how Indians walk through the woods.

The group started from the door; they pretended to be a group of hunters with bows and arrows, walking single file. Visiting teacher explained that a bang on the drum meant it was time to shoot. The children obeyed the signal, killed their animal, dragged it to camp, cut it up; built a fire, smoked the food, then cooked it over the fire. Two of the Indians went to sleep, two kept guard. This group's turn was now over.

The time was going fast. Two groups were combined. They took the part of Indians and the Dutch. The children acting as Indians made their way through the thick underbrush, gathered wood, built a fire. One of the Indians walked down to the beach; saw a big boat with the Dutch traders on it; put up his hand to his brow, gazed at the boat; thought it was a bird; ran back to tell his Indian companions what he had seen. The

Dutch came ashore in small boats; saw the Indians; gave them gifts. The two groups, Indians and Dutch, pretended to trade with each other. The Indians pretended to go to work with the things the Dutch had given them, digging, etc.

The classroom teacher said that the time the children were to stay was nearly up. Visiting teacher quickly showed the children how to do the Indian toe and heel campfire dance. In no time at all the children got on to the step, and danced around a circle at the front of the room.

Most of the group then sat down on the floor. Watched the Dutch people put up their sails on their big boat and sail away.

The children gave the visiting teacher a few suggestions as to what they thought they could do next. Then the classroom teacher had to hurry them down to the yard and dismiss them.

The group of teachers remained a few moments and discussed the children in the group. Their teacher thought the children had done very well—under the circumstances. She seemed greatly pleased at the response the visiting teacher had got from children she didn't know at all.

This record is a perfect illustration of what we mean by an "outgo" experience. In this dramatization, the children organized the information they already had and expressed it in their own images on their own level. The teacher acted as a guide, but in order to release the children to free expression, not to dominate or put over adult techniques. Also, it was a social, a group experience. These children felt they *were* Indians and Dutchmen. Identifying with other people, in the present or the past, makes for healthy social growth.

In Creative Language: Individual and Group Stories

Language is an art medium—perhaps the most important one, since everyone uses language. Children play with language long before they have learned to use adult forms correctly—grammar and, later, punctuation, paragraphing, etc. That is, children spontaneously enjoy and experiment with sounds, with rhythm, with a patterning of words.[22] These are the art elements in language at any age. They are what raises language to literature, what adds the emotional

[22] See Chapter 8, p. 137.

heightening to the meaning of words. But language is not only an art medium. It is our chief method of communication. In art the individual expresses himself, and the pleasure and release it gives to the artist comes primarily from the creative act. The "other fellow" is in the offing, to be sure, and his understanding and enjoyment of the artist's product adds to the artist's satisfaction. But communication fails of its very purpose unless it is understood by the "other fellow." It is obvious that the communication aspect of language is of prime importance, and equally obvious that correct grammar, punctuation, paragraphing, and all the other adult matters should be taught to children sometime. But not too early, not at the expense of enjoyment of the art element. Yet that, historically, is just what has been done in language more than in any other art medium. Free or creative language has suffered more and suffered longer than the other arts. Free art (meaning graphic art) was permitted in schools before free language. "Correctness" as a standard for children in speech or writing his dried up the creative springs which bubble up so spontaneously in the language of all small children. By eight years of age most children have stopped using language creatively in school. Most of them are fairly indifferent to "literature" that is read to them at intervals to give them standards in language art. They concentrate on getting the meaning of words— communication—and have stopped enjoying the sound, the rhythm, the patterning of words—art. And later as adults they seldom read for enjoyment. They read, if they read at all, solely for information, for "improving" themselves.

To get creative language started with children in the older grades, one must first release them from inhibitions built up by adult disapproval. The first moves can almost be called therapeutic. The teacher must not merely refrain from correcting the child's language every time he speaks or writes. She herself must join in language which has an art element, which draws upon her own images. This, more than anything else, will make children feel self-confidence in drawing upon their own images, their own ideas. We give one record of how one Bank Street member helped a group of second-grade children to get their images into action in words. Note that she started with an immediate experience which had interested all the group.

Children began telling about army parade (yesterday):
"Tanks scratchin' up the street."
"Every time I looked up in the sky airplanes were going by my house—
eight by eight."
"I was in the place where squirrels were hoppin' across the grass."

Bank Street member said the parade had started in Washington Square. Questions came about directions, busses, where the parade went. Led into river interest by comparing with Navy Day. "Now we're going to make a story about that river. We are going to have fun with words. I'll think up some words and you'll think up some. This is the beginning." (Words underlined were supplied by Bank Street member.)

STORY OF A RIVER

Part I

Down on that river near our school
    there was some ice.
And the ice was swimming in the water. The boats were shooting fire.
And the fire looked red, and blue, and white.
    The river was cold.
It was so cold that we froze.
Down on that river near our school
    there was President Truman.
He was standing on a ship.
And he was the President of the United States.
President Truman was rolling in a car around the river.

Part II

Down beside that river I saw a lot of people.
Waiting to see all the ships.
There was smoke.
Smoke was coming out of the boats.
Down beside that river we saw some trains.
They were going underneath the bridge.

The wheels sounded rum-rum-rum-rum
And every car was rolling.
It was rolling down the track.
And in the cars fresh milk—
In an icebox in the cars.
Every car carried food—milk, eggs, cows, hens.

Part III

Across that river near our school
Busses, rocks, Palisades,
Cows, a tugboat, Jack Frost sugar,
Houses, ferryboats,
Little boats you could ride in.
Bond Bread Company, newsreel signs
Cars riding to Palisade Park,
Horses, people riding.

Part IV

Far up the river near our school
An airplane riding in the air
And the George Washington Bridge.
Cars riding on it.
Busses, taxis, trucks, lumber trucks,
Jeeps from the Army.
And under the George Washington Bridge
There is a little red lighthouse.

Acting Parts of the Story

One child acted. Others guessed.
1. Boat crossing river
2. Boxcar on trains

Two children planning and acting together.
1. Subway train
2. Taxi with passenger
3. Airplanes
4. Hammering tracks to see if O.K.
5. Steam-shovel
6. Coal truck dumping coal
7. Locomotive

Because of their desire to write like grownups, the children paid much attention to rhyme in their own writings. The exigencies of rhyme have sidetracked many an adult poet into saying what he could rather than what he wanted to! We tried various devices to make the children content with unrhymed, rhythmic language if it said what they wanted it to. We wrote their stories (when they had rhythm) in verse form. We asked them to sing words to their own tunes. Above all, we asked the teachers not to concentrate on rhyme as the only art element in language.

We give a few samples of stories told or written by children.[23]

STORY BY SECOND-GRADE CHILDREN
AFTER WATCHING ANTS AT WORK IN THE YARD

One day I saw a little ant and he was carrying a crumb of bread.
And the ants all over the yard came into the house to get some more
    bread. If my aunt dropped any on the front porch they would get it
    and pull it to them.
I said to the ant, "Hello, stop eating the food. Stop eating the bread.
    There will be plenty."
But the ant said, "No, no, leave me alone. I will not stop eating."

STORY BY TWO THIRD-GRADE CHILDREN
AFTER TRIP TO INWOOD

On our way climbing the mountain
I liked the sound of the trains.
And we sat and listened
to the noise the caves made,
and we climbed over a wall.
We walked down a pathway singing a song.
We saw a motorcycle
resting by itself.
We saw a rowboat
going across the river.
And the water flowed very, very fast,
and it met with the Hudson River.

[23] For stories by first-grade children, see p. 138 and Appendix 12: First-Grade Charts.

STORIES BY FOURTH-GRADE CHILDREN

Snow

Such a twinkling glow,
   Comes from flakes of snow,
Especially in the moonlight,
   Does the twinkle glow.

School

I like school,
   Do you know why?
I don't know myself,
   Do I?

Arts and Crafts

One day Billy's class,
   Had Arts and Crafts,
When that day came,
   Billy was full of laughs.

In May

It was a beautiful day
   in May
So I went out to play
And I was very gay.

So one day
   my mother went away
I was not gay
When my mother went away
On that beautiful day
   in May.

A Glowing

A glowing in the moonlight.
A glowing in the sky.
A glowing in the starlight,
   the little star and I.

STORY BY FIFTH-GRADE CHILD

(studying the Western movement)

With my pack on my back
I found a spot on which to build my cabin,
Chopped down trees and cleared the ground
And built a rude, strong home.
For my windowpanes greased paper
Through which I could not see.
My door swings on wooden hinges.
Wide, rough slabs were my floor.
From trees I made stools and tables.
I whittled my dishes, too.
There were bowls and spoons
And knives and forks
Of wood and pewter gray.
On the floor I laid the skin of the bear
Which I hunted and shot in the forest.
That was the home of a pioneer,
Do you think you could live that way?

In Group Expression: Original Murals and Plays

In the fifth and sixth grades, social attitudes take on a more mature tone, as seen in their art expression. These children get tremendous satisfaction from a group expression. Indeed, we in the Workshop felt their satisfaction in a mural painted by the group, or in a play written and given by the group, was greater than their satisfaction in individual paintings or stories. The climax of a long study by the group should be a group expression. And surely it is not necessary to turn art into a competitive affair. Children get more than enough experience in competition in our culture. Into the construction of a play or a mural, children while working together can pour much of their individual thinking and their feelings. Both murals and plays challenge the children to select what they consider most important to express. It practically always leads to research when they find they do not have enough information, clear enough images to complete an episode, to make costumes, to design a backdrop. A play will change in the making many times. Ideas by an individual or a small group will be tried out with spontaneous language and acting, considered by the whole group in comparison with other ideas, and the one the group considers best will be accepted. It is exciting for children and teacher alike to see a play grow. The teacher takes an active but not an authoritative part, giving her suggestions and criticisms as a member of the group. The techniques of language and of dramatic action become important and are worked on seriously by all the group. The experience of giving an original play with original backdrops in assembly was a new one to both children and teachers. The first one was greeted with wild applause. And it proved to be a real stimulus to other children and other teachers to do likewise. The appreciation of *their* play was received by the group as a reward of joint effort—a group creation.

We give a series of records by a Bank Street member which shows how a play develops. These were sixth-grade children considerably disturbed by the war, which was then going on.

NOTES ON PLANNING AND PRODUCTION OF A PLAY
BY SIXTH-GRADE CHILDREN

October 31

There was little opportunity for just observing in this class, for even on the first visit I was drawn into reading with a small group and very soon found that we were dramatizing the poems in the book we were looking at.

The atmosphere in the room is most relaxed, very easy to step into. The teacher and the children all seemed to accept another person cordially and know how to make use of her.

From the material around the room I judged that the core of the social studies is the war—"Our Heroes."

November 14

There has been some talk of a play for the group's assembly program but up to this point very little has been done about it. The presentation of something dramatic and entertaining which is nevertheless related to the program of the group became very acceptable to the sixth grade at this point because Mrs. B's play (the first original play) had just been given and was a smash hit. Quite spontaneously, the children wanted to discuss their play and wanted to be assured it would be even better, and so we plunged right in. Their contributions were the kinds of things that they had been taught to give as reports—"Countries and Products." There were many such ideas, none of them dramatic, none of them offering opportunity for plot development. There did seem to be some agreement on the peoples that they wanted to portray—Greece, China, and Russia, and their part in the war, were pretty well agreed on and I promised to try to get them some of the music.

November 21

Discussion of the play: Lucy and another girl had written the whole Greek episode for the play and they were quite ready to begin assigning roles with themselves in the leading roles, of course. The adults offered no comments when she was finished reading except to ask for the children's criticism. They brought out every single point that I had written for discussion and handled them so well that Lucy only suffered a moderate rejection of her play. Further discussion brought up the fact that perhaps we could begin talking out what we wanted to see in our play rather than writing it out and so save ourselves the trouble of learning words. Just to show them what we meant, we got a group of youngsters to dramatize a bit of the setting for the Chinese episode in the play. This was little more than a rehash of a bit of *Dragon Seed,* the movie that had been playing in the neighborhood theater, but the children were convinced that they could begin to do a play without learning a script first.

November 28

My appearance in the classroom is becoming the signal for the play, so there has been practically no opportunity to observe any of their work and we have plunged into rehearsal or play discussion as soon as I have arrived, ever since.

At this point we stopped to talk about what they really wanted to show in the lives of the people they were telling about. The most dramatic thing they could think of in terms of the Greek situation was the starvation. In the Chinese episode the emphasis seemed to center about the rescue of an American flier, and in the Russian situation (which was later dropped) they wanted to show victory coming to the Russian people.

The children had found some child in the school to teach them a Greek dance and I had brought some music which could be used. But the real problem was to put these large ideas into some kind of material that they could handle. With some help they arrived at the conclusion that they would have to show what was happening to the country by showing some family and its problems, so discussion typical of children's original plays began to develop—eating supper, and the food is limited and bad; the neighbors coming to call and telling about further injustices.

The children wanted to get in their dance and so they developed the device of talking about the good old days and planned to have older people show the children what a Greek festival was like. This seemed of paramount importance at this point in the play's development but was dropped out of the finished production completely. The Greek episode at this point ended with the entrance of the Gestapo, their searching the family and taking one of the boys off to a concentration camp.

December 5

The children wanted to rehearse what had been done the last time I was with them but they were dissuaded from doing so and attempted the Chinese episode instead. After a few false starts which they turned down pretty quickly as being undramatic or too much like the Greek scene, we began to develop an episode here. To get some activity rather than talk, I suggested that the scene open with a group of Chinese farmers planting their seedlings and even went so far as to offer the possibility that they do this with a Chinese music background. Thanks to the Hollywood influence, this was quickly accepted and did offer the children the release that made it possible for them to lose themselves in dramatization. They played out the noises of the airplane, the falling plane, picking up a wounded flier who had descended by parachute, giving him first aid, and hiding him when a Jap patrol appeared.

January 5

There was a hiatus of several weeks caused by my absence and Christmas, but the play was a very lively part of the class program when I returned. There had been some work on it and the children and the teacher were troubled for the lack of a connecting thread between episodes. Many suggestions were given, such as many refugees coming to our country. Someone suggested the possibility of their coming on the boat together from the two lands. I suggested that the inscription on the base of the Statue of Liberty be presented as a program in choral reading, but this was not well received.

The teacher told us of a song called "The House I Live In" which gives us an America-for-all feeling. He promised to bring this to the children, and we thought it would serve as a good opening for the play.

We finally hit upon an idea that satisfied the children deeply, namely, that the play would open with the meeting of two brothers who have suffered at the hands of Nazism and who relate the stories of their escapes—one having come through the Balkans and Greece and the other all around the world, through China, to be reunited in New York.

January 12–23

From here on we were really working on refining the dialogue and action, learning songs, painting a large backdrop, making some props, and putting the whole thing together. It looked like an almost insurmountable task and even the final rehearsal on the afternoon before the play was woefully ragged. But when I arrived on the morning of the play the children were shiny-eyed and scrubbed and polished.

Olive, who seemed a very inarticulate youngster, had written a perfectly charming announcement. The wonder and satisfaction of having made their own play seemed the most dramatic aspect to them. As Olive put it, "Every day more and more ideas kept coming and then when we put them together, we found we had a play."

The performance one might almost call inspired. There was a complete lack of rigidity and shouting of lines. There was some very genuine dramatic expression. There was intelligent ad-libbing when someone would leave out part of the planned dialogue or put in some new refinements thereof. The response of the audience was excellent. The children not only enjoyed the play—they seemed to value the fact of its having been really made in its entirety by children.

TEACHERS AT END OF YEAR AND A HALF

Ready for a Second Workshop Approach

All the preceding story and records of our Workshop in action show early curriculum experiences for the children and teachers. None of them shows how the teachers began to build those isolated experiences into integrated programs based on long-term planning, yet flexible in the carrying out. This did begin to happen at different speeds with nearly all the teachers. An examination paper of a first-grade teacher written after being a member of the Workshop for a year and a half shows the extent to which some of these teachers had made their own the attitudes and thinking that had developed in our

Workshop discussion and were putting them into practice in their classrooms.[24]

In the older grades, where our work in the classroom had been largely centered around units, the teachers developed new attitudes toward units. Instead of thinking of them as "extras," units came to be thought of as progressive experiences in a program of subject matter which was based on the interests and needs of children. This development is illustrated with records kept by a fourth-grade teacher: first, an outline of units; second, a log which she kept currently.[25] This teacher, who had chosen China as a unit in the first term we were in the school, decided in the second term (with different children, a class of "difficult" children, many of whom were non-readers) to begin with the study of Manhattan as lying closer to the children's interests. Her records show that while keeping the required setup of units, she built a real social studies program of progressive learning experiences—discussions and activities—one leading into another. She was thinking now in terms of a program, not merely disconnected units and information, and that child development was firmly integrated with both subject matter and teaching techniques.

By the end of our first year and a half, most of the teachers had passed through the early stage of wanting chiefly to know how to conduct the new teaching techniques. The Workshop members, Bank Street members, teachers, and administrators felt that the group had grown beyond the first approach of the Workshop—curriculum experiences—and was ready to go on to the second approach of true curriculum building where not only the content from the one-time separate courses of study is drawn upon in a related program but where the thinking about children is used in choosing subject matter, in teaching techniques, and in attitudes toward children. The story of this second Workshop approach in one school with one principal, with Bank Street Workshop leaders, follows in the next chapters.

[24] Appendix 17: Examination Questions and Paper by a Teacher of First Grade.
[25] Appendix 18: Outline of Work on Units: Teacher's Log.

10

Building for the Whole Child and the Whole School

OUR WORKSHOP TRIES A SECOND APPROACH

IN THE last chapters we have told how our first Workshop approach through curriculum experiences was determined by the teachers' initial interest to learn how to conduct the new teaching techniques largely in connection with units; and how, during the first year and a half in this school, our Workshop had developed to the point of trying a second and distinctly new approach to our job. The particular form which our Workshop took on was unexpected and in a sense accidental. It was determined more or less by the appearance at that time of the new official curriculum bulletin in tentative mimeographed form. Even in its tentative form, this bulletin gave us much more clearly than anything had previously the lines of newer thinking and attitudes toward children and curriculum content that the final official revision would eventually take. It superseded the old separate courses of study and outlined eight areas of learning which, it was stated, overlapped and were not to be taught as rigidly separate fields. On the contrary, it was suggested that content from any of the areas should be drawn upon for a rich experience for the children. It put much more responsibility on the teachers and encouraged initiative and experimentation on their part and on the part of an individual school for organizing programs within the general framework stated in the bulletin. Thus, much that we had been working toward in the Workshop received the support of an authoritative official statement—a matter of real psychological as well as practical importance for us all.

What really determined the second approach in the Workshop, however, was in no wise accidental. It came from a year and a half of hard thinking, hard work, and experimentation on the part of the school administration, the Bank Street staff, and, above all, the teachers. The picture as we neared the end of this first year and a half had developed in significant ways. Most of the teachers were thinking and planning in terms of a year's program of consecutive, progressive experiences which were based on a study of their children's needs and interests. That is, they were *building a curriculum* in a broad sense in which child development and the planning of curriculum experiences and curriculum content were closely interrelated; and teaching techniques were tools, a means to an end, not an end in themselves.

We shall not tell the story of our second Workshop approach uniformly by grades with all the kinds of intake and outgo experiences and curriculum materials for each grade or grade grouping. Instead, we shall emphasize a particular curriculum development which seems significant and appropriate in each grade, although this development really extended throughout all the grades. From the beginning we in the Workshop had put most of our thinking and time into the area of social studies with the related areas of science and the expressive arts,[26] because, as we have said before, social studies give the best chance to think in terms of children and to plan programs for total growth.

Now seemed a propitious time to begin to think of social studies not only in horizontal grade programs but vertically, for the whole school; that is, in terms of the experiences and curriculum content a child would have as he progressed from kindergarten through sixth grade. The Bank Street staff therefore proposed that we—administration, teachers, and Bank Street staff—work on a joint project,

[26] We are here following the areas as outlined in the official bulletin.

thinking out and writing up tentative social studies curriculum content and materials for this one school, for these particular children and their particular neighborhood. The group accepted the plan for the second term of our second year (1944–45). The story of our Workshop growth during the next year and a half now moves on to this second and maturer Workshop approach—our work in genuine curriculum building in social studies (as contrasted with isolated curriculum experiences) for the whole child and the whole school.

Inherent in the situation were difficulties that made the planning and writing of such curriculum materials far from ideal for a real group undertaking. To begin with, the teacher group was inevitably made up of teachers who had been working and experimenting in the Workshop for a year and a half, and teachers who were coming to the Workshop for the first time. To meet this situation, we planned some meetings for "new" members which were more or less repetitions of those in our first Workshop approach in curriculum experiences—with one significant difference: now the "old" members, more and more, became leaders in planning for such meetings and conducting the discussion.[27] The Bank Street staff worked with the new teachers in their classrooms in ways already described. With the old members our role became more that of consultants, available when they sought us.

The second difficulty was that none of the teachers, either new or old members, had time for much writing and few of them had had much writing experience. The Bank Street Workshop was on a year-to-year basis. We hoped, but had no assurance, that we should be asked to carry it on another year. Yet if tentative social studies materials were to get down on paper in time to be tried out in the classrooms in the second term, the actual writing had to be done at high speed. But what we wrote had to represent the joint thinking of the whole Workshop group—teachers, administration, and Bank Street.

[27] The teachers suggested that experienced Workshop members work with new members in their classrooms on special techniques. Though everyone thought this a good plan, it proved impractical to release the teachers from their own classrooms for this purpose.

Through preliminary discussions, the group proceeded to outline in broad terms our approach to such curriculum materials with suggestive but not fully worked out details.

There was a third difficulty. It was obviously important for the entire group to understand the new organization of subject matter and the new attitudes in the recent tentative official curriculum bulletin. The administration and the Bank Street staff had studied carefully the few available copies of the long mimeographed statement, and though these copies were passed around among the twenty-six teachers as fast as possible, the teachers inevitably had to look to the administration and Bank Street members for detailed information.

PRELIMINARY GROUP DISCUSSIONS AND THINKING

In our Workshop meetings preliminary to writing a tentative curriculum, we began by discussing what changes the teachers hoped would be made in the old official curriculum. What the teachers now considered a desirable curriculum forms an interesting contrast to their curriculum thinking as shown in their early discussion (pp. 90 ff.). Even more striking evidence of their growth is shown in what they wished their share to be in determining the social studies curriculum for their school. In the first preliminary discussion the teachers brought out a number of significant points, both in criticism of the old curriculum and in what they hoped for in the new. We list some of the points made by the teachers:

that the New York curriculum needed to be adapted to the neighborhood from which the children came; the teachers should be given leeway to do this;

that the old curriculum shows very little connection between history and geography; that the teachers couldn't teach social studies as an integration of history, geography, and civics with the present textbooks that isolated these fields; that minority groups needed consideration. Most of them were reluctant, however, to see Negroes [28] singled out as a "unit"

[28] See pp. 365 ff for further discussion on Negroes.

as too suggestive that they were a "problem" rather than Americans. (They referred to a section in the new official curriculum on minority groups.)

Other specific criticisms of the present situation were:
that the books for children were too difficult, with hard vocabulary. When children couldn't understand a book, they just copied out a part as a "report";

that the syllabus in arithmetic was too difficult.

In the discussion, the Bank Street members brought out the conception of social studies in the official curriculum which was the same as what we in the Workshop had been working toward. Social studies were conceived as an integration of history, geography, and civics; a variety of books and source materials was to be used for both children and teachers. "Units of work" were discussed in relation to themes in social studies to cover two years of work (in kindergarten, first and second grades, it covers three years); all of the themes are focused on ways of living and working; units are treated as progressive steps in developing the theme which, taken together, one step at a time, could be called a program of work; teachers are given great leeway in choosing which units will best further the development of the theme. A teacher summed up the discussion on units: "A unit should be thought of as a means to an end, not an end in itself." This, again, was very different from the initial attitude toward units.

WHAT IS A CURRICULUM BUILT OUT OF?

In one of our later preliminary discussions, in order to clarify the new and broader meaning of curriculum, a Bank Street member asked the group, "What is a curriculum built out of?" An immediate reply was, "The needs of children." Then followed, "Curriculum content"; to which another teacher immediately added, "Subject matter related to the children's own lives." Ideas poured out: "Experiences which help children to understand the world they live in —the work aspect, for instance." . . . "Also, the physical world, which is explained by science." . . . "Expression through the arts." . . . "Participation in the world around them—with young children that might mean just their home and the school." . . . "The curriculum should cover all aspects of a child's development—emotional and social as well as mental development."

The Bank Street member said that all these suggestions of what should go into the building of a curriculum seemed to center around either children—what they are like—or the world they lived in—the environment. She started a simple chart with these two cornerstones for curriculum building.

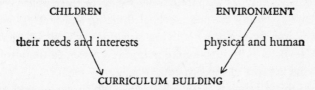

CHILDREN   ENVIRONMENT

their needs and interests   physical and human

CURRICULUM BUILDING

Under the cornerstone "Children," a Bank Street member asked what we meant by the "whole child." The discussion that followed brought out the following points: the expression "the whole child" had degenerated into a cliché. Yet, we all believe it has real educational meaning. Basically, it means that a child is not to be regarded as a sum of special faculties to be trained or developed separately; he is to be regarded as a person, an organism, reacting to experiences as a whole. We agreed that for purposes of discussion a child may be divided into a physical body; an intelligence with certain capacities and limitations; a social being reacting to others—either adults or his peers; a creature capable of definite emotional responses. But no one has ever met such a split-off division of a child all by itself. Someone said that a child meets life situations, he learns, he develops by reacting as a whole—physically, intellectually, socially, emotionally. Though some experiences may involve more of him than do other experiences, he remains a "whole child," with interacting major or minor reverberations throughout the artificial divisions into which our analysis may split him. This thinking about *all* children came from teachers whose initial interest in child development had been largely confined to "problem" children.

Then we discussed what happens to curriculum building if children are planned for as organically whole people instead of as bundles composed of bodies and brains and membership in society and an outfit of emotions, each to be attended to one at a time. If we face this question literally and almost naïvely as modern educators and students of child development are trying to do, we find ouselves discarding such traditional school thinking and practices as separate courses of study, confining body activities to recess, separating pleasure from learning, as inappropriately trying to teach split-up children; and accepting the newer school thinking and practices which give children experiences in living situations which will develop them as whole, fully functioning persons. We seemed to agree that this is the keynote of modern education.

From this discussion came subheadings which we entered under "Children" in our chart. We also discussed the meaning of environment—both the physical and man-made in which children live—and entered subheadings under "Environment" on our chart.

We then discussed whether these two cornerstones were enough to support all that we meant by a curriculum. The needs and interests of children could have many interpretations, depending upon what one wanted children and the world they were to live in to become. The Nazi philosophy developed schools which would fit the children to understand and participate in a Nazi environment. For instance, science in Nazi schools—content and experiments—was to fit the children for efficiency in war. Their teaching methods were good in so far as they gave children firsthand experiences not only in science experiments but in trips. They "got" the children's interests. Why, then, don't we approve of the Nazi curriculum? One teacher replied, "We would if we believed in the Nazi philosophy. We believe in democracy." Another teacher said, "Teaching democratic thinking and living is certainly one of the central aims of our schools."

After some discussion we decided we needed a third cornerstone in a chart of curriculum building. Soon we had the following chart with arrows showing interrelationships:

PHILOSOPHY OR SOCIAL IDEAS
(what you want children and the world to become)

CHILDREN AND THEIR
DEVELOPMENT

ENVIRONMENT IN WHICH
CHILDREN LIVE

their needs and interests and the way they learn at various maturity levels; their backgrounds; their individual personalities.

physical—physical phenomena and people's use of them in inventions and work—expanding from neighborhood to world; social—expanding from family to world groups.

CURRICULUM BUILDING
(with teaching techniques)

When this generalized, theoretical chart was interpreted in terms of our immediate job, the Workshop group came through to the following principles or statements which they wished our curriculum materials in social studies in all ages to include. The parentheses following the statements are our (the authors') own annotations.

1. Statements of general maturity level of each grade level in terms applicable to the school situation (recognition of child development as basis in curriculum building).
2. Statements of basic social ideas underlying the curriculum for each grade (indicates a wider conception of "social" than formal behavior or verbal expression).
3. Concrete suggestions in terms of experiences for children—trips and classroom activities and other experiences with materials to be used. Among the classroom experiences specified were:
   a. Map thinking and map making.
   b. Science experiments appropriate to the maturity level of the children and to the curriculum content. (Recognition of teaching techniques as tools in the learning process, not ends in themselves.)
4. The ways of living and working of any people (history, past and present) are to be studied in relation to the lands they lived in and used. (This human geography approach was, in general, in keeping

with the new official curriculum and had received special emphasis in Workshop thinking.)

5. Civics is to be brought in primarily (some said entirely) through current events. (This came from the teachers.)

6. Background content in child development and curriculum content to be included as a help to teachers. (Recognition of their need to keep up-to-date professionally.)

7. A bibliography for teachers and children.

The group agreed that the themes for social studies for the three grade groupings stated in the new official curriculum should be the themes in our tentative curriculum. Our job was to interpret these general themes in terms of our children, our neighborhood, and our social ideals for children and the world.

In small meetings with the three grade groupings, we worked out, on the basis of our past experiments in this school, an interpretation of these three general themes in terms of our children, our neighborhood, and our social ideals for children and the world. This gave us outlines of horizontal programs for each grade. Now came a new step—to work out these programs vertically so that children's progress from kindergarten through sixth grade would not only give them situations for all-around growth but would also cover the curriculum content as it was stated in the new bulletin. At this point one of the Bank Street members tried to put the Workshop thinking into a form which would present this thinking in terms of children at any grade level and also in the development of children as they progressed through the grades. She made a large chart which attempted to outline a social studies curriculum for our whole school built on the three cornerstones in our chart of curriculum building and on the principles and statements agreed upon by the group, using the theme for social studies in the new curriculum. This chart, read in the horizontal columns, showed social studies materials and techniques for each grade; read in the vertical columns, it showed the official themes around which experiences and subject matter centered, with teaching techniques and maturity levels, including interests and social ideas, arranged from grade to grade under these same large headings. Two of the large headings used the definition of social studies given in the official bulletin: (1) relations of people to environment, and (2) relations of people to people. We added another large heading, "Science," which in the official bulletin was one of the eight areas of learning. Our fourth heading, "Map Thinking and Map Making," did not appear in the official bulletin. The chart went through many changes in the course of the next year and a half of trying out our social studies materials in the classrooms.

See pp. 194–195 for chart as developed in our second revision.[29]

HOW WE WORKED

Throughout this period of writing and trying out a tentative social studies curriculum in the classrooms, one member of the Bank Street staff was asked to meet with the official revision committee as an associate member. The committee was interested to have the new official curriculum in its tentative form tried out in many schools and hoped to have concrete reports from such schools.

The teachers took the chart and the outlines as a point of departure for Workshop discussion, not as something final, to be accepted or rejected. Our general procedure was to discuss appropriate learning experiences for children with the whole group from kindergarten through sixth grade through which they would develop wider interests and a body of information. These preliminary inclusive discussions accomplished two things: first, the reporting of teachers from each grade on their own experiences with their children sharpened the thinking of each teacher about what her own children were interested in and what she could do about such interests, what subject matter they could understand, how far along they were in social ideas—in brief, the thinking about maturity levels and also about "whole" children; second, the teachers in each

[29] The completed plan appeared in pamphlet form under the title: *Tentative Social Studies Curriculum from First Through Sixth Grade*. Copies are available at Bank Street Publications, 69 Bank Street, New York 14, New York.

	Themes	Work related to Neighborhood and Land	As Individuals	In Communities
Kindergarten	Living and working in home; school; around the block; from river to river	Home and school in relation to immediate environment	Largely individual. Some play and work in groups	Work in the home and its relation to neighborhood
Grade 1	Living and working in home; school; around the block; from river to river	Home and school in relation to upper Manhattan	Largely individual. More play and work in groups	Relation of neighborhood workers to children's own lives
Grade 2	Living and working in home; school; around the block; from river to river	Home and school in relation to Manhattan Island	Less individual. Beginnings of more organized play and work in groups and in games	City housekeeping and its workers
Grade 3	Living and working in kinds of communities now and long ago in Manhattan, Great Plains, Southwest, and on the coasts	Work in Manhattan Island now; in Indian times; Dutch times. Great Plains now, in Indian times; Southwest now, Indians now and before Europeans came. North Pacific Coast	Beginnings of organized dramatizations, and of ability to work in committees	Workers in the city related to children's own lives. Workers in Indian communities long ago or far away
Grade 4	Living and working together in N. Y. C.; differences and likenesses: N. Y. and other regions	Life and work as conditioned by earth situations in deserts, in tropics, in far North, in mountains	"Clubs" in school. Further development of group expressions in various arts and games and committees	Group life developed in various regions. "Teamwork" among members of exploring party
Grade 5	Living and working together in the U. S. and world. Land and people of U. S. Ties with American nations	Beginnings of American nations: explorers and lands they found; settlers, early life in these lands. How we became a nation; Western expansion; cities grow; Civil War; new roads. Other American nations grow	Neighborhood groups. Organized social life: scouts, church, etc. Children take over more group responsibilities	People seek freedom in new world. Federal Government. Slavery
Grade 6	Living and working together in the U. S. and world. Our country and its ties with rest of world	We became a modern nation; an industrial nation; regional work and interdependence of regions. Global roads, trade, raw materials. Eurasia: lands and peoples. Europe; Mediter. world; England; Commonwealth of Nations, Empire. Asia; China; Russia. Science and inventions still going on	Neighborhood groups. Organized social life: scouts, church, etc. Children begin to take over some neighborhood responsibilities	Now: postwar conditions. Past Reconstruction postwar period; slavery; people from all over the world built our nation

| TO PEOPLE | | SCIENCE | | MAP THINKING AND MAP MAKING |
National	World	Earth Science	Man-Made Inventions	
		Simple experiments; wondering how things behave, then watching	Furnace; radiator; coal truck; cement-mixing truck	Orientation in school; own room in relation to another on floor; to principal's office; school library; lunch room. Near-by streets
		Water supply. Sound-conducting materials. Coal and cement, etc.	Electric engine, fire engine, tug-boat, derrick, mail-canceling machine	Orientation: school in relation to rivers; to play with floor blocks, rivers and land work they have seen
		Steam, refrigeration, banana ripening	Steam engine, ferry, Borden bottling machinery, mailbag escalator	Orientation on Manhattan Island. Making rough map. Playing out, on maps, work they have seen
Attitudes among Indians; Europeans and Indians; N. Y. and other people in U.S.		Simple experiments in erosion; with seeds; with food preservation	Experiments in handwork of Indians; of Dutch. Pump drill, loom, windmill	Rough orientation in U. S. Sense that "far away" in U. S. are mountains & big plains. Rough modeled maps with Atlantic and Pacific Oceans; east and west mountains; rivers running down them to two oceans and through Mississippi Valley to Atlantic Ocean
	People in earth conditions different from N. Y. C.	What makes soil, rain, seasons? Why deserts are dry. Why far North is cold, has long dark and long light	Adaptation of plants & animals to these regions. How earth has changed. How plants & animals have changed	Use of graphic relief maps, erosion of mountains making plains; rivers. Use of globe: bands of climate; of vegetation; great circle routes of ships and airplanes
ndian cultures	Good Neighbor Policy	Experiments in handwork of early U. S. Development of work techniques in roads	Inventions: canals, early railroads, auto, airplane	Graphic relief map of Americas as basis for cultures of Indians & work of modern American nations. Make relief map of U. S. basis of regional earth resources; soil, rain, rivers & divides, coal deposits. Routes of explorers, pioneers, present railroads, highways
uture: freeom for all eople; deocracy still rowing in . S., in orld	The United Nations	Earth science applied to world climates, soil, topography	Inventions: application of wheel, lever, screw, pulley in modern machines	Paint relief map of Europe or Eurasia: northern and southern plains; early civilizations in warm river valleys of southern plains (China, India, Mesopotamia, Egypt, Mediterranean world). Distribution of earth resources needed for modern industries; coal, metals, oil

grade thought of the work they did with their children in relation to the children's past and future school experiences and thought of their grade curriculum as a part of a *school* curriculum—in brief, they were thinking about child development and also about the "whole" school.

After the curriculum in outline form had been more or less thrashed out in the whole Workshop group and broad grade divisions in appropriate experiences and subject matter decided upon, the Bank Street staff wrote a long but still very tentative social studies curriculum for the whole school and gave it to the teachers in mimeographed form, for experimentation. After a period of experimentation in their classrooms and discussion in small groups, we all met together again to get once more the sweep of a child's development from kindergarten through sixth grade, and to make adjustments—and they were many—where we agreed the tentative curriculum did not fit a grade. This procedure led to detailed suggestions for our first revision of the tentative curriculum at the end of one term—that is, at the end of the second Workshop year.

At this time came a new development in our Workshop growth. The Workshop teachers, who included about half the teachers in the school, were eager to have *all* the teachers in the school try out our social studies materials. They asked one of the teachers to discuss this possibility with the principal. At this moment, the principal walked into the Workshop meeting and joined in the discussion. He decided to make the social studies curriculum which had been worked out by the Workshop group the official school social studies curriculum. Furthermore, he decided to turn his monthly conferences with the whole faculty into curriculum discussion and to use bulletin boards and mimeograph sheets for the many necessary announcements which had hitherto been made at these faculty meetings. Bank Street members were invited to attend these faculty discussions. It was, however, the Workshop teachers who did most of the explaining of what the Workshop curriculum was trying to do.

Within the Workshop, the procedure of the previous year was

followed through the two terms of this third year, and once more we finished the year with detailed suggestions for a revision which, once again, the Bank Street staff wrote during the summer. This social studies curriculum, though twice revised, was still tentative in the minds of all Workshop groups. Indeed, we believe *any* curriculum material must be permanently tentative. Any curriculum plan must adapt to changing times. A fixed curriculum is an anomaly if we consider "children" and "environment" two of the cornerstones upon which a curriculum is built. Indeed, the third cornerstone, "social ideals," should not remain fixed. One of the major problems in a school system is how to keep a written curriculum plan flexible and up-to-date in a rapidly changing world.

Space does not permit a full picture of Workshop thinking and activities as, for a year and a half, we worked experimentally on social studies materials and techniques for each grade level; and also on how experiences, curriculum content, and concepts developed at each grade level fitted into one another and covered the entire spread of curriculum content outlined in the official bulletin. All that we can do is to show our chief problems and how we attacked them both in discussion meetings and in the classrooms.

The real interest in the story of this second Workshop approach of building a curriculum in social studies lies not in *what* we did, *what* we wrote. The real interest lies, rather, in the teachers' growth in this joint undertaking. Their approach to their job became more and more scientific—studying their children's growth in an experiential curriculum and modifying it accordingly. Their approach also became more and more creative—planning a good life of learning situations for the children, entering into this life themselves with increasing zest and satisfaction.

11

Building a Social Studies Curriculum for
Kindergarten, First and Second Grades

*PRELIMINARY DISCUSSIONS: CURRICULUM
CONTENT RELATED TO MATURITY LEVELS*

IN ORGANIZING a social studies curriculum for the younger groups in the Workshop, we had from the beginning encountered fewer problems than we had in the older groups—or rather the problems were of a different kind. This was partly because, in the old curriculum, subject matter in the younger years had not been so narrowly defined or played so dominant a role—always excepting the three R's. In the new curriculum the theme for these younger groups—*Living and Working in Home, School, and Neighborhood*—really put it up to each school to gather its own subject matter for its own children and their neighborhood along lines outlined in a general way. There is, however, another reason which explains the relative lack of "problems" in putting a curriculum for these younger groups on paper. These younger children have been much more intensively studied than older children. There is, among psychologists and increasingly among school people, a general acceptance of some outstanding characteristics of children at these younger maturity levels: young children live in the here-and-now world about them; they learn more through active use of their bodies and senses than through words alone; their play is a way of learning and can be developed constructively—not merely as "busy work" to make life easier for grownups; the younger the children,

198

the more help they need to feel secure, to feel a part of a group. By the end of our first year and a half, most of our Workshop teachers had accepted these characteristics of young children not because of "therapy" but because they had had evidence of the growth of the children when they were given firsthand experiences in exploring the here-and-now world of school and neighborhood and when they were encouraged to express their experiences in the classroom through constructive dramatic play and other expressive arts.

When we began to write a social studies curriculum, there was general agreement among most of the Workshop teachers of the younger ages as to the maturity level characteristics of their children, and also as to the implications that trips, dramatic play, free painting, music and dance, and even simple science experiments were essential parts of their programs. Indeed, the old Workshop members took an active part in convincing new members that these teaching techniques made their children eager to learn and also made them feel secure. At this stage, the writing of our social studies curriculum involved not so much discussions of what young children were like or the kinds of experiences which make for their total growth, as in finding concrete neighborhood opportunities for trips; materials and equipment for constructive free play and free art; bibliographies of books to enrich the slender information children could gather for themselves; situations which interested children to explore through simple science experiences. In short, the groundwork had been laid in the earlier stage.

The whole statement of social studies curriculum in the new bulletin written for these younger grades gave official backing to our effort. Our job was to fill in the general outlines with details drawn from our children's homes, our school and neighborhood.

What still troubled these teachers was the tool subjects, particularly teaching the children to read, which many of them had considered their chief function as teachers of young children. Here again, the new curriculum was much less rigid than the old. The bulletin put much emphasis on reading readiness and distinctly stated that the technique of learning to read was not to be forced upon any child in the first grade, or even in the second, if tests showed he was not "ready." Some teachers were skeptical; others thought this "too good to be true."

The first draft of our social studies curriculum was a more detailed and organized statement of the materials given the teachers in the first stage of our Workshop.[30] To this material we added "social ideas" which the group thought were within the understanding of these young children, though often not within their power to express in words. Social ideas were specifically stated because new teachers often thought that the primary aim of a social studies program was to teach behavior—sometimes just manners. We wanted to state clearly that social studies had a broader basis, that interest in work processes and workers was a "social" interest. The following are the social ideas which we placed at the beginning of the social studies curriculum for each of the three younger groups with the statement that these were ideas for the teacher to keep in mind and to develop whenever appropriate rather than to teach verbally.

	Kindergarten	Mother's work; father's work. There are many kinds of workers. Beginnings of ideas of our dependence on many workers.
Social Ideas	First Grade	*How* work is done rather than why it is done. Like kindergarten, but developed to include wider range out into neighborhood.
	Second Grade	Beginnings of sense of organized city care for people. Interdependence of city and country.

HERE-AND-NOW: THROUGH PLAY AND PERSONAL EXPERIENCES

The first version of the Workshop tentative curriculum in social studies in mimeographed form was given to the Workshop teachers

[30] Chapter 8 and Appendices 3 through 13.

in the middle of our second year and tried out by them in their classrooms. The next year (our third) the Workshop social studies curriculum was discussed both in the monthly faculty meetings which the Bank Street staff was invited to attend and in grade conferences attended only by teachers. At grade conferences the teachers in each grade drew up a report upon the Workshop curriculum and presented it to the entire faculty at the monthly faculty meeting with the principal.

The following excerpts are from a meeting at which teachers from all grades reported on the social studies curriculum a year after it had been written. The Bank Street member's analysis of the Workshop curriculum was primarily to explain to our District Superintendent what we were trying to do.

WORKSHOP MEETING

January 7

The Workshop meeting was held in the principal's office at 3:30 P.M. Present were twenty teachers, the principal, two assistant principals, three Bank Street members and two visitors, the District Superintendent and a visiting teacher.

A Bank Street member said that the Workshop has been trying to make specific for this school some of the generalizations found in the new curriculum.[31] The new curriculum is still very general. *Bank Street member* felt that this was intentional. She felt from the new curriculum that each school in the city will be expected to go on doing the kind of thing we have been doing this past year at our school.

Kindergarten, First- and Second-Grade Curriculum

The discussion was started with the statement that in the kindergarten, first- and second-grade area the new official curriculum is in general agreement all the way along the line with the Workshop curriculum. Our curriculum adds some things such as bridges, boats, and trains. The new curriculum roughly takes in the here-and-now world for the kindergarten, first- and second-grade area. In our school's curriculum in the first and second years we have taken in a great deal more than is sug-

---

[31] *Curriculum Development in the Elementary Schools,* Board of Education of the City of New York, Curriculum Bulletin No. 1, 1945–46 Series.

gested by the new curriculum of the Board. First, environmentally we are right in the midst of boats and trains and bridges. And second, we feel that the children as a group are ready for these things.

A second-grade teacher said that her children enjoyed the study of coal tremendously, getting a lot out of it. They started their study with the coal bins in the cellar and went on up to a study of how coal is found. They had planned to see coal trucks being filled, but were unable to do so because of the snow. They studied tugs, and brought in rather sketchily other uses of coal—to run trains, etc.

A Bank Street member said that in addition the new curriculum included a good deal of geographical orientation—for example, a trip to 125th Street to see the Harlem and East Rivers join—which is a good deal more geography than seems to be implied in the Board of Education curriculum.

The District Superintendent said that the argument against the interrelated social studies program is that one omits significant areas. In the new setup this possibility should be kept in mind.

TENTATIVE SOCIAL STUDIES CURRICULUM WRITTEN FOR KINDERGARTEN, FIRST AND SECOND GRADES IN OUR SCHOOL

The second revision of the Workshop social studies curriculum contained the actual experiences of these grade groups taken from our records. The general theme, which remained *Living and Working in Home, School, and Neighborhood,* was broken down into three subheadings suggestive of the widening meaning of "neighborhood":

Kindergarten: Around the Block.
First Grade: From River to River.
Second Grade: The Island We Live On.

The outline of topics follows:

    I. INTRODUCTION, WITH MAP.

   II. LIST OF KINDERGARTEN TRIPS, WITH MAP.

 III. WRITE-UP OF A SAMPLE KINDERGARTEN TRIP AND ITS OUTCOME.

The curriculum materials as written up in detail for the three grade levels is much too long to include; besides, much of it repeats in different words what has already been said.[32] We shall give, INTRODUCTION, which contains many quotations from the official bulletin with interpretations of them; lists of kindergarten, first- and second-grade trips including references to stories and songs for each grade. We omit the write-up of actual trips and the outcomes for all three grades since these experiences will be described in Chapter 16 for first-grade children. Under SUMMARY OF IM-PORTANT TECHNIQUES we shall give the sections on How Social Aims Are Fulfilled through Social Studies, How to Set Up and Conduct a Work Period, and How to Introduce Science Experiments, but omit the other sections since all these "how's" repeat in more detail much of the material already given.

[32] The complete statement may be obtained through Bank Street Publications, 69 Bank Street, New York 14, New York.

SOCIAL STUDIES CURRICULUM

Kindergarten, Grades 1 and 2

INTRODUCTION. The social studies program for kindergarten, grades 1 and 2 is based on trips or other vital group experiences which follow each other at intervals of a week or two in some organic pattern, providing stimuli for classroom activities and guiding the selection of reading materials, visual aids, songs, etc.

The trips listed here for this school are based on those actually taken during 1945–46, with a few additions, and slight changes in placement. They are planned especially for the neighborhood of this school but may be used as a general guide in any neighborhood.

The order given here, based mainly on the concept of expanding geographically, is not arbitrary. Groups differ in their interests, and adventures in the classroom or on the street often change the direction of the social studies program. For example, one day when the children were playing in the outside yard, a cement mixer came up and men began to work on the sidewalk right in front of the children's eyes. This was so dramatic that the teacher discussed it with the group in the classroom and followed it up by a trip to the Harlem River, where they could see the barges of gravel, cement, and sand, and the hopper which supplied the cement trucks.

If a group is high-strung and easily overstimulated it is wise to look for shorter and quieter trips; if the group is steady and reliable, a teacher can allow for more complications. But whatever the direction, it should develop from the known to the unknown, from the simple to the complex, and from the near-at-hand to the faraway. By watching and listening to her group a teacher can pick out the highlights, the points of emphasis, and learn what to reject and what to accept and build upon. It is desirable that each trip have some relationship to the one before it, as each act of a play develops out of the preceding one. There are many related incidents, facts, and images in a play but there is one theme which carries it along, and at the end one comes away with a feeling of completion. Children feel this, too, at the end of a year when their experiences hang together and come to a logical climax. As the official bulletin says, it is important for children "to understand facts and their relationships . . . not only to other facts but also to large areas of experience." In the kindergarten, the final trip to Fort Tryon is a kind of high point in terms of growing up and seeing relationships as well as a high place from which to look down on that part of the city which enfolds the school neighborhood.

The Bulletin on Curriculum Development states that one of our aims is "to develop an awareness and appreciation of economic processes, and of all who serve in the world of work." . . . "The worth of the worker, the value of his contribution, standards of workmanship and technical skill, and the place which the child himself will one day take in the world of work, are matters for exploration, discussion, and thought."

In the light of this aim, the following questions may be of value in thinking out a pattern for social studies.

1. What are the steps in the economic processes of providing coal, water, food, shelter, transportation, etc., for the community?

2. Which of these steps may be seen by the children in the immediate community?

3. Which of these steps are suitable for special observation by a particular age group?

4. How far back to the sources of these commodities can one go?

5. What relation has "father's work" or "mother's work" to the economic pattern?

6. What stories and pictures are suitable to help round out the child's understanding?

In our listing of the trips we have attempted to show how those of the first grade are an extension of the ones taken in kindergarten, and how those of the second grade are built upon the foundations of the two preceding years, expanding the child's world from the home to the extreme ends of Manhattan Island, and reaching farther and farther out along the trail back toward the source of the things which the child first meets at home or at school. With this foundation of firsthand observation, supplemented by discussion, stories, songs, dramatic play, painting, and construction, he has a good solid foundation for the years to come, in which books and imagination play a greater and greater role in his understanding of the world.

A LIST OF KINDERGARTEN TRIPS
with appropriate stories and songs

Theme: *Around the Block* (home, school, and their relation to the immediate community)

TRIPS	TO HELP CHILDREN BECOME ORIENTED IN THEIR SCHOOL AND AROUND THE BLOCK
1. Classrooms	Where they have friends or brothers or sisters
2. Outside the building	To locate the windows of their own classroom
3. The nurse's office	Where they have been individually
4. The principal's office	To see the school bells
	To borrow a story book
5. The school library	Where some have their lunch
6. The lunchroom	As a first experience outside the building
7. A dairy store	

"The Milkman's Horse"—From *Keep Singing, Keep Humming*— Bradford and Woodruff—Scott

8. A grocery or a bakery	To see another kind of store

This is the Bread That Betsey Ate—Irma Black—Scott
The Delivery Man—Charlotte Kuh—Macmillan

9. The school furnace room	To meet the custodian when the heat is first turned on

Here and Now Story Book—Lucy Sprague Mitchell—E. P. Dutton & Co.

10. The coal truck	To see delivery of coal to houses and to the school

People Who Work in the Country and in the City—Judson—Rand McNally (good for pictures)

11. Around the block	To point out children's homes

I Live in a City—Tippett—Harper (poems)
The Tale of Two Houses—Caroline Dyer—Whittlesey House

12. Following the postman — From the post office across from the school to the near-by houses

> *The Postman*—Charlotte Kuh—Macmillan
> *Here Comes the Mail*—Disraeli—Little, Brown & Co. (for the teacher)
> *Here Comes the Postman*—Park—Houghton-Mifflin

13. Sidewalk repair in the neighborhood — Watching the steamroller

> *Cement Work for Sport and Skinny*—Grace Paull—Viking
> *Diggers and Builders*—Lent—Macmillan

14. Watching window repair — Where it is going on in the school

> *Here and Now Story Book*—Lucy Sprague Mitchell—E. P. Dutton

15. Watching fire engines go by — Wondering why they come through this street

> *The Fireman*—Charlotte Kuh—Macmillan
> *The Little Fireman*—Brown—Scott

16. A furniture store — More on what is sold in stores

> *Busy Carpenters*—Tippett—Grossett and Dunlap

17. A shoe-repair shop — To watch the shoemaker

> "The Shoemaker"—From *Around the World in Song*—Gordon—Scott

18. Down in the subway station — To watch the trains and the people

19. Riverside Drive — To see freight trains and boats

> *Pogo's Train Ride*—Jo and Ernest Norling—Henry Holt

20. The flower shop (in spring) and flowering pear tree, 145th Street between Broadway and Riverside Drive — An experience in sensing the changing seasons

21. Fort Tryon Park — To look down on the river and city, and "find" the school

> *Along the Busy River*—Keeler—Edward Stern & Co.
> *I Go A-Traveling*—Tippett—Harpers
> *I Live in a City*—Tippett—Harpers (poems)

A LIST OF FIRST-GRADE TRIPS

with appropriate stories, songs,
poems, or science experiences

Theme: *From River to River* (home and school in relation to upper
Manhattan)

TRIPS	HOW THEY BUILD UPON THOSE TAKEN IN KINDERGARTEN
1. A classroom on each floor	Further geographical orientation within school building
2. The yard, to locate windows of rooms visited	Relation of rooms to outside streets and directions
3. Stock rooms, which serve all classes	More awareness of the needs of the school in relation to its size
4. The lunchroom (review)	Ordering, division of work
5. Street trips to see vegetable wagons, grocery trucks, and dairy store (review)	Further awareness of food distribution

Streets—Co-operative School Pamphlets—John Day [33]
Another Here and Now Story Book—L. S. Mitchell—E. P. Dutton
& Co.
Mr. Brown's Grocery Store—H. S. Read—Scribner

6. Riverside Drive to see milk trains and refrigerator cars (review)	Milk and food come from the country—relationships reach out away from the city

Trains—Co-operative School Pamphlets [34]—John Day
The Little Train—Lois Lenski—Oxford Press

7. Tracing overhead pipes in the boiler room to radiators upstairs, and to hot- and cold-water faucets in halls, and lunchroom	Develops from previous experience. More about relations of furnace to water and steam

Here and Now Story Book—L. S. Mitchell—E. P. Dutton & Co.
[33,34] Out of print.

8. Street trip to see street washing, use of fire hydrants, repair of underground pipes

Connection between pipes in the street and those in the school—also between water coming out of hydrants and out of faucets

Streets—Co-operative School Pamphlets—John Day [35]

9. Garage to see car washing and inflation of tires

More use of water from underground pipes

Science (air in tires): *Let's Find Out*—Herman and Nina Schneider —Wm. Scott

Mr. Bradley's Car—Caroline Leach—Stokes

10. Fire Station, Engine Co. 69 (must get permit)

Further use of water from pipes and hydrants managed by "the city" for the people's protection

Speedy, the Hook and Ladder Truck—Hurd—Lothrop, Lee & Stoddard
Jamie and the Fire Engine—Johnson—Harpers
"Firemen"—From *Songs for the Little Child*—Baker—Addington Press

11. Street trip to note fire escapes

Safety measures at home

12. Trips through school to note fireproof building and alarms

Safety at school

13. Street trips to see coal and cement trucks

Review and also preparation for next trip

Jamie and the Dump Truck—Johnson—Harpers

14. Trolley to Harlem River—get off on the Bronx side of the bridge and walk across to Manhattan

Further relationships in distribution of coal and cement

The Annie Moran (tugboat story)—Hurd—Lothrop, Lee & Stoddard
Boats and Bridges—Co-operative School Pamphlet [36]—John Day
A Steam Shovel for Me—Edelstedt—Stokes
How the Derrick Works—Jones—Macmillan

15. Riverside Drive to compare boats and bridges with those on the Harlem River

More on how things are brought to the city—why so few barges on Hudson River

Manhattan, Now and Long Ago—L. S. Mitchell—Macmillan (barge story—simplify for first grade)

[35,36] Out of print.

16. Public Library to check out a book about bridges. Look at other picture books, meet librarian | Compare with school library, learn when to come for storytelling, start interest in future use of books

A Story About Boats—Read—Scribner
  Science: Uses of corks (which the teacher has cut with designs or letters), pressed on ink pad and then on paper

17. Print Shop—145th Street between Broadway and Amsterdam | Further evidence of how books get printed

  Science: Glue a row of corks onto a ruler, and show how a whole row may be printed at once
  Watch mimeographing work in school office
  Have group stories printed by mimeograph and staple into books

18. Post Office to see letters canceled and sorted | Another kind of printing machine —also follow up on kindergarten interest in the postman

19. K Bus to 3rd Avenue and 125th Street (without changing), walk about one block east and walk up the ramp of Triborough Bridge as far as Randalls Island. Can have picnic there | Comparison of Harlem and Hudson River bridges with Triborough. Count cross-town blocks. Compare with 145th Street. Bus to the Harlem River. Manhattan Island much wider here

Bridges (picture book)—Borman—Macmillan
Boats and Bridges—Co-operative School Pamphlet [37]—John Day
Write to Triborough Bridge Authority for booklet. Randalls Island, New York, N. Y.

A LIST OF SECOND-GRADE TRIPS
with appropriate stories, songs,
poems, or science experiences

Theme: *The Island We Live On* (home and school in relation to Manhattan Island)

TRIPS | HOW THEY BUILD UPON THE TWO PRECEDING YEARS

1. Repeat many school and neighborhood walks | Review of home and school needs, and pattern of distribution. Ask grocers and drivers of vegetable wagons where they buy their produce

[37] Out of print.

The Little House—Burton—Houghton-Mifflin
The Horse Who Lived Upstairs—McGinley—Lippincott

2. To Bronx Market just on the other side of the bridge. Walk down sidewalk toward river freight yards, coal hoppers, unloading of refrigerator cars

Getting more distant relationships in food distribution. Another step in the process. Also further exploration of coal barge to hopper to truck

The Tug Boat—Lent—Macmillan
A Squash for the Fair—Paull—Doubleday
The Merry Shipwreck—Georges Duplaix—Harpers
The Little Fisherman—Margaret Wise Brown—Scott

3. Riverside Drive to compare freight cars with those at Bronx Market. Read words on cars to see what they contain and where they came from

Why cars on Riverside Drive come by land and those at Bronx Market come on barges

The Wonderful Locomotive—Cornelia Meigs—Macmillan
What Engineers Do—Walter Bing—Norton

4. 125th-Street Ferry to New Jersey *and* Borden's Bottling Plant, which may be watched from the sidewalk on the way from subway

More on milk. Also more on distribution, watching what the trucks carry to and from New York by ferry

"The Ferry Boat"—From *Singing Time*—Satis Coleman and Alice G. Thorn—John Day

5. 23rd-Street Ferry to Hoboken, 8th-Avenue Subway to 23rd Street. Walk to ferry. Get off ferry at Hoboken and visit place behind station where mail bags are sorted and put on trains

The same river as the one near school. George Washington Bridge in distance. More on mail

Engine, Engine No. 9—Edith Hurd—Lothrop
Let's Find Out—Schneider and Schneider—Scott
Story of Steam—Ann Coolidge—John C. Winston
"The Steam Engine"—From *Keep Singing, Keep Humming*—Bradford and Woodruff Scott
"The Engineer"—From *Songs from "Now We Are Six,"* by *Milne*—H. Fraser-Simpson—Dutton

6. A walk on the George Washington Bridge

To look up and down the river. To see the lighthouse

The Little Red Lighthouse and the Great Gray Bridge—Swift—Harcourt, Brace, Inc.

Science: Experimenting with ropes as cables over orange crates used as towers

7. Real train ride to Spuyten Duyvil Station. Two ways to go
  a. Take transportation across Harlem River to New York Central station at 138th Street, Bronx
  b. Take Amsterdam Avenue bus to High Bridge at 174th St.
	Opposite upper end of Manhattan Island. Meeting of rivers under Henry Hudson Bridge
	Old-fashioned railroad station and grass for picnic. Tower man willing to explain signals to children

Too Fast For John—Emma Brock—Knopf
The Little Stone House—Hoden—Macmillan

8. Battery Park by 7th-Avenue Subway (picnic). Walk through narrow streets made in olden days of Dutch village	Lower end of Manhattan—contrast with upper end. Where two rivers meet—New York Bay. To see Statue of Liberty, Fireboat at Pier 1, Canal-barge terminal on East River, and Brooklyn Bridge

Little Tim and the Brave Sea Captain—Ardizzone—Oxford University Press
Tim and Lucy Go to Sea—Ardizzone—Oxford University Press
"My Boat"—From *Songs of Many Lands*—Surette—Houghton-Mifflin

SUMMARY OF IMPORTANT TECHNIQUES AND ATTITUDES

Social Aims Are Fulfilled through Social Studies: As we have seen through the descriptions of trips and their outcomes, there are unlimited opportunities to develop the social aims of education.[38]

Children are helped to "develop the ability to think constructively" by experimenting with materials; wondering, trying out, and getting results; asking questions of workers who are the "experts" on their particular jobs, and by sharing their ideas and memories with their classmates and teacher. . . .

And there is probably no better way "to develop pride and faith in American democracy, and respect for the dignity and worth of individuals and peoples, regardless of race, religion, nationality or socio-economic status," than through taking children on trips where they see

[38] As stated in *Curriculum Development in the Elementary Schools*, Board of Education of the City of New York, Curriculum Bulletin No. 1, 1945–46.

these Americans all doing necessary work, and taking pride in doing it well. By questioning and talking with the ferryboat captain, the driver of a vegetable wagon, the Sanitation Department worker, the children begin to feel a part of the larger family which is America, knowing that their parents, too, have functions to perform by which they earn their living and which are necessary to the rest of the population.

The excerpts which follow are given here as examples of (1) the kind of materials teachers will need to develop in a curriculum such as this, and (2) the techniques and methods in classroom procedure.

How to Set Up and Conduct a Work Period: The teacher sees that materials are ready for use and are placed where the best use can be made of them.

Crayons, paper, and clay should have their special places on low shelves or in cubbies where the children can reach them, and may get them of their own accord.

Paints should be mixed and ready, and clean paint brushes standing on end ready to be chosen. Cups for water should be available.

Blocks neatly arranged on low shelves should be near an open, unobstructed floor space.

The doll corner or playhouse should be arranged where it will not interfere with block play.

In rooms where there are stationary desks and no blocks, the teacher should try to have a group of unnecessary desks taken out, substituting a big table (low enough for children to work at) or long boards supported by "horses." This serves as a place for map schemes on a small scale, for which the children can construct trucks, trolleys, fire engines, houses, bridges, etc.

A workbench or heavy table (with vises and a few tools) is necessary if the children are to get the most out of their work period.

Though the teacher remains in the background and lets the children choose the kind of materials they want to work with, she keeps close watch on what they are playing and saying, and steps in with questions and suggestions when she feels it is necessary, for this helps them to enlarge the meanings and relationships in their play.

As stated in the official bulletin, one of the aims is "to develop a love of learning—to refine and extend the child's interests and to provide for a steadily growing competence with objects and *tools,* both *manipulative* and intellectual."

The teacher supplies new materials to help the play along, when she sees that they are needed, rather than giving them out all at once. Thus when she sees children attempting to push along on the floor the boats that they have made, she may provide some flat boards for them to build the boats on. This factor alone will prove to be a great stimulus to good boat play.

In the daily "work period" a child should largely determine his own activities, but if materials are limited, sometimes it is wise to plan first with the group, finding out how many would like to paint, how many would like to work with blocks, etc. If there is too large a group for the supply of paint brushes, the children themselves can suggest ways of sharing or taking turns. This is good social thinking, and develops the attitudes mentioned in the beginning of this summary. Also, if there are arguments during work, or if some child interrupts or spoils the work of another child, it affords an opportunity to make the meaning of group co-operation clear.

The end of a work period is important, too. It is well to have carefully thought-out rules for "putting away." The children may help plan these rules in advance, perhaps involving a list of jobs and certain children to be responsible for them each week. A good plan is to have the children gather round the piano for clapping games, or to be shown a picture book, as they finish their particular clean-up job. This is an added incentive for getting through quickly, and avoids confusion which comes when some have finished and others have not. When the group is all together, one or two "inspectors" may go quietly around the room to see that all is in order. This is always a good time for the group to hear a quiet story.

How to Introduce Science Experiences: Science "experiments" in kindergarten, first and second grade can be thought of as "experiences" which show the way things behave. It is enough to mix the paint powder and watch it dissolve, mix salt with water and see what is left when the water evaporates, put water outside in a closed jar in cold weather and see what happens, without delving into the *why.* Still there is the beginning of the scientific method in all of these experiences. For young children it is, "I wonder . . . Let's try it and find out."

Every trip suggests many of these experiences. We will list a few. Additional suggestions are given in the curriculum bulletin.

1. A visit to the pear tree. "I wonder when the buds will open." Go back each day to see.
2. Bring back a rock from Riverside Drive. "I wonder what it looks like inside." Break it open with a hammer.
3. Hang a green banana in the window. "I wonder when it will get ripe." Watch it each day to see.
4. Put the pet turtle on a big piece of white paper on the floor. "I wonder which direction he will go." Watch and see. "I wonder if he will come to me if I sing to him." Try it and see.

In these experiences, the teacher can "wonder" too. It is good for children to feel that one is never through learning, that there is always something more to find out. If the children ask questions beyond their grasp tell them a little, and then say, "And you will learn still more about that in such and such a class." It is pleasant once in a while to ask a child to come down from an older class and show some simple experiment which is related to their own "wonderings"; or to arrange to have the group invited to an older classroom where they can see this progress in learning, and feel a part of the school family.

CONCLUSION. "Learning should be a continuous process. It begins in those experiences of the child which determine his readiness for further related experiences. Transitions should be gradual, with one experience growing naturally out of the preceding one. The child participates in new experiences because of their (a) meaningfulness, (b) purpose, and (c) satisfyingness."

We might say that this applies as well to the teacher and to all who are taking part in the creative process of building a new curriculum for our city. We hope that this outline will be used in that creative spirit, not as something which must be followed in unthinking routines, but as something with which to experiment further, accepting here, rejecting there, finding better solutions wherever possible, and judging the whole by its meaningfulness to those who use it.

12

Building a Social Studies Curriculum for Third and Fourth Grades

*PRELIMINARY DISCUSSIONS: CURRICULUM
CONTENT RELATED TO MATURITY LEVELS*

UNLIKE the earlier grades, there was no lack of subject matter problems in writing curriculum materials for social studies for eight- and nine-year-old children. The curricula for these grades all over the United States show larger variation in subject matter than any others in the elementary school. We think this is due, in a large measure, to the fact that the maturity levels of children at these ages have been less carefully studied than those of the younger years and those of the older years who are approaching adolescence. As far as subject matter was concerned the central problem was: When are children ready to profit by leaving the here-and-now world of their immediate experiences? This problem, of course, was basically a question of maturity, which had to be agreed upon first. As a corollary to this central problem were the questions of how to approach subject matter dealing with the faraway and long-ago in the third grade; in the fourth grade. Again these were questions of maturity levels on the basis of which we would plan in detail the kind of experiences which were most valuable to these children. Also these questions involved the social ideas, more or less inherent in the subject matter, which we thought children of third and fourth grades could understand and use in their own ways.

The first mimeographed version of the official Board of Education curriculum suggested that in third and fourth grades the social studies curriculum be treated as a unit with the theme: *Living and Working Together in New York City and in Communities Different from New York City.* The illustrative units suggested for the two grades put the emphasis for third-graders upon an expanded environment but still largely in New York City, and took the fourth-graders to communities scattered all over the world. The statement, however, admitted of much leeway in interpreting the theme which covered both third and fourth grades and left to a school the determination of the concrete subject matter appropriate for each grade. The Workshop group had decided on the general principle that, for all grades, the ways of living and working of people should be studied in relation to the earth environment which they used. Behind this general principle lay still broader educational principles which applied to all grades. First, that children should steadily progress in understanding the ways of living and working of the people around them. Second, that the study of people or cultures in communities different from their own should also contribute to the children's understanding of their own community and own culture. We now discussed how these general principles worked out in detail for third and fourth grades.

To this discussion the third- and fourth-grade teachers brought definite opinions based on the experimental work they had for a year and a half been carrying on with the children. The experiences of the teachers and the Bank Street staff alike showed a real maturity difference in the way these eight-year-olds and nine-year-olds approach distant and past people and lands. Eight-year-olds in our environment can "identify" with people whose culture is very unlike their own in a dramatic play way which means largely *how* these people live and work; whereas nine-year-olds eagerly pursue problems of *why* their lands are so different one from another and from our own. Fourth-graders can also get some idea of why the great natural regions are distributed as they are on the earth globe; whereas, to third-graders, these types of regions are just "somewhere" and no questions asked.

NOW AND LONG AGO; HERE AND FAR AWAY: THROUGH IDENTIFICATION WITH STRANGE PEOPLE AND PLACES

Though we felt that learning about "communities different from New York" would have most meaning to our eight-year-olds if approached in a dramatic play way, we felt it of extreme importance that the children should believe that the faraway and long-ago people and lands they studied were *real* people and *real* lands—not just imaginary, storybook people and lands. The most convincing proof of unseen people or lands lies not in words, not in completely vicarious experiences, but in gathering some actual evidence of their existence through some direct experience. Consequently, the first approach either to the faraway or to the long-ago should be closely tied up with the immediate world around the children which they can to a certain extent explore at first hand. Through trips children can gather actual evidence of the past life on Manhattan, whether of Indians or the Dutch, for past living and work have left some tangible traces everywhere in the present. Children can also gather actual evidence of present-day distant people and lands through other trips where they see things that have been produced by faraway work and workers which cannot be produced in New York and often see these products actually coming into New York for our use. This use of present-day New York as a laboratory in the study of the past and distant was in line with the educational principles we have just stated. For all these trips furthered the children's understanding of the ways of living and working of the people around them. We felt, however, that eight-year-olds, who are still young children, should not be plunged simultaneously into the past and the distant. Either they should take their first step back in time to people who long ago lived in the same place in which the children live, or their first step should be far away in space to living people with whom their own lives have a real and tangible relation. For eight-year-olds as a first experience outside the here-and-now world we chose the past life in Manhattan rather than the life of the Eskimo in the far North, or Indians on the Amazon, or Negroes on the Congo, or a Chinese village, or an imaginary island—all suggestions in the official bulletin—for two main reasons: first, it tied up closely with further exploration of the ways of living and working in present-day New York; and second, past life in Manhattan, whether of the Indians or the Dutch, could be explored directly through trips. In brief, their social studies program *both* of now and long ago could be pursued by using their immediate environment as a laboratory. We believe this to be a far sounder approach to their first study of other people than written accounts of people with whom we have slight or no relation who live in unfamiliar or imaginary lands.

Nine-year-olds still need many direct experiences in the world around them to make past or distant peoples and lands real to them. But fourth-graders can profit by vicarious experiences—being told about things and people—to a larger extent than can third-graders. Faraway and long-ago happenings, if they contain adventure, do not need to be as closely related to their own lives. They move more readily and without confusion as to reality into different parts of the world and different cultures. They can understand and are interested in more complicated relationships in both the physical and the social world.

These general differences in maturity levels made a natural general division of subject matter between third and fourth grades, putting more emphasis in the third grade upon situations the children could relate to their personal lives and which they could investigate directly, and leaving to the fourth grade more remote situations. Such a division was therefore made the basis of the detailed social studies curriculum which as a group we were to write.

The actual subject matter to be written up was determined after teachers of the two grades had again pooled their experiences in the experimental work they had been carrying on. Thus the curriculum write-up became the building of a year's program for each grade through a selective ordering of the more or less separate curriculum experiences for children and teachers which we have described in Chapters 8 and 9 as our first Workshop approach. The teachers also wished our tentative curriculum to include some of the thinking that lay behind our choice of content and teaching techniques. They wished the written statement to begin with a description of the maturity levels of the children.

When the official curriculum bulletin [39] appeared in printed form during our third year, the subject matter for third and fourth grades was reversed. The Workshop members, however, were unanimous in feeling that curriculum content which took third-graders for the first time into long-ago or faraway lands and people should be closely tied up to their own environment, whereas curriculum content for fourth-graders could profitably range over the globe. Since we were given permission to experiment in detail and were told that the bulletin was not in its final form,[40] in our second revision we worked out an adjustment thus: first we stated the themes as they appeared in the official bulletin and then our own interpretation of these themes in terms of subject matter.

Curriculum for Grade 3: Living and Working in Different Kinds of Communities Now and Long Ago in Manhattan, the Great Plains, the Southwest, and on Pacific Coast.
Curriculum for Grade 4: Living and Working Together in New York City: Compared with Other Regions of the World.

The statement,[41] which, like all written curriculum, was still tentative, is far too long to give in full. Instead, we give first the topical

[39] *Curriculum Development in the Elementary Schools,* Board of Education of the City of New York, Curriculum Bulletin No. 1, 1945–46 Series.

[40] *Social Studies, Grades III & IV,* Board of Education of the City of New York, Curriculum Bulletin No. 5, 1947–48 Series. In this publication the grade level organization of subject matter was reversed again so that in its final form there is agreement as to what is suggested in the official bulletin and what is projected in the social studies curriculum presented here.

[41] Tentative Social Studies Curriculum from First through Sixth Grade. Copies are available at Bank Street Publications, 69 Bank Street, New York 14, N. Y.

outline of subject matter; then under each heading or unit we give some of the thinking in the Workshop that led up to this sequence of materials, with a few illustrative excerpts and a few sample records which show how the Bank Street staff helped individual teachers to carry out the various suggestions contained in the statement.

OUTLINE OF CURRICULUM FOR GRADE 3

THEME: Living and Working in Different Kinds of Communities Now and Long Ago in Manhattan, the Great Plains, the Southwest, and on Pacific Coast.

I. NEW YORK CITY: NOW AND LONG AGO.
> Our City Today.
> Kinds of Workers in New York.
> Mechanical Inventions That Make Our Life Easier.
>> Our Water Supply.
>> Our Ways of Transportation.
>> Our Ways of Communication.
> Indian Life on and near Manhattan.
>> What Was the Land around Us Like before People Changed It?
>> How Did the Indians Use This Land?
> Dutch Life on Manhattan.
>> How Did Europeans Happen to Discover Manhattan?
>> How Did the Dutch Use Manhattan?
>> How Dutch People Lived in New Amsterdam.
>> How the Dutch Finally Lost New Amsterdam.

II. FROM ATLANTIC TO PACIFIC: NOW AND LONG AGO.
> The Western Plains, from Buffalo to Grain and Cattle Lands.
>> Life of Plains Indians.
>> Present Homes on Great Plains.
> The Southwest Desert, from Rivers to Springs to Irrigation.
> The Northwest Pacific Coast, Salmon and Big Trees, Past and Present.

III. OUR WHOLE COUNTRY.

As had been decided in preliminary Workshop discussions, our tentative social studies curriculum began with a section giving the approach to subject matter for third-grade children—really a statement of what the Workshop considered to be an eight-year-old maturity level. We give in full this opening section.

TENTATIVE SOCIAL STUDIES CURRICULUM WRITTEN FOR THIRD GRADE IN OUR SCHOOL

The first step in organizing a social studies curriculum for third-grade children is to find out how thoroughly the children have become oriented in the here-and-now world around them through their experiences in kindergarten, first and second grades, and whether their interests and curiosities now extend beyond the present and immediate world that they can explore at first hand.

Third-grade children are still "little children" in many ways. They are still keenly interested in what goes on around them. But during the year their capacity to understand the long-ago and faraway begins to blossom.

The phrase from a poem, "Where we walk to school each day, Indian children used to play," is enough to start them off on a fascinating adventure in imagination, turning the city that they know into the world of long ago.

If they know the neighborhood—well bordered by its two rivers and the Palisades, which have existed for unknown ages—it is an easy step back into the past, learning to know this same land as the Indians knew it. Indians knew it as no one else ever will. The animals, stones, trees, rivers, were as intimate to them as their own brothers. And the children, through trips to old camp sites, followed by stories and more trips to the museums, can through imagination, crafts, and dramatic play begin to relive that life. They will begin to see life through the eyes of children very much like themselves, yet different in many ways.

In the preceding years, the children will have learned different points of view by listening as well as talking in discussions, by questioning workers on trips, by joining with the teacher in helping to settle arguments, by living and working together on common projects. Instead of characterizing the contributions of the classmates as superior or inferior, they are able to appreciate the contributions of each.

As they have learned to respect differences among their classmates of the same culture, now they will take a further step and learn to appreciate people of a different culture, a different kind of community from the one which they know so well.

Again the starting point is New York, but this time it is New York in relation to its past, specifically the Indians and the Dutch.

The fall is an ideal time to plunge into the Indian life of New York. Every schoolroom can become, for a time, a real woodland scene. If the teacher or some of the children are fortunate enough to have a week end or two in the country, it is fine to bring in great bouquets of corn-stalks, tall beach grass, gourds, and ears of corn—exhibits of shells, rocks, bones, small logs, and supple branches—everything that Indians used. If the teacher is not so fortunate, a call to the Bronx Botanical Gardens may put her in touch with some willing sponsor who may help get some of the materials for her.

At first, merely decorations, each one of these things may later be used as a craft material. Dried corn husks, when wet, may be braided into mats and moccasins. Grass may be woven, logs dug out into canoes, corn pounded into meal, gourds dried and weighed as a study in evapora-tion, and later cut into dippers and spoons.

Through original stories about their own experiences with turtles, snakes, fishing, and swimming, the children will soon find what they have in common with Indian children and will appreciate Indian stories all the more. And, as in the younger grades, both free and planned dra-matics play a most important role. Far from being a war-whooping, tom-ahawking program, the children actually begin their first historical re-search, in the comparison of communities and cultures, learning to know their own land from those who knew it best.

When the children have been Indians long enough, the Dutch may naturally arrive. The story of "Ride the Wind" introduces Henry Hud-son beautifully from the Indian point of view. Along with original rec-ords of the Dutch settlers, extracts of which may be read to the children, this story provides fertile material for a discussion of what these very different people thought of each other. This is a good time to appreciate the fact that because a person cannot understand a foreign language, it is not queer.

In the study of the Dutch, the children will through dramatic play and stories, as well as trips to the museum, live through the experiences of digging wells and canals, building windmills, filling in swamps, pip-ing off brooks, widening trails into wagon roads—in fact, they will ex-perience through the activities of these new settlers the beginnings of their own great city.

If the group is mature enough the study can spread into New York's relation to our country as a whole—not in great detail, but enough to show the main features, the coasts, the great plains, the mountains and the desert of the Southwest.

Therefore the curriculum includes materials on the Indians from the main regions of our country, to be used at the teacher's discretion.

Throughout the whole study, it is possible and desirable to make comparisons with the past and present of these regions.

The introductory statement was followed by the *social ideas* which were more or less inherent in the subject matter which we thought third- and fourth-grade children could understand and use in their own ways. We did not expect the children to be able to express these ideas in words, nor did we think that teachers should verbalize these ideas for the children. Rather, we thought of these ideas as basic relationships that the teachers should keep in mind in planning experiences for children which would gradually make these relationships clear to the children. We give here these social ideas as they were stated in the first draft of our social studies curriculum.

The chief *social ideas* to be brought out wherever the situation is appropriate are:

We use the earth. So do all people.

Many kinds of lands produce many kinds of work and workers.

All peoples have developed some inventions and tools. The Indians in the United States had not learned to use metals. They used the animals and plants they found around them.

We live in groups. So do all people. Different people in the group do special kinds of work.

New York, the South, the Great Plains, the Southwest, and the Northwest Coast use each other's products today.

Our ways of living in the United States have become more interdependent since we developed cities and new ways of transportation.

From here on the curriculum statement dealt with subject matter under large headings or units.

NEW YORK CITY: NOW AND LONG AGO. The curriculum as developed by the Workshop began the year with some study or unit of New York City, both because each teacher needs first to find out what experiences and information her children bring with them to third grade and because talking over familiar ground brings a group together. The teacher will make this unit long or short according to the past experiences and the maturity of her particular class. We quote the first paragraph in full.

Our City Today. This will be a sort of exploratory introduction in which the teacher will become acquainted with how much her children have learned about New York in previous grades and will draw together and supplement their knowledge. Before leaving this subject the children should be thoroughly aware of Manhattan as an island, of the part of the island on which they live; of Brooklyn, the Bronx, and Staten Island as parts of New York City; of Long Island, New Jersey. They should become aware of some of the complicated factors that make up life in New York, the magnitude of the job of supporting seven million people in such a small area, how dependent we are upon other parts of the country, and upon means of transportation.

Then followed suggestions for *Introductory Discussions* about:

Kinds of Workers in New York. This drew on the children's past experiences; suggested a few trips; suggested having some parents come to tell about their work; suggested the children act out little skits— "Suppose something happened to all the postmen," etc.—to show how each of us is dependent upon all other kinds of workers.

Mechanical Inventions That Make Our Life Easier. Specific suggestions were made for trips, stories, and pictures about our water supply and our ways of transportation, including comparisons with Indian ways of meeting these needs. Under Trips, Dramatization, Art Expression, were specific suggestions with reading references to our Bibliography in the Appendix.

The second step or unit was back into the past life on Manhattan. We have already told the basis upon which we chose this subject matter for eight-year-olds. It was not intended that the teachers should follow this outline slavishly. Indeed, most teachers did not attempt to cover both Indian and Dutch life fully. Rather, they felt either one or the other should be taken at a slow pace with plenty of time for dramatizations, trips, and craft, and the other done quickly, largely through stories with one or two trips and one or two handcraft experiences and informal dramatizations. The Workshop group, however, felt that it was well to have more in the curriculum than most children could take so that the teacher could choose what she felt was best suited to her children.

We quote from *Introductory Suggestions* under the heading:

How Did the Indians Use This Land? What was the value to Indians of the following (get children to reason this out):

woods   —   wild animals and plants for food (no wild cows, horses, pigs, sheep in America); wood, protection
river   —   canoe transportation, fish.
land   —   (aside from natural features) agriculture (limited).
swamps   —   to trap animals.
hills   —   for lookout and defense in war.
caves   —   as homes and for storage.
sea   —   fish for food and shells for implements and decorations.

Activities based on information gathered from books or firsthand observations and experiments.

Read plenty of stories and descriptions of Indian life. Many of these the children can read to themselves. Many others should be read by the teacher. There is a wealth of excellent material.

A wealth of concrete suggestions for Craft and Activities with full techniques described were written up covering: Corn, Clothes, Feathers, Mural, Cradleboard, Collect Seeds, Stories, Canoes, Mask, Gourds, Map, Fire, Indian Legends, Trips, and Dramatizations.

We give two sample records to illustrate how this subject on Manhattan Indians worked out in practice.

Notes by Bank Street member given to two third-grade teachers summarizing trip to Inwood on which on separate days she accompanied each teacher and her class.

Trip   November 13, 14
Eighth Avenue Subway, a train to 207th—end of line. Great thrill to ride on subway. Interest in sounds, opening and closing of doors, smoke from oil, lights, passing other trains; *Bank Street member* explained what end of line meant—that this was the "uptown end of Manhattan Island." Bronx train went under the Harlem River and on to the Bronx, but this train just went uptown and downtown in Manhattan.

Walking west to Inwood Park. Amazed at big rocks, nice houses. Would like to live there. High house on hill with walls to hold up terraces and steps. Began to talk of what they would find: Indian arrowheads? etc.

Walked to stump of big tulip tree that stood there during Indian and Dutch days. Compared largest living tree near by. Guessed at height of tulip tree when alive. "Might touch the sky." Mrs. A.'s group took shelter from light rain in real Indian cave. Large enough for whole class. While

there we talked of how Indians could keep warm in it. Doors of wood—
but no saws. Stones for wall. Or animal skins. Noted tall grass that could
be woven into mats. Squirrels.

Then walked to see Hudson River, New Jersey, and Henry Hudson
Bridge. Pointed to Bronx and back to school, Riverside Drive. School
62 blocks back.

Inwood Park

Noted sheltered lowland by Harlem River where Indian village stood
and boats were beached.

Mrs. B.'s group picked up sticks that would bend for wigwams. All
children brought back rocks.

Notes to Mrs. A. and Mrs. B.

After this experience the children are ready to begin a map of Manhattan which they will really understand.

A. Materials to have ready for map:

1. Space on floor for large paper (to be provided by assistant to
principal)—scenery paper.

2. Better still—six or eight orange crates of the same size packed
close together to make a table. Large paper on top. With this we
can make real hills and houses and canoes.

3. Chalk, crayons, blue paint for rivers.

4. Clay for hills, bowls, and Indians.

5. Sticks, bits of bark, long grass for wigwams, canoes, and weaving mats.

6. Scraps of brown wrapping paper.

B. Other crafts.

1. Wampum belt weaving.

Materials—¼-inch macaroni (I will bring this).

       purple tintex.

       string and large needles.

       cheese boxes, hammer, nails.

C. Large scenery wigwam with opening to go in and out.

Materials—large paper and brown paint.

D. Papooses of stockings and cotton. Cradles of grape baskets from
grocery store.

To: Mrs. B. November 21

Your children were so creative with making the clay animals, canoes,
and Indians, it would be fine if they could have an opportunity to work

with clay three or four times a week. The clay from our map can be soaked and used again next year, and I believe there is enough clay in the school so that you could use it often.

Also, I suggest that you invite two or three of Mrs. A.'s children in to show your children their wampum weaving, and if your children want to do it, they can tell you what materials are needed and teach yours the technique. This interclass sharing is very good as long as it is rotated. Later your group can learn something the others do not know, and teach it to them. In Miss C.'s class the children are making little Dutch figures of pipe cleaners, cotton, and crepe paper. They could show you how they do it and your class could make Indian figures in the same way, using tan crepe paper of different shades for body and "skin" clothing. Cotton covered by stretched crepe paper forms the head.

Following our discussion, in which the two children talked of their partial Indian origin, I thought we might send a letter to the parents, with Mr. B.'s (the principal) approval, something like this:

"Dear Parents: This year we are studying the geography of the United States by learning how first the Indians, and then the early settlers, used the land, beginning with New York and going westward. History and geography mean so much more to children if they can actually see and feel the things that Indians and pioneers made and used. If you have things of this kind at home which you think would be of interest to the whole class and would be willing to loan it for a day, we might set a special day for the children to bring things. Some of them have spoken also of objects their fathers have brought home from various war theaters, and these would be welcome, too. Will you let us know if you would like to lend something?"

This seems to me to be a very good opportunity to begin appreciation of the many different kinds of people who make up America, the study of which is carried out in more detail in the fifth and sixth grades.

By the way, "Ride the Wind" by Phillips is a very fine story of New Jersey Indians and ends with the coming of Henry Hudson. We could go from that into the Dutch very easily. I believe it is in our school library.

Mrs. B.   November 28

Summary

1. Children showed things they had made or brought. Crayon designs, pictures, Indian stories in books, carved coconut.
2. Told Indian words and Spanish words with meanings.

3. Practiced for Assembly:
    A. Beaver song with Indian words.
    B. Indian music by one at piano, one dancing story of hunt, others with tom-toms.
    C. Poem—"Where We Walk to School Each Day."
    D. Indian group dance.
4. Grass braiding while I demonstrated Eastern woodland method of grass-mat weaving.
5. Child from Mrs. A.'s class came to show her wampum weaving.

Dutch Life on Manhattan. The section was written up in detail. It included: suggestions for introducing the Dutch on Manhattan— how they happened to come here; what things we use today that had not been invented when the Dutch came; what the Dutch brought with them that the Indians did not have; how the Dutch changed Manhattan; how they lived. A wide variety of possible experiences were written up in detail. They included: making a large relief map of New Amsterdam; trips on Manhattan to see where the Dutch lived and trips to museums; a great deal of craft activity in making candles, lanterns, horns, books, etc.; science experiments with windmills and construction of windmills; experiments with water displacement and construction of simple boats; a variety of possible dramatizations; concluding with the story of how the Dutch finally lost New Amsterdam and the naming of New York.

As we have said, all the Workshop members felt that the total curriculum as written up could not profitably be covered by any one class—probably not more than two sections or units could be done fully. Some teachers felt it better for their children to study both Indian and Dutch life on Manhattan and not attempt to go to any remote parts of our country. Many of the teachers, however, felt their children would get more from studying either Indians or Dutch life on Manhattan fairly fully and the other only sketchily and then studying fairly fully life in a different region in the United States. So it was decided to write up *From Atlantic to Pacific: Now and Long Ago,* so that each teacher could choose what she felt best for her own program. The regions were chosen largely on the basis of

their striking contrast to the Eastern woodlands in which New York
lies, and the consequent striking difference in the work done in New
York and the work done in these other regions by the long-ago Indians and by people today. As the children were strongly identified
with Indians by this time, the first approach to these regions was as
homes of the Indians.

The Great Plains, more than the other regions, give opportunities
for dramatic identification with both Indians and cowboys, and also
for showing an important relationship of a faraway land with our
own way of living through the products of wheat and beef cattle. We
therefore quote from this section:

The Western Plains, from Buffalo to Grain and Cattle Lands. Introductory Discussion: Life of the Plains Indians. Have many pictures assembled of flat plains. A land of grass which grew scarcer and shorter
the farther West one went because there was less and less rain.

What kind of food would these Indians eat? Complete dependence on
the buffalo, supplemented slightly by roots and berries. Had to keep on
the move to follow the buffaloes.

What kind of houses would they have? Need to pick up and move
frequently. Lack of wood except on edge of streams. Therefore made
tepees of buffalo skins.

What would they wear? Animal skins.

How would they travel? Did not have horses until Spaniards brought
them. Had dogs to drag travois.

Crafts and Dramatizations of Plains Indians.

Tepee: A few bamboo poles and some old sheets painted with Indian
designs will make an excellent tepee that the children will enjoy getting
inside. If your room is not large enough for this, toy tepees can be made,
but of course they are not nearly so good for dramatic play. Or the children can paint a large mural of a tepee to use as a background.

Buffalo masks: Can be made of papier-mâché. The children will enjoy
thinking up grotesque faces. The masks should be used in a *buffalo
dance.* Try to make drums to use for the dance; otherwise, borrow some.

Buffalo hunt: Before or after the Indians had horses.

Indian village on the march: Pantomime setting up of tepees by the
squaws; building fire; cooking buffalo meat the braves bring in.

Present Homes on Great Plains. Study relief map. Explain that there is less and less rain as you go West over the plains to the mountains. The grass gets shorter and sparser.

What do you think we would use the Great Plains for today? Explain that the buffaloes were killed off. What animals have we that might use the same sort of land? Could New York get its milk supply from cows living on the Great Plains? What else are cows used for? Go into some detail on life of cowboy on the open range. Almost all cattle ranches are now fenced. Place the "cow country" near the mountains on the map.

Read cowboy stories.

Play cowboys, emphasizing the real work that they do.

Sing cowboy songs.

What kind of food do all of us eat? Bread. It needs large space to grow wheat. Wheat needs more rain than cows do. It can be stored and shipped easily by railway. Place wheat ranches on map. Farms.

Activities: Get some wheat grains and plant them. Experiment with them as you did with corn. If possible visit a grain elevator (Brooklyn). Visit a bakery unless children have already visited one.

For mature third-graders life in a desert, both now and long ago, holds great interest. We quote again:

The Southwest Desert, from Rivers to Springs to Irrigation. The Southwest is a land of little rain. Rain is important both to the Indians and to all other people who now live there. The Pueblo Indians, a settled village people, dependent on their fields, need rain for their corn. The Navahos, a seminomadic people, need rain so that their sheep can find grass. Our modern farmers need water for their crops. The Indians perform ceremonies to bring the rain. Our modern engineers build a Boulder Dam and an irrigation system. And the government gradually is helping the Indians to understand erosion and is taking steps to solve the problem of drought on the Indian reservation.

Activities: Popular crafts for children in connection with this region are silverwork and weaving.

Wool may be obtained, carded, spun, dyed, and woven. A simple spindle that works is a sharpened dowel stick with a wooden wheel near one end of it. Wool cards (combs) may be obtained from the Industrial Arts Cooperative.

Experiments with dam building and irrigation may be tried in a sandbox.

A trip to the Cactus Room at the Bronx Botanical Gardens, in which the temperature is very high, gives a realistic feel of desert atmosphere.

The Northwest Pacific Coast. This region can be contrasted with the Atlantic Coast. Reading the legends of the Northwest Indians, a trip to the Northwest Indian Room at the Natural History Museum, and some photographs would be enough to make this part of the country real to the children.

OUR WHOLE COUNTRY. Use the whole room for a map of the United States. Pile up coats on desks to represent mountains. Use a central aisle for the Mississippi River. When possible use the northern end of the room for North. Let the children play out stories they have read of pioneers or Indians, traveling from one part of the country to another. Or play out the things that come to New York from other parts of the country. Try this several different times so that the children will have a number of opportunities to figure out relationships and to play experiences.

Draw a rough map of the United States on wrapping paper on the floor. Let the children put in whatever they remember.

Finally, let each child try drawing his own map, or use plasticine. Try to stop them from worrying about detail and instead to get the rough features.

OUR WAYS AND OUR LAND COMPARED WITH OTHER WAYS IN OTHER LANDS: THROUGH SCIENCE AND VICARIOUS EXPERIENCE

For fourth-graders the social studies curriculum content was to include New York and communities different from New York with distinct emphasis on faraway parts of the world. We chose explorers as our guides and companions—relatively recent explorers who had gone to "hard-to-reach" places. We felt that nine-year-olds need adventure. They seek it in movies and radio programs and on the street. We quote just one of many notes in our records of remarks made by children in fourth-grade classes.

Found three boys deep in discussion of Frankenstein movies. Teacher listening with interest. One child told of a boy who was shot in movie theater. Another boy said he couldn't sleep because of excitement of movie.

This love of adventure makes it easy for nine-year-olds to "identify" with explorers. We began each unit—the study of one region—with the story of one expedition. The hardships which explorers encountered create a lively interest in the lands which the explorers found—the plants and animals, the topography, the rivers, the climate. And this interest is readily extended to earth science—what makes some regions flat and others mountainous, some regions hot, dry deserts and others hot rainy jungles, and still others cold deserts or forest lands; how mountains and soil are formed; how plant and animal life adapts to the environment. The children become interested in scientific discoveries made by the explorers they are following, as, for instance, knowledge of weather conditions in polar regions and how they are related to our own weather and to airplane routes. The experience of both Bank Street and Workshop teachers who had tried science experiments had convinced us that nine-year-old children are ready for many science experiments and that science should be a part of their social studies curriculum. Indeed, we felt that the social studies curriculum for the fourth grade should be primarily on the level of adventure and science.

The children are always interested in the people the explorers found living in these hard-to-reach places. These people, just because they are cut off from the cultures of other peoples, use what they find around them in their work of meeting the common human needs of food, shelter, clothes, and roads. Human geography is seen in its simplest form in relatively primitive cultures. It becomes clear through the children's own reasoning why people are nomads in the half-desert regions of Central Asia and in the cold nearly plantless North polar region; why a jungle is a hard place in which to develop farming; why mountain people developed herds of tame animals. People's work becomes related to the lands they use.

An exploring expedition holds more than adventure and science for fourth-graders. The careful planning necessary in equipment and food, the necessity for teamwork, is a good vicarious experience in group living.

In our curriculum throughout the year we related all these natural regions and their people to New York, the homes of our children. We suggested many trips, all of which formed the basis for discussions of the differences and likenesses of our own environment and our ways of using it and that of the faraway environment being studied. Some trips were to see products (largely foods) from these various regions which we ourselves used; some were to see plants and animals of these regions; some were to museums; some to stores which sold equipment to explorers; still other trips were to the Weather Bureau to show how we ourselves use science discoveries.

As in the third grade, the teachers needed much background content. In the fourth grade most of the teachers needed background in earth science and in the interpretation of the physical characteristics of various world regions as homes of plants, animals, and human beings. Much of this background content was given in our after-school Workshop meetings, and some was written into the curriculum. Concrete science experiments appropriate for each region were suggested. Also, in the curriculum, there were many suggestions for dramatizations, free art, creative writing, music and stories, and selections from books to be read to the children.

Our Workshop discussions after a period of experimentation in the classrooms showed that the teachers felt the first version of the curriculum was overcrowded. The committee of teachers working on the second revision recommended cutting the explorations to four regions. They were Roy Chapman Andrews Explores Deserts of Central Asia; David Livingstone in the Jungles of Africa; Explorers of North and South Polar Regions; Some Mountain Climber Explorers: In Andes.

The following are records showing several ways in which the Bank Street staff members worked with the teachers and children in their classrooms to introduce and develop the techniques for working out this curriculum in practice.

This fourth-grade class had been studying present-day New York and the Dutch on Manhattan. They had just begun a unit on the far North.

February 3

Discussion of North Pole under way. What would you take? Children suggested clothes, food, weapons. Discussed animals. Looked in books for information and listed what found in notebooks. At teacher's request

I told them a little about Russian explorers—left Papanin's diary with teacher. I told about bathysphere—one child had seen one. I explained water pressure a little. Paul asked where thermometer was that recorded temperature at sea bottom.

February 20

Teacher produced ice they had frozen. Asked if it got larger or smaller. Children said smaller! No mark on glass so couldn't tell. We reminded them of how ice breaks jars, milk bottles overflow, etc. Agreed it must take more room than water. I asked if heavier or lighter. Put some water in and watched it float. Drew picture of ocean and imagined what would happen if ice sank. One child said ocean would overflow.

Paul asked why icebergs have part out of water. Discussed how wood floats. They drew their ideas. We floated a pencil and observed it was part in water. I took two jar tops. Placed one flat in the water. Children saw that it sank a little in the water but still floated. Placed another tilted so that the water flowed into it. It sank. Asked children why boats floated. They emphasized air. I put ink bottle into jar of water. They saw that bottle with light air in it displaced an amount of much heavier water. Dropped things into ink bottle. It sank lower and lower—that is, displaced more and more water. Sank when ink bottle with things in it weighed more than the water it displaced. Teacher interested.

Darkened room and showed day and night on globe. Children seemed to understand. I asked what part of globe was hit directly by sun's rays. They figured it was center part. Recalled flashlight on board. Reference made to up and down. I asked which was up on South Pole. Confusion.

Much interest and continual questions. Teacher said she would go over material with children.

March 1

Dramatization of Stefansson's adventure. Considerable teacher dictation—insisting on details of story. I thought children showed plenty of initiative.

Also dramatized shooting seal. Much enthusiasm. I helped two children make igloos of plaster of Paris at teacher's request.

March 6

Several reports read on Eskimo material—well written and good information. A class book in process of formation.

Teacher read to children from *Northward Ho,* stopping frequently for questions, comments, and even dramatization. Not much story element in what she read.

Teacher asked group for words that reminded them of arctic—cold, windy, hunting, etc., suggested. Teacher asked them to think of doing something specific. Words still rather general.

This fourth-grade class had been following the old curriculum in a unit on China before they began to study polar regions. The following outline of a discussion led by the Bank Street member with this class had been recorded and the notes given to the teacher.

December 11

Q. What has happened to the weather since yesterday morning?
A. Cloudy—snow—much colder.
Q. Where did the cold air come from?
A. World turned around in twenty-four hours.
A. Wind came from far away.
Q. What is the wind?
A. Wind is something like a breeze.
A. Wind is a strong bit of air.
Q. How tall is the wind?
A. Ten miles?
A. Half a mile.
A. We never know how tall it is.
A. All the way up to the sky because when it blows, it blows all over.

Discussion of stratosphere—where winds do not blow—no storms. Scientists have discovered much about the height of air by use of airplanes, and by measuring northern lights by means of cameras and mathematics.

Children's remarks:
The northern lights are like a rainbow.
Like electricity—yellow and different colors.

What science has discovered: Magnetic storms on sun throw out tiny particles (electrons)—radio waves go through atmosphere.

Children's questions and remarks about life in the arctic:
How thick is the ice?
How long are walrus tusks?
How heavy is a walrus? A seal?
Why don't Eskimos get sick from eating raw meat?
(From child): If fish had been lying around in stores it might be dirty, but right out of the water it's clean.

How do they find the meat they have buried in meat pits?
(From children):

> Put marker in.
> A big tall pole.
> A whale bone.

If airplane goes there, where would it land?
Discussion followed of how cold preserves food.

Story of Soviet scientists from *The Chelyuskin* saved from ice by airplanes. Problems of flying in the arctic—of landing on ice, freezing motors, ice on wings.

The children were so absorbed in this discussion, sitting very quietly for almost an hour, and they had so much to contribute, I think they could take a weather map discussion. I would like to go further into the air mass idea if you think it is feasible.

Also, more on the magnetic pole with an experiment that I did with Miss C.'s class on magnetizing a needle.

The children responded eagerly to the suggestion made by the Bank Street member that a real explorer visit their class. All the children wrote letters. . . .

Suggestions to teachers studying the Gobi Desert. Notes to teacher.

October 7

I investigated the possibility of a trip to the Bronx Botanical Gardens (Cactus Room) to fit in with your study of the desert. Mr. N., who is in charge, asked that we notify him one day in advance so that he could have someone to answer the children's questions.

October 23

These are some things I think might enrich the play about the explorers to the Gobi Desert. The trip from Peiping, China, takes them in trucks across a high mountain pass and down across the grasslands before they reach the desert. I think it is important for the children to know where the Gobi Desert is in relation to the land around it, as well as its relation to New York, where the children live. I will give you just a few passages which you might read to the children with a map of Asia at hand, and perhaps some of the incidents with the truck might be added to the play.

Page 64, *On the Trail of Ancient Man,* by C. F. Andrews. Description of trucks winding up mountains. You might discuss what a mountain pass is, and why that was the only way they could get to the Gobi Desert from Peiping. Talk about views they have seen from high places.

Notes to another fourth-grade teacher.

Preparation for making Congo scenery.   October 16

Discussed kinds of trees and plants, shapes, density, swinging vines, big leaves, ferns. Children gave experiences from woods in the South. Grapevines they had swung on.

Had the children dramatize swinging vines—swinging arms.

Then they went to the board and tried out jungle plants and trees with white chalk. Then discussion of what had been drawn, followed by another group filling in spaces. Made a continuous jungle scene around the room.

Then practiced two acts of play about Stanley going to find Livingstone. After first act, the audience gave suggestions. Encouraged them to give positive suggestions rather than negative criticisms.

TENTATIVE SOCIAL STUDIES CURRICULUM WRITTEN FOR FOURTH GRADE IN OUR SCHOOL

After a year and a half of experimentation in the classrooms with our fourth-grade curriculum, we decided to revise it a second time. Though no one thought four regions could profitably be studied by any one class, we nevertheless wrote up four so that a teacher could choose whether she and the children would explore a desert, a jungle, a land of ice, or a mountain. In practice, usually two regions were studied fairly fully with trips, science experiments, dramatizations, and other art experiences. The statement for all four regions is too long to include. We give excerpts from the introduction, one region in full, and the summary at the end as they appeared in the second revision. It was not presented as a finished product. The teachers regarded it as suggestions which should be submitted to further trial and experimentation.

OUTLINE OF CURRICULUM FOR GRADE 4
THEME: *Living and Working Together in New York City, Compared with Other Regions of the World.*

I. EARLY AND LATER EXPLORERS DISCOVER HARD-TO-REACH PLACES.
Roy Chapman Andrews Explores Deserts of Central Asia.
Desert Land: Its Plants and Animals.

What Makes Rain?
The Way People Live in Desert Islands.
What Desert Products We Use.
David Livingstone in the Jungles of Africa.
Jungles: Their Plants and Animals.
What Makes the Tropics Hot?
The Way People Live in Jungles.
What Tropical Products We Use.
Explorers of North and South Polar Regions.
Polar Regions: Their Plants and Animals.
What Makes the Polar Regions Cold?
The Way People Live in Cold Regions.
Relation of Polar Regions to Our Weather.
Some Mountain Climber Explorers: In Andes.
Mountains: Their Plants and Animals.
How Mountains and Soil Are Formed.
The Way People Live in Mountains.
What Use Mountains Are to Us: What Difficulties They Make.

II. SUMMARY.
III. SCHOOL JOB.

The fourth-grade child is a little more far-reaching in his questions than the third-grade child, a little more boisterous and vigorous. He also needs plenty of firsthand use of materials. He can begin to generalize about and to understand more distant places and times. He feels very strongly the need for approval by his companions and should have plenty of group experiences to which he can contribute. He has a rather keen sense of fairness and values in human relations, though he is still markedly individualistic. He enjoys fantasy, humor, and above all adventure. His heroes are people who accomplish difficult physical feats. New York children are particularly in need of wholesome adventure and the right kind of heroes to offset undesirable street adventure and heroes drawn from some of the comics and movies.

With these characteristics of our fourth-grade children in mind we suggest a year of exploring the world, with emphasis on the adventures and scientific discoveries of explorers, but always comparing the lands and peoples found by them with life here at home. We have not selected the explorers solely for their personalities and the excitement of their explorations, though these have been important considerations. We have selected those whose explorations would acquaint the children with many of the outstanding regional types on the surface of the earth—

mountains, deserts, tropical jungles, and the poles—and with some of the peoples who are using these various regions (grass plains and cool forest lands come in Grade 3). We have looked for explorers whose discoveries have been significant science contributions which affect our own lives. These explorers are suggested rather than the traditional ones who opened up North America because during the war our children became conscious of and interested in the globe, with its wide variety of geographic phenomena and peoples, and because science is increasingly significant in understanding our modern world.

These explorers will take the children into many distant regions of the globe where people's ways of living are different from our own.

Because legends and fanciful stories are keenly appreciated by fourth-graders we suggest that this material be used freely in connection with whatever region of the earth is being studied. It is an excellent way of building up a feeling for the way people react to the earth conditions around them.

Political boundaries are confusing to children of this age and can be largely ignored. The emphasis in geography, therefore, is not on the nations but on the lives of people as they are conditioned by the variety of land forms, climate and other natural phenomena, and on what these regions can contribute to us and to the world. Such a program should build a sense of global geography. It should give many opportunities for understanding the world of science: weather, the development of communication and transportation including future air routes, glimpses of geology and of astronomy. It should finally build an understanding of man's relation to other animals and of the oneness of the human race. All of these are legitimate and important aspects of a social studies curriculum. They can be supplemented with discussions of current happenings that will add reality and immediate importance to these various earth regions: soldiers in the tropics, airplanes over the arctic.

The exploring expeditions themselves were severe tests of character involving heroism, co-operation of an intense sort, boundless curiosity and energy. Through identification with such people the children can grow and expand their human values.

Incidentally, this material should lend itself readily to the use of primary sources of information, a valuable experience in itself. It also gives particularly rich opportunities for dramatization and art expression.

The chief *social ideas* to be brought out wherever the situation is appropriate are:

In New York we use the products of lands and workers all over the world.

Development of idea of variety of lands of the earth.

All people seek to meet their physical needs and have a good life.

People are alike as well as different: it is of great importance to understand their likenesses, not merely their differences.

Under the heading *Subject Matter Suggested: Discussions, Activities, Reading References* were suggestions for introductory discussions which would link New York with whichever faraway region was first taken up, and also tell the teacher how much background the children brought to this adventure with a hard-to-reach land. We give just one of the four explorations into four regions which were written up.

THE EARLY AND LATER EXPLORERS DISCOVER HARD-TO-REACH PLACES.

David Livingstone in the Jungles of Africa. Read the stories of the expedition with the background of the jungle, vegetation and animals, and rivers as roads. Take time to play it out and to feel like explorers. Pause for discussion or dramatization. Put a big outline map of Africa on the board and get the children to trace Livingstone's route. Supplement with pictures wherever possible. Discuss the difficulties of the Negroes and the white men in understanding each other. The people Livingstone found were a very old people who had some powerful kingdoms. *In the far past some of their ancestors may have intermarried with Semites and other Mediterranean people to form the earliest real civilization we know about in Egypt.* But for a long time these people had lived cut off from the rest of the world. Europeans had found their way to the land of this people only a fairly short time before Livingstone went there. Europeans, with the tools and weapons they had invented, found it easy to overpower the African people and take them away as slaves.

How were the people living whom Livingstone found? They were using what they found around them just as Indians did on Manhattan and our Great Plains and our Southwest. People in hard-to-reach places have to invent everything themselves because they do not come into contact with other peoples. What did people in hot forests find to use? Depending upon the children's interests, elaborate and play out ways of living in hot forests. Bring out that people in different parts of Africa developed different tools. In some places people discovered *how to use iron and how to weave cloth at a time when ancestors of white men in Europe were using stone tools and dressing in animal skins.* They made beautiful things of wood, ivory, pottery, and jewelry. In some places they had developed farming. A jungle is a difficult place in which to develop real agriculture, as jungle plants quickly encroach on the farms. Some tribes were nomad farmers. They burned down a patch of forest and raised crops. After a few years they moved on. They used jungle plants, fish, and wild animals for food. They were skilled hunters and trappers. They used rivers as their roads. They danced with drums. They invented musical instruments and were the first people to use stringed instruments.

Geography and Science combined. Discussions and Activities. Why are the tropics so hot? Experiment to show that direct rays of the sun bring more heat than indirect. Point a flashlight directly at the blackboard. It will shine directly on a small round area. Mark this with a chalk. Keep the same distance away from the blackboard and slant the flashlight. It will cover a much larger oval area and the light will be less bright. Emphasize that you have the same light, the same amount of heat. Which region will be hotter, the small area or the large? Children should be able to figure this out if it is stated clearly. Now ask which rays of the sun warm the most, slanting rays or direct rays. Illustrate with a globe. Why is the equator hot? See where the sun is in the sky at noon. If possible make some record of this with the date. Record the place of the sun in the sky a month later. Connect the directness of the sun overhead with the seasons of the year.

Why does it rain so much in the tropics? Tropical forests are in hot valleys. Water vapor is constantly steaming up from the swamps, rivers, and plants into the cooler air above and causing rain. Rivers and seasonal floods result from rains. Refer to spring floods in Mississippi Valley.

Why do plants grow in such profusion? Because of good soil in the valleys, rain, and heat.

Visit Botanical Gardens. Make sketches in tropical rooms. Make a terrarium and watch plants grow in warm moist air. Try to grow some tropical plants. Experiment with the amount of heat and water needed and contrast with the desert plants. Botanical Gardens would probably help us get a tropical plant.

What animals live in African tropical forests? What are their habits? How do plants and animals help one another?

Study some particular animal in detail, showing his relation to plants. Elephants are particularly interesting. Read stories of elephant hunts.

Make papier-mâché animal heads and use them for jungle play. Paint a jungle mural and use as background for dramatics. Paint great tropical forests on the globe. Note that they are in a broad band close to equator.

Read Mukerji's descriptions of the jungle and some animal stories and legends. Perhaps some of Kipling's *Jungle Book.* Try asking the children for brief descriptive writing on animals and jungle. Emphasize feeling. One technique for doing this is to get from the group as a whole adjectives and verbs expressing motion appropriate to the jungle and write them on the board. On a later day, after they have been erased, ask the children to write. (If they write while the adjectives and verbs are still on the board they are apt to copy each other's feelings too much.)

Depending upon the class, elaborate and play out ways of living in hot forests. Experiment with drum beating. Get the children to work up codes and try sending messages to each other. Get them to reason out why drum messages were valuable in the jungle. Let them also figure out rhythms and try dancing to them. Use rubber bands and boxes—preferably cigar boxes—to experiment with stringed instruments.

Relations of tropical forests to us: What tropical foods do we eat? Bananas, Brazil nuts, tea, cocoa, coffee, etc., from South America and the Orient.

Visit neighborhood groceries and fruit stores to answer questions about tropical foods—where and how do they grow? How do they get to us? If possible buy something to eat.

Visit a boat from South or Central America. (Advertising material from shipping companies is often valuable.) If this trip is impossible substitute the banana room of the A & P Warehouse in the Bronx.

What other tropical plants do we use? Rubber, quinine—both originally South American plants taken to East Indies, now being replanted in South America because of transportation difficulties from East. Enlarge on story of rubber and its discovery, how it is obtained, its uses, and synthetic processes discovered during the war.

What animal products from tropical Africa do we use? Elephants were hunted for ivory, which is no longer of major importance. Piano keys. See Bibliography in Appendix.

We quote the closing sections of the curriculum statement.

SUMMARY. Everywhere, in every land, we have found that people were using the earth. We found that we, in New York, use products of lands all over the globe, brought to us by railroads, boats, trucks, airplanes. Some of these products are raised in farms by people in faraway lands. Some are manufactured into foods, clothes, machines, etc., by people in faraway factories. Some of these products are taken from the ground by faraway miners. Discuss the food, the clothes, the houses, the roads, the machines which the children know at first hand and trace everything back to its source as a product of some earth force somewhere. Bring out that the earth supplies raw materials (soil, rain, sunshine, water, plants, animals, metals, coal, etc.) but that people have to *work* to make these materials of use to them.

We found that people in hard-to-reach places used the things they found around them. We found that the kind of lives they lived, the kind of work they did, depended largely upon the kind of land they lived in.

In exploring the earth, we found people living in many different kinds of lands. Has the earth always been the way it is now? Have there always been oceans, rivers, mountains, soil?

From discussion of mountains, we learned that some mountains are made by the wrinkling of the earth crust as it cooled; that some mountains rose a very long time ago and some more recently. From discussions of tropical forests we learned that soil began to be made when small pieces of rocks from mountains were washed down into valleys. All soil on the earth began with rock erosion somewhere, through rain, frost, ice, or wind.

We learned that all air holds some water; that the sun draws water vapor up into the air and forms clouds; that clouds drop their water as rain when they come into contact with something cooler than they are. We learned that climates have not always been the same as they are now —the deserts of Asia must once have been a land where there was plenty of vegetation (refer back to dinosaur egg found there). We learned what made the tropics hot and the polar regions cold.

In our year of exploring, we found a great variety of plants and animals living in the great variety of lands on the earth. People everywhere are dependent on other living things—plants and animals. Have the living things now on the earth always been the way they now are? How did plants and animals come to be so well fitted to live in the lands and climates where we find them—camels in deserts or half-deserts, polar bears in the arctic, elephants in tropical forests, etc.?

Today we say we are living in the Age of Man because men have learned to use the earth and living things fairly fully. New Yorkers today live as they do because we can use things from all parts of the world —the cold, the hot, the dry, the wet, under the ground, under the sea. Lately we have learned to use the air as a road. New discoveries like the atomic bomb make possible great changes in our way of living. Whether or not these changes will make life for people of the earth much better or much worse will depend upon how we use our discoveries, whether we wish changes to benefit only ourselves or all the peoples of the earth. This might be the closing discussion.

SCHOOL JOB. Participating in School Living. As a school job for the fourth grade we suggest the responsibility for a picture file for the school. Most pictures fall into some geographic category. In the course of classifying these the children can get a great deal of knowledge about other parts of the world. At the same time they can do a useful job for the school. If they become interested in cutting out pictures, mounting them where appropriate, and filing them under useful headings, they may very well become inspired to bring picture material of their own from home. They might also stimulate other classes to co-operate. If mature enough, the class could help teachers to find the picture material that they need for teaching.

13

Building a Social Studies Curriculum for
Fifth and Sixth Grades

THE problem of organizing the subject matter for fifth and sixth grades was even more difficult than for third and fourth grades. In the new official bulletin it was suggested that curriculum content in social studies for the two grades be planned together under the general theme: *Living and Working Together in the United States of America and in the World,* leaving the division of subject matter between the two grades largely to individual schools. To be somehow covered in the two grades there remained the subject matter covered in the old separate courses of study: History of the United States from Explorers to Present; Geography of the United States and the Rest of the Western Hemisphere; and Europe; to which was now added Living and Working Together in the World. In the official bulletin this broad sweep of subject matter was suggested under large topics in which history, geography and civics were integrated.

In the course of our preliminary discussions, we in the Workshop all agreed that whatever division of subject matter should be decided upon, our Workshop social studies curriculum in both grades should be based upon the following approaches to subject matter:

(1) A human geography approach to people—past or present, around us or far away. That is, how people lived and worked to-

gether was to be consistently studied in relation to the earth situations they used—the kind of land forms, natural waterways of rivers and harbors, climate, natural vegetation and native animals, natural underground resources. (2) The opening topic or unit in both grades was to be in the present. And in both grades the study of present ways of working and living in New York was to be carried on throughout the year. (3) Chronological history was to be approached through the development of big movements or happenings which brought about significant changes in the lives and work of people, as, for instance, when people came to use new lands or new inventions. This approach would leave out many details of dates, wars, and political history which we thought more suitable to high school children. (4) Relationships of people to people, or social values, to be more emphasized in fifth than in fourth grade and much more in sixth than in fifth grade.

The question of the actual division of subject matter between fifth and sixth grades had a practical, almost a mechanical side to which the teachers were very sensitive. Any large area taken out of one grade had to go into the other grade. In our Workshop discussions with teachers of the two grades together, three outstanding practical questions were constantly raised.

1. How to cover the old curriculum content and add global relations? Should some portions be omitted or only touched upon? Which portions?

2. How much of the chronological history of the United States should be put into fifth grade? (In the old curriculum, the history came down to the Civil War.) How fully could living and working together in the world be covered, even if the sixth grade took that as its central theme?

3. How to study the past ways of living and working of people in relation to the study of their lands? Or, as the teachers usually put it, how to combine history and geography? (This question meant not so much that the teachers were still thinking within the framework of the old separate courses as the practical difficulty of using

textbooks in which history and geography were treated separately. One teacher developed a transition plan.[42])

WHAT IN OUR PRESENT AND PAST CULTURE HAS MEANING TO FIFTH-GRADE CHILDREN? TO SIXTH-GRADE?

Everyone recognized, however, that the actual division of subject matter between fifth and sixth grades was far more than a mechanical one. It really involved considering what in our present and past culture has meaning to ten- and to eleven-year-old children. On what basis should we divide the whole sweep of the development of United States history from "Explorers to the Present"? Interpreted broadly, this development includes our ties with the rest of the world from our original tie with the mother country of England to our role in the United Nations, which was coming into existence even as we planned this curriculum. Our first division of the subject was simple but somewhat arbitrary and did not work out well for either grade when it was tried out. We put all of United States history into Grade 5 and all of the relations with the rest of the world into Grade 6. The fifth-grade teachers felt their curriculum was greatly overcrowded; the sixth-grade teachers felt theirs was too mature for their children. In our second revision of the curriculum we tried a different alignment of subject matter, putting United States history to the beginning of the industrial era in the fifth grade and later history to the present in the sixth. The theme for the fifth grade became *The United States: Our Lands and People; Our Ties with American Nations;* the theme for sixth grade became *Our Country and Its Ties with the Rest of the World.*

The thinking that lay back of this division was based on what we considered the difference in maturity levels between these ten- and eleven-year-olds and what opportunities to follow the special interest drives of children of these ages and experience the subject matter afforded. The first part of the chronological story of our country, told

[42] Appendix 19: The Americas.

as a dramatic sweep of big happenings in the New World, makes the strong appeal of adventure and heroes to ten-year-olds. Explorers hold this appeal. But thinking of our fifth-grade curriculum as following our fourth-grade with its strong emphasis on explorers, we felt little emphasis should be placed on the exploration period in our history. The early settlers and the Western movement show people of European culture adapting their ways to a situation which demanded "self-help" under difficult but readily imagined circumstances. These situations present dramatically and convincingly the kinds of work which naturally developed in various kinds of lands in our present country, which was one of the basic relationships we wished children to understand. The excitement of the freer life in the New World to people used to the crowded Old World, the struggle against the mother country to form a new nation, the problems of the young nation trying to fuse widely separated parts each with its own regional work and regional thinking, the differences in regional thinking finally resulting in war—all these situations are easy for fifth-grade children to identify with. Also in terms of building a sound attitude toward another culture, the relationship between Indians, the old Americans, and settlers, the new Americans, is simpler and more readily understood than the present-day relationship among nations in the United Nations. It seems possible to approach all this early part of our country's story on a younger level than the later part, beginning roughly from when the industrial revolution started us on our modern ways of living and working.

The same kinds of experiences came to people all over the Americas. Everywhere Europeans had to adapt their ways of living and working to conditions completely new to them, everywhere they met a culture strange to them, everywhere they finally broke from their mother countries and formed new nations. They did not all go through these stages simultaneously or at the same speed. Their lands were different, the cultures of the Indians were different, the mother countries had different attitudes—all of which makes up the individual stories of the American nations. But the dramatic sweep of big happenings is essentially the same in the Americas. That led us to put "Our Ties with American Nations" into the fifth grade along with the early part of our country's story.

In the sixth grade, the chronological story of our country was picked up after the Civil War, which roughly coincides with the beginnings of the industrial age for us. Here came the sweep of big happenings in the machine age, from the cotton gin and railroads to airplanes, diesel engines, and atomic energy. Here came the development of roads and trade which bound together the early, almost independent regions to form a whole with vital interdependence; and finally the evolution from isolation to modern United States as a vital part of the whole world.

Obviously, the sixth-graders could not cover "the whole world" thoroughly! We took a broad look at Eurasia—its lands and peoples —as a preliminary to the study of one European and one Asiatic country.[43] We wrote some background content on Eurasia into the curriculum statement. For the European nation to be studied more intensively we chose England both as the country from which we received our largest cultural heritage, including our language, and as an ally in the war through which we were then living. And as countries wholly or partly in Asia, we chose and wrote up both China and Soviet Russia, two more of our war allies, to give the teachers a choice.

In Workshop discussions it was decided to begin the written statement of our social studies curriculum with a selection on the interpretation of themes for fifth and sixth grades. This was prepared as an integral part of the curriculum and came before the sections on subject matter. It was written not just for ourselves in the Workshop but for teachers who had not been through the discussions and experimentation out of which this statement evolved. We give it here with a few parts omitted, though of necessity it repeats some ideas already expressed in this book.

[43] Appendix 20: Earth Forces in China. This provides the kind of background content on Eurasia given in Workshop meetings.

". . . the general theme suggested for the fifth and sixth school years is: *Living and Working Together in the United States of America and in the World.* Since the child will still need help in adjusting to home, school, and community life, problems related to these areas are also an important aspect of the social studies program in these as in earlier years. Furthermore, the social studies program will draw from the significant current happenings and ideas as well as from the more conventional subject matter of geography, history and civics." [44]

The theme for fifth and sixth grades covers an immense area of subject matter. *Living and Working Together in the United States* covers both the present and the past as it did in the old course of study in history. Also, *Living and Working Together in the World* sounds very mature for ten- and eleven-year-old children. Global thinking is fairly new for many adults including teachers and perhaps even newer among nations. It is imperative to interpret this inclusive general theme in terms that will have meaning to fifth- and sixth-grade children. Specifically, we must decide what aspects of the ways of living and working in present-day and past United States, what kind of world relationships, will help these children to grow in interest and understanding of the world they live in, which, after all, is the most important outcome of their social studies program.

In the following curricula the selection from the wide sweep of subject matter is based on what we believe to be significant characteristics of ten- and eleven-year-old children: their desire to find out about things, which can be called intellectual curiosities; their desire for adventure, which is closely allied to their ability to identify dramatically with heroes and stirring events; and their expanding sense of values in the way people treat one another. The suggested techniques for carrying out the program are based on what we believe to be their need to get into action, their skills, and their ways of learning.

RELATIONSHIPS OF PEOPLES TO THEIR ENVIRONMENTS. Direct experiences are still a basic approach in helping fifth- and sixth-grade children to understand the world they live in just as they are in younger years. But these children bring to these experiences wider interests, greater capacity to generalize, to see complex relationships and implications, and to gather and organize their information from new sources. The smiting quality of direct experiences—seeing and hearing things for themselves, thinking out implications, hunting up evidence for them-

[44] *Curriculum Development in the Elementary Schools,* Board of Education of the City of New York, Curriculum Bulletin No. 1, 1945–46 Series.

selves, expressing their ideas their own way—gets these children into action and makes informational subject matter real and significant. Direct experiences transform the world into a laboratory, a place in which to find out about things they are interested in. This "finding out" is the first step in the learning process—what we call "intake." The second step is doing something about what they have found out—what we call "outgo." If our informational subject matter is to be really learned, we must provide some direct active experiences in both the intake and outgo steps in the learning process.

What in our ways of living and working together interests these children? What kinds of direct experiences can we give them to satisfy their interests?

Their interest in how things work has not diminished. Rather, it has developed so that now they can explore new aspects in the physical world, whether natural phenomena or man-made mechanisms and inventions based upon the way natural phenomena (earth resources) behave. To illustrate: these children are eagerly interested in finding out both how air behaves, and how inventors have utilized the behavior of air to make heavier-than-air planes fly. They are interested in finding out both what earth resources made natural phenomena such as forests, coal, and oil in certain parts of the earth, and how people have learned to use these natural resources as fuel for heat and transportation.

These children are growing up in a world where science and applied science (inventions in work processes) play an enormous role in the way people, at home and all over the world, are living and working. The world these children live in is a mechanized world. New York holds almost inexhaustible possibilities for observing inventions in work processes. Trips can be planned to see an important link in almost any kind of work that ties up with the subject matter. To illustrate: a trip to a clothing factory was taken by a sixth-grade class who were studying "Consumers." In connection with the same topic the children wrote a play.[45] The teacher wrote that the trip and the play together made clear and significant the whole elaborate work interrelationships beginning with the sheep, carried through transportation and various factory and distribution processes, to the coats which the children wore. The program, of course, included much information and many activities besides the trip and the play. But the trip was a high point in the intake, and the play was a high point in the outgo, by which the children learned an

[45] Appendix 21: Notes Kept by Bank Street Member Working in the Sixth Grade on "Consumers" and "Mary's Coat."

important aspect of the present ways of working together in the United States.

Moreover, some appreciation of our modern elaborate work processes forms a basis for appreciating the work in early United States which people had to do largely by hand, without the help of modern machines. It lends zest to the study of how work patterns gradually developed through scientific discoveries and inventions. It gives an appreciation of the dependence of the modern mechanized world upon natural resources and of the urgency of nations to secure these natural resources for themselves.

Science is an important aspect of living and working together in the United States and the world which can help these ten- and eleven-year-old children to understand the world they live in. These children show eager curiosities and corresponding satisfactions in straight science experiments. Many simple science experiments or demonstrations can be done in our classrooms with such simple equipment as our Workshop School has in its source material library.

We believe that science and man-made inventions as a part of "what men have done, are doing, and will do in their efforts to solve basic problems of living" [46] should be given considerable weight in a social studies curriculum for fifth- and sixth-grade children. In the curriculum we have suggested a few specific trips. Also we have included descriptions of a few science experiments. In the Bibliography we have included a few simple science books which these children are capable of using for their own "research."

We all want our children to think. Thinking is seeing new relationships. Thinking is an active creative performance. It is not a passive memory performance, though obviously memory plays a large role. Our job throughout the school is to use the subject matter in the curriculum so that children think, that is, see new relationships in the way people live and work together now, or the way they did in the past. A mere statement of relationships, whether by the teacher or in a book, is less likely to stimulate genuine thinking than some direct experiences or what may be called raw source materials in which the children have to find out the relationships themselves. This is really the basis of the "problem approach." The situation is put up to the children, but thinking out the solution, the implications, discovering the relationships remains an active creative performance on the part of the children themselves. It

[46] *Curriculum Development in the Elementary Schools,* Board of Education of the City of New York, Curriculum Bulletin No. 1, 1945–46 Series.

depends upon the teacher whether any subject matter challenges the children to think or merely to memorize. In sixth-grade discussion of people and their lands in Europe (described in the Introductory Overview [47]), the children knew many facts about political boundaries, natural resources, and products of various countries. That is, they had raw source material. But it was in the discussion that they discovered the significant relationships between the earth and work, between people and the lands they use, between modern mechanized ways of working and relationships among nations.

Among the basic relationships which we believe lie behind living and working together is the relationship between the earth and work—the way people use the earth. This is our interpretation of "the relationships of peoples to the environment in which they live," which is stated in the official bulletin as one of the "bases of social studies materials and activities." Everywhere in the curriculum for fifth and sixth grades, people and the land they use in their work are considered together. Living and working together in the United States in the past—which is a large part of the subject matter for fifth grade—is interpreted for these ten-year-olds with emphasis on the way the new environments people moved into conditioned the way they lived and worked. Living and working together in the world also lays emphasis on global work—trade and roads. ("Roads" is everywhere used to mean any kind of road: water roads— rivers, oceans, etc.; land roads—trails, railroads, highways; airways.) There is no separate geography, no separate history. The way people live and work is history-geography integrated.

RELATIONSHIPS OF PEOPLE TO ONE ANOTHER. Relationships of people to their environment does not, however, cover all the subject matter in our big theme *Living and Working Together in the United States and in the World.* "The relationships of people to one another" is stated in the official bulletin as the second "basis of social studies materials and activities." Fifth- and sixth-grade children, unlike younger children, are beginning to think of the relationship of work to a "good life" for the worker. When they visit a factory, for instance, their interest in the worker is not merely what he does and how he does it, but often extends to what kind of life he is getting through his work. That is, ten- and eleven-year-old children are beginning to think in terms of values in human relationships, and to care about how people treat one another.

[47] Introductory Overview for Curriculum from Kindergarten through Sixth Grade has been omitted. The same sixth-grade discussion appears on pp. 163 ff., Chapter 9.

They are beginning to build up a conception of "a good life," beginning to identify with larger groups of people and consequently to wish them to have a good life. This is social thinking on a more mature level than social thinking in terms of work processes, of how people use the earth.

Ten- and eleven-year-old children are very uneven in their development of social thinking that involves social standards or values. Even the less mature, however, have codes or standards of behavior for themselves and their personal groups. The more mature extend their standards far beyond their personal groups, even to nations discussing global peace.

These children have lived through a war which affected most of them through their parents, through either actual service or war work. They are living in a postwar period of adjustments which affect many of them directly through their families and all of them through newspapers, magazines, and movies. It is our job to help them, according to their maturity level, to understand this and other complex aspects of living and working together in the United States and in the world.

In discussing social values in current happenings, such as the United Nations or the Good Neighbor Policy, or in historic happenings such as the struggle for independence or the slavery aspect of the Civil War, a teacher can determine how mature her particular children are. Probably all fifth- and sixth-grade children should be given the opportunity to discuss some of the current social happenings and social ideas which are a part of the general talk and atmosphere around them. Nevertheless, there is a distinct danger that these children may form the habit of using words such as "freedom," "democracy," "global peace," without much meaning behind them. Using words without understanding is a dangerous and persistent habit which may well retard genuine social thinking, seeing relationships.

There is less danger of using words without understanding if the children can work out the meaning of these social value words in some kind of action. Even in a discussion, the situation can be dramatized. An unusually mature sixth-grade class wrote a play in which the theme was atomic energy.[48] Another sixth-grade class built up social interests and got them into action by studying the neighborhood.[49]

Ten- and eleven-year-old children are beginning to think in abstractions. But they respond most to abstract social ideas when embodied in individuals or in big, stirring events which they can live through dramatically. Also they need to express abstractions such as "democracy"

[48] Appendix 22: Sixth-Grade Play about Atomic Energy.
[49] See Chapter 16: Glimpses of Teachers in Action.

and "freedoms" in their own ways really to digest them. All the expressive arts—painting, language, music, the dance, drama—help to clarify their ideas as well as give them satisfactions that only creative expression can give. Some outgo aspect is necessary in learning any complex relationships. Probably it is even more necessary in relationships of people to one another than in relationships of people to their environment. These expressive activities meet the need for adventure—trying something of their own—so characteristic of ten- and eleven-year-old children. Planning and executing a group mural is an adventure. Writing and giving a play is an adventure. Planning and carrying through a neighborhood or school undertaking to meet some social need is an adventure. Moreover, all are adventures in "groupness," the development of which underlies all social studies programs.

The following topical outline of subject matter was what the Workshop worked out for the fifth grade after a year's experimentation with different alignments of subject matter.

OUTLINE OF CURRICULUM FOR GRADE 5

THEME: *The United States: Our Lands and People; Our Ties with American Nations.*

I. NEW YORK TODAY: ITS RELATIONS WITH OTHER LANDS AND PEOPLE.
   Trade Relations.
      What Do We Need from Rest of Country?
      What Does Rest of Country Need from Us?
      Why Is New York the Center of Many Roads?
         New York as Port for the Nation.
         Relation of Port to Other Roads.
      Why Have American Nations Surplus Food Materials?
II. THE AMERICAN NATIONS: HOW THEY BEGAN.
   Explorers: How They Found the Americas.
   The Lands and Peoples of the Americas in 1492.
   Settlers in Our Country.
      Why People Left Europe.
      First Homes on Atlantic Coast.
      Settlers Spread to Mississippi.
      Pioneers: Working and Living in New Lands.

III. HOW WE BECAME A NATION.
      Revolution: Struggle for Independence.
      Individuals Who Helped Make Us One Country.
      National Government: Problems in Agreeing on How to Govern
         Ourselves.
IV. YOUNG UNITED STATES GROWS.
      Homes across the Mississippi.
      Far West Becomes a Part of the United States.
      Cities Grow.
      Regional Work of North, South, and West.
      Civil War or War Between the States: Peril to the Union.
      New Roads Help to Build Many Regions into One Nation.
         Canals; Early Railroads; Pony Express.
V. OTHER AMERICAN NATIONS GROW.
      Comparison of Lands and Work of American Nations.
      Canada.
      Mexican and South American Nations.
        Brazil.
        Mexico.
VI. OUR RELATIONS WITH AMERICAN NATIONS.
VII. THE NEED TO BE GOOD NEIGHBOR TO WHOLE WORLD.

Before giving excerpts or summaries of the material written up under the headings of this topical outline, we give one sequence of records to show how, within a unit, one curriculum experience led to another as the Bank Street staff worked with individual teachers.

Records by Bank Street Member on a Fifth-Grade Class.

These first records show an attempt to help children organize their own scattered information about the modern United States into relationships: of work to land; of work to natural resources; of work to science and inventions: to help them get images of the land of the United States as the explorers found it. The later records (from November 7) show how the children expressed their new thinking in a mural and then in an original play. All this kind of thinking was fairly new to the teacher and to these children. The records show the children's responses.

                                October 8

The subject in social studies for this class is "How We Became What We Are." Has begun with explorers of Americas. Has not discussed our present, except in current events. Thinks present should come at end. Formal approach. Using old history curriculum with no modifications. Asks how she can get in geography of New York State. (Old curriculum.) Class has been discussing Columbus. I promised to bring his Log.

October 15

Took class on discussion of the present, "What We Are." Children had information but not organized. Wrote following on board from their suggestions:

Our Country Now
Great nation.
Powers—Navy, Army, Air Force.
Sciences—atom bomb.
Industries—power houses, machines.
Farms—dairies, animals, vegetables, fruits.
Roads—water, highway, railroads, air.
Cities—parks, bridges, zoos.
Country—woods, metals, coal, waterfalls, rivers, oceans, mountains, volcanoes, coal, iron, oil.
People.

I asked children to write about any of above—what use it was to them—what would happen if we had none. . . .

Note to Teacher: October 21
Here are a few thoughts after our discussion in class on October 15th and reading the children's papers.

1. The *combined* information and thinking as shown in their papers makes a fair picture of "What We Have Become." There was no evidence, however, that they differentiated different kinds of lands, food for different purposes, and most of them assumed that coal, metals, were necessary for life—not just for our kind of life today. It was this kind of thing that I was probing for in the discussion with your class, but, as I told you, I probed too far and wide for one session!

2. I suggest that as you proceed with your history-geography, you keep in their minds the various kinds of growth that show "How We Became What We Are."

a. Discovery of various kinds of lands.
b. Settlers who developed the use of these lands.
c. Industry that developed natural resources of coal, metals, oil.

    d. Roads as a necessary development with industry.

    e. Growth in number and kinds of people.

    f. Growth in national unity.

You are started on this now.

3. Also I suggest that as you proceed, you let me help on the geography side, using geography in the large sense to mean kinds of lands and how people learned to use them—all the natural resources from soil to oil. This might mean making a map! We could decide that later.

October 22

I read to the class all the papers which the children had written last week, and the class discussed them.[50] The classification under headings is mine. The spelling and grammar is the children's. In the discussion I tried to lead the children's thinking from the present to the time of explorers which they were studying.

October 29

The teacher thought the next step in making history (explorers) come alive to the children might be a big mural. We discussed various possibilities. Contrast between past and present. Explorers going through different kinds of lands. . . .

Notes by another Bank Street member on this same class.   November 7

Since most of the emphasis in the preceding class discussion had been on how hard it would be to get along without the things we have today, I first tried to get them to think of how to build houses, bridges, etc., on different kinds of land, plains, desert, woodlands.

We talked of what a mural is. They told of some they had seen, in the Museum of Natural History, in the school hall, and of one they had made last year.

Summary of children's answers: "All kinds of things in a mural." "Tells a story." "Can have now and long-ago, here and faraway." "Things you think of together."

After this the children were given paper and crayons to make sketches of anything they chose from today's discussion, from the papers they had written, or from their stories. It could be now or long ago, here or far away. From these we would plan our mural. After sketching, the children stood in turn by groups and explained what they had made.

[50] See Appendix 23: Samples of Children's Papers: Fifth Grade.

Note to Teacher: November 14

There is a great deal of variety in the children's sketches, and I think each one should be appreciated. Even Dorothy did a very good one. Her "Indians in the Boat" is a good attempt. . . .

You might like a trip to the Museum of the City of New York before we actually start the mural. Then they could compare fire engines, loco-motives, ships, etc., of today with those of long ago.

Next time we might have the large paper ready and talk about where to sketch in the different things but not actually do it. This should point up what more they need to know before beginning, and lead to further research.

Note to Teacher: November 19

Summary of discussion of roads:
    Animal trails.
    Railroad followed buffalo trails.
    Mountain passes.
    Modern highways.
    Air routes.
    Ocean and river roads.
    Wagon trails.

At end of short discussion children were asked to sketch some ideas for the mural about roads, showing history or combining ideas in any way they wished. The teacher will carry on during the week and she with the children will decide on a theme for their large mural. . . .

. For the children it would be well to make a list of the ideas you decide to include in the mural and ask the school librarians (sixth-grade chil-dren) to have books out on the various topics when the children go to the library.

A trip to the public library would be in order too, to sit down and do actual research. I'm sure the librarian would be glad to have you come as a class if you arranged for it ahead of time and gave her a list of subjects.

November 26

The teacher worked with part of the class on a play while I took four or five children at a time for work on the mural. They were chosen on the basis of small pictures they had drawn. Discouraged tendency to copy from books. They have very little confidence. While some sketched on the mural, I encouraged others to try things they had not tried before: buffalo, Indians, ponies. Some really got good results.

Record Given to Teacher: January 3

Mural was ready for background. Talked about music, an orchestra, instruments blending together in a pattern.

Mural has many small things. Needs a background that will blend it all together—make it seem like parts of *one* thing.

Children and teacher gave suggestions. . . .

Results

Children's pride in their work has grown steadily. One boy, who was afraid to paint a little car without the teacher's showing him each stroke, proudly painted Indian designs and pointed out to teacher how well he was doing it.

The mural shows a combination of care and freedom in the children. Some things are put on in stiff lines copied from textbooks; some, such as the Indians and pioneers, are drawn from imagination.

In the beginning, the tendency was to be afraid to make a line for fear it wouldn't be just right. Toward the end, and especially in the background, there has been more freedom to experiment a little.

I would say these children need a great deal of encouragement in creating fantastic pictures of their own. Children often get over their stiffness and need for perfection by such suggestions as these:

1. Paint an animal or flower or trees that never were and never could be. Just make them up.
2. Paint a farmer's barn being swept away by a flood.
3. Paint a disaster by fire. . . .

Notes to Teacher: January 9

Your play was very successful and I noticed the audience was really absorbed in it. I believe that we could use both the play and the mural, which have similar ideas, as centers from which to broaden out the children's conception of our country in human terms.

The Trading Scene was very good because it really made history real, as the little girl said.

How about trying to dramatize the people in our mural someday? That would lead into questions of "what kind of people were these anyway who made the roads across our land, who built our cities—where did they come from? In what parts of the United States do they live now? What kind of work do they do?"

In Workshop discussions we worked out the chief *social ideas* to be brought out through experiences and discussion whenever there was an appropriate opportunity. We give these social ideas as they appeared in our first revision of our social studies curriculum.

Fifth Grade:
Each individual is also a member of larger groups: family, Harlem community; New York City, the United States.

Interdependence of regions with different natural resources and workers with different kinds of work.

Our national heroes represent the social thinking of the people.

Natural resources are important to everyone: they should be conserved.

How many kinds of people have built our nation: contribution of workers, now and in our national development; of "immigrant" and "minority" groups, Negroes and others. All are immigrants except Indians.

Democracy, with its freedoms (Declaration of Independence), is an ideal, not yet fully achieved. Present struggles for freedoms—minority groups, unions, etc.

Sixth Grade:
The interdependence of nations: in trade and in threat of war.
The responsibilities of United States in the world.
The struggle for freedom is age-old and still going on.
Every freedom brings a responsibility with it.

TENTATIVE SOCIAL STUDIES CURRICULUM WRITTEN FOR FIFTH GRADE IN OUR SCHOOL

THEME: *The United States: Our Land and People; Our Ties with American Nations.*

In dividing the wide sweep of subject matter in social studies between fifth and sixth grades, we have attempted to postpone the more mature aspects (particularly *social values* in world relations) to the sixth grade. Since the whole world is covered in the official outline of subject matter for the two grades, we have placed all the American nations in grade five. Their early history—explorers, settlers, struggle to become independent nations—parallels our own history in many ways. Also, the lands and peoples of the Americas found by explorers seem a good introduction to the settlers in our own country. Far more time should be spent on the United States, past and present, than on all the other American nations put together. Probably only two, or perhaps three, American nations other than the United States should be studied in any detail.

NEW YORK TODAY: ITS RELATIONS WITH OTHER LANDS AND PEOPLE. Before they reach fifth grade, we hope our children will have had a good many experiences and have gathered a good deal of information which will give them a background about New York today. The emphasis in earlier years, however, is more upon the functioning of the city itself than upon relationships to other lands and people. The first discussions should be to find out what the children know and to pool their information. Such discussions lead naturally to any of the following questions which concern New York's relations with other lands and other people.

Trade Relations.

What Do We Need from Rest of Country? Sources of raw materials for: food (milk, meat, vegetables, fruit), clothes (cotton, wool, rayon, silk), houses (building materials, utilities), machines (metals, coal, transportation, factories). Might discuss where things in room came from—kinds of places and workers. Pull together whatever children know. Might locate sources of raw materials on relief map. Political map undesirable as it does not suggest earth resources.

What Does Rest of Country Need from Us? They need our *products* —largest industries are clothing, printing and publishing (both require many workers and little space). In discussions develop idea of great variety and wealth of our natural resources; of kinds of necessary work; of interdependence of regions and workers. Some trips to show New York's dependence on rest of U. S. (docks at Harlem River or Hudson at 125th St. or Riverside Drive, or big station), and our contribution to rest of United States (clothing factory or equivalent).

Why Is New York the Center of Many Roads? Discuss New York as *port for the nation.* Three water roads meet at New York: routes over ocean, opposite Europe; routes from New England over Long Island Sound; route to West over Hudson and Mohawk Rivers and Great Lakes. New York *Harbor*—channels, pilot maps, etc.—is in charge of Federal Government because of its national importance in trade. Railroads, trucks, boats handle goods for shipment or goods arriving. New York also center for air roads. Study transportation maps. During war large proportion of troops and war materials were shipped from New York;

in present postwar period food is shipped for starving nations of Europe.

Why Have American Nations Surplus Food Materials? Discuss food shortages in Europe: contributions from United States; from other American nations. This or any other relevant current happening might be made an introduction to the Americas and to a plan for the year's work.

The study of New York today should be continued parallel to study of past of United States and of other countries. These opening discussions are by way of orientation rather than detailed information, and should not cover too much time.

Suggested science experiments as background for understanding work processes and inventions used in transportation and industries: water displacement and buoyancy of boats; power of steam; tides and Spuyten Duyvil and Hell Gate.

Suggested reading for children and materials to read to them in Bibliography.

THE AMERICAN NATIONS: HOW THEY BEGAN.

Explorers: How They Found the Americas. Here we suggested that some time be spent on Columbus as a person and as a representative of his time—what Europeans knew of the world; the stage of scientific development; the urge to reach Asia by a sea route; a good chance to make their social studies program synchronize with celebration of Columbus Day (appropriate for an assembly play). If it is brought out that Columbus's explorations were for Spain and that Spain followed up discovery by vigorous explorations in both North and South America and established claims to vast areas, the transition to next topic is a natural one.

The Lands and Peoples of Americas in 1492. The Americas might well be approached as a whole before beginning details of explorers or settlers. Have the children look at a graphic relief map of North and South America together. Get them to pick out the broad physiographic features, what geographers call the "continental build." High land, close to the western shore, runs from Alaska to the southern tip of South America. The Aleutian Islands are parts of this same great mountain range which have sunk so that now only the tops of the mountains show above water. The high land is broad in North America—two high mountain ranges with high, dry plateaus between. Mexico is just the southern continuation of this high land—the two mountain ranges with high plateau between. The two ranges join and form the narrow, twisting strip of land, the Isthmus of Panama, connecting the two continents.

East of the mountains in North America is the vast lowland, sometimes called the "great depression," built in past ages by erosion from western and eastern mountain islands. In South America is another vast lowland, the Amazon basin, also built from western and eastern mountain islands. Highlands of Brazil were once an island. The three great river systems, Orinoco, Amazon, and La Plata, all rise near one another in land so flat that in floods the three systems join. The Great Plains of North America (in United States and Canada) are similar to the pampas of South America in climate as well as topography.

There will not be time to go into the many differing Indian cultures that the explorers found in these differing lands. The relation between the ways of living and working and the lands the different Indians used should, however, be brought out. The three great Indian cultures in Mexico, Central and South America—Inca, Aztec, and Mayan (absorbed by Aztecs before 1492)—were all in the warm climate zones—as were early advanced cultures everywhere. All of them had developed farming to a high level; also metalworking. The lands of these advanced Indian cultures were explored and later settled by the Spanish. In the lands that are now the United States, the Indians were hunters, knowing little about farming or about working metals. The Indians in the harsh climates of the extreme north (Eskimos) and the extreme south (Patagonians) were even less advanced. No animals in either North or South America were very good for domestic use—no cows, horses, pigs, or sheep; the llama probably the best. Everywhere, however, Indians had skillfully adapted their work to meet their needs of food, clothes, and shelter from what they found in their particular environments. Appreciation of the ways of working of various Indians, through museum trips or dramatizations, makes the lands they used seem real and significant.

Science experiments to explain types of land, rainfall, and temperature.

Indians everywhere had beliefs, laws, and codes of behavior in human relations. The social standards of the Incas is worth some time. . . .

This meeting of two cultures—two ways of living and working—and what happened, should be discussed as explorers and then settlers spread over the New World, as Europeans called the ancient homeland of the Indians.

It is suggested that only a few explorers be taken up after Columbus, and that they be chosen from the point of view of kinds of lands that are important in the present-day American nations rather than from establishing political claims.

Settlers in Our Country. Emphasize that land hunger brought settlers from crowded Europe and kept them moving west into new "free lands"; the search for different kinds of freedoms; applied to any appropriate current happening.

First Homes on Atlantic Coast. Opposite Europe. Emphasis on kinds of lands settlers used and what work and attitudes this made them develop rather than on details of separate colonies. Description of differences in land in South and in North. South became agricultural—big plantations with slave labor; North turned to shipbuilding and early industries run by water power. Northern mills needed Southern crops, particularly cotton, and Southern colonists needed finished goods that Northern colonists imported and later made. Pressing need for roads developed *post roads*. Locate both Boston and Albany Post Roads on modern automobile map. Old milepost 167th St. and Amsterdam Ave. Model map of Atlantic coastal plain and Appalachians.

Settlers Spread to Mississippi. Why settlers went West: to have own land in hard-to-reach places where they could arrange their own lives. Emphasis on using up good soil in South; more need of slaves on plantation than in Northern mills and trade; indentured servants—reasons why they gained their freedom, whereas few Negroes did; new crops in South today partly to displace cotton; experiments with peanuts and soya beans; work of George Washington Carver.

Science experiments for children: water wheel; erosion.

Pioneers: Working and Living in New Lands. Stress the *natural* roads they used and *man-made* roads they developed; adventures, hardships, and freedoms they had; the kinds of lands they came to as they went West.

Model map of Rocky Mountains.

How pioneers met their needs for food, houses, tools in these various regions; what Indians they met and how they treated the Indians. Discuss what settlers cared about—land of their own, schools, religion. Dramatization of pioneer life centered around an individual such as Boone or a region.

HOW WE BECAME A NATION.

Revolution: Struggle for Independence. Conflict in interests of England and colonists, different conflicts in North and South. Dramatic presentation of Stamp Act; tax on tea; Boston Tea Party; Lexington; Declaration of Independence. War itself done briefly. Emphasis on why people fought: how North and South united against England.

Individuals Who Helped Make Us One Country. Make these people human beings. Use direct source materials. (See Bibliography.)

Washington—bring out that he was a surveyor as a boy and after the Revolution he planned the great highways and canals which were later built to connect East and West. . . .

Use relief map to show draining of rivers.

Jefferson—bring out his desire for free schools, his inventions in White House, his belief in the workers.

Franklin—bring out early life as printer, his scientific curiosities, "Unite or Die," which led him to suggest our two houses in Congress, his acquaintance with Europe and European ways as well as American ways.

Alexander Hamilton—because he lived near our school.

Tom Paine—See Bibliography.

National Government: Problems in Agreeing on How to Govern Ourselves. Dramatic scene in Hall of Independence, Philadelphia, with delegates from states trying to agree on Constitution. Bring out difference in interests of North and South, of large and small states. . . .

States were admitted in pairs—a slave and not-slave balance. Who were the first voters? Negroes and women excluded. Jefferson, a Southerner, wanted Negroes to have vote. Idea that democracy is still growing —still needs working on.

YOUNG UNITED STATES GROWS.

Homes across the Mississippi. Pioneers found the great flat grass plains stretching to Rocky Mountains. New kind of land for farming settlers. No steel plow to cut the sod. No trees to build houses out of. Buffaloes everywhere. Sod houses and slaughter of buffaloes on the Great Plains, and changes in agriculture with invention of steel plow. No stones. Good land for big wheat ranches. Farther West near mountains too dry for wheat. Became the *cow country* after slaughter of the buffaloes. Cowboy life and songs.

Discuss increasing dryness as you go West, which means thinner, shorter grass. Work out rainfall and temperature on a relief map. Pioneers were stopped for a time by the Rocky Mountains, the great stretch of high half-desert land, and the Sierra Nevada, which separated the Great Plains from the fertile valleys near the Pacific Coast.

Far West Becomes a Part of the United States. Spaniards had settled the Pacific Coast almost as early as the English had settled the Atlantic. Spain had explored all of what is now South America (except Brazil),

Mexico, southern and southwestern parts of the United States of America, and the Pacific Coast.

The French had explored up the St. Lawrence, around the Great Lakes and down the Mississippi to the Gulf of Mexico. France therefore claimed the land near those waterways and land west of Mississippi. (Pioneers found Indians everywhere. At first Indians were friendly, but when they found that the pioneers intended to take their land away from them, they became hostile. So pioneers had Indians to fight and sometimes the French. But the French had not made homes in this inland country and could not defend their rights. They had established trading posts and missions on the great rivers. These they defended. But there was plenty of good land where pioneers could settle and the French hardly knew it. Squatters took possession of unoccupied land. This brought about rival claims to land among European countries.)

Spanish claimed Florida and all south and west of French possessions to Pacific Coast.

After the Revolution our pioneers began to cross lands claimed by both Spain and France west of the Mississippi. Explorations of Lewis and Clark.

Discovery of gold in the Sierra Nevada. This began the gold rush to California. What roads could the "Forty-Niners" use? Across the Isthmus of Panama; or across Great Plains, over Rockies, across high, dry plateaus, over the Sierra in covered wagons—and no road! Stories of Donner party, gold miners, development of great ranches in valleys of California. . . .

We could not use this land of the Far West fully until better roads from Mississippi Valley to Pacific Coast had been built.

Cities Grow. Roads and cities are necessarily closely related. Cities are distributing centers for surrounding areas. Interesting to have children study map from Atlantic to Rockies and explain why our chief cities grew up where they did. . . .

Cities brought new kinds of needs, new kinds of work relationships between different regions. City people cannot raise or mine materials needed for food, clothes, shelter, or local factories. The self-sustaining community became rarer as work interrelationships between farms and cities developed.

Regional Work of North, South, and West. Development of characteristic work based upon natural earth conditions. The North had poor soil and poor climate for farming as compared with South. The North early began trade, business, and industrial development, but its great industrial growth came after the Civil War. The South, with its good soil, warm climate, flat plains, remained primarily agricultural; only in recent time has South developed many industries. The newly settled lands west of the Mississippi were also suited to agriculture. Wheat left the Atlantic Coast for the flat, stoneless Great Plains; cattle (for meat) grazed on the drier lands to the west when the buffalo had been slaughtered. Rivalry between industrial, business North and agricultural South for the products and markets of the West was one of the great causes of the war between North and South. Mississippi River with its many tributaries was a natural road for the products of the West. This threw the trade to the South. The North, therefore, was eager to build man-made roads in order to secure the trade with the West—receive the farm products of the West and sell their own industrial products. The great road-building period, however, was interrupted by war.

Civil War or War Between the States: Peril to the Union. It was not easy for a big new country with many kinds of people doing different kinds of work to develop unity. Conflict of economic and work interests between agricultural South and business and industrial North influenced their attitudes toward slavery. . . .

The sides were divided largely by a climate line, for climate largely determined the work interests. . . .

(Would not go into battles; rather keep the war on level of social ideas and regional work. Union is saved.) Partial democracy extended to Negroes in Emancipation Proclamation. Chance for a unit on Lincoln and Lee as two great Americans. . . .

New Roads Help to Build Many Regions into One Nation. The War Between the States and freeing of the slaves left the agricultural South depleted. The North boomed ahead in industry and business and in road building. After the war we needed new things and ways to use our land. Inventions begun long ago were now developed and used. We explored and opened up our rich natural resources. We built many new factories. We needed and built new roads.

Present dramatically the building and use of *Canals, Early Railroads;* the *Pony Express.*

OTHER AMERICAN NATIONS GROW.

This section should be brief as compared with time spent on the growth of the United States. No attempt can be made to cover all American nations.

Comparison of Lands and Work of Other American Nations. Their development and their lands should be constantly compared with that of the United States. Refer back to *Lands and Peoples of the Americas.* Are same kinds of lands used for same kinds of work? In discussions with good relief maps, the children can readily figure out the chief work of various regions. Also the main features of climate (temperature and rainfall). They will see that the great grass plains in Canada and Argentina would be used for cattle grazing as they are in the United States. They can figure out where the good farmlands would be—where soil would have accumulated from erosion and where there would be enough rain. The temperature (distance from equator combined with height) would determine the kind of crops grown. . . . Difficulty in transportation through Amazon basin has kept white men from settling there. Native Indians have gathered rubber from wild rubber trees until recently. Rubber plantations have been started there. Great coffee plantations near the coast. In the mountains would be the metals and consequently mining. In South America transportation has always been difficult and still is. Slight development of roads as compared with U. S. Comparatively small coal deposits, water power far from eastern coast, has delayed industrialization. Therefore, South America has remained primarily agricultural and mining land.

Science. This general discussion of the lands and climates of the Americas and their use in modern times is a strategic time to find out what the children have digested in scattered experiments and what more they need to pull their information together into generalizations on earth science and the implications for human work everywhere.

As a background for the growth of modern Mexican and South American cultures the children should recall that the various native Indian cultures were very different from one another. Three great Indian civilizations developed in the warm band flanking the equator, with primitive culture in cold south (just as in cold north of North America). These Indian cultures in tropic zone had developed agriculture and mining, particularly gold and silver. To plunder these riches was the chief purpose of the early Spanish explorers. Later, settlers used these agricultural Indians virtually as slaves.

All of above must be done briefly but dramatically, if not already covered.

The history of all modern American nations began in Europe. All were explored and settled by Europeans. All had pioneers; they were all colonists at first; they all finally became independent of their mother countries—all except Canada fought revolutions to become independent nations. In broad terms, the American nations have much in common.

The question might be raised why so many nations grew in South America—why Spanish colonies did not form a United States of South America as the English colonies formed the United States. Two reasons largely determined the growth of separate nations. (1) The policy of Spain was to keep trade relations of each colony confined to its mother country, Spain. Trade between the colonies was discouraged—even forbidden. (2) There was, therefore, no urge to build roads connecting the colonies such as there was in the United States. Moreover, distances and difficulties in road building were even greater in South America than in the United States. The Andes are almost twice as high as either Rockies or Sierra. Either the Andes or the vast swamps of the Amazon basin (in Portuguese Brazil) had to be crossed to connect northern with southern colonies. Only in recent "air age" has quick travel in South America become possible.

Of the twenty American nations (besides the United States), only two or three can be studied, and even these not in great detail. In this curriculum originally we included notes on Canada, Mexico, and Brazil, though other nations might be chosen, particularly if any current happenings turn public attention to them. The notes were merely a synopsis of the chief social and historic happenings in Canada, Mexico, and Brazil. These factual notes were to be supplemented by direct experiences: trips to museums, to docks where produce is arriving, or to stores where products are sold; by research and crafts, which might well eventuate in a play written by the children with stage sets.

Canada was written up with more emphasis on the present than the past; similarly to U. S. in geographical forms, ways of living, use of same machines. Also how we share in the use of the Great Lakes, Niagara for electricity; and that we have preserved friendly relations over a long period of time across the long, unfortified boarder.

Mexico and South American Nations. Under this heading the first approach was through heroes: *Bolivar,* who came from Venezuela but belongs to all South America because he led the revolutions of all Spanish colonies in South America (that is, all except Brazil), and *San Martin* of Argentina. Bolivar was called "The Liberator" and "The George Washington" of the south. He was not satisfied with independence of separate nations but dreamed of a great American league of nations. Some dramatic background history was written up, as, for instance, how during the revolution the President of Haiti, the Negro republic, gave Bolivar ships and money, asking only that Bolivar free the slaves if he came into power. Slavery was outlawed in the Spanish colonies in 1825.

We felt that one modern nation in the south should be done more intensively. Mexico and Brazil seemed to offer the best possibilities, and their past and present were written up through heroes with a background of their lands and natural resources, past relations with their mother country, and present trade relations with the United States. (Two sixth-grade classes developed original plays when studying this section. One play was about Bolivar and Washington, the other about Juárez and Lincoln.)

OUR RELATIONS WITH AMERICAN NATIONS.

In this unit the information children had already gathered in previous units was pulled together and supplemented. Our ties with other American nations were brought down to date through discussion of the *Good Neighbor Policy* and Franklin D. Roosevelt, the part American nations took in World War II and are taking in the United Nations.

The curriculum closed with:

THE NEED TO BE GOOD NEIGHBOR TO WHOLE WORLD. This section should be omitted or developed according to the maturity of the children. Discussions of any current world problems such as food shortages, possibly some current happening in the United Nations, would form a natural transition to world relations in grade six.

We have already told how the subject matter for fifth and sixth grades was planned together throughout the year and a half in which our school experimented in a social studies curriculum for the whole school, and the basis upon which we divided the subject matter between the two grades. The outline of the subject matter planned for the sixth grade as it appeared in our second revision follows:

OUTLINE OF CURRICULUM FOR GRADE 6
THEME: *Our Country and Its Ties with the Rest of the World.*

I. PRESENT POSTWAR CONDITIONS IN THE UNITED STATES.
II. HOW WE BECAME THE MODERN UNITED STATES.
    Reconstruction Period.
    How We Became an Industrial Nation: The Machine Age.
        Inventions and Science.
    Regional Work and Interdependence of Parts of Country.

How We Became a Nation of People Drawn from All Over the
World.
III. MODERN UNITED STATES AS RELATED TO THE WORLD.
Our Country Is Now a Part of Whole World.
Global Roads.
Global Trade and Raw Materials.
The United States in Two World Wars.
IV. OUR TIES WITH THE OLD WORLD.
Eurasia: Its Lands and Peoples.
Our Ties with Europe.
The Mediterranean World: Our Heritage.
Our Heritage from England.
England and Commonwealth of Nations and Empire.
Our Ties with Asia.
China: Its Lands and People.
Soviet Russia: Its Lands and People.
V. MODERN UNITED STATES AMONG WORLD NATIONS.
Postwar Conditions in the World.
The United Nations.
The Future.
Science and Inventions Still Going On.
Democracy Still Growing in United States; In World.

It will be seen that once more we began with the immediate present in which children and all the rest of us were living. The discussion of postwar conditions which we felt sixth-grade children were
mature enough to profit by highlighted the United States as an industrial nation and made a natural transition to the unit that followed: the development of the machine age. (Our curriculum for
the fifth grade had taken us chronologically to the Civil War, which
coincided with the beginning of the machine age.) In moving toward global thinking with children, we took up the more objective
work aspect of roads and trade, and continued to use New York as
a laboratory with a new emphasis—that of a port for the nation. The
teachers of fifth and sixth grades agreed readily on this introductory
unit in the curriculum for grade six.

There was much more disagreement, however, when in the second
part of the curriculum (IV and V on Outline) we came to the prob-

lem of how to acquaint eleven-year-old children with the cultures of
other peoples of the world. Everyone felt that the organization of
the United Nations in San Francisco and later the meetings in New
York were current history of the utmost significance. Our problem
was how to give sixth-graders experiences which would help them
to sympathetic appreciation and understanding of cultures unlike
our own as a background for the United Nations and for the place
of our nation among world nations. Some teachers, still wedded to
the old curriculum, were content to locate other nations on the globe.
Most of the teachers, however, agreed with Bank Street that we
should attempt a few intensive experiences (units in the school vocabulary) in the cultures (the ways of living and working) of other
nations. The question remained: Which nations?

After much discussion the decision was reached that children must
be given some real background on Europe, with emphasis on England but including the Commonwealth of Nations and the Empire,
and on one other nation composing the Big Five. The teachers
wished both China and Soviet Russia written up in our curriculum
so that a teacher could choose between them. The task of writing
the sixth-grade curriculum with the necessary background content
proved so heavy a one for the Bank Street staff that the suggested
firsthand experiences for children through trips and science experiments were never written up in detail. However, the Bank Street
staff members working with the teachers developed some firsthand
experiences out of the content of the curricula described here. From
our wealth of records we have chosen just one sequence which shows
how a group of children, beginning with a study of the land and its
people, go on to expression through creative language and finally to
identification with these people through free dramatization. The following notes give the details of the process which led up to a play.[51]

October 2

I hung up a large graphic relief map of the Americas. Mrs. E.
turned class over to me. Asked children to look at South America,
think what people could use this land for. What do modern people need?

[51] Appendix 24: Sixth-Grade Play: A Visit to Mexico.

Children at once said, "Farms," "Food." Children came up to map and picked out good place for farm. Wanted sun, rain, and soil. Quite articulate children. Discussed climate from map. Too hot and low. Jungle. Decided to have farms nearer coast. Suggested coffee and banana crops. Grasslands. Decided to raise cattle there.

Another child said people needed metals. Would-be miners raised hands. Immediately said they would use mountains for iron, gold, and silver. Some said coal? One child said little coal in South America. I showed them where it was. Child suggested people needed cities. Decided cities needed harbors. Located industries near coal. Discussion whether water power in Andes was available. Thought it too far from east coast.

Very intelligent children. Eager. Ready to think. Mrs. E. seemed to have easy friendly relation with them. Pleased that children were thinking. At end she said, "Next time we must do some geography." I answered, "I think we've been doing geography." She seemed surprised so I volunteered, "You mean political geography?"

October 24

Mrs. E. turned the class over to me. I began by asking what things in Mexico or South America they would like to see or hear. Answers were, "Condor," "A mountain," "A llama," etc. Difficult to get them to think in terms of images. I asked how they thought it would feel to be a condor. Almost every child answered with gestures rather than words. Mrs. E. asked them to write imagining they were an animal, or a person, or an object in Mexico or South America. I picked up their papers the next day. Wrote a few words on each trying to make them *feel*. Children's language is all intellectual. They need to be released in dramatic action.

October 31

Passed gourds around for children to see. Gave back their papers. Asked the mountain climbers how they would feel if they were really climbing. They said they would get hot. Finally that they would start in a hot valley and have to put on clothes when they got to cool top. One child said you would be breathless. We discussed other papers in the same way. These children have never thought of expressing *themselves* in language. To them, language is a way of reporting what other people have written about.

November 8

Gave back their papers with good parts marked with appreciative remarks. Tried to make them show how they would act if they really were the animals they were writing about. Boys crazy to act like burros. They acted out being stubborn most realistically. One boy made it into a kind of stylized dance. A girl was a snake. A boy was a condor. Children got very hilarious. All wanted to act at once. The papers which they wrote after this show much greater freedom and imagination.

Following are a few of the papers which they wrote:

The Condor is a very huge bird. It's eyes and nose is more sharper than ours. If it is flying through the air and smells a dead animal it circles down, down, and down. The Condor's feet are pulled up like the wheels of an airplane. On the way down it uses it's sharp eyes. As soon as it spies it's pray it glides. You can imagine how it's wings go. One wing goes down while the other goes up. Then the other goes down while the other goes up. As he is landing his feet are stuck out and he land. When he starts eating imagine a farmer coming, the Black Condor grabs his pray and soars into the air. It goes to it's nest and the Condor family have a feast.

I can imangin myself being a lama withe my fur and long neck and when I got mad at somebody I would turn arond and spit in his face but I think it is sort of silly to spit at somebody when I got mad at somebody. If I were a lama I would turn arond and kick him in the face it would do much more harm than just spiting at him and so thats what I would do if I was a lama

Have you ever closed your eyes and imagined you were some sort of animal or a high mountain. If you would like to be a mountain just close your eyes and imagine that you are a high, beautiful mountain with a lake and some grass beneath you. Overlooking feilds. Cattle grazing, farms houses tall trees and rivers flowing out the sea and all sorts of beautiful things and when you open your eyes you might still think your a mountain.

November 14

Tried an experiment with the children. Asked them to close eyes while I said common words and afterwards to tell what they saw or heard or felt. First word was "high." Second was "soft." Third was "green." An extraordinary range of concrete images came out. Almost every child wanted to tell what he saw. Told them they should get these concrete, vivid images into their writing if they wanted the reader to see and feel what they themselves were seeing and feeling. Took the general word "go." They named many things that go. Train, boat, airplane, victrola record, submarine, horse, rabbit, clock, sun, etc. Mrs. E. wrote these on board. The children then gave words which would describe concretely how these various things go. A surprisingly large vocabulary and a good sense of the sound quality that some words possessed. All they need is encouragement.

Note written to teacher during this period.   November 21

Dear Mrs. E.:

Since there is so little time when we can talk, perhaps it would be well for me to write out what I have been trying to do with your children in language. I have not aimed at correct forms—grammar, spelling, punctuation, etc.—not because I think these techniques are unimportant but because I take it for granted you are attending to them. I have been trying to make the children sensitive to language as an art; to thinking in terms of images, sound and muscle images as well as visual; to choosing exact words rather than general words; to enjoy expressing their feelings in words in the same way that they enjoy expressing them in paint. I think their response has, on the whole, been satisfactory. The question is what next?

If I were to go on with creative writing with your class, my next step would be to read them some prose or verse with strong rhythm, sound quality and pattern, and attempt to get them to analyze it. Then to experiment with their own language. I don't know how much more time you want to spend on this. Perhaps you can carry on as well without me? I wish your children could do some group writing like a play with language and dramatic expression combined. I believe they would do it well and get real satisfaction from it. [This class later wrote its play, "A Visit to Mexico." Appendix 24.]

It is interesting to note that in this chapter we have referred to three original plays developed by the children out of the content of their social studies program. Actually, each is different from the other with respect to the kind of satisfactions and creative experience which the children enjoyed. In "Mary's Coat" [52] the jingle form and play with language that was involved was even more important to the children than the social concepts which were being clarified. Between the jingle form of "Mary's Coat" and the sweep of dramatic

[52] Appendix 21: Notes Kept by Bank Street Member Working in the Sixth Grade on "Consumers" and "Mary's Coat."

movement which the children created in their atomic play there was impressive contrast closely related to the contrasting meanings and feelings of the material. This is so naturally achieved by children that it is often not recognized for what it really is, namely, a basic aesthetic experience. This same general idea is once more illustrated in the forms which the play about Mexico took on.[53] Vastly more significant than the dialogue of this play were the beautiful props that the children assembled, the choreographic pattern which developed almost spontaneously, the rich use of music in songs and dance. Here was content which had its fullest expression through color and motion, in contrast to the more deeply dramatic form and content in the play on atomic energy or to the light, lilting quality of the play about a child's coat.

TENTATIVE SOCIAL STUDIES CURRICULUM WRITTEN FOR SIXTH GRADE IN OUR SCHOOL

We now give the written curriculum materials as planned for our school. Only a few parts can be given in full.

THEME: *Our Country and Its Ties with the Rest of the World.*

In this period of transition from separate courses in history, geography, and civics to an integrated program in social studies, it is particularly necessary for a teacher of sixth grade to know what subject matter her children have covered. Also, since the subject matter in grades five and six is treated together in the official bulletin, and the divisions between the grades left largely to the individual schools and teachers, a teacher of sixth grade should know in detail the curriculum planned for fifth grade and, more specifically, what aspects have been studied by the children.

The subject matter in the following curriculum begins the study of past United States and our ties with the rest of the world on a relatively young level where many firsthand experiences can form a background for understanding, and postpones to the end of the year those aspects of world relations in which the children cannot have an active part. Much time is planned for the development of inventions and science, with trips and experiments. The study of world relations begins with global

[53] Appendix 24: Sixth-Grade Play: A Visit to Mexico.

roads and trade, where, again, appropriate trips and experiments are available.

Sixth-grade children, however, are in the preadolescent stage where concern for human relationships begins to bulk large—their own place in their families and their community—and, with many children, concern for the *values* at home and in world relations has more meaning than in fifth grade. By the end of the year, most eleven- or twelve-year-old children are interested in the social values of the United Nations, for instance, though they cannot usually sustain a prolonged interest in a situation where their only active part is in "research."

PRESENT POSTWAR CONDITIONS IN THE UNITED STATES.

Some brief discussions about current happenings related to postwar conditions might be a good introduction to the year's program in social studies. Probably most of them will be aware of rise in prices; of the struggle for increased wages among workers; of difficulties in securing jobs; of the United Nations as an effort to secure global peace. This opening section should be for orientation rather than detailed information. It should give the teacher a sense of what information and interests her particular class brings to social problems and ideas at home or in the larger world, and give the children a sense of what the year's program will cover.

HOW WE BECAME THE MODERN UNITED STATES.

Reconstruction Period. Compare the adjustments in North and South after War Between the States with present adjustments after World War II. Bring out the difference in industrial development in the two periods. Recall (from grade five) that the South was primarily agricultural and the North was turning more and more to industry and business. The South was left depleted from war and loss of slave workers. . . . The North boomed ahead in industry and business. Exploitation of South by North. . . . Did emancipation of slaves give Negroes equal freedom with white people? Have Negroes yet equal opportunities? Carry this discussion as far as it seems wise.

How We Became an Industrial Nation: The Machine Age. (Allow plenty of time for this section.) Machines created new needs, new ways of using our land. We explored and opened our hitherto unused natural resources now needed for new factories, for new inventions. United States, which had been a great agricultural nation, now became also a great industrial nation.

New Industries. First need was machines to make machines. Factories and mills needed coal and steel. Great activity in coal mining, both hard and soft; in opening iron mines and steel mills. Why were industrial centers in the North? Locate early ones on map in economic atlas by nearness to coal and iron.

New Roads. Recall development of roads (in grade five). What are our most recent inventions in transportation and communication? Automobile Highways. Superhighways. (Possibly study U. S. 1, Lincoln Highway. See Triborough Bridge.) Airways.

New Ways of Communication. Telegraph built same time as railroad to West. Trouble with buffaloes. Trains held up. Telegraph poles rubbed down. Buffalo Bill killed buffaloes for food for railroad builders. Cowboy period followed slaughter of buffaloes. Telephone, Cable, Wireless, Radio.

Modern Inventions and Machines. New technique in mass production. Effect of machines on farming. Science of soil. (George Washington Carver could come here if not taken up elsewhere.)

Oil Fields. Why so many derricks; oil pipelines and pumping stations; refineries—gasoline and lubricating oils. Find out where oil used in New York comes from, how it gets here.

Steel. Discuss its many uses; its production; raw materials of coal, iron, and limestone; locate these raw materials, explain why these are found in these regions. Locate early and later steel mills, discuss why they were in those places.

Power. Early mills run by water wheels; later use of water power through building dams as source of electricity; coal for direct power or to make electricity; oil, diesel engines. Atomic energy: if this is discussed, extend the idea of atomic energy from destructive bomb to possible use in industries. Arrange for some trips to show big industries. Discuss work in factories as compared with farms; work on early farms as compared with modern mechanized farms.

Science. As much background for understanding modern inventions as possible. Simple explanations of origin of soil, coal, oil. Experiments in classroom and research in books. (See Bibliography.)

How We Became a Nation of People Drawn from All Over the World. Early growth in people. After Civil War and Reconstruction, we needed people to develop our large land; to open mines, work in new factories, build new roads. These were the days of great immigration—in one year a million people came to the United States. Where did people come from? Where did they go? What kind of lives did they have? Feature any national group in class.

Ancestors of people in present New York City and United States. Everyone except Indians are "immigrants." Place old homes of present United States citizens on globe. Examine names on neighborhood stores. Trips in New York to centers such as "Little Italy," Chinatown, or any other group of special interest to the children—perhaps have luncheon at some of these places.

MODERN UNITED STATES AS RELATED TO THE WORLD.

Our Country Is Now a Part of Whole World. (Discussion and research according to the maturity of the children.)

First discussions should pull together what the children know about other parts of the world and our world relations, and orient them in thinking of our land on the globe, and our nation as a member of a world group of nations and races. The earth should be thought of in broad terms—great land masses and bodies of water, bands of climate (rain and temperature), natural vegetation, elevation, and what products these great regions yield. This kind of thinking about the earth should precede and form a background for thinking about the kinds of lives people live in these regions, and the division of these regions into nations. Complicated political relations can only be vague to eleven-year-old children. Relations should be emphasized throughout. Classrooms should have a large globe which can be painted or chalked on without injury. A number of small globes (Woolworth, 15¢) are also desirable.[54]

The war and the United Nations have made everyone talk and think about the *global* world. The United States has become linked to faraway places that seemed unimportant to us a short time ago, some places that we never even heard of before the war. Our country used to think of itself as largely apart from other nations, not needing them much and not being threatened by them.

Global Roads. Panama Canal shortened global road for boats. (Grade five.) Now the two great oceans no longer separate us in time from the Old World. Now all parts of the world can be reached quickly by airplane from every other part. Discuss need for international air route agreements such as United States has with Canada. In the war neutral nations did not allow planes to fly over them. Discuss need of *air bases*. On the globe pick out important points for air bases. Importance of Alaska in air transportation; of Canada; of Philippines and other Pacific islands; of Dakar, of Natal, etc. Children can judge of these places by flying distances without knowing names.

[54] See fourth-grade material with less mature concepts.

Global Trade and Raw Materials. What we get in products. The war showed us how much we depend upon products of other lands. The sources of the chief products which we import because we cannot produce them in our own country might be spotted on the globe with color symbols.

What we give in products. Discuss our exports before, during, and after the war. Needs of other countries due to war. Possibly explain UNRRA (now it would be Marshall Plan). What foods have we in excess of our own needs? What manufactured goods? What raw materials? Europe's, Russia's, China's needs for food, manufactured goods, raw materials. Make simple chart of what we have and what we need for ourselves.

The United States in Two World Wars. Let the children tell what they know. Our industrial and farm response during war. Discuss *why we were involved.* Spot countries involved on globe. Tie this up with what raw materials these countries have or need and do not have. No need to go into war campaigns.

OUR TIES WITH THE OLD WORLD.

To understand other nations we must know something about their lands. For the lands in which people live condition the work they do and, in a large measure, how they live.

Eurasia: Its Lands and Peoples. Here followed background content.

Europe and Asia are really one great land mass. There is no natural boundary between them. The Ural Mountains are so low in places that the Russians took boats over them during the war. The Western (European) nations developed around the Mediterranean (Middle-of-the-Earth) Sea and near the Atlantic Ocean. The Eastern (Asiatic) nations developed near the Pacific and Indian Oceans.

Our Ties with Europe. Until recently we in the United States have not thought much about other nations except those in *Europe.* Reason for this is largely historic. Study of our history and ancestry of people in New York and United States shows our ties with Europe. European settlers brought over their ways of living, working, believing, which we have developed into our American way. . . .

The Mediterranean World. Our Heritage. Under this heading were suggestions as to how to trace briefly a few of our inheritances from the Mediterranean cultures. For instance: Egypt, language and writing; Greece, first experiment in democracy, yet they maintained slavery (as did the United States in its early years); Rome, science and inventions (aqueducts, roads, etc.), laws.

Recall the Mediterranean world at the time of Columbus. Recall fifth-grade discussion of his times; of revival of interest in art and science; what the Europeans then knew of the rest of the world; the urge to explore for trade.

Discuss any current happenings in Mediterranean world which have meaning for these children, particularly trade and raw materials; possession of Gibraltar; why England feels she needs Suez Canal; immigration of Jews to Palestine.

Our Heritage from England. Our closest historic ties are with *England.* She was the mother country of the thirteen colonies that banded together to form the United States. From England we inherited our language, our form of government, our jury system, the idea of unions. However, in the United States people whose ancestors came from every European country, from Africa, from Asia, built our nation.

England and Commonwealth of Nations and Empire. Very briefly discussed largely in reference to recent war happenings which the children know about.

Our Ties with Asia. Before airplanes and before the war, Asia seemed so far away as to be almost unreal to us. Now we think and talk all the time about two Asiatic countries—Japan, who attacked the United States in December 1941, and China, who was our ally in the war and is one of the Big Five in the United Nations. Another one of the Big Five is Soviet Russia, which stretches over part of Europe and all of northern Asia. *Asiatic or Eastern nations* today and their recent past can be done only in broad terms.

We felt that one nation should be chosen for more intensive study; most teachers preferred either China or Soviet Russia. Both were consequently written up. We give the classroom approach in the unit on China, but omit all the rest of this section since a good deal of the subject matter concerning China, India, and the Soviet Union which was worked out by the Workshop group is now actually out-of-date.

This, we believe, is a very important point in all curriculum planning. Curriculum, particularly in social studies, does get out-of-date, needs revision and constant evaluation. Curriculum today cannot be static because of the changing world we live in.

China: Its Lands and People. Classroom Approach. If the children have already discussed and studied relief maps of Eurasia before marking the political boundaries of China on their group or individual maps, they will have a foundation for understanding some of the complexities of modern China. As far as possible, keep the children wondering *how* and *why* the Chinese developed their particular ways of living, how these ways are different and how like our own ways. For sixth-grade children a study of a foreign country should constantly refer back to their own country. They should be learning more about our ways as they study the ways of other people.

Try to get the children to put themselves in the place of the Chinese; to see the beauty and variety and size of their land; to work with them in the paddy fields and on the canal boats; to understand and feel what it would be like to live in a country with few schools, few railroads, few highways; to understand what Westerners like ourselves, with Western customs and traditions, would seem like to these people, with their age-old customs and traditions. Try to make the children feel that having different ways from ours does not necessarily mean being inferior to us, that though we are superior in industrial developments and in money-making pursuits, these are not the only human accomplishments that make for a good life.

Dramatization, either brief and impromptu or a longer play written by the children, with stage sets and costumes, is one of the best ways of having the children digest new content material as well as "feel like" the people they are studying. Give the children as many firsthand contacts with Chinese things and people as possible. Go to the Metropolitan Museum of Art to see the ancient art products of the Chinese; have a meal at a Chinese restaurant in Chinatown; invite a Chinese to tell about what his country is now trying to do. Bring out the human qualities in the Chinese people and the fact that their broad human ideals are essentially like our own.

MODERN UNITED STATES AMONG WORLD NATIONS.

The United Nations.[55] Can be approached as an effort to prevent another World War; would be far more destructive than previous wars because of atomic bomb and new rocket mechanisms; inability of any nation to defend itself from these new weapons. Global thinking about people came later than global thinking about products. Interest in trade relations long before interest in freedoms for other people. World War II made all nations our neighbors, whether enemies or friends. Oppressed peoples mean war. War anywhere now becomes world war.

---

[55] Many suggested themes in this section are no longer timely.

Study globe with great circle routes to see who are our nearest neighbors. Outside of North America (Canada and Mexico) our nearest neighbor is Soviet Russia. Japan was near enough to attack Pearl Harbor. Discuss first meeting of a world organization at San Francisco; the Big Five; who are members of the United Nations; any current happenings that the children will understand.

The Future. At close of year, the teacher will want to try to help the children pull together whatever social thinking they have achieved during the year; to think of the present as growing out of the past, and the future as growing out of the present. This can be done only on a young level. A few national and world trends can, however, be understood by mature sixth-grade children. The following are suggested as possibilities for discussion.

Science and Inventions Still Going On. Our country became a great industrial nation by science and inventions, which are still going on. We may expect new inventions in synthetics, airplanes, television, and above all in atomic energy applied to industrial uses. New parts of the world are opening up their earth resources and using them through new techniques of work. Through science and inventions once separated parts of the world may become more and more closely related. Interdependence of nations in trade; in use of earth resources; in prevention of war. If children wish to, let them go into fantasy about the future.

Democracy Still Growing in United States; in World. Struggle for freedom is age-old and still going on. Trace growth of democratic living in past United States; the search for freedoms that brought people to our country; Declaration of Independence, its high words not yet completely fulfilled; freeing the slaves; giving women vote; unions; ideas of jobs for all, that freedoms carry responsibilities with them; the Four Freedoms; Atlantic Charter; United Nations as a new venture in cooperation. Teachers must be guided, always, by the maturity of their children to think in terms of social values. If this final section is attempted there must be something for the children *to do.* Just talking is too intellectual; it would be more likely to confuse the children than to help them.

BACKGROUND CONTENT AT WORKSHOP MEETINGS: ALL GRADES

During this year and a half during which the school was experimenting with the Workshop social studies curriculum, most of the after-school meetings were naturally discussions of aspects of the curriculum. We did, however, have a number of meetings which gave background content for the curriculum. Much of this content was similar to that described in the story of our early Workshop approach. It was given again partly because of new teachers and partly because the old members felt they would get more out of it than they did before. We had talks on the environment of New York with special emphasis on the work of New York in relation to its natural environment; talks on Eurasia, its lands and people; talks on children's language, their map thinking, and on various teaching techniques such as trips, discussions, dramatic play and organized plays, creative language, map making, etc., in all of which the actual experiences of the teachers with their children were discussed. Since similar background material is given in the preceding chapters and in the appendices, we shall not here repeat it.

Two other kinds of background content are reported on here, since the teachers' approach to them was different from that in the earlier period of our Workshop growth. One development in the teachers' interest was in science. A second was interest in discussing social values, not only in terms of social ideas which children in various stages of maturity could understand, but on their own mature level.

When we first began the Workshop, all the teachers were afraid to try science experiments in their classrooms. They felt this was a job for a specialist and quite beyond their powers. By the time the Workshop group began to work on building a total social studies curriculum, they all wished science to be written into the curriculum at every grade. Not that many teachers were not still afraid of science —still lacking in self-confidence in a field where they had little background. But the attitude now was that it was a part of their job to acquire this science background and techniques of doing simple science experiments in their classrooms. At the end of the second Workshop year the teachers themselves suggested that the Workshop group work on a specific science curriculum from kindergarten through sixth grade. Such a science program was never fully developed. But this was due to lack of time rather than to lack of interest.

Each year a committee of teachers composed of volunteers from various grades made recommendations to the Workshop group as to what they wished in the way of science at the Workshop meetings. These recommendations were of several types. First, general fundamental background content which they felt they themselves needed. Excerpts from the minutes of one of the Workshop discussions follow.

Workshop Meeting   November 13

The science committee composed of three teachers representing first grade, fourth grade, and sixth grade reported to the group. One of the committee said that the committee felt that, since the science specialist would be able to present very few experiments in the short time he would be working with the group, it would be preferable to have him give the group content material when he meets with them. They would like material on solar, mechanical, electrical, and atomic energy. Under astronomy they wanted information on the solar system and on weather. *A sixth-grade teacher* said the teachers wanted information on communication and radar. These are things which particularly interested the children.

Bank Street member asked the group to give a more specific idea of topics on which they want information. For example, what sort of material does the group want on weather?

The following topics and areas were suggested: machines, radar, atomic energy and the atomic bomb, astronomy; weather (winds, as applied to airplanes; as applied to geography); air map analysis; mechanical and electrical energy as applied to transportation and communication—contrast between the airplane and the locomotive.

After some discussion the group decided that they would like the science specialist to present information on the following topics in lecture form:

First lecture:
    Energy—mechanical, electrical, atomic
           radar
           with information on machines demonstrating these types
              of energy
           transportation and communication.

Second lecture:
　　Weather—transportation
　　　　　　　agriculture
　　　　　　　weather as applied to geography.
Third lecture:
　　Synthetics
　　Soil conservation and reclamation
　　Dams and irrigation
　　Soil erosion.

A teacher suggested it would be helpful to the teachers if they could have a bibliography on these topics. This the science specialist gave and it was distributed to members of the group.

A second type of Workshop science meeting was when the trained scientist helped the teachers themselves try certain simple experiments which they could repeat with their children in the classroom.

Still a third type of science meeting was when the lecturer read our Workshop social studies curriculum and based his discussions on science immediately related to the subject matter, suggesting and sometimes demonstrating experiments for teachers to do in class.[56] This approach brought more questions from the teachers than did other approaches.

Probably all three types of meetings are desirable for teachers without much science background—straight background content, actual practice in conducting experiments, and discussions of science immediately related to social studies subject matter. Unfortunately, there is seldom time to cover all three in a Workshop with teachers who are engaged in active teaching.

In a social studies curriculum the teachers, naturally, had always been interested in the problem of social values. In our Workshop we had many times discussed the questions of what social values children could grasp at various stages of maturity and how such values could be made real to them.

It was not, however, until our third Workshop year that we de-

[56] Appendix 25: Notes on a Workshop Meeting with Science Resource Leader.

voted any Workshop meetings to the discussion of social values on our own adult level. In this year we had two outside guest speakers. One guest, who had accompanied Mr. Willkie on his round-the-world trip, spoke of the One-World concept. At the following meeting the Workshop group discussed this One-World concept for ourselves and how it could be applied within our programs for children. A second guest, from the Intercultural Education Workshop, spoke on contributions to American culture of various racial and national groups. Her general thesis was that we should *"ignore* racial differences and *understand* (not merely tolerate) religious differences and *share* (not merely appreciate) cultural differences." One part of the lively discussion which followed was this general thesis applied to Negroes. Each teacher in our school, where a large majority of children were colored, met *racial* difference within the American culture in her own class.

END OF FIRST STAGE OF WORKSHOP GROWTH

We have been quoting throughout from the second revision of the Workshop social studies curriculum for the whole school, which was written in the summer of 1946 after a year and a half of discussion and experimentation in the classrooms. Many details had to be worked out before the close of school. The regular fifteen sessions of the Workshop were over. A group composed of at least one teacher from each grade volunteered to thrash out these details with some administrative school members and members of the Bank Street staff. These teachers understood thoroughly what they were doing in building a curriculum. They discussed subject matter in great detail: subject matter in relation to the needs and maturity of their children, in relation to experiences which could clarify and vivify information, in relation to new needs in the new world we were all living in. Moreover, they were articulate and earnest in defense of what their own creative teaching had taught them when a representative of the official committee in charge of curriculum revision came to a Workshop meeting. Their attitude toward their job was not that of unquestioning followers, as it had been three short years ago. Not that they wanted to organize a curriculum outside the official framework. Not that at all. But now they knew what they wanted a curriculum to be for. They had worked hard and co-operatively on the building of a social studies curriculum for the whole child, for the whole school. Meeting regularly through June, we came through to the decisions which are incorporated in the revision from which we have been quoting.

The story of our Workshop has now reached the point forecast in the Preview in Chapter 5. What did the Bank Street staff feel had happened in the three years of our Workshop? What did the teachers feel had happened? In answer we repeat what we said in the Preview:

"Our curriculum was a second time revised in the spring of 1946 in the congestion of the end-of-the-year work and agitation of impending changes in administration. This second revision involved all the Workshop members. It was no light task for the Bank Street members—but it was their job. It was no light work for the teacher members—but *they considered it their job, too.* The teachers' professional attitude, their conception of their job as teachers, *that,* not the written curriculum, was what all of us in the Workshop—teachers, administration, and Bank Street staff alike—counted as the real result of our three-year experiment in helping teachers to understand and enjoy their new job."

So ended what we have called the first stage in our Workshop growth. In the first stage we worked in one school, with one principal, and with Workshop staff composed entirely of Bank Street staff on part time. We felt ready to extend our experimenting along new lines. We moved on to the second stage in our Workshop growth.

14

Our Workshop Changes Its Pattern

PUBLIC SCHOOL TEACHERS JOIN THE STAFF

IN THE fall of 1946 after three years of working together, the Bank Street Workshop and the Board of Education were ready for a new stage in the development of their joint program. One of the major goals, the training and development of Board of Education personnel as leaders in the Workshop group, could now be realized. Before the close of school that spring, the suggestion was made that we begin to expand these services into other schools. The work in one school had had sufficient recognition so that the Board of Education was willing to underwrite our expansion by releasing three teachers who had been members of our Workshop group from the classroom responsibilities and assigning them to serve as full-time members of our staff. We knew how many complex problems there would be to meet in this next step, but we were also exhilarated by the achievement of an important goal in the program and stimulated by the challenge of this next objective.

HOW SHOULD WE EXPAND OUR EXPERIMENT?

First, where were we to find schools into which these services could best be fitted? Where were we to lay our experimental emphasis? This was a period in our city when juvenile delinquency was receiving vast public attention, and many programs in social work, recreation, and education were being developed in neighborhoods which came to be known as tension areas. Would we become an agency to help curb juvenile delinquency through education? Would we become another community agency working with parents and neighborhood groups in order to provide children with better neighborhood services?

Our answer to ourselves was to continue as specialists in education. We would proceed as a teacher education service, working specifically in terms of a teacher's needs in her own classroom. Also a research program had got under way in our public school, and we wanted situations where we would find appropriate material for the further development of psychological as well as educational research. Although this was not a major criterion in our final selection of schools, it was nevertheless an important one. It was with these ideas in mind that we began to look about for schools to which we might offer the services of the Bank Street Workshops.

It seemed prudent to remain within the same school district, since this would mean a simpler supervisory setup and would entail less traveling about and therefore a more efficient use of staff time. The district in which we had been functioning was sharply divided into rather distinct social and economic patterns; the southern end was almost entirely Negro and Puerto Rican slum and near-slum areas, while the northern end presented a rather solid middle-class American pattern of mixed origins, predominantly of the Jewish faith. Our original school was almost midway in this geographical area and had only within recent years become a school largely for Negro children from families of a social-economic level somewhere between middle-class and lower-class groups.

We had been working in a school with special problems—underprivileged living conditions, the devastating influence of racial discrimination on children's lives, many children had been moved from one region of the country to another, and to some our culture and language were totally foreign, etc. It had been a challenge to us to see what the new program in education could become under these instances. Now we were interested to see it tried out under other conditions, with children not so enmeshed in a struggle against social-cultural impediments and where problems of academic adequacy might not be so acute. The needs of children in a more typical middle-class city school, though not so desperate, were nevertheless important in the larger context of experimentation in curriculum revision. Here, then, was another factor to be considered in choosing a school.

Perhaps most important in our consideration would be the staffs of the schools we were investigating. Our original experiment could never have grown so quickly and healthily had it not been for the cooperation of the supervisory staff. And so in visiting schools in the district, we were anxious to find other staffs as eager for what we had to offer as we were for the opportunity to work in their schools.

The two additional schools finally selected for our program are geographically and socially at opposite poles in the district. One of these schools, School III, is housed in one of the older buildings of our city system, presenting, however, none of the major building problems of our first school. Here there are fairly good and well-kept play areas outside of the school. The inside yard is fairly light and adequate. There is a good auditorium, the building has an air of being well kept, and with its wide, white-pillared front facing a park, the river, and a majestic bridge, the school building professes the typical American faith in children and their education.

The other school, School II, in which we were to work is housed in one of the newest buildings in our city, set wall to wall with the surrounding dilapidated houses on two sides but having a good-sized, paved play yard in the back, which faces on the next street. The surroundings eloquently express the slum quality of the neighborhood —the typically littered streets, the poor, meager little stores, and steaming, smelly stable (which, incidentally, provided real trip opportunities), the general grayness of poverty. Indoors, however, there is a light and cheerful yard, fairly good lunchroom facilities, a fine auditorium and gym, some delightful kindergarten and first-grade classrooms, a science room, a cooking room, a library, and the much-proclaimed movable seats throughout.

The staffs in these two schools afforded interesting contrasts also. The solid middle-class picture of the neighborhood carried over into the staff setup in School III. In this school there had been a markedly limited turnover of staff. It was considered a good teaching spot, with bright, clean, well-behaved children and co-operative parents. We found teachers working in this school for upwards of twenty years. In fact, when we entered the picture, practically all of the members of this staff had achieved maximum salaries and were therefore no longer required to make any gestures in the direction of further self-development and education. The supervisory staff had also been a long-established one up to within a few months of our beginning efforts in this school. It was the advent of a new principal who was not averse to the new program that encouraged us to begin our work here in spite of many misgivings as to the reception our program would receive. This school dramatically looks out upon a great bridge. Yet in accordance with the highly traditional curriculum that we found here, the children had never been taken on trips, even across the bridge.

In our other new venture, School II, we found a very different situation in terms of staff. The teachers in this school were a much younger group attached to the purposes of the school through unusually warm, human contact with the supervisors. This was in a tension area, with its all too typical broken home and family pattern: mothers working, fathers out of the family picture completely or unable to provide wholly for their families. In such a setting teaching is hard, offering challenge and a sense of dedication to some, only frustration and despair to others. In this school there had also been a recent change of supervisory staff. The new principal had been a member of the staff in the role of assistant to the principal for several years, however, so there was not the unsettling atmosphere of adjustment to new supervision in the school. In fact, the morale of this group was most unusual; there was an honest pride in the school together with a sincere recognition of the woeful inadequacies in some aspects of the program.

In this school we were to find an unusually large number of special classes for children who were suffering from orthopedic and cardiac difficulties, classes run by teachers with special training but now meeting new concepts of education for the deviate child. The parent body was not highly organized or very articulate, but we were to find that these parents could be counted upon to help the school's program despite their extremely limited resources.

For two years our program functioned only in these three schools, as we worked intensively with all of the staff who joined with us, attempting to make our Workshop a real and lively influence in the whole structure of the schools' program. At the same time new ways in which we could be of service to the schools in the district were germinating.

Recently a new school had been established in a neighboring district in charge of a principal under whom a member of our public school staff had worked as a classroom teacher. In this school we were asked to assist in working out some new patterns for the first grade, to plan such fundamentals as the use of space, the choice of equipment, the scheduling of the day, and also to develop with the teachers an understanding of the larger needs and program implications for these very young children. Such an invitation was important to us in that it implied acceptance of our role as well as methodology. This was a new pattern. Not a whole school but only a section thereof was involved; teachers were not volunteering to work with us; we had been called in as specialists in answer to a specific need and would not necessarily develop any further program of our own.

At this writing still another new school is under construction in our district. The principal assigned to the new school is, interestingly enough, one of the teachers who was with us as a member of our Workshop when she was herself teaching in one of our schools. When this school opens to receive its children, we shall be at work there. Perhaps one of the deep gratifications of our program has been her request for our services in the school which she is to head. Here is not only a school new to us but new in every sense, where literally we can have a hand in the very building of setup and program and where, at least from the point of view of administration, we do not need to build contact but have in our common background a working relationship that is so essentially sound.

The choice of expanded staff was our next major undertaking. We were to be assigned three teachers who had been members of our Workshop and had received classroom consultation from our Bank Street staff. What we needed in these people were qualities of leadership, a sense of zest in exploring new educational fields, an appreciation of teachers' needs as well as children's needs, and, perhaps most important of all, a rich equipment—a large kit of teaching tools and techniques. We felt also that it would be wise to select people who represented the spread of the elementary years, namely, people who had taught for many years at the fifth- and sixth-grade level, or the third and fourth, or had worked primarily with very young children. We were fortunate in finding in the public school one teacher who had had some of her training and experience at our own Bank Street School. And it was perhaps just as sound policy that the two other teachers chosen had had their initial training in a most traditional setup and all of their experience in public schools.

And so, equipped with a broadened concept, an expanded staff, a backlog of experience, and supplied with a field of operation, we were ready to begin on another step in the development of our program.

OUR FIRST JOB IN OUR NEW PROGRAM

Our first job was to help members of our new staff to develop security and competence in their new roles. For these teachers there were wondrous possibilities but also serious problems in this special assignment. What was required was a way of working together that was new to everyone. How would their so recent colleagues react to the leadership and guidance offered by them? After all, there had always been a tacit assumption of equality of competence in a school staff. Particularly in a large school system leadership implies status, often another rung of the hierarchy ladder climbed. Relationships such as these are delicate, and the violation of feelings can easily wreck an experimental program. We proceeded with the utmost caution.

Considering the human relations factor, we thought it wise to begin by assigning the teachers who had come from classroom teaching in our first school to the new Workshop schools and to use Bank Street workers and one public school staff member who came from another school to continue the program in our original school. After a period of about a year the Workshop teachers (as they came to be called) felt ready to work out their leadership role with teachers in the school from which they had come and were gradually assigned first as classroom consultants and later as leaders in the Workshop course. When later our staff was further enlarged to include a fourth public school teacher, the structure of help and guidance from within one's own status group was sufficiently well established to permit us to make assignments without regard to this special consideration.

So we tried to build for security in the feelings of all of us involved in this performance. But we also needed to develop new competence for new functions. Perhaps it was not so great a misfortune as we thought it at the time that the teachers could be released to us only very slowly. We received them into our program one at a time and were able to give each one an individual apprenticeship in the ways of procedure demanded by her new role.

When we began to work with a full staff it became necessary to set aside a full afternoon each week for planning and discussion times. Our conferences needed to be devoted to the mechanics of assignment of duties, records to be kept, plans to be made for the Workshop sessions, progress notes on classroom services to be discussed, and at the same time we needed to train and develop our new personnel in terms of some of the deeper aspects of our approach and method. They needed to become true members of Bank Street.

We also had another problem, namely, that of specific responsibilities shared with the public school system. There were simple mechanical problems of accounting for time, where to sign attendance books, from which school pay checks would come, to whom were these teachers responsible—Bank Street, their own school principals, the district superintendent?

It is important to note that mechanics of administration have worked with the utmost ease throughout this joint program. Workshop teachers have been expected to sign in, largely for purposes of auditing, and they have kept a log of their activities for the superintendent's office, but beyond this their program has been left entirely in the hands of the Bank Street Workshops to plan, supervise, and evaluate. Throughout the relationship there has been a friendly, comfortable, understanding atmosphere. There have been many informal conferences and an annual accounting of our accomplishments and further goals to the Board of Education.[57]

We had many other newness problems to cope with. Our center of operations needed to be shifted from our own building to a working center in one of the new schools. Fortunately, one school could provide a fine office, and here we began to build a small teachers' library of books, pictures, and materials. Here we held our meetings, worked on records, planned and prepared for our classroom undertakings. We needed to explore our new neighborhoods, to find out about our new children, to become acquainted with the teachers with whom we were to work.

To introduce what we had to offer to these new schools was not easy. In School II the principal cut down barriers with an insight that was almost brilliant. She introduced our group to her staff by saying that our coming into the school marked a new epoch in public school education. Here for the first time teachers would have the opportunity to receive consultation and advice from fellow workers who were really their peers, who had no supervisory power, who would work with them entirely in terms of the children-teacher process and

[57] Appendix 26: Annual Report of Bank Street Public School Workshops, 1948–49. (Excerpts.)

without any of the evaluation and rating procedure which is almost per se a part of most school supervision. They would also have the benefit of a Workshop course that was custom-made out of their own questions and needs and problems.

In School III our staff, in consultation with the principal and the district superintendent, decided to proceed very slowly with the proposal to set up an after-school Workshop. Our suggestions to this staff were made most tentatively. We worked for the first half year entirely as classroom consultants and only in those classrooms where teachers took the initiative in asking for assistance. We were surprised to find ourselves working in a fair number of classrooms after only a few weeks of the term had gone by. And by mid-year we were being asked why there had been no Workshop developed in this school. This was our cue, and we decided to exploit this interest even if the group were a very small one in the beginning. The district superintendent was present to introduce our Workshop staff to the small group of teachers who showed up for that first session. This was important in this situation, since it gave the nod of official approval to our efforts and speeded our beginnings.

HOW WE WORKED

By mid-year a pattern somewhat similar to that developed in our first school emerged. We were taking the responsibility for leadership in a Workshop course given once a week after school hours, and were also working in classrooms in somewhat the same fashion that had proved successful in our first Workshop school.

In the Workshop Courses

We began to look upon our classroom services as analogous to the laboratory sections of a course, with the afternoon Workshops as the lecture and discussion periods. In the first years of our program in these schools, we felt that these parts of our services were so closely integrated that we limited our Workshop membership to those teachers with whom we were also working in classrooms. In fact, very often the material for Workshop discussion grew out of problems arising in the classrooms where we worked, and again the techniques developed in Workshops were often made immediately applicable in the classrooms. After a first year of beginnings we were serving a substantial portion of our new schools' faculties. In School II almost the entire school was involved in working with us. In this school the principal and two assistants were in regular attendance at Workshop sessions and took an active part in discussions. In School III we were working with approximately half the teachers. In our original school the numbers of teachers remained pretty much the same from year to year and added up to about half the total number of teachers in the school. For the three schools the total number of teachers involved in the program at any one time was in the neighborhood of a hundred people in the Workshop courses, which were held in the three school buildings where we worked. About ninety-five classrooms were being serviced by our group, consisting at this time of three full-time Board of Education teachers and three part-time Bank Street Workshop staff members.

In our new schools the pattern of reception of our philosophy and outlook in education adhered quite closely to that which we had found true in our first school. There was first the demand for practical aids in the development of the new program, a demand often tinged with hostility to all these newfangled notions. Ofttimes when there was acceptance of the new program in theory, teachers expressed a sense of helplessness and frustration in the light of the inadequacy of equipment and materials, the size of classes, and their own untrained approach to the new ways of doing things. Their questions were invariably of the "just how" variety—"How do you set up a unit?" "How long should it last?" "How do you do group reading?" "How do you keep children quiet in the new program?" The teachers wanted practical aids of the kind they could take back to their rooms the very next morning. This was all reminiscent of our early sessions in our first Workshop school. They were not yet interested in the "why's" of children's behavior and certainly not ready to tackle a program in education as an answer to children's needs. In this stage of our growth with teachers, our classroom services were specific in nature: showing the teachers how to plan a mural; how to make and use reading aids; how to divide a class for group work; how to conduct an arts and crafts period; how to plan, take, and use a trip and what trips to take. To a degree, this was a period of educational gadgeteering for these teachers.

In this second stage of the Workshop we were far better equipped to meet the teachers' needs during the first phases of their own development than we had been at the very beginning of our experiment. The new members of our staff who had been teachers in the public school had developed unusual proficiency in using original teaching techniques (classroom gadgets) to adjust to the hampering realities of scarcity, crowding, regulations, etc. They had themselves worked under these conditions, and known the limitations imposed by them, at firsthand. They knew, for instance, how to work soundly and with integrity on parts of a program if that was all that was possible or wise to undertake. A good unit by itself was an accepted and acceptable undertaking, an interesting mural related to social studies an end in itself, a successful work period a sound, final entity. They, themselves, as new Bank Street workers, were only now in the process of developing their own concepts of the new program so as to embrace the whole challenge of broader and deeper organization of curriculum.

In the classrooms it was our job to find materials and methods which offered enrichment to programs already set up. At the same time we needed to begin to work slowly and cautiously toward a next step, namely, the questioning of the total existing program and its appropriateness to child needs.

In School II this was an easy next step. In this school behavior problems were of major concern. Teachers felt more pressed toward the area of understanding the child because they could not proceed with the presentation of a program without first coming to grips with the serious problems of individual children. This was a school with a relatively large number of academically retarded as well as emotionally disturbed children, where court appearances were not uncommon, where in many classrooms the major problem was the maintenance of satisfactory means of control in order to set up an atmosphere in which learning could take place. These teachers, therefore, looked to the area of child development as a tool for their own teaching proficiency and very soon after the initiation of our program were eager to explore this aspect of their need. The psychologist of the Bank Street Schools entered into the Workshop program both as a leader in Workshop sessions and as a visitor consultant in the classroom. The particular behavior problems of these particular children were made the subject matter for a series of child development discussions.

In School III, on the other hand, traditional controls had been a safe stand-by in the hands of the teachers. There was a disinterested attitude, even suspicion of "progressive" education. Many Workshop sessions were needed before there was an atmosphere in which basic work could be begun, in which there was discussion and examination of ideas rather than heckling.

If the new program in education is to be built upon an understanding of child needs, it has implicit responsibility to develop and to provide suitable experience as a means of growth. This requires teachers who have experience rather than textbooks to offer children and who stand ready to participate with children in experience which leads to learning. With the recognition and understanding of the meanings of the new program, teachers began to see the need for some new tools in their trade. They needed to develop some adequacies of their own. They needed to grow toward a broader grasp of our culture if they were expected to teach without undue reliance on texts and syllabi prepared by higher authorities. These were the years when a group such as ours was backed in its approach by the pronouncements of the Board of Education authorities. There was a turning away by the school authorities from didactic courses of study and an approach to elementary curriculum that offered teachers areas for development which they were expected to fill in in terms of their experiences with the children.

The teachers looked to us for help, therefore, in the interpretation of these new programs as set forth by the Board of Education and for ways in which they might begin to develop these new programs in their own classrooms. We needed to seek out experts from the fields of arts and crafts, music, science, and bring to these teachers some firsthand experiences of their own with these materials. We needed also to bring constantly to them an enrichment of their own background in relation to their environment. These teachers too became learners, and in many instances they had first to learn how to accept the proposition of learning from their peers. They went on trips with us and saw the process of planning, preparing, and living through a trip to its outcomes through their own participation in such an undertaking. They became the makers and doers in the field of map making or puppetry and performed science experiments. The sessions planned for the after-school Workshop reflected these varied needs and interests.[58] In some schools teachers were now ready to integrate their experience and to think of a curriculum as an organic whole made up of the deeply interwoven natural needs of the child and the cultural needs of his society.

In Classroom Services

In classroom services which went on concurrently with the Workshop program described above, there was also a developmental pattern. At first we provided material supplementary to the program set up by the teachers. We would bring to a classroom an appropriate story, a needed map, some visual aids materials. We would tell a teacher about an appropriate trip; we would show her how to get a mural started for her unit; we would rehearse with her children for a play or find a song that she needed for her assembly program. With a special appropriation from the Board of Education for materials, we could supplement the schools' supplies of paints and

[58] Appendix 27: Sample Schedules of Workshop Sessions.

paper, brushes, and other materials that were so woefully meager in all of our schools. We were willing to be used in just this way. In fact, after a year of service in one school we were gratified when the principal said about us that we had been instrumental in opening the doors of her classrooms, that teachers no longer looked upon people coming into the room as an intrusion and a threat.

Our next objectives in these schools too were to be taken into the broader planning and into developing larger areas of program. We were eager to be called upon in the initial planning stages, whether in the setting up of a total program for a year or the development of an assembly play or the introduction of a new social studies area in the curriculum. This began to happen in all of our schools. In the kindergarten, first-, and second-grade classrooms, our staff was being called upon to help with such things as room planning in terms of function, to give teachers help with time schedules, even to help in formulating new methods of writing lesson plans. We were constantly improvising or finding new materials inexpensive enough to be practical. One of our public school staff members built such a piece of dramatic play equipment, which has had large acceptance by first- and second-year teachers in all our schools. This was made of orange crates, prune boxes, and planks nailed together for permanence and suggesting the façade of a store, a ticket window, a gas station, or any other scheme for the children to embellish and use in play. This simple piece of equipment provided a base for as good social and creative play as we have ever seen anywhere and might well be considered an appropriate material even in situations where the ample supply of blocks would seem to make it unnecessary. Here was an interesting philosophical compromise between the "pure" unstructured blocks of our experimental schools and the finished "dollhouse" type of play equipment found in many traditional first grades. Perhaps this structure expressed quite succinctly how we were living through a bridging-over experience, how well we had learned that there are many pathways to a goal.

These years of our function in the schools coincided with the directives from the Board of Education which attempted to give teachers in the first grade much greater leeway in methods of teaching reading than they had had before. In fact, if one interpreted Board of Education directives literally, reading could now be put off until the second year. One would have expected teachers to be greatly relieved by the removal of the burden of teaching the very young children to read. We found, on the contrary, that first-year teachers were at a loss in the development of a program for these children which was not focused on academic learnings. When we consider the paucity of equipment in the schools and the ideas with which the traditionally trained teacher comes to her classroom, it is not to be wondered at that these teachers felt their most solid props withdrawn, nor is it to be wondered at that the response to this new program was largely negative. However, for our purposes the new program meant authoritative backing for our approach, which had seemed idealistic and impractical to many teachers for many years. Now all teachers needed to learn how to develop a play program in the early grades because this was becoming the official program. We could now serve them in their own professional needs by showing them how to become successful teachers in the new program. More specifically, for instance, the introduction and use of blocks was now the responsibility of the public school teacher, and when the Bank Street consultant was able to offer ways and means of building a successful block program, she was not only a desirable resource but a much-needed one. Similarly, in the upper years the concepts developed in the curriculum bulletins which were being brought out by the Board of Education laid so much emphasis on experiential learning, free expression, and creative activity that Bank Street consultants were the much-needed experts who had the know-how and ofttimes the physical materials with which to implement their knowledge. Instead of being asked to help with the mural of a play or the rehearsal of a song, we were now being asked to help with the development of the ideas for plays which were likely to be made up in their entirety by the children and based upon some common school experience in social studies. Instead of being asked how long the unit should be, we were often consulted on the proposition of setting up an experience appropriate to the total program of study for the term or year.

Also, because our staff now included people with public school experience, we no longer limited ourselves to the social studies program as our main area of service. Previously, we had included science as part of our work in social studies. Now we were called upon to help develop a curriculum in science per se. We began to take part in the language program and even helped with academic skills as another important area of our classroom work.

But most important from our point of view was the sense that we were developing into more than resource people who could be used for the minor specifics of classroom operation. We had become most valuable as policy makers, if one may use such a term to denote the broader aspects of curriculum formulation. This followed quite logically from the line of development that we were beginning to perceive in our Workshop sessions. In our new schools, as had been true in our first school, we were leaving the stage of development which calls for the answers to the "just how do we" questions and taking our thinking into the realms of "why we do what we do" in terms of our understandings of children's growth and development.

CONTRIBUTIONS TO TOTAL SCHOOL PROGRAM

Although work with the individual teachers and their classroom needs has occupied our major attention, we have felt from the beginning that some school-wide services were very much a part of our contribution. In our first school it was relatively simple for us, an outside agency with no status on the hierarchical ladder and yet with considerable community-wide acceptance and prestige, to have a share in general school policy making and planning. When, however, our Workshop staff began to be made up of public school teachers, our roles in the school assumed a somewhat different quality. It was through specific service to the schools that we could best make ourselves felt at this point. One of the natural ways to do this would be to enter into some school-wide undertaking, and one year we were offered this opportunity in both our new Workshop schools.

In School II we were asked to help develop a pageant to be presented at the time when the Freedom Train came to New York City. Although this was a school-wide function, it was our Workshop group that developed the form this presentation was to take. We used Workshop sessions to discuss the desirability of one content over another, the music that would be appropriate, the groups of children who would participate, and how. In final form the pageant presented a cavalcade of American life as the children told or sang or played out in pantomime the stories back of some of the major documents exhibited on the Freedom Train. The organization of the project and the actual work with the children was taken over by the classroom teachers, with only an occasional bit of advice or assistance at rehearsals from us, but the finished performance bore the imprint of our assistance in the childlike quality of the lines, the fresh and unstudied quality of the performance. In School III we were asked to help with the assembly program to be given before the winter holidays. The principal of the school felt that the presentation of a program based purely on the Christmas story was hardly appropriate in this school and asked our help in developing a new kind of program. The weeks that followed might be described as stormy. Feelings were tense and raw. We were seeking a simple device for telling the story of the winter festivals celebrated by the peoples of the major religious groups represented in this school. One plan after another was discarded. Some teachers felt that here was a real encroachment upon their deep-seated and up to this time completely respected principles of faith. The story as given was a much-diluted version of what was originally intended by some members of the group, namely, to symbolize in this performance the breakdown of some of the barriers between faiths. The simple device was employed of two families of different faiths enjoying the holidays in their special ways with children visiting each other and becoming aware not only of differing patterns of observance but also of the similarity of feelings and meanings attached to these festivities. After the final performance parents were moved almost to tears, not necessarily by the quality of the play but by the fact that at last the American school was open to more than one interpretation of the winter festivities. But there was also much deep rejection on the part of some of the teachers. In fact, one teacher took no pains to cover her feelings and practically assailed the principal of the school for permitting such a presentation.

In another of our schools the total responsibility for a rather special project was turned over to the Workshop staff. This was the time in our school history when, because of changes in administrative policy, the schools began to admit children six months earlier than they had heretofore. Since it was also the time when the policy of the Board of Education as it concerned the teaching of reading was considerably changed, this meant a much longer period for children to attend school before major attention was to be given to the teaching of academic skills. The play program for young children almost overnight became not only desirable but necessary. The principal of this school offered us a large, light, cheerful classroom to set up as a playroom for first- and possibly second-year children. This was a rich opportunity indeed and an exciting one. Although the economic status of the families in this neighborhood is very low indeed, parents were so interested in this program that they wished to contribute money for it in small sums, and very generously gave time to build equipment, make curtains, and paint and decorate the room for the children. The project found support on all sides, and within a period of a few weeks we were able to open a well-equipped playroom for the children of the first grade. This room has functioned as a laboratory in creative play and an important spot for demonstrating the meanings of play of young children to their teachers. It is not merely a place where children go to spend time happily. It is integrated into what we think of nowadays as the social studies curriculum for this age level—an investigation of their here-and-now environment.

This undertaking has had important use and outcome in more ways than one. Here was an opportunity for our public school staff worker really to show "what she could do." For some time she took over the direction of groups of children in the playroom while the teachers of these children had an opportunity to observe her techniques. She was able to work with all of the first- and a good many of the second-year teachers, whether they were associated with the Bank Street Workshop or not, and more important, she was then able to follow through this experience in the classrooms of these children. Teachers began to develop a greater interest in the play corners in their own classrooms. They developed a good eye for appropriate materials that could be improvised. They began to participate in children's play without embarrassment and with a sense that this was teaching too.

The playroom has had meaning for some groups of the oldest children in this school too. For a long time we had been hoping to develop some interclass services beyond the milk service which functioned in this school. Our group had for a long time worked with the concept of a school service job as rich and rewarding in possibilities for the total program of a group. In this situation we saw a natural and honest opportunity for the older children to take on the job of helping these first-grade children. One group of sixth-graders became the maintenance crew for our playroom. At first they were merely glamourized monitors who went in to wash paint brushes, straighten out shelves, and clean up the floor. We soon found, however, that these grown-up eleven-year-olds were almost as anxious to play with and use the equipment as the little ones whom they were presumably serving. It was a natural next step to give these older boys and girls opportunities for making equipment rather than simply maintaining it, and from then on there developed a rather fine interclass performance in which the older children took responsibility for smoothing the way for the first-graders' use of their playroom.

It has always been our belief that a good job for children serves as a springboard into a new activity, and this has proved to be the case here too. We were interested to see how these children, beset by deep emotional and social problems, wanted to observe the younger children in play, welcomed the opportunity to play out some of their needs, and used this experience as the beginning of a simple projective experience of their own. Puppetry grew naturally out of the experience of this group, and it then became our undertaking to provide trained personnel to carry on. For the teacher in charge of this class, this whole episode opened up the meanings of child behavior as no courses or Workshops could possibly have done. Its value for the school as a whole lay in the fact that the pattern of interclass services and function had been demonstrated. We were confident that in this school further opportunities for developing such a program would be sought.

It is interesting to note in passing that this is the school which we have referred to time and again as the one in which the areas of child development had been a first consideration in Workshop planning from the very beginning, and so it seemed to come about quite naturally that the emotions and behavior of children played such a large role in teacher growth and development too.

In another of our schools—and, parenthetically, it is also interesting to note that this is the school in which the children had the greatest academic adequacy and in which the teachers might be said to have had the most highly developed technical teaching skills—the school library was being reorganized, and the classroom teacher in charge of the library grew to depend upon our staff worker as a very important aid in the project. The undertaking and the service which a sixth grade was developing were in the realm of the intellectual, as one would expect in this school. But the outcomes have been manifold. The children's initial job here was to help organize and catalogue the books that would form the nucleus of the school's growing library. A number of books was purchased after the parents' association had contributed a generous sum of money for building up the library collection and the choice of titles was turned over to our Workshop staff. What became a much more childlike part of this undertaking was a little book review section in the school paper. The children wrote to many publishers for books to review and received a considerable number which have been added to the library collection. This group undertook to spread the awareness of what is available in the library and to "sell" a love for reading through the reviews and also through a story unit which they conducted. This latter job entailed the thorough preparation of the reading and dramatization of a simple story. Often the children made intriguing illustrations for the stories which were sometimes pop-up and sometimes movable pictures. They followed a regular program of presenting their stories to first- and second-year groups. Their teacher remarked recently that this job had been of inestimable value to slow readers in her sixth grade because it had given them an opportunity for easy reading without loss of status. Our concept of a school job program has always been to seek honest relationships between the actual service performed and broader social implications—to use the job as a springboard experience into the further study of a "spot" in our historical-social development. This library job provided sound reasons for studying the making of books and paper, the invention of printing, even the history of writing. The children dramatized and gave art expression to the new, well-grounded information that they discovered in tracking down these aspects of our culture.

In all of the schools we have an indirect but important role with regard to the ordering of books and supplies. Each year at requisition time supervisors use us to help them make decisions as to the amounts of materials to be ordered, the kinds of books to be purchased, the building up of one type of equipment rather than another. Indirectly but very specifically such advice works its way into school programs.

BROADENING THE BASE OF OUR
CONTRIBUTIONS

A major dilemma in a program such as this is the constant choice that one needs to make between intensive and extensive development. The program in these three schools has been, as school programs go, of an intensive nature, even though it would be folly to assume that these schools have been fundamentally remade by the Bank Street Workshop. We constantly come to grips with the enormousness of our task even in these few schools, and yet it is obvious that no small group could possibly hope to reach even a substantial portion of our school system through this approach. The ways in which a whole system could be affected have been a constant source of concern because of the ever-present threat either of thinning out one's contribution or of developing it into a meaningless stereotype while in the process of extending and expanding.

After three years of work in these three schools, which, in effect, means six years in our first school, we have come to some decisions made in part because of requests which have come to us and in part as a next step in policy. We are seeking ways and means for a broader base of contact with all public schools, but we are putting our major effort into an intensive program in our own district. Also in keeping with our original goals, we are beginning to remove some of the intensive work which has been done in the school where we began to function first. Here perhaps more fundamentally than in our other schools the die has been cast. The concern of the professional staff is truly in terms of children and their program. There is emphasis on teachers functioning as a co-ordinated faculty rather than as a group of subordinates. There is an awareness of the possibilities of richer materials. There is consciousness of the use of the environment as a major factor in curriculum building. This is not to say that there are no problems left in the school. They are many and deep, but our experiment seems to have achieved its major goal, and it is in line with our conception of this program that we now function with this group less intensively and more in terms of an advisory group. So we are releasing some of our energies for services in other schools or areas and continuing to serve in a general advisory capacity in this school.

In another school our Workshop course has developed a rather special pattern in that we have begun to accept teachers who do not teach in our Workshop schools as members of the Workshop courses. We have had some misgivings about this procedure, because teachers in our community take too many courses that have scarcely any relation to their actual daily work in the classrooms. In this special Workshop course, however, we have found the process to be stimulating to the group coming from within the Workshop school and, judging from the response of the teachers coming from outside schools, of value and importance to them. We have been asked to visit the classrooms of some of these teachers in their schools, and perhaps there will develop an extension of our program that we had not planned, namely, working with individuals in many schools rather than holding to the original plan of working through an intensive whole school approach.

A most satisfying extension of our contribution to individual teachers has come when teachers in our program have transferred to other schools and, on their own, stimulated thinking about children and curriculum along these lines in the schools to which they have gone. Although our follow-up of Workshop teachers is not an organized one, we do make personal contacts simply because so many of the teachers we work with are our friends, and we hear time and again of former Workshop members who are making grass roots attacks on some of the inadequacies of the schools to which they go.

After three years in our Workshop, one of the teachers left our school on a leave of absence. When she returned to her work, it was to another school. This is her account of what happened in her first term there.

"I walked into my classroom in this old-fashioned building and looked at the rows of screwed-down desks, many more than there were children to fill them, but no space for dramatics, carpentry, or painting. I called in the principal, explained my need for space and a table. In a few days the extra desks were gone, and the principal said, 'Come along through the school and we'll see what we can find in the way of a long table.' We found a small one and he asked if that would do. 'Oh, I need a big, long table,' I said, 'so the children can use tools, make big relief maps, and scenery for our plays.' Believe it or not, in two weeks a long, new table, painted a nice light green, was all set up, and we soon got started on constructive work. Fortunately, our school had clay and paints, the children brought boards and tools, and I gathered in the other necessary materials. I spent until five o'clock every day, those first weeks, just getting my room the way I wanted it, pictures up, and a color scheme worked out, with crayons, drawing paper, folders for the children's work, charts of suggestions, paint and clay all in their places within reach of the children.

"I didn't say a word, but the teachers began to drift in, and exclaim, 'Why, this is just the way I'd like to have my room.' It wasn't long until the principal was swamped with requests to have desks pulled out and tables put in.

"The teachers who are new in the school meet every Thursday afternoon to talk over our common problems. One day we worked with clay, discussed its preparation, how to use it in connection with social studies. But many of the teachers were hesitant about working with it. One especially would not touch it. Later I said, 'Come into my room at lunchtime. I'll help you.' And she accepted. We locked the door and I got out two balls of clay. I urged her to experiment a little with it and see what came out. She tried but was really too timid, and was sure she could make nothing worth while. She felt she needed to be taught before she could teach the children. It was just before Easter, and I knew the children would all want to make rabbits, so I suggested we try one. She began pinching off bits and sticking them back on for the ears, so I showed her how to keep it all in one piece and pull the ears out gradually, smoothing and forming them as she went along. As soon as the rabbit began to take shape her whole attitude changed. By the time we finished she was glowing.

"I'm planning a trip soon, and have invited another class to go along. This neighborhood has its possibilities, too. At our old school we had the Hudson River and the George Washington Bridge, and all those historical places. But here we have the East River and other bridges, and best of all, a short subway ride will take us to the spot just opposite the new site for the United Nations. I've got to do a lot of exploring before I plan my trips for next year.

"The teachers asked me to be chairman of one of their committees, but I said, 'I don't want to shirk, but I'm a new teacher here, and I'd rather take my turn later on, after I've settled in.' I didn't want them to think I know it all. That would spoil everything."

As this teacher spilled out her story to us in an informal get-together, it was evident that she had little sense of planned strategy. She was just being herself, going about her job—enthusiastic, wanting to share. But it bears out our deepest philosophy about the way our Workshop work must spread. When it is genuine, practical, and of superior quality it cannot help being contagious.

The members of the Bank Street School staff have always considered it an important function to set down their attitudes and approaches. In Chapters 10 through 13 the story of the joint curriculum undertaking in the first school where we functioned has been told. In that situation we worked closely with a group of teachers, helping them to develop a social studies curriculum for their own school. But the final organization of the materials and the actual writing were in the main the function of the Bank Street Workshop group. Now, after two years of working together, the Workshop staff drawn from public school personnel has been found ready to work independently on the preparation of written materials for teachers. In one case this material was developed into a science curriculum for fourth and fifth grade prepared in co-operation with other Board of Education personnel. Other materials have concerned themselves with varied aspects of school program. Within the short space of two years these teachers have moved into this new role, preparing written materials for teachers and short articles for publication wherein they feel competent to take a leadership position that is much broader than even the one that they occupied as Workshop teachers in the three schools. We also find it appropriate and acceptable to have our Workshop teachers serve as members of curriculum committees set up by the Board of Education and to contribute articles to publications of the Board.[59] We find the public school members of our staff now ready to take speaking engagements, ofttimes with fairly large groups, to discuss Workshop methods and materials. And so in the space of three years the goal of developing from within the public school group people who can take over the direction of teacher growth seems to have been demonstrated quite completely and successfully.

PROBLEMS WHICH THIS PATTERN OF WORK PRESENTS

Teacher growth is the goal of this program, and with the many signs of its accomplishment we sometimes neglect to report some of the negatives or obstacles to the developing pattern. We want to give reality to a story of this kind by at least enumerating some of the difficulties, even the barriers, to a smooth upward line of progress in the specific direction of our goals. It has been at least implied that acceptance of our program is not complete. There are individuals—groups, even—who sense that in a program of this nature lies some real danger to the educational *status quo*. One is sometimes aware of the questioning of the whole social philosophy back of our educational formulations. There were a number of sessions in one school in which the "laxity" of our own present-day morality was laid at the feet of progressive education, in which the teachers almost upbraided us for what they thought of as our attitude of superiority, in which the old cry of "Look at me; I was brought up in an old-fashioned school" was heard. These were hard hours, and if they are no longer so definitely brittle in tone, there is often still injected into the discussion the question which is no question really, but in effect a challenge, "This sounds very fine, but I'd like you to come into my classroom and try to do all this." And invariably there is the pattern of response which says, "We would like to do all these things, but our supervisors still demand quiet classrooms, obedient children, and

[59] *The Play Is the Thing,* Board of Education of the City of New York. *Curriculum and Materials,* Vol. 4, No. 1. October, 1949.

high academic outcomes. How can we do all this?" And in all honesty one must often ask, how can they?

Less profound, perhaps, in its origins, but just as difficult to surmount are some of the school problems which are so common that they hardly need mention again. But for teachers these are the hour-by-hour irritations and frustrations with which they have to cope. In all schools clerical work is an incredibly heavy load. In one school teachers are constantly interrupted by collection of milk money, attendance books, borrowing of materials, announcement of change of plan, and each of these breaks into a teaching-learning flow that is so difficult to establish, even under ideal conditions. In another school the loud-speaker interrupts all too often to permit a good atmosphere to be sustained. These are necessities of a large school in a large system. Administration has its own problems, and one cannot be too critical, but administrative requests often constitute a heavy burden for our teachers and children to carry.

The individual teachers who have come to work with us form in the main a fine and dedicated group of professional workers. Among them, as is to be expected in any group, are also people with a less professional attitude. Among these are some who come to our courses because they provide the necessary credit for advancement, others who begin with an attitude of proving to themselves and to us, if possible, that the ways they are used to are best. There are still others who come out of professional loneliness and seek our work largely as a means of contact. Though comparatively few in number, they can introduce an alien atmosphere which slows down progress in the early stages of new Workshop courses. Those of us who have been at it for some years have learned to expect these slow beginnings and not to allow the reactions of a few to distort our impressions of the underlying eagerness for professional development which characterizes the group as a whole.

Then there are practical problems. In at least two of these schools there is a fairly large staff turnover, which in terms of the Workshop means that each year we are working with "beginners" and advanced students. In fact, one year we attempted to break up our group into two such sections but found that this was not practically possible in terms of covering two sessions with our small staff. Teacher turnover also means classroom service on differing levels, but here adjustments are not in group situations and are easier to handle.

Perhaps the most complex of the problems presented in this part of our work is the incredible difficulty which grows out of the professional ethics of our setup. We come to these teachers as peer consultants, but by the very nature of our relationship with the principals and their assistants we find ourselves in a somewhat supervisory role. It is hard to talk with the principal about what one as a Workshop consultant has been able to do in a classroom without giving him evaluation material on the teacher. In fact, all of the recording of our work was seriously jeopardized by the near phobia which teachers have of being marked or evaluated. Even when we were a completely private group we needed to be meticulous and precise in recording classroom situations. Only our own classroom activities and the children's responses were set down, and the teacher's part in a situation was largely implied. Now, with a public school staff in the position to record, it becomes doubly difficult. Almost out of loyalty to their colleagues they hesitate, even balk, at setting down reports on classroom activities.

It is all very well for us to set ourselves up to seek out teacher leaders, but many times a principal wishes us to work with a teacher of whose ability he has some real doubt. In an honest attempt to help a teacher the principal may suggest that she seek our help. If then she needs to be graded "unsatisfactory" our program finds itself in a dire dilemma. Were we "telling on her"? And why couldn't we make her into a "satisfactory" teacher if teacher education is our forte? We would be doing ourselves a basic disservice if we became a reporting agency in any sense of the term. Yet our contact with supervisory staff is of the profoundest importance to our program. And how to build a working relationship with a principal and his assistants while at the same time protecting the integrity of our relationship with teachers is sometimes walking a tightrope indeed. Then when we have succeeded in developing a person with the qualities of leadership and wish to use such a person on our Workshop staff, one can see the principal's real dismay over the loss of a superior teacher. It is a rare principal (but there is at least one such in our program) who can see the largest good for the whole system with a clear and absolute understanding of the necessity for drawing upon teacher leadership. This principal was most generous in releasing one of his teachers to this program. The development of a teacher in a school can never be considered wholly a Bank Street performance. It is only as the total picture of the school comes into it that the teaching staff develops those attitudes and skills that we are so concerned with. And it is not only just, it is a profound necessity, that principals should feel themselves to have had a decisive role in teacher development.

In a sense, therefore, our program is somewhat self-annihilating. Even with individual teachers it is part of our role to step out of the picture when the job is done, to take little or no credit for the quality of the performance that emerges, to refer lightly and carelessly to our contribution in the school, and then to back out gracefully when it has been made. It is not always easy in terms of natural human needs to function in such a fashion.

AS WE LOOK BACK AND FORWARD

How far have we come? In this chapter we have attempted to outline the beginnings of an expanded program carried on by a from-within group. Several important concepts have been clarified as we have worked. The hierarchy pattern has been challenged, at least. We have found that teachers can and do accept leadership from within their peer group and also that there is fine leadership material awaiting development in teachers' ranks. We have found that even in a large system schools have individualities, that each school is unique not only in the problems it presents but also in the way in which it meets them, in tradition, mores, and even curriculum. There is greater challenge but deeper hope for change and growth in such a situation. We have found the "system" open to suggestion, genuinely co-operative, even eager to receive and use the new ways in education. Perhaps most important has been the acceptance by the public schools of the slow, intensive, personal approach which is inherent in the method of this program. In such an atmosphere the role of experimental education is real and vital and on-going.

In the following chapters we shall look back in order to give a more detailed analysis of the growth of teachers at the period prior to the one discussed in this chapter.

PART III

Broad Learnings and Implications of Workshop Experience

15

Growth of Teachers in Professional Maturity

AN OLD professor once said that the proof of the pudding is not in the eating but comes several hours later. This holds true of more things than puddings! The results of an educational experiment such as the Bank Street Workshops do not show until several years later. It takes time to do what we were attempting—to explore what experiences, approaches, and techniques in an inservice situation are best adapted to further teachers' growth toward professional maturity. Both we and the teachers had to learn on the job. Growth is a slow process. One cannot expect quick results. In the second place, when one is immersed in the daily exigencies and details of a job, one cannot get far enough away from them to see things that are happening slowly. If one does not see a child for a number of years, one is actually startled at his growth—far more than his parents, who have seen him daily. So is it with a long-term experiment. It is only later when one can study the day-by-day records with a detached attitude that one can get a total picture. That is the reason for keeping records—to have something more reliable than memory as a basis for an analysis. When records of several years are put together they form a kind of moving picture of what has happened.

In Part II we told the story of our Workshops largely as that of technicians. There we made a report based on the day-to-day records of what happened in six years. In such a report one can hardly see the forest for the trees. Now, in Part III, we shall turn from detailed reporting to analysis, from what the Workshops did to what we and the teachers learned through the doing.

We begin with an analysis of the growth of the teachers in understanding and enjoyment of their new job, which, as has been repeatedly said, was the central aim of our Workshop experiment. Throughout the experiment we measured the success or failure of our Workshop techniques in terms of their contribution to the teachers' professional growth. We shall go back to the initial attitudes of the teachers toward their job and what they wanted from the Workshop and analyze what kinds of situations hinder or aid the growth of teachers, and the stages of growth by which teachers progress toward professional maturity. This will take us rapidly over some of the same ground covered in Part II, since our analysis is necessarily based on the record of what happened in the Workshops.

INITIAL ATTITUDES TOWARD THEIR JOB AND WORKSHOP

Obviously, teachers cannot be lumped together as people with similar characteristics and personalities or attitudes toward life any more than can parents or miners or cooks or lawyers. What any of these groups have in common is not personality characteristics but a kind of work. When we come to analyze the growth of teachers we shall concentrate on professional thinking and attitudes and largely ignore the wide variations in personality, background, interests, and prejudices which they bring to the teaching job, though all these factors affect their professional growth. If we find a group of highly diversified personalities holding similar attitudes toward their work, we shall examine the conditions under which this work is carried on and ask how far these conditions explain the attitudes common to the group.

So we begin by recalling the initial attitudes of the Workshop teachers toward their job as shown by what they wanted from a

Workshop.[60] The situation in the New York schools when we began our Workshop was typical, we think, of the situations prevailing in many, perhaps most, of our schools throughout the country. The thinking and attitudes about children and curriculum to be planned for them were in a state of transition. The "new curriculum" embodying the new thinking and attitudes had been given to the teachers but in practice had not genuinely superseded the old curriculum. In varying degrees the teachers clung to the familiar old curriculum (which to them meant largely subject matter) which had been set up over twenty years before under twenty or more separate courses of study. Within this old framework they were trying conscientiously to carry out the newer methods of teaching which, for a number of years, they had been instructed to use. A common complaint of the teachers was that, though they were willing to follow the new curriculum, they were handicapped by the conditions under which they worked—large classes, lack of space in the classrooms, old equipment, etc. They devoted "periods" to activity programs, units, trips, research, conferences, and "show and tell periods" in which children "expressed themselves," but for the most part these periods were thought of as extras, as episodes which interrupted the *real* work, "the desirable information" contained in the old syllabus.

Many teachers still depended largely upon the traditional source of "desirable information"—that is, textbooks which contained facts to be memorized. They were not tied to a single textbook as they were in the early traditional schools; but most of the added books were still heavily weighted with factual information—a variety of textbooks, encyclopedias, etc. For the most part, "research" meant reading one of these books. There was little use of genuine source material for research—pictures, maps, written materials which children were called upon to interpret, which challenged them to think out relationships for themselves. Few teachers thought of the functioning world outside of the classrooms, the world in which their children lived, as a laboratory where children could have firsthand

[60] See pp. 90 ff.

experiences, carry on investigations on a young level under teacher guidance, which would start new interests and give meaning to factual information contained in books.

The teachers had also been given instructions in regard to their attitude toward children and methods of "handling" them. Here, again, the teachers conscientiously tried to follow out these instructions. In order to let the children freely express themselves in conferences, many teachers simply handed over the situation to the children and stepped out of any participation in or responsibility for these "free" periods. The children were both young and inexperienced in handling such responsibility. Without teacher guidance, they got nowhere and the listening children were simply bored. In subtler ways the new instructions concerning the "atmosphere" of the classrooms brought difficulties to many teachers. In an attempt to let children be "free," they relaxed the old repressive kind of discipline before building up self-discipline within the group or an individual child. They confused freedom with license, with disastrous results for both themselves and the children.

In this situation the teachers were practically unanimous in what they wanted from a Workshop. They wanted to be shown *how* to conduct the new teaching techniques they had been instructed to use, not *why*. Their primary interest was not to understand the educational and psychological basis of the new curriculum better. They stated emphatically that they wanted "no theory" from us—that they had had enough theoretical talk. They wanted "practical help" in carrying out instructions. These teachers obviously felt insecure as technicians in their "new job." This was only natural in this transition stage from old to new curriculum and was typical of teachers wherever school systems were trying to introduce new thinking and attitudes. For, broadly speaking, the experienced teachers nearly evrywhere have been trained with major emphasis on subject methodology and have taught under a system which has upheld this traditional approach. These experienced teachers—who had self-confidence when officially supported by courses of study which gave detailed content to be covered in each term, by textbooks with recitation, by disciplinary punishment, gold star rewards—lost their self-confidence when their instructions became less rigid and less detailed. They attempted conscientiously to carry out whatever new instructions were given to them in the way of new techniques—units, trips, conferences, research, children committees, etc. But as a whole, these teachers felt little responsibility for studying their children and for planning experiences for them on the basis of such study. In some schools the teachers were told to be experimental, but few of them were or wanted to be.

In brief, the teachers' initial attitude toward their job was to follow instructions, to put new teaching techniques into practice without much responsibility for understanding the psychological and educational thinking that lay behind these techniques. What had brought about this attitude toward their job? It is important to try to answer this question. For such an attitude toward their job must profoundly affect the growth toward professional maturity of teachers everywhere who have a similar attitude. It is important to know whether psychological conditions under which the teachers carried on their job might explain the common attitude toward their job of a group of highly diversified personalities.

PSYCHOLOGICAL EFFECT OF ADMINISTRATIVE SYSTEM UPON TEACHERS' ATTITUDES

In telling the story of the development of our public school Workshops in Part II, we described the stage set of that six-year experiment with one important omission—the psychological effect upon teachers of the vast administrative system under which they worked and in which most of them had had all their teaching experience. A large proportion of the teachers of our country's children work under somewhat similar systems. So it seems well to attempt some analysis of the nature of administrative systems and how such systems psychologically condition the attitude of teachers toward their job and consequently their growth toward understanding and enjoyment in their new job.

A big school system is organized as an administrative hierarchy with responsibilities for decisions (which means instructions given or permission granted) belonging to a graded series of officials. At the top is the Superintendent of Schools; at the bottom are the teachers, whose job is directly with children, for whom the whole system has come into being. Each successive step up the graded responsibilities is one more step removed from children. A good principal knows the children in his school, but not in the intimate way the teachers do. He deals more with teachers than with children. A good district superintendent knows the children and the teachers in his district only as he sees them in occasional visits to the classrooms. He deals more with principals than with teachers and more with teachers than with children. Step by step up the administrative ladder, officials acquire wider and wider responsibilities and power and become more separated from children and their teachers. And promotion up the rungs of the ladder means increase in salary, which inevitably enhances the higher positions and stimulates the desire for promotion. Such is the nature of this hierarchical type of organization, whether in a school system, a government, an army, or anywhere else.

What psychological effect has this type of administrative organization upon the members who compose it? Since wider power and higher salary depend upon promotion to the next rung of the ladder, it tends to turn the eyes of the members at each level upwards to the occupants on the upper levels, to make them look to their immediate "superior" for instructions, to seek the superior's approval—all of which tends to mean following out *his* instructions, *his* thinking and planning, rather than concentrating their thinking and planning upon the responsibilities at their own level and acting according to their own judgments based upon their own experiences. At its worst, an administrative hierarchy can draw the attention and energies of an ambitious member at any level away from developing his immediate job, and make him an authoritarian in respect to those on the level below him, perhaps to offset the power exercised over him by his immediate superior. An ambitious teacher who is at the lowest level of administrative authority may have his eyes drawn from children to promotion; he, too, may become an authoritarian in his classroom to offset emotionally the power the principal has over him. How to conduct the complicated machinery of a vast school system without the evils of minimizing the importance of the job at each level and without breeding the authoritarian attitude is one of the major problems of public education.

At its best, any administrative ladder has to some extent a psychological effect upon all teachers—not merely upon the comparatively few who are more interested in their own promotion than anything else. The very nature of graded responsibilities (leaving out the salary aspect) is to make teachers who are on the lowest level look to their immediate superior, the principal, for instructions and to conceive of their job as following out his instructions and the instructions issued by those faraway supreme powers, the Board of Education and the Board of Superintendents. Their whole experience within the administrative setup of a big school system has been away from their taking the responsibility for planning individually for their particular children, away from experimentation and initiative in their classrooms, away from trusting their own judgments based on their own experiences, away from taking part in or even following educational efforts which do not affect them personally—in short, away from *taking their teaching job as a profession*. It is an anomaly inherent in this form of administration that the teachers, who are on the lowest level both in responsibility for educational decisions and in salary, are the ones who really control the school lives of the children for whom, presumably, the whole towering system has been erected. It was striking that, as the teachers relaxed in the informal atmosphere of the Workshop, they again and again expressed their sense of this anomaly. They posed this question as one of their greatest problems—How could they take responsibilities for educational thinking within their classrooms though they still remained on the lowest level as far as general decisions for educational thinking in the system are concerned?

It may be that all of this is but a reflection of the total society in which our public school system evolved—a time when the hierarchical ladder prevailed in business, in family, in social organizations. To succeed meant in all walks of life rising step by step, away from the actual work of the job nearer and nearer to management—to giving instead of taking orders. All institutions shifting from the old hierarchical form of structure to one more consistent with democratic ideals find difficulty in the transition. And this on every rung of the ladder, those on top trying to develop a more liberal approach as well as those below trying to use a new freedom. Historic lags are characteristic of all institutions in transition. It is all a part of the evolution of democracy.

STAGES OF TEACHERS' PROFESSIONAL GROWTH

As we came to know the teachers, we became sure that their early concentration of their interest on learning-teaching techniques grew out of their attitude toward their job—an attitude which had been built up within an administrative ladder system in which they had been expected to follow instruction from "superior" officials rather than to think through educational and psychological problems for themselves. Their new job asked many new things of them besides using new teaching techniques. It asked them to study their children's needs and interests. It asked them to be flexible, to adapt their programs to their children. It asked them to take responsibility for planning, to be experimental. But psychologically they had been conditioned by what had been asked of them under a hierarchical ladder system in which they stood on the lowest rung. Their role had been to follow instructions handed down from above. No wonder that they did not trust themselves to take on new kinds of responsibilities and initiative, to be experimental. No wonder their anxieties centered upon learning *how* with only secondary interest in learning *why*.

First Stage: Self-Confidence in Thinking, Planning, and Experimenting

This, then, was where the Workshop began. The teachers, for all their differences in personality, in background content, were impatient of talk about what children are like and how to fit a curriculum to children's needs; they said such basic concepts were "mere theory" and of "no practical use" to them; they were unanimous in wanting from us practical help—to be told or shown *how* to handle "the activity program" or *how* to organize and conduct a "unit." Since we believed teachers, like everyone else, learn better by experience than by words, we began what they called "demonstration teaching" of children in the classrooms, followed in our Workshop meetings by discussions of the children's responses. We planned and took trips with a teacher and her children; we helped to get dramatic play started, or to organize an original play, or to make a map or a mural; we conducted a science experiment, and led follow-up discussions with the children.

After such demonstration teaching, the teachers tended *to repeat what we had done* rather than to work out new experiences for the children adapted to a new situation. A few illustrations: After a staff member had planned and taken a trip with a teacher and her children, a teacher repeated the same trip with her next group of children though a different trip would have contributed more to the current study. Teachers continued to use the source material we had brought rather than hunt for new materials themselves. After a staff member had helped a class of sixth-grade children to organize an original play by starting them off on writing jingles for each step in the process of making a woolen coat, from the sheep to buying the coat in a store, the teacher repeated this same pattern in the plays she later helped the children to write. That is, the teachers followed rather than taking initiative and experimenting along new lines. We were convinced that this pattern of following was not due to lack of originality or ability. Nor did we think the teachers were particularly resistant to a new way of teaching. Rather, they lacked self-confidence in what was genuinely a new job. We felt their pattern of following was a holdover of attitudes built up by their old job, in which they had been expected to follow in detail the instructions handed out to them. So long as they held to this old pattern, they could not throw themselves wholeheartedly into what was genuinely a new job. But to break this pattern they needed a degree of self-confidence, and that required time. The assurance that we were not supervisors trying to rate them was accepted only slowly. When it was finally accepted, they became less afraid of failure. The first stage in their growth was when they acquired enough self-confidence to experiment, to try out something new and not be unduly upset if their first trial was not altogether successful. Only then did tension begin to give way to satisfaction in this new way of teaching.

Naturally, it took some teachers longer than others to reach this first stage of self-confidence. We continued to give concrete suggestions and to encourage any attempt at independent planning until a teacher felt secure enough to use us as advisers rather than as guides to be followed.

Second Stage: Desire to Acquire Background Content

At first we supplied the background content and source material necessary for any particular project or unit. Each of us arrived at school staggering under some load. We brought relevant books for both the children and the teachers. We brought pictures from our Bank Street files—even enormous graphic relief maps difficult to manipulate in the subway. We also brought some educational materials and tools such as simple science equipment and our Bank Street tubs of plasticine when the teachers modeled maps. In all our informal discussions with the children or at Workshop meetings, we naturally drew upon the background content which we had accumulated through years of teaching children and teachers. Much of it was new to the teachers. Most of them used our source materials and background content eagerly when they saw how interested their children were and how children began to observe new things and ask questions which showed genuine intellectual curiosity.

By the end of our first Workshop year, a common remark was, "We don't know enough to teach this way—we haven't the background content." The group, as a whole, asked us to devote considerable time the following year to talks on straight background content. Many asked for a list of readings for the summer. As a group they decided to work on gathering such material for a school source material library. Here was a big step forward in the teachers' growth—a step which meant an appreciation of how the use of all sorts of sources could enrich the children's curriculum experiences. It meant more than that, too. Eventually it meant an acceptance of more after-school work as a part of their job. It meant a sharing of their experiences and problems and a sharing among themselves of precious "private" stores of pictures and other source materials. It meant an extension of their interest and their sense of responsibility from their own classroom to the school as a whole.

Third Stage: Growth of the Concept of Curriculum Building

The teachers' understanding and interest in their new job broadened gradually along two lines—subject matter and child development—until they finally merged into the concept of curriculum building.

Their growth in thinking about child development had gone through several stages. At first their interest was largely limited to disturbed children. Nearly every teacher had some children whose behavior showed maladjustment, and some teachers had classes composed entirely of such children. The teachers' initial approach to child psychology was in terms of the troublesome problems they had to handle in their own classrooms. Many of the teachers began by rejecting children with behavior problems. "You can't do anything with such children." "You can't change their homes, so why try to do anything?" "They oughtn't to be in school anyway." This attitude of rejection gradually grew into an eagerness to understand why these children were so disturbed and disturbing, a challenging of a quick judgment that nothing could be done for them in school. Of course, a number of children *were* too unstable to be in school. But more and more, the teachers wished to give understanding help before saying, "They oughtn't to be in school."

From this limited interest in disturbed children the interest of most of the teachers eventually broadened until it included the total growth of all children. They came to recognize that all children have emotional needs which teachers must meet; also, that a child's ability to learn is closely tied up with a satisfying life. They began to question some of the old techniques of human relationships such as praise cards and gold stars. What did such rewards do to those unsuccessful in this competition? To those who succeeded? Did such rewards split the group into rival camps? Did they turn attention to achievements rather than to interest? Most of the teachers came to feel such rewards were harmful, that children were as genuinely interested in co-operation, group undertakings, as they were in competition. They told the principal how they felt and he accepted their point of view.

This growth in understanding children was brought about in a large measure by the Workshop discussions of actual children in this school—children these teachers were teaching—rather than of "the child" in general. The Bank Street psychologist observed the children in their classrooms and then discussed them in the Workshop. The principal had asked each teacher to make a case study of one child. Since most of these case studies were of disturbed children, the psychologist asked each teacher to make at least one study of a child the teacher felt was growing satisfactorily. Discussion of these case studies of their own children helped the teachers to understand the emotional needs of all children and the special needs at different stages of maturity as a basis of teacher-child relationships as well as the other human relationships in the home and with other children.

Understanding children's emotional needs made a marked difference in the atmosphere of the classrooms of many teachers.

Another closely related aspect of child development was how children learn at various stages in their process of growing up. Such words as "children's interest drives," "direct experiences," "maturity levels," passed from the realm of theory into the realm of practical curriculum planning. Understanding how children learn had direct bearing upon teaching techniques. The teachers' interest in *how* to acquire skill in the new techniques broadened to *why* these techniques helped children to healthy all-around growth.

The teachers began by thinking of curriculum content as a series of separate courses of study and separate units. From this, bit by bit, they grew to think of a total program for their own children, a year's program built up of progressive experiences and activities centered around basic relationships in various kinds of information that the children were gathering. When the teachers began to reach this point we suggested that the Workshop plan curriculum materials in social studies for the whole school. The working out of this curriculum revealed a startling growth in the teachers whose interests only a year and a half before had been largely limited to the acquisition of new teaching techniques. Not only did they now think clearly and constructively about progressive steps in the total curriculum subject matter in social studies which children from kindergarten through sixth grade were ready to take: they extended their thinking to the children in the whole school system. That is, they did not want to do something for just their one school, though the Workshop had received permission to work out a fairly independent experimental curriculum. They distinctly wished to work within the prescribed framework of the official curriculum. But within this official framework they wished to experiment, to find out how to interpret the prescribed curriculum content in ways that were best for children's growth.

At this point, they were actually combining child development with curriculum content. Children's needs—physical, intellectual, and emotional—became a basis not only for teaching techniques but for selection of subject matter as well. When the two basic concepts—child development and fitting the curriculum to the child—became thus closely interrelated, the teachers were ready to *build* a curriculum. The social studies curriculum which the Workshop wrote (teachers, administration, and Bank Street staff) was based on the two fundamental concepts—what children are like and what subject matter, experiences, and activities best further their growth. These were exactly the basic concepts which at the beginning of our Workshop the teachers had said were "mere theory" and "of no practical use" to them. That the teachers were able so quickly to understand and apply these concepts shows, we think, that as a group they were learners. And what better can be said of a grownup than that he is still a learner?

Fourth Stage: Relating Their Job to the World Outside the School

As their own jobs became more creative, we thought we noticed that the teachers were keeping more closely in touch with educational thinking and happenings elsewhere. Current books and magazine articles were constantly recommended by teachers at our meetings, as were interesting exhibits and lectures. We thought this indicated that the teachers felt more closely identified with the broad aspects of education everywhere.

As the teachers became more responsible for building their social studies curriculum, we heard more and more talk about national and world issues. We are in no position to judge whether their social thinking had been stimulated, for we had not known them in their lives outside the school. But this we think we can say: the social problems of the world had become more related to their job as teachers and they shared their thinking both as adults and as professional teachers. The suggestion that we ask someone to talk at a Workshop meeting about intercultural relations came from the teachers. One such meeting considered intercultural relations from the point of view of teaching techniques at various maturity levels. Another was frankly a thrashing out of points of view about the One-World concept on an adult level. We thought it significant that the teachers felt a Workshop for teachers in school was a suitable place for such discussions. We are reasonably sure that they would not have felt so at the beginning of our Workshop experiment.

TEACHERS DEVELOP A PROFESSIONAL ATTITUDE

All these growths, which we have somewhat arbitrarily enumerated as stages though many took place simultaneously, worked toward a professional attitude. Their attitude, their conception of their job, certainly expanded. And not merely in the kinds of work which, as we have indicated, they undertook in order to be better teachers. The most refreshing aspect of the growth of teachers as we watched it was subtle yet evident. There was an atmosphere of stimulation. Their new job was a challenge—not a frightening chore. Every Workshop teacher we met was bubbling over with some tale of "what her children had done." These teachers, as we have said, had a deep interest in their children. When they saw their children taking on new interests, new zest for observing and finding out, new habits of tackling a problem by thinking out relationships, new ways of expressing their thinking and feelings, the teachers themselves became excited. It worked, this new curriculum! They became inventive, experimental—and industrious, too. For this new way of teaching means hard work. The lazy, the indifferent will never teach this way except in superficial forms, but they are a small proportion of the teachers. Most of them got deep satisfaction in having a creative job. For that is exactly what their new job is. Creative jobs are always hard work, yes. But they are fun too.

We believe that only a negligible percentage of the teachers who have experienced creative teaching would wish to give it up. As they grow in creative power in their classrooms, they are more aware of and impatient at the practical handicaps under which their work is done and which are not inherent in this way of teaching—poor equipment, little space, large groups. Any school system that really wishes its teachers to do a creative job must implement its new curriculum. Any community that wishes its children to be taught by enthusiastic, creative teachers must insist that unnecessary handicaps be done away with. It may be that teachers themselves will become a force in bringing about clearer community thinking which will demand better working conditions for children and their teachers in our school. It may be that the teachers, once they are released from the psychological handicaps of authoritarian supervision to creative teaching, will become our educational leaders. They are closest to our children in their school lives. Is it too much to ask that we should look to them for educational guidance?

16

Glimpses of Teachers in Action

W E HAVE just analyzed how the teachers grew toward professional maturity. No amount of analysis, however, can give any adequate picture of these teachers in action. Nor can the day-by-day reporting of curriculum building in Part II give a picture of the kind of life teachers and children live together when a curriculum is being built in a living situation. It is difficult to describe what happens when teachers are in action—watching their children, meeting their needs as they arise. Evaluation is difficult because the picture is complex. Yet, the real human quality of the experience can best be seen as teachers work—the atmosphere created, the children's interest, the sense of groupness, the teachers' devotion to their children, their creative teaching, their satisfactions, their conception of the responsibilities of their profession. We of the Bank Street staff who watched these teachers at work felt this human quality, which is of such vital importance in a good life both to children and to teachers. We hope our readers may sense some of it through the following sketches made from our records. Some of the illustrations we have chosen are of teachers of children who were slow in acquiring academic skills. This is not so much because in this school we had many children from low-income homes who had been handicapped by having had very inadequate cultural and educational opportunities (some ten-year-old children from the South had never been to school at all). Rather, it is because in this school the best teachers were quite commonly assigned to classes which presented

the hardest problems. Also, it seems fair to argue that if the new
education can succeed with "slow" or "difficult" children, it can
succeed with children less handicapped by the conditions life has
brought to them. The sketches give glimpses of only a few teachers
in action. All of them show only patches of a year's program, or how
a teacher handled one situation with a particular group of children.
They are in no sense designed to be "case histories" of teachers.
Rather, they are designed to show how teachers with markedly different personalities, backgrounds, and talents *analyzed the needs of
their children and built a curriculum creatively to fit these needs*—
which is, perhaps, as good a definition of professional maturity as we
can give.

READING AS A PART OF LIVING: A FIRST-GRADE TEACHER IN ACTION

One experienced teacher of first-graders was a good teacher,
sensitive to children as young human beings, sensitive to the wide
social values in the world inside and outside the school, long before
she came to the Workshop. She felt cramped by the old courses of
study, which she still followed conscientiously, and was feeling her
way toward giving her children a richer, fuller school life. In our
first contacts with her she showed an eagerness to understand and to
put into practice the newer thinking about children and a curriculum
for them. But she was shy in our presence. Indeed, she was more her
real self with a group of children than with a group of adults in the
Workshop. Nevertheless, she welcomed us in her classroom and
talked with increasing freedom about her teaching problems and
about children whose behavior puzzled her.

She began almost immediately to experiment with the new teaching techniques in giving her young children firsthand experiences,
keeping intelligent and understanding watch of the children's reactions. She, like all first-grade teachers, faced the problem of teaching reading. How could an academic skill like reading be tied up
with six-year-olds' interests in how things and people worked in the

here-and-now world in which they lived? How could these young children learn something of social value to them along with a necessary academic skill? Early in her year's program she took her children on a trip—not a long trip, for her children were numerous and young and not yet accustomed to trips. Before the trip she found out from the custodian when coal was to be delivered to the school. When the truck arrived, she and the children gathered on the sidewalk and watched. This teacher did not talk much. She watched the children, and this is what she noted. Even the children speak little. Their eyes and ears are too busy for much talk. They watch the driver grind the crank that raises the body of his truck, take the cover off the hole in the sidewalk, put up the chute. Then the coal begins to slide. Subdued noises from the children—not words, just noises like the coal. They watch the driver put the cover over the hole. Now they know what that round thing is for. They watch the driver climb up into his seat. "Good-by!" they yell. Now they know a driver of a coal truck. He is a strong worker. He is their friend.

Back in the room the teacher does not at once ask the children about the trip. She knows that six-year-olds take a period for digestion before an experience becomes a part of themselves. The next day the children gather for a discussion time. On the board she writes, "We heard the coal." She asks what the coal sounded like when it slid down the chute. A chorus of sounds follows. One by one she writes on the board what various children say. With excitement the children read the sounds. They have made up a story! They can read it!

> We heard the coal.
> The coal said,
>   "Bang, bang, bang, bang,
>   Sh, sh, sh, sh,
>   Bump, bump, bump."

and so on down the list. That was the first of many charts about the coal.[61]

[61] Appendix 12: First-Grade Charts.

There were charts about what the children saw in the school cellar—the big pile of coal, the big furnace, the hot glow as the custodian's helper opened the furnace door, the way he shoveled in the coal, the big pipes from the furnace, the little pipe connected with the radiator in their room. Now they knew how their room was kept warm. They could read it over and over.

More charts about what they saw and heard on the East River— little tugboats, barges heaped with coal, big derricks unloading it. Machines and men doing work. More strong workers.

This was a shared creative language experience for the group. But six-year-olds need more and other expression than they can get through words to make information their own. The children dramatized almost everything they saw. They were drivers of coal trucks; custodian helpers; men unloading barges, derricks, tooting boats. Gravel was coal. Blocks were furnaces, trucks, barges—anything.

According to instructions, these children's curriculum in social studies should be stated in terms of units. In her report the teacher stated this series of trips, discussions, and dramatic play as a unit on coal. It was not, however, an isolated episode. Rather, it was a part of a study of home, school, and neighborhood (the official social studies theme for first grade) on a six-year-old play level. Other workers, other city work, entered the developing curriculum—the scissors grinder who sharpened the butcher's knife and the tailor's scissors, the neighborhood butcher using his sharp knife, the tailor using his scissors, the bakeshop, the garage, the milk truck bringing the little bottles of milk which the big children brought to their room, trips, discussions, dramatic play, and a whole series of stories about themselves which the children could read. She read the children more stories about things they could not go to see. She hunted for printed books with relevant content. When she found none she began experimenting in writing such stories herself. (She was one of the group who joined the Workshop class in writing which met after school on days other than the Workshop.)

Trips, discussions, and dramatic play were the chief but not the only new techniques with which this teacher experimented. As she gained in self-confidence, her conviction grew that her children not only developed wider interests and better work habits when they were given wider school experiences in their familiar world but that they actually learned academic skills faster and more soundly.

This teacher later spoke to the school faculty when the Workshop plan was under consideration for another year. She said she didn't know how she could now teach "the old way." She now plans a flexible school program for the year based on experiences in the here-and-now world that six-year-olds live in. She has found out through her experience and thinking the many ways in which her children were growing while at the same time they were taking the early steps in the difficult technique of learning to read.

They were growing as *thinkers.* Thinking is seeing relationships. They were seeing the relationships in the world they lived in—their homes, their school, their neighborhoods, their city. They were learning about work and workers.

They were growing as *scientists.* They were making observations and recording them. They were growing by the scientific method of research.

They were growing as *artists.* Their experiences turned into paintings, dramatic play, dancing, stories. They were learning not only by taking in information but by giving it out in their own terms.

They were growing as *social beings,* learning social techniques. A trip is a big social experience. So is dramatic play. So is a discussion. So is creating stories. All these shared experiences helped to build a sense of groupness as well as to develop independence.

All of these growths were a part of the children's total school life. They were not scheduled—one period for bodily growth, one for mental, another for social growth. A child is an organism, and an organism reacts as a whole to a situation. It is only for convenience in our talk that we split these growths into separate compartments. A happy child learns better than an unhappy child, an active child better than a passive child. Reading was a part of a total experience, a part of living, a skill which helped the children to do something they wanted to do, namely, to record and read a pleasant experience. A teacher who has learned this through her own experience and thinking will *build a curriculum* based on the total needs of her children.

EXPERIENCES IN WHICH SLOW CHILDREN CAN SUCCEED BEFORE LEARNING THE THREE R'S: A THIRD-GRADE TEACHER IN ACTION

Another experienced teacher had a class of third-grade children who had made little progress in the second grade either in self-control or in academic subjects. She had been given this group because the principal felt that she could and would establish friendly relations with any children and would not take a disciplinary attitude toward the non-readers and the profoundly disturbed children in the class. She had been in our Workshop the previous year and had begun to experiment in the new way of teaching with the class of fairly fast learners and fairly well-adjusted children that she then had.

Later, she told us what happened this second year:

"After I had had this difficult class for two or three weeks, I went to the principal and told him, 'I can hold this group and I can teach the old way, but I can't do anything more.' And he just looked at me and said, 'Are you kidding?' Well, I went away and thought it over. That was when I learned to start backwards. But it was slow! I got clay and the children began to work—even the difficult children. There were about eight of them—one girl ended in Bellevue. One boy had been so very difficult—well, that boy was so skilled with his hands that all you needed to do was to give him something to work with. But these children couldn't read. They couldn't write. And I didn't even try to make them.

"Then I got some carpentry tools. We had no carpenter's bench but we managed somehow. This particular boy made a most beautiful little box. The others began to go to him—this happened very gradually, you understand. The other children would go to him and say, 'How do you do this?' 'Will you help me?' And do you know that by the end of the year that boy was up by my desk struggling away with an original story, saying, 'Miss ——, how do you spell this? Miss ——, how do you spell this?' They were all writing stories by the end of the year. And reading, too. You ask the teacher who had them the next year. She was amazed how well they could read, for they were a 'dull group.' But it's hard to work this way. I never thought I could do it. But what a satisfaction! Sometimes you just have to start backwards. Those children needed that clay in their hands. They came around to reading and writing later."

The next year this teacher had another group who were largely non-readers. One morning Dicky, one of the boys, came to school very agitated. He told the teacher that a few days ago a white rat that had been someone's pet had come down from an upstairs apartment into his room. His mother had let him keep the white rat as a pet until the rat began to chew her curtains and other things. Then the mother told the older brother to sell the rat. Dicky had hidden the rat in the garbage can so his brother couldn't find his pet. "Miss ——," said Dicky with tears running down his cheeks, "will you let me bring him to school for just this afternoon?" This teacher, frankly, did not like rats, white or otherwise. But she saw that this disturbed little boy loved his pet. So she said, "Yes." That was the beginning of the story, "Mickey Goes to School," [62] which was written as easy reading for these children from the teacher's records. It is all true—how the children made a house for Mickey, studied diets for him, shared responsibilities for his care, and finally on their own initiative took their pet to a medical center because they had heard that the doctors needed white rats in studying how to make sick people well. Through sharing this great emotional experience, these difficult children became happy and co-operative, and academic skills became less difficult.

YOUNG CHILDREN ACHIEVE SOCIAL THINKING ON THEIR OWN LEVEL: A FOURTH-GRADE TEACHER IN ACTION

The difficult third-grade children who had learned to read and write by being "taught backwards"—that is, by getting interested

[62] Included in the new edition of *The Here and Now Story Book*, Lucy Sprague Mitchell, Dutton, New York, 1948.

in something they could really do, clay modeling, carpentry, taking care of a pet before instruction in academic subjects—went the next year to another of our Workshop teachers. This teacher had read widely on child psychology, had a rich accumulation of background content and a deep interest in human relationships in the classroom and in the world at large. She was one of the teachers to whom the newer thinking about children came as a great release to her real creative ability as a teacher. When we first knew her, however, she lacked self-confidence in putting the newer thinking into practice. Naturally experimental, she worked hard on the new techniques. The log she kept of her classroom work in an earlier year appears in Appendix 18. She now took over the slow and difficult fourth-grade children we have met as third-graders with Mickey. We quote her own description of how this group of children developed their own concepts of world events and added to their social development. The dramatized discussion by the children was taken down nearly verbatim by a Bank Street student placed in her class.[63]

Children often show a social awareness which is way beyond their years, their background, or their scholastic abilities. I have ample opportunity to observe this phenomenon daily in my fourth-grade class in a school situated in a mixed racial and depressed economic area in Manhattan. My class of twenty-four boys and girls, whose mental equipment ranges from an I.Q. of 76 to 110 and whose scholastic advancement has been very slow, are nevertheless very interested in world events.

A regular feature of our daily program is a morning get-together where we exchange experiences, sing songs, discuss current events, and occasionally dramatize freely any interesting occurrence in school or out of it. The children in my class, coming from poor homes and broken homes, have, as a result, little opportunity for social intercourse and resultant social discussions. However, the movies, the radio, the picture newspapers, and the comics, as well as their own needs, do contribute to their social awareness. This is brought out daily in these morning get-togethers.

When the daily papers featured the progress of the United Nations

[63] This appeared as an article titled "We Dramatize the United Nations," in *Childhood Education,* May, 1947, pp. 435–436, by Tillie S. Pine.

Organization, I waited for an opening during the morning discussion period to bring the issue to the attention of the class. One morning events played right into my hands. Fred walked in with just the right book, *Photographic Record of World War II.* He showed the pictures to the class and we discussed the many nations and places that were involved in the war just ended. I took the opportunity to open the discussion on the United Nations Organization by asking such questions as: What did the people of the world decide to do in order to avoid another war? How many countries make up the United Nations? Is Japan one of them? Is Germany? How were the people chosen to go to San Francisco? Who sent the English, the Russians, the Chinese?

We talked about the United Nations Charter and I read the preamble to them, asking them to see how many words they could remember. They remembered "no more war" and "peace always." I suggested that they might like to dramatize the United Nations Conference at San Francisco. This is the way they did it:

Eugene is appointed chairman and to represent the U. S. A. He names other children to represent Russia, China, England, Turkey, France.

"I'm American," said Eugene. "When they come in I shake their hands." He greets each one cordially as he comes from the coatroom where the planning had been done. Each representative names his country as he steps out.

Several children had wanted to represent China, England, and Russia. One member of the class said as they were arguing over who was to be China or England, "They'll have a war there if they keep this up."

Soon all the children who represent the United Nations are lined up facing the U. S. delegate.

Eugene: "First we will have our famous song." He begins to sing our national anthem, joined by the class and delegates.

I suggest that since the other delegates will not know our anthem one person usually sings for all the rest. Thomas then sang "My Country, 'Tis of Thee."

Eugene: "We the people brought you here for a serious matter. We are trying to form a government, a court for the whole world. Anyone have anything to say?"

Mexico raises his hand (Laurence) then gets confused: "I don't know what to say. I think if one country starts a war and all countries got together . . ." His voice trails off.

Rudolph (China) stands on chair and insists on talking in Chinese. The children say they won't understand him. Eugene says he will interpret when Rudolph finishes. So Rudolph imitates Chinese language and does very well.

Eugene interprets (stands on chair and pretends to talk into a mike): "He said his country lost a lot of people. They don't want war. They want peace. That's why he came here. They want food. The Japs burned the rice fields. They have been at war a long time. He was glad the conference was going to be. The United Nations are good people. He said all his people would be grateful if they have peace."

All applaud.

Robert: "I am from Turkey. The Turkish people need peace. They do not like to fight."

I ask, "This is fine, but what do you want the United Nations to do?"

Several voices say, "Peace all the time."

McCarvin: "I'm from England. My country was fighting against the Germans. We want peace."

Fred wants to speak for France. Eugene objects and says France gave up.

"Right," I interrupt, "but they became one of the United Nations. They went over to our side."

Fred speaks: "My people want peace. Most of our people were killed by the Germans."

England asks to speak again. Eugene objects. I explain that as the conference lasted several weeks delegates had a chance to speak several times.

McCarvin (England): "My country has been burned and bombed. We need food. Some of my people were hung by the neck and shot by a firing squad. We want freedom, no Germans breaking in. I don't want war. I want freedom of churches, freedom to get a job, freedom to take care of your child, freedom to see that you raise 'em right. Instead of letting them run in the streets, build playgrounds. I want parks, hospitals. Children nice and healthy and strong. Nothing to worry about. If they get in trouble someone to do them a favor, maybe nice and kind to them. No war. That's all, ladies and gentlemen."

Applause.

Eugene makes a speech for the U. S. A.: "Ladies and gentlemen, we must have peace. I want all of you to sign this. Then we'll get along more better. We want no arguments like this: 'My people is better.' 'No, my people is better.' If you do that you'll be like Hitler. All people are the same, even if you have different color skin or hair or anything. No people are better. Sign this and get along with one another. They are your next-door neighbor even if they are countries. Step up like brave men and sign. Pound Hitler into the ground."

Applause.

"What will happen if one country goes to war?" I ask.

Eugene: "We'll get together, have a club, and talk. Every country will talk."

The delegates sign the charter and the play is over.

The free dialogue gives the children an opportunity to express their ideas without worrying about spelling and form and to crystallize whatever knowledge they have gained during the discussion periods. The emotional maturity of the group has a chance to be channeled in directions that will contribute toward their intellectual growth. Dramatization gives the dull an opportunity to identify themselves with famous people who may have an effect on their own future. Thus dramatization emphasizes the "intelligent use of the principle that interpretation and generalization . . . are valuable only when based on an understanding of the facts to which they relate." *

This teacher was not only creative and understanding in her own classroom, she was a leader. She is one of the public school teachers now released from the classroom to work with us as a member of the Workshop staff.

FROM GANG LIFE TO NEIGHBORHOOD RESPONSIBILITY: A SIXTH-GRADE TEACHER IN ACTION

One more sketch of a teacher in action. Because of her deep interest in social problems, her sensitive awareness of the influence upon children of social and economic conditions in the homes and neighborhood, and her unstinted devotion to her work, she was given a sixth-grade class which contained a number of overage children—overage not because they were mentally retarded, but because they had been bored by school to the point of truancy. This teacher was used to children who were labeled "misfits" in society. She understood them; she liked them. Long before we came to the school, she and her classes had taken on responsible jobs for the school, such

* From the Harvard Report on General Education.

as, for instance, getting the cards and rooms ready for giving out ration books in the school. When the Workshop came, she and her children took on jobs for us such as preparing the clay in the storeroom, grown hard from long standing, for the use of Workshop modeling of maps, and mimeographing the social studies curriculum. If these jobs helped to give her children a sense of "belonging," a pride in carrying responsibilities, she unhesitatingly took on after-school work to carry them through. From the Workshop she wanted largely ideas and techniques for new concrete work which would help her children to become interested in aspects of the neighborhood and the world which their own experiences had failed to develop. She quickly made her own the map-thinking and map-making techniques which we gave to our Workshop teachers. She developed maps in an original way in her program as an additional tool to use in answering the fundamental questions she asked herself: What could geography, what could American history, mean to adolescents who had found street life more interesting than school life? What could civics, what could democracy, mean to children whose standards and play were largely influenced by movies of gangsters and whose adventures had often led to encounters with the law?

She began with here-and-now American history—the life of the community where the children lived. The principal of the school wanted a map of the school district recording block by block the house numbers, many of which had been recently changed. The class undertook the neighborhood survey which such a map entailed. Many of the children worked after school by themselves or with their tireless teacher. In class they began to discuss what they had seen— the kinds of living quarters in the district, the kinds of stores and public services. From these discussions developed a large pictorial map of the district.

The children became curious about what went on inside some of these buildings. The teacher arranged trips—not only to firehouse, police station, and telephone buildings but also to settlements, clinics, Y.M.C.A. and Y.W.C.A. centers, clubs, housing developments, nurs-

ery schools. The class was invited to swim in a swimming pool—
the boys one afternoon, the girls another. They visited a children's
court, though this was not in the neighborhood. Nor was it a new
experience to all of these children.

Discussion of all these neighborhood and city sights led in several
directions. How had this neighborhood grown into its present pattern? The children plunged into history, at first local history. But
they soon discovered that their neighborhood was an outgrowth of
large social and economic movements through which the United
States had developed from the past to the present. History took on
meaning. They discussed what present situations were responses to
war needs; what developments were undesirable and should be done
away with.

Gradually from their own experiences they formulated standards
for the community. Among the community needs which were not
being met but which bulked large in their thinking were housing
developments, nursery schools, play opportunities for children of
their own age—not just playgrounds but swimming pools, brass
bands, carpentry shops.

That these children knew the neighborhood gangs was shown by
the play they wrote. The plot: Two gangs have a street fight, are
arrested by a policeman who wants them "sent up the river," are
tried at a juvenile court where neighbors testify against them, and
are finally put in charge of a probation officer who makes an elo-
quent closing speech in which she says that the community is partly
responsible for these gangs and their misdeeds since it provides
neither play space nor interesting occupation for its boys and girls.

Two large maps developed—one a section of the school district
as it is now, the other the same section as the children would like to
see it. On these maps stood a hundred or more small clay buildings.
The first map, modeled from the world they knew, showed fire escapes down the front of walk-up apartments and tiers of clotheslines
with fluttering wash from the windows in the rear yards—little open
space, no trees. The second map, modeled from their vision of a

future, showed a housing development with buildings radiating from a center to insure light to all. Around the grounds they placed tiny sponge trees, a wading pool beside the nursery school building, a ball field near the clubrooms for boys and girls. They painted the windows of the building with phosphorescent paint which glowed in a darkened room with realistic cheer.

The class discussion, however, ranged beyond these physical improvements which could be expressed in their map. Unemployment and discrimination in hiring had been experienced by many of these children through their parents. War, too, had a personal significance to them. Many had fathers in active service; many had fathers or mothers in war industries. A historical approach to these present-day problems helped these children to a better understanding of the present harsh world in which they lived. They began to feel responsible for their neighborhood, not merely antagonistic; they organized and took part in a campaign to clean up the dumps in the neighborhood back yards.

These children absorbed facts about history-geography-civics as a hyphenated study. Many of them developed an eagerness in writing. How? Not merely through exercise of bodies, minds, and emotions, but through what might be called exercise in living. In analyzing the world they lived in, they became participants in their community in constructive ways. They were also projected into the future as participants. This teacher was *building a curriculum* to fit the *special needs of children* who had refused to conform to the school and society's standards.

TEACHERS GIVING THEIR CHILDREN A GOOD LIFE

All these glimpses of four teachers in action show them following the prescribed subject matter and at the same time giving the children rich experiences and guiding them toward social thinking. On the young level, six-year-olds learning to read while exploring the work and workers in the here-and-now environment of their homes, school, and neighborhood; difficult third-grade children overcoming their resistance to academic skills through hand work and the group interest in taking care of a pet; these same children as fourth-graders struggling to solve the problems of the United Nations; overage children entangled in gangs and street adventures, approaching the same neighborhood as the first-graders with developing social standards.

All these teachers took an active part in the children's school experiences. All these teachers *guided their children*—helped them to think, to take in, to explore new source materials both in the world around them and in books, to organize and express their experiences through discussion, dramatizations, and art, to work out relationships between people and the lands they use and, as they grew more mature in their interests, human relationships among people. All these teachers helped their children to *feel* as well as to think. They all built a curriculum which gave their children a good life in school, a life which met the particular needs of their children at their various stages of development, to grow in power to think, to observe, to express themselves, to live with others, to care about others outside their own narrow personal group.

We have sketched only a few teachers. These few illustrate their quality as human beings as well as professional educational thinkers of these public school teachers as we came to know them. All these illustrative programs contain an orderly progression of subject matter. But with subject matter these teachers integrate what they know about the world and what they wish their children to become. Like all teachers who really build a curriculum, they add much of themselves to subject matter. For they are teaching and caring about more than curriculum content. They are teaching and caring about the most sensitive of all human beings—children. And such teachers make children their job.

17

Special Work Related to School Problems

ANY experimental work conducted by a group has ramifications —work that reaches out from the central and planned experiment to special and related problems. Any Workshop staff who attempt to meet a particular situation—the specific needs and interests of a particular group of teachers and children in a particular school neighborhood—will find themselves doing unexpected special pieces of work which they might not do in a differing situation. Also, individual members of the staff will approach their job with specialized as well as general interests and backgrounds which lead to other special pieces of related work. So far we have told the story of our central experiment and analyzed the techniques and results. Now we wish to tell of the techniques and results of some special pieces of related work that developed in response to special situations or special interests and backgrounds of individual members of the staff. These special pieces of work cover a wide range, including written materials, organization of source material libraries, work with student teachers, discussion with leaders of the Harlem community, and research.

WRITTEN MATERIALS

Almost from the beginning of our Workshop, the staff found themselves involved in considerable writing. Our first writing was for the teachers in the school in which we were working. It came from an effort to interpret the new official bulletins and to imple-

ment the new curriculum these bulletins contained. Our aim was
to apply the general statements of the bulletins to our particular
situation. It became one of our regular Workshop techniques to write
and give individual teachers notes we had taken in classrooms or on
trips, and concrete suggestions for possible development in their
programs, often with a brief résumé of relevant background content;
and to give the whole group of teachers written materials summing
up the chief points that had been covered in talks and discussions
in Workshop meetings.[64] The full minutes of Workshop meetings
were open to the teachers but were seldom used except by a teacher
who had missed a session. In addition we compiled full annotated
bibliographies for both teachers and children for every grade. These
reference materials were largely in connection with the *Tentative
Social Studies Curriculum* (including some science), which was our
largest piece of writing.[65] These curriculum materials were the joint
product of teachers, administration, and Bank Street staff, but the
actual writing was done by Bank Street.

One of the Bank Street staff also found herself writing stories for
the children in our school. This was partly to meet the need for
stories with content familiar to these children or directly related to
their programs, of which there are very few in published form;
partly to interest the teachers in writing such stories themselves. All
the teachers were interested in a plan to develop a *Neighborhood
Story Book*. Many of them suggested specific subject matter which
they felt their children needed in story form. Nine of them were
sufficiently interested to ask for a Writers' Workshop in addition to
the regular Workshop. This writers' group met eight times on days
other than those of the regular Workshop meetings. At these meetings we discussed what language meant to children, children's own
language, and techniques of writing stories for children of different
age levels. Each member handed in experiments in "direct language"
and in using rhythm, sound quality, and pattern which heightened

[64] Samples of such written materials are given in Appendices 3–11, 13.

[65] The story of how these curriculum materials came to be written for the
whole school has been told in Chapters 10–13 with some excerpts.

the subject matter. Then each wrote stories for her own children, using these language elements, which the group discussed. We also analyzed some of the stories the teachers were reading in class from the point of view of content and form.

The tangible results in stories for a *Neighborhood Story Book* were slight: three first readers based on reading charts and teachers' records written by the Bank Street member in collaboration with three first-grade teachers,[66] and the story of "Mickey Goes to School" based on the records of a third-grade teacher and written as easy reading for her children.[67] The intangible results are difficult to evaluate. Some few teachers carried this work over directly into their classrooms. Teachers, particularly those of the younger grades, wrote stories based on various experiences that the class had had together, incorporating images and expressions that the children used in discussion. These stories they read back to the children and modified according to the children's reactions or at times their concrete suggestions. Even those teachers who did no writing for their children said they listened with more understanding and pleasure to the way their children were using language, what we have called "the play of language." They also evaluated the stories they read to their children with more attention to the language and content.

In another year, another Bank Street member worked on story writing for children with the whole group of Workshop teachers with marked satisfaction to the teachers themselves. Getting teachers to write stories is a valuable but rather specialized Workshop technique. Perhaps it requires a staff member who has had experience in writing stories for children. We recommend it when there is a writer on the staff for the intangible results, even if the tangible results are negligible.

But meeting needs within our central experiment was not the only reason we found ourselves doing so much writing. We were concerned not only with problems within the Workshop but with prob-

[66] Appendix 12: First-Grade Charts.
[67] See p. 345 and footnote 62.

lems in the broad field of education. We were concerned about the language and setup of most books on education and particularly of official bulletins which were interpreting the newer thinking about children and curriculum to teachers, and this concern led to what has proved to be an important piece of writing.

Traditionally, the language of curriculum bulletins is not only general: it is formal. The very setup of the pages with innumerable I, II, III's and a, b, c's carried a didactic atmosphere rather than a challenging, thought-provoking one. Such language and setup is appropriate only for strictly instructional matter which is to be followed in detail. Though the new bulletins we were following do not have the rigid form of the old syllabus, the language and topical headings still convey little of the challenge of new curriculum to the teachers. There is little translation of the formal statements into images of children—thinking, feeling, acting—though some of the newer bulletins contain a few illustrative photographs. We felt that one of the genuine problems of inservice education or any teacher education situation was to express the newer thinking about children and curriculum for them in language which would give the teachers a new interest and insight into the why of children's behavior and give them enthusiasm for their new job with its new responsibilities. Ultra-formal didactic language is not appropriate for a curriculum statement which is intended to be a guide to teachers as to how to tackle their job of understanding children and of planning a program for them. Discussions of what children are like and how they learn, of teaching techniques and what children get out of an experiential program, even statements of general aims of the school can be stated dynamically—not merely be statements under topical headings. Formal, didactic language is neither convincing nor stimulating. Yet the purpose of the new curriculum is to convince and stimulate teachers—not merely to give instructions to be followed.

At Bank Street we had long been writing about children and curriculum, trying to express the newer educational ideas in language that would be thought-provoking rather than formal and didactic.

So a member of our staff who was also carrying on a piece of research in this school wrote *Teacher! Are These Your Children?* and offered it to the Board. It appeared as a Board of Education bulletin in 1946.[68] Sixteen thousand copies have been distributed to officials and classroom teachers. All the material is based on actual records of children in kindergarten, first and second grades in their classrooms. But the children are not presented after the manner of case histories. Rather, we watch these little human beings behaving with their fellows and with their teachers. Along with the author, we wonder what lies behind their behavior and what we can do about it in terms of what each child is unconsciously groping for. It has proved thought-provoking to the teachers.

A brief excerpt will illustrate the approach to one of the children and the easy informal language which brings the child himself before us.

Michael

So Lively!

His teacher complains that she just can't keep him down. He can't stop talking or sit still, always wants a turn at everything, dashes around the classroom. In fact, he's always so much in the foreground, piping up, doing this and that, that sometimes she's hardly aware of the other children in the room at all. She's always having to speak to Michael, send him back to his seat, or tell him he has to let the others have turns, though he is agreeable enough and seems to mean well.

Let's see what she means. Let's look in on Michael in his first-grade room. . . .

Dismissal time. The teacher, who is standing near the door, has asked Michael to go and get her purse and keys from her desk. Delighted at this chance to move around, he starts right up to the desk. But is it a boy or an airplane, a boat, approaching? He holds his hands pointed in front of him, and steers his way along the aisles, making little motor-like put-put-put sounds.

"Michael! Do you have to make that noise?" his teacher calls.

[68] This bulletin by Claudia Lewis is also available at 69 Bank Street Publications, New York 14, N. Y.

Michael reaches the desk, drops his pointed hands, and turns into a little boy again. He finds the purse and keys and takes them over to the teacher, with little-boy steps. . . .

What is the trouble with Michael?

The only trouble in the whole wide world is that he is a lively, intelligent, imaginative, well-adjusted boy trying his best to get along in a schoolroom that has not yet been able to make the best provision for him, for all its many excellent beginnings.

"Trouble?"

Michael is probably as "normal" a child as we could hope to find in any school. . . .

In fact, he is as pleasant a child to handle as any in the class. The teacher herself has explained this—"He's willing enough, so it seems, but just can't stay put in his seat, or stop talking."

Michael could be the very child the educators had in mind when they planned the active kind of program for the schools—Michael, the normal, happy, eager, lively boy.

SOURCE MATERIAL LIBRARIES

Another piece of work closely related to our central experiment of the Workshop was developing source material libraries in schools. We believe the use of source materials for teachers and children is fundamental in the new curriculum.[69] A source material library in a school is an important way of implementing the new curriculum, one which we believe every school should develop. One of the schools in which we worked already had a good head start on such a library. In our first school there was a children's library which contained some reference books for teachers. A small room called "Reference Library" contained largely reading "Work Books."

In our first school the initiative for collecting and organizing source materials came from the Bank Street staff. A number of teachers, however, soon expressed their willingness to work on it though it took out-of-school time. We had been drawing on a fairly large collection of source materials at Bank Street for the use of individual

[69] See Chapter 9: Extending the Range of Experiences and Ways of Learning, pp. 154 ff.

teachers or as illustrative material in our Workshop meetings. One day when the school was not in session, two teachers met at Bank Street with two Bank Street members. They went through our source library carefully. Our library was organized under headings suitable for the use of our student teachers in their regular course with us. The group discussed what headings would make source material of most practical use at the school.

We started files of printed matter and pictures. Much of this material consisted of clippings from current newspapers and magazines, pamphlets issued by industries showing work processes, travel bureau material, and bulletins issued by the government, particularly by the Department of Agriculture. Nearly all of it was free. Much was brought in by teachers and children who had gathered it for use in their own programs. To supplement the collection of current materials, someone donated to the school past files of magazines such as *Life, Fortune, Asia, National Geographic,* and a number of science magazines. All these materials were cut up and filed under headings with appropriate cross-references to other headings.

Some materials written by teachers or children were filed in the library. The teachers' materials included: a series of original reading charts; typed stories for children; a list of possible trips compiled by a teacher for the school. The children's written materials were largely original plays. A few particularly good murals were preserved in the source library.

Other kinds of source materials began to accumulate, some made in school, some acquired through special purchases. The school bought some simple science equipment from a special fund. The school also bought a set of new graphic relief maps (ten sheets), which covered the world. These were the first relief maps in the school. Several fine maps made by fifth- and sixth-grade children were added. By the end of three years this school had quite a respectable source library.

The room which housed the source library was small. More serious was its position, which was too far away from any classroom to have a class, with teacher supervision, take charge of it. The children's library in this school was managed by a sixth-grade class whose room was next door. We had hoped another sixth-grade group, under teacher supervision, could carry a similar responsibility for the source library as a school job. This plan was never feasible in this overcrowded school. In one of the other schools where we conducted a Bank Street Workshop in our fourth year, the source library files were placed in the children's library. There a sixth-grade class worked efficiently and enthusiastically at building up a source library.

Obviously, a source library is worth while only to the extent to which the teachers use it. We spent one of our Workshop sessions showing the teachers in small groups all the materials which had been gathered. We knew, too, that the more teachers and children were actively involved in gathering such materials, the more they would use them. There were many teachers who had precious private hoards of pictures, for instance. It was a genuine extension of their identification with the whole school to contribute to a school library. Furthermore, the more the teachers took over the building up of the library, the more it became "theirs" and the more likely they were to carry it on after Bank Street had left the school. Certainly the work of building up a source library brought to the teachers a new awareness of the wide gamut of source materials suitable for themselves or for children to use.

But teachers are too busy to organize and keep up such a library without help. The only alternative to such a school source library is to ask each teacher to gather the material she herself needs. Every good teacher is on the lookout for source materials and is constantly adding to her private collection. But again, teachers are too busy to supply even their own needs. Even if they were not, it is a wasteful procedure not to have the gathered materials available to all. Looking over a collection of source materials is in itself a stimulus to enriching the curriculum content. The more a source library can be made the responsibility of the teachers, the better. We do not believe, however, that organizing and keeping up a source material library can or should be the sole responsibility of the teachers. We believe such a library should be a recognized need in implementing the curriculum, should have its own appropriation, which need not be large, and should be in charge of a school official with a supporting teacher committee.

STUDENT TEACHER PLACEMENT IN PUBLIC SCHOOLS

We at Bank Street were interested in the relationship between teacher education centers and public education. We believed such a relationship could be a two-way service, of benefit to both. We were now working both with teachers in public schools and with student teachers at the Bank Street School for Teachers and at New York University, where two of our staff were on the faculty. This seemed a strategic position. So, to our central experiment with teachers in the Workshop, we added the related experiment of placing student teachers with these Workshop teachers.

From the point of view of teacher education centers, it seems obvious that their student teachers should get oriented in the problems of public education, no matter what their background or where their future teaching jobs are to be. Public education is one of the greatest social forces in our culture. As members of the teaching profession, teachers should know and care about what is happening in our schools. As adults, they have a responsibility to take part in moving our schools in the direction they believe in. As in any situation, a firsthand experience in public education should be a learning situation.

From the point of view of a school in which student teachers are placed, the gains may be great. The new education, far more than the old, demands attention to individual children from the teachers. This makes the large group even more undesirable than formerly. Though, in general, schools are trying to reduce the size of the group, the teacher shortage in our present school dilemma has not only prevented reducing the size of classes but in many cases has actually increased them. Both teachers and principals welcomed the idea of student helpers in the crowded classrooms. On our part we felt that having the responsibility for student teachers in their classrooms would further the professional growth of the teachers—that an extension of their job to help in the education of future teachers would be a broadening experience.

So far, so good; a two-way service seemed likely to develop. But not automatically. It requires special work both on the part of the teacher education center and on the part of the teacher with whom the students are placed. By the nature of the case, student teachers need much guidance. Every student teacher needs an adviser who follows her work personally and helps her interpret her school experiences. It is up to the adviser to plan with the principal and with each teacher with whom a student teacher is placed how to make the classroom work a genuine educational, a genuine learning experience. For *the student is there to learn.* Teachers need to be worked with to understand what their job with students is and how to do it. They have to take on a new responsibility. They have to teach the student teachers, not merely leave them to do classroom chores, which is often the attitude of teachers who have never before had students placed with them. They have to teach students classroom techniques by letting them participate, not merely observe. They have to include the students in their thinking about the children and the program planned for them, not merely tell them what to do. Teachers have to learn how to give educational experience to the students, how to watch their growth and gradually hand over to them larger responsibilities. This is a new teaching situation for teachers and one which requires a new technique. Some teachers regard this teaching of students as merely an extra burden; others welcome help on this new aspect of their job and find real satisfaction in doing it well.

A principal, too, sometimes regards the students placed in his school largely as helpers in school situations which require an extra pair of hands. He, too, has to recognize that student teachers are in his school to learn and that their experience will have little educational value if they are constantly called off their own classroom work to help out in other classrooms or on special office work. Principals, too, have to extend their job to the education of future teachers.

Practically, what did our student teachers do in the schools? Their chief work, of course, was in the classrooms with our Workshop teachers. There they were useful in practical ways, which was a part of their job. The Workshop teachers, as a whole, did not limit the students to doing practical chores—or not for long. They responded to their role of teaching the students and welcomed suggestions as to how to give students genuine educational opportunities. Some of our exceptional students made genuine contributions to the teachers themselves. They came with newer teaching techniques and some few with background content which the teachers themselves lacked. Our Workshop teachers took this as a learning situation for themselves. In these exceptional cases, the student became almost an assistant teacher. Our students also took on jobs for the school which seemed educational. They worked on the organization of the materials in the source library, scouted for appropriate trips and for particular source materials. A group of student teachers from New York University contributed to the school source library the source materials they had collected about New York in their own work. A group of Bank Street student teachers who were placed in our first Workshop school chose to write a curriculum study—the culmination of their year's work—about this school. We have already referred to our use of their study of the neighborhood.

To conclude: We believe a two-way service between a school system and teacher education centers will not develop unless both sides feel it worth while to work together. Without such working together, the placement of student teachers in public schools is not likely to give either the student teachers or the classroom teachers an educational experience. But these two groups—school systems and teacher education centers—have much in common in their work.

Both are working on teacher education—one preservice and the other inservice education. If the two groups have common aims and beliefs, if both are trying to get the newer thinking and attitudes toward children and curriculum into action in our schools, if both are trying to move our schools in the same direction, each group should get something worth while and contribute something worth while through a working relation with the other.

DISCUSSION WITH LEADERS OF THE HARLEM COMMUNITY

We believe in having educational content in the curriculum closely related to the lives and needs of the children in any school. The school in which we had our first Workshop happened to be in a neighborhood where both Negro and white people, including many Puerto Ricans, lived. When we began, about 70 per cent of the school children were Negro and 15 per cent were Puerto Rican. The proportion of both Negro and Puerto Rican children increased until in four years there were few others. The children who were learning to speak English were placed in what was called the Foreign Class. Formerly these children came from many countries; later almost all came from Puerto Rico. These children went on trips planned especially for them. On the anniversary of the unveiling of the Statue of Liberty, they climbed to the top of the Statue and afterwards in their classroom had a birthday party for her. By special permission the whole class was allowed to see two hundred people sworn in as citizens of the United States in the courtroom.

Naturally, the question often arose: Should curriculum content and experiences planned for the children in our school be influenced by the fact that so many of these children were Negroes? And, if so, how and in what ways? These questions reached down to the kindergarten and younger grades. Should the dolls these children played with look like Negroes? Did these children react differently to Negro and white children? To Negro and white teachers? At what age? These questions reached up into all the older grades, where curriculum content included history, current events, and science. Should African culture be taught? Should such times in the history of the United States as the Reconstruction period receive special emphasis? Were the children conscious of race discrimination in housing? In jobs? If so, should discrimination be discussed with these children? Did these children have a special need to have their self-esteem built up? In discussing progress in any field, should contributions of Negro scientists, Negro explorers, Negro writers and artists be emphasized? Be labeled?

All these and other related questions were discussed in Workshop meetings; also in a meeting of the Bank Street staff with the principal and his two assistants in our school. There was not complete agreement about whether or not there should be special emphasis in curriculum content highlighting the problems or contributions of Negroes. On one basic question, however, the whole group seemed in general agreement. The native endowment of Negro children is not inferior to that of white children. If their average academic achievement fell below the average achievements of white children as measured by I.Q. tests or age ratings in academic skills and background content, this was due to their lack of cultural and educational opportunities, not to race inferiority. That is, our questions about curriculum content and experiences for our Negro children were never tainted by the assumption that Negroes, because of their race, were fitted to fill an inferior role in our culture. Rather, they were questions such as we would ask about any group of children: What are the environmental influences under which these children grew up? Had these influences created special needs? If so, in what ways could the school meet these needs?

Who could help us to think more clearly about the needs of our Negro children and how our school could meet these needs? We felt our best help would come from both Negro and white people who had lived through and were living through the so-called "Negro problem" at first hand and who had thought deeply on all its aspects. We needed to see our particular school problem against a wider background, to test our own thinking against the thinking of those who had had long experience and had arrived at some conclusions based on their experience. We asked a group of leaders of the Harlem community if they would talk over our particular problem with us and the principal of our school. They accepted and we met one evening at the home of a Bank Street member.

These men and women showed us the broader implications of our questions. From the minutes of the discussion, which ranged over many subjects, we give a few highlights which affected our thinking and so our practice:

In response to the specific question of whether we were right in introducing the story of David Livingstone and Africa into the curriculum content these points were made:

Africa is not the homeland of the Negroes. It is the home of their past origin. We should teach African culture—the great art, ivory and ebony carving, early use of metal before it was used in Europe. We should not link the Negroes entirely with their past in Africa or with slavery in the United States. The myths of the Negro past are the main support of prejudice against Negroes.

Any modification in curriculum content for Negro children will be interpreted by the Negroes themselves as supporting the assumption that Negroes are inferior and require only such education as will fit them for work with their hands.

In discussing the question of emphasizing any period in history or of featuring contributions of Negroes, the points were made:

In teaching the Reconstruction period, get at the real picture—the way it is presented in *Freedom Road.*

Children need to understand reasons why they live as they do—they have to repudiate the conditions they come from. This problem has to be faced head-on—must know the sort of society they live in—get away from the feeling, "I'm from Georgia and proud of it." Must know what conditions lead up to being a tenant farmer—must develop a realistic understanding of modern life, not a fatalistic democracy.

The problems of the Negro are the problems of the country as a whole. The Negro problem is same as that of other groups. It would be fallacious to overemphasize certain prominent Negroes. Successful Negroes are not exceptions in terms of their ability. They just happen to be the ones who have had the breaks. There is this kind of danger in overdoing the prominent Negro.

If George Washington Carver is introduced as a Negro scientist, then call the Polish scientist a Pole, the Jewish, a Jew.

Discussion of the prejudice of Negro children against Puerto Ricans brought out several points of view concerning the problem of prejudice: that prejudice against Jews in Harlem is on the wane lately, landlords are not dominantly Jewish in Harlem, we hear less of this idea than we did five or six years ago; that there is anti-white prejudice which is not deep-seated and could be wiped out easily if the whites were to give the Negroes a square deal; that there is a deep race problem with many Negroes finding it hard to get over the feeling that there is a limit to the degree of acceptance by whites, that Negro children feel deeply the lines that may not be crossed and expect to suffer if they trust the whites.

In discussing the attitude of Negro children toward themselves as well as toward white people, the following points were made: Idea of Negroes having difficulty accepting themselves as Negroes has been overdone. If the school system is concerned over not having Negroes grow resentful it should work on changing the attitudes of the non-Negro, rather than the Negro. It is essential to avoid the hush-hush attitude. Psychologically it is true that the Negro in a hostile environment builds up suspicions, a chip-on-the-shoulder attitude. White teachers with good intentions have been misunderstood at times. The need is for all of us to get to know people in our community, look frankly at racial and religious prejudice. This is a process that should be part of school life.

Some of the general conclusions we in the Workshop reached after this discussion with the leaders of the Harlem community were: that the part played by Negroes in the present and past development of our country should be given somewhat greater emphasis in the social studies curriculum in our school than is usual but that such emphasis should be put in the curriculum for *all* children; that the present trends in schools to have a "unit" on Negroes, or a "Negro Week" in a city program, was false though well-intentioned. This singling out of Negroes, we felt, tended to set them apart as a group instead of having them take their place just as do other Americans who have shared and who share the culture of our country.

Furthermore, we felt that though the universal child need to be accepted was probably more acute in our Negro children than in average children, this need could be met better through the attitude of the teachers toward their children than through modifications of the curriculum content.

RESEARCH RELATED TO SCHOOL PROBLEMS

This discussion with leaders of the Harlem community and other similar contacts and discussions influenced the direction of our work in curriculum building and in the program of study and research which was inaugurated at the very beginning of the Workshop experiment. From this group as well as from teachers in the school we had been told that the youngest children showed no color awareness with respect to their teachers. They were sensitive to the ones who were warm and responsive to them and, when a close emotional bond was established, seemed to assume commonness of color. This problem—the relation between affect and color awareness—we are now studying experimentally, working with children up through the sixth grade.

One phrase, "these children," impinged upon us in many different contexts. There was no problem in combating the myth of inherent inferiority; there was no difficulty in sensing the latent spontaneity and originality of the children whenever they were given appropriate stimulation and an opportunity to relax and be themselves. But there were problems to face, questions to consider and to study concerning the specific life situations of "these children." The teachers were deeply impressed with the high degree of instability of family life in the children's homes, in the high incidence of traumatic life experiences, with the poverty of cultural background, with the frequent exposure to intense, exciting experience right in their own neighborhood and indirectly through frequent unselected movie-going.

Obviously, we were not in a position to undertake an extensive socio-psychological study of the children and their families. We did feel the necessity to penetrate some part of these larger questions experimentally. At least, to make some connection between what the

children were bringing *to* their school experience and what we were
advocating as beneficial for them to derive *from* their school experience.

Experience is important as residue rather than as event. The main
questions which we set ourselves experimentally became what attitudes, what values had these children already absorbed as a residue
of their experience, what did these attitudes lead them to expect from
school as a part of life and from teachers as people and as authorities, and how could these attitudes and expectations (which the children bring with them) be effected by the kind of teacher attitudes
which they would actually encounter in school. Teacher attitude,
teacher-child relationship, as has been said previously, was one of
the cornerstones in our approach to total curriculum revision. Good
teacher-child relationship needs to take into account not only what
is good ideally but what is best under given conditions, with specific
children in mind. Through our research we hoped to make "these
children" more specific to the teachers and to help the teachers to
see more concretely what the effects, in terms of inner values, of
teacher-child relationships can be. Following are excerpts from a
monograph [70] reporting the results of our first experimental study,
which was conducted in our Workshop school referred to as the
North School and in a private experimental school called the South
School where children with contrasting background and experience
served as a control group.

A projective picture technique was devised to explore the feelings of
children about their relationships to their teachers, and their life in
school. Thirteen picture situations, with explanations, and questions
were used to elicit from children expression of their feelings in the
areas of trouble, happiness, good and bad behavior, punishments, and
anger. . . .
The test was given to a total of 94 first- and second-grade children
in four classrooms in a New York City public school, the North School,

[70] *An Experimental Study of What Young School Children Expect from
Their Teachers.* Barbara Biber and Claudia Lewis, Genetic Psychology Mono-
graphs, 1949, 40, 3–97.

and, for purposes of comparison, 25 first-grade children in a private experimental school, the South School.

The majority of the North School children revealed strong pressures to obey in a compliant, blindly obedient fashion. Their concepts of punishment were rather heavily weighted with the expectation of violent handling; however, they took spontaneous pleasure in parties and surprises and had a strong drive to play and work with materials, and in general saw their teachers as sympathetic and helpful, though unemotional. . . .

In general the South School children had a great deal more freedom from pressures and fears in the areas of good and bad behavior, and punishments, than the North School children had. Their concept of the teacher was a warmer one, and they placed more emphasis on constructive *social* aspects of behavior in the classroom. . . .

The fact that the children of one teacher in the North School—the best teacher, whose values were fairly close to South School values—gave responses that were in many ways similar to those of the South School children, led us to believe that it is entirely possible for a teacher to mold attitudes and values through the classroom atmosphere she creates. This is not proved by the findings in this one group, but is offered as a hypothesis for further study. . . .

It is interesting to study the difference in the structure of the value systems, as reflected in these responses of these two groups of children. . . . Thus, we see that the South School children show not only greater absorption of social values but also markedly fewer values that would lead them to expect compliant, obedient behavior of themselves. Their concepts of goodness and badness have much less to do with passively and quietly pleasing and minding the teacher or blindly obeying her than do the concepts of the North School children. Not that they do not take pleasure, as has been noted previously, in being good, in being approved and accepted by their teachers. The fact is they are moving beyond the range of satisfaction through submission. Their heightened social values are evidence of one of the ways, alternate to compliance and obedience, through which they can find pleasure in acceptance by the adult. The difference lies in what is conceived as the essential ingredient of goodness rather than any false independence of the need to be accepted as essentially good.

In the South School children's responses we noted that their concepts of what constitutes good and bad behavior were not only different in content but were also both more specific and more highly differentiated than those of the other group. These concepts were embedded in the ordinary workings and the exigencies of the daily school situation. They were not merely gross counterparts of the nod or the frown of the teacher. The authority of the teacher had already been partly diffused into the needs of the situation, and virtue in the eyes of the teacher lay in making things go right for the group rather than smoothly for the teacher. The implication here seems basic to the whole large question of education for democratic living. The teacher's role leans toward that of an instrumental rather than an arbitrary authority.

Closely tied in with children's concepts of what constitutes bad behavior are expectations of what will happen if one is bad, of how one's bad behavior will be censored, disapproved of, or punished. In the North School, the teacher was much more likely than in the South School to mete out some form of arbitrary punishment rather than deal with the bad behavior in terms of its specific aspects, and punishments conceived by the children were very often violently destructive in nature. The violence expressed was fantasied far beyond the reality of school experience and probably was also in excess of the children's home experiences, in the main. Putting this finding beside other findings such as the concern over compliance and the relatively undifferentiated authority vested in the teacher, another relationship suggests itself which is worthy of further study on other groups of children, in other situations. Children's concepts and fantasies of punishment are a function of the strictness of the code (related to compliance and the authority figure) under which they are expected to behave. In the South School, where children's codes are structured to a greater extent around the specific needs of a social situation and where the teacher, the figure of authority, is partly an instrument for the situation rather than an authority, per se, infringement of the code has less devastating psychological overtones. Broader study of this relationship would be exceedingly valuable as a way of substantiating the claims for positive mental hygiene values implicit in the atmosphere of the modern school. The indications from these findings are that the children of the South School were absorbing a less stringent system of values, conceiving basic relationships (of which the teacher-child relation is certainly one) with a lesser degree of servile compliance and fewer fears of devastating disapproval or punishment. . . .

Throughout it has been pointed out that the values of the children in either school reflect partly school atmosphere and partly home atmosphere. Often, teachers working with children where home mores do not coincide with the philosophy and practices of the modern school feel deep futility concerning the value of what they do. For them, the findings of the group which we have called C46 seem to us to have special importance and should be further studied and checked. If the atmosphere of the school can have as much effect on the development of values and attitudes as seems to be the case in this instance, then the psychological atmosphere of the school as a whole can be seen to be a major factor in counteracting the harsher aspects of reality which many children meet in their out-of-school lives.

The question of retraining teachers is a prominent one. We are impressed, from the experience of our work, with the difficulty in changing psychological atmosphere in a school for several different reasons. Perhaps too much thought has been given to what teachers should be and what they should give children without sufficient thought and analysis of what the children within the larger context of the life atmospheres can really absorb. We are hopeful that a technique such as the one we are working with may illuminate this problem of what the child can learn or become in the sphere of values and attitudes rather than merely what the teacher can give to him. In the intellectual sphere, this point of difference between what is taught and what is learned has been more clearly recognized. The question of the application of mental hygiene to schoolroom atmosphere begins basically with what the teacher feels about the children and what her own ideals for human relationships are. How much these can be passed on to the children will depend on the total school atmosphere, on the children's preconceptions of school as a constellation within which the children have to absorb the values and attitudes of a particular teacher, and on a broader plane it will also depend upon the general life atmosphere of the children, which is an important, decisive factor in determining how readily and how selectively they absorb teacher values.

We found this research program to be valuable in a variety of ways. Primarily, of course, it put us on the trail of reliable answers to perennial questions, especially those heavily laden with futility: What use is all this when a child is only in school a few hours a day? What good does it do a child to trust his teacher if he can't trust other people? From a wider point of view, it helps to relate our work in our school with broad problems of education and even of theory in the field of psycho-social development.

There were values more closely related to our scheme for inservice teacher education. Long before we had arrived at the stage of analyzing findings and drawing conclusions, we used research material in some of our regular Workshop sessions. Our technique lent itself readily to active participation of the teachers. Pictures which had been shown to the children were now shown to the teachers. The teachers were deeply interested in guessing what their children's responses might have been and then hearing their guesses checked against what had actually been the children's responses.

That their guesses were sometimes right and sometimes wrong was not of major importance to them or to us. What mattered more was that this proved a highly effective way of stimulating empathy with children—an inside-out process rather than an outside-in. The teachers became vitally interested in what might be behind the growth of certain attitudes and expectations and, consequently, much less defensive as to whether the children thought well of them or not. More quickly and more directly we found ourselves discussing questions of motivation, relationship, inhibitions, etc., than we would have been able to do without benefit of the research material. This give-and-take relationship between teaching and research is one which proved highly fruitful in this school and has great potentialities for other schools and situations as well.

18

What We Learned

THE Workshop was a learning situation for the Bank Street staff, as is any real teaching situation. Our Workshop job was exceedingly hard work and at times discouraging—which is true of nearly all learning experiences. And as we took on more and more related work, the job became complicated, at times confusing. But we got immense satisfaction out of our work, which is the great reward that should come from teaching. The fact that one is constantly called upon to learn on the job is what makes the profession of teaching so challenging.

The big all-inclusive thing that we learned in our Workshop experience was that it could be done in public education, in the schools that most of our children attend. What do we mean by "it"? Fundamentally, we mean a good life for children—a life that arouses their intellectual interests, gives them emotional satisfactions, develops attitudes of social comradeship with others—all this along with the acquisition of information and skills.

There are many factors which enter into the complicated situation within our schools today and condition the kind of school life children will have. First of all, we saw how some of these various factors, directly or indirectly, affected the children's lives.

ABOUT OUR CHILDREN

We have already said a good deal about these children: that most of them came to school suffering from the lack of cultural opportunities, as do most children in our country who grow up in low-income homes; that many of them came from the South, with inadequate previous schooling, some with none at all; that most of them belonged to that group of Americans whom other Americans penalize for having dark skins; that this school was in a tension area with marked friction between colored and white people. We have told of various Workshop discussions within the school family—administrators and teachers—and of the general attitude within the group that society at large, not the school, not racial inferiority, was responsible for the handicaps which our children brought to school with them; that this attitude produced a school atmosphere where there was little to no friction between the Negro and white members of the school family, no sense of "superior" and "inferior."

But these children showed that something had happened to them which happens to most of the children in our schools regardless of their particular background, something for which our past schools have been responsible. The effect of a big administrative system upon the various members of the school family has been implicit and sometimes explicit in the story of our Workshop. The children showed the effect of large groups (forty or more) where individual initiative is hampered and where individual personalities, particularly those that do not conform to expected achievement or standards of behavior, receive less attention than is possible in small groups (twenty-five to thirty). Our children showed in our research studies as well as in observation in the classrooms that their conception of being good in school was to be quiet and docile and to remember facts which the teacher wanted them to remember. Many simply accepted school as a place where boredom was to be endured and lived their real lives, followed their real interests and drives, outside the school. Their behavior as we watched their play on the streets proved this conclusively. Their eager response and quick learnings when given a chance to learn through firsthand experiences along the lines of their own interests proved to us that these children were fundamentally like all the other children we had taught before. If their behavior in school was more apathetic, less interested than that of the children we knew in experimental schools, it was due in part to the regimentation to which they had been subjected in past school life rather than to native apathy or dullness.

These children had to be taught that even in school it was *all right* to express their opinions in discussions, *all right* to draw what they wanted to and as they themselves saw and felt, *all right* to do active things if they did not disturb or interfere with others. Or perhaps it is more accurate to say, they had to be untaught what old attitudes and methods of teaching had taught them. Once this was accomplished, these children functioned in the new ways adequately—some of them brilliantly. No, there was nothing wrong with these children except what had been done to them by a society which had permitted them to grow up without the full opportunities we like to think we accord to *all* our children, and by traditional school standards and traditional teaching methods, now fast disappearing, which had been a repressive rather than a releasing experience. As far as the quality of our children as human beings endowed with abilities and talents to become young thinkers, young artists, young scientists, young co-operators is concerned, the new education can succeed, can give our children a good life in our public schools.

ABOUT THE WHOLE SCHOOL

A good school life for children depends not upon the children, who, with all their differences in background, have everywhere the same basic needs and interests. It depends directly upon the whole school and indirectly upon people outside the school—the public—and what they wish their schools to be like.

By "the whole school," we mean all the members of the larger school family in the school system from teachers to the Superintendent of Schools and the Board of Education, and all the complex interrelationships among them. If children are to have a good life in our schools, these various members have to function toward that end.

So we give a brief summary of what we learned about some of these members within a big city school system from the experiment we tried out with them.

About Working with a Big City Board of Education

Bank Street is a private organization conducting educational experiments and research related to children, to teachers, and to schools. Why should a big city Board of Education wish to work with such an "outside" organization? Because within a big city school system there are always problems concerned with the direct, practical functioning within the school which need to be approached experimentally—such problems as inservice education of teachers, and related problems—which need more knowledge that only intensive research can yield. Experimental work in its early stages can be carried on in small fluid situations better than in the big unwieldy and less flexible situation usually found within a big public education system. Such small fluid situations are found in private schools that have an experimental approach and in organizations set up for research. Such schools can and should be regarded as laboratories for public education. But the findings of experimental schools and research cannot be absorbed into public schools without further experiments—experiments in techniques of adapting those findings to conditions within the public schools themselves. These experiments in techniques conducted within public schools require a staff with experience and training in experimental work with teachers and with children. It may be that eventually public education will take over the work that private organizations are now doing, will set up its own special and smaller laboratories for preliminary experimental school work and research on a full and satisfactory basis, and so have an adequate staff of its own for working out techniques adapted to larger-scale school situations. But that time has not yet come. Until it comes, the staffs of private organizations with such experience and training can and should be used to carry on experiments for the Boards of Education within school systems.

Now we reverse our question: Why should private organizations wish to work with a big city Board of Education? We give our own answer, realizing that many private organizations would disagree with us. Because private organizations working on problems related to children or to school problems should regard themselves as laboratories for public education. The time may come when the public will regard private schools as justified only when they *are* working experimentally and thus are potential laboratories for public education. Until that time comes, the responsibility for having private organizations make contributions to public education rests upon those who regard their work as preparatory laboratory experience ultimately to be of use to public education. For such organizations the chance to work with a big city school system is a chance to fulfill their ultimate aim, a chance to fulfill their deepest hope.

So much for the general basis of a working relation between a big city school system and a private organization like Bank Street. To make our Workshop and its related work really function meant we had to be accepted for what we were. Our experimental approach to our work and our general philosophy about a good school life for children had to be acceptable to the official authorities in charge of our work. We, on our part, had to accept and work with whatever factors in the school system condition the kind of school life the children were having. The general administrative system and the official curriculum, the officials and teachers, the physical conditions within a particular school—these were all parts of the framework within which our work had to be carried on. Once again we take a brief backward glance, this time at how our relations worked out with administrative officials.

About the Administrative System

A good life for children is obviously conditioned by the framework within which an individual school functions. The educational thinking and psychological attitude within the administrative system filter down from the highest officials and the highest boards to each and every child. Within an individual school the psychological attitude and educational thinking of the principal can dominate, not merely condition, the kind of school life the children will have. So true is this that a school may become a genuinely different school with the advent of a new principal and each child have a better or a worse school life. We have already analyzed the dangers of the hierarchical ladder system, which is the typical administrative pattern of big city school systems.[71]

The danger of breeding an authoritarian attitude in those on one administrative level toward those on the next lower level; the danger of developing the attitude of too great subservience in following instructions handed down from above rather than the experimental attitude of thinking and finding out for oneself; the danger of over-attention to promotion from one level to the next higher level—all these dangers we believe are real. We found individual people who had succumbed to these dangers. But on the other hand, we found on every administrative level people who had not succumbed to them, who recognized these dangers and were striving to bring about more democratic interrelationships among the various members of the whole school. We found principals who were working toward giving teachers more initiative in planning for their children, a more experimental attitude, more recognition of their work, a larger share in basic curriculum decisions—and principals who were not. We found principals who welcomed a Workshop by "outsiders" in their schools and who regarded the experiment as theirs as well as ours—and we found principals who did not. We found higher officials who were willing to take a gamble on us, who were ready to stand as our sponsors in the higher boards where permission for our Workshop had to be granted. On every administrative level we found people who were working for a good life for both children and teachers in the same terms that we were and who, therefore, wanted us—members of a private organization—to work with them

[71] See Chapter 15, Growth of Teachers in Professional Maturity, pp. 327 ff.

and wanted to work with us. These lower and higher officials were all working within the framework of a hierarchical administrative system. But they were free from the evils a hierarchy often breeds.

In short, we found in the New York City school system a situation which we believe is fairly typical of school systems in our country today. Administrative systems, like everything else in our schools, are in a state of transition. They too are leaving the traditional authoritarian attitudes and moving toward new, more democratic attitudes. And as in any transition period, among our school administrators are people who have moved little in their thinking in the past thirty years, and those who have moved far. That administrative attitudes are in a stage of transition means much to those who are working in and for public education. It means that so far as administration is concerned, a good life for children can be accomplished in public education.

About Our Teachers

As for our teachers, we shall say briefly what we have said repeatedly and at greater length. We found, as in any group, all sorts of people, some of whom should never have become teachers in the first place. But most of the teachers had the qualities which make a good teacher: interest in children and an eagerness to work for their children's good; a willingness to work both within and outside their classrooms in order to become better teachers. They had or developed professional zeal, which implies a readiness to study and an eagerness to learn. Moreover, many of them proved that they were capable of becoming creative teachers and educational thinkers. And, as has been said before but bears repetition, the growth of their professional attitude turned them from followers into colleagues and made the Workshop a joint undertaking. A large part of the satisfaction we got out of our Workshop job was learning that so many of the teachers had the human qualities and the capacity, enthusiasm, and flexibility to become creative teachers once they understood how to attack their new job. As far as the quality of our teachers is concerned, a good life can be given to our children in our schools.

About Interrelationships within the Whole School

The question of whether our teachers can give a good life to children in our schools does not, however, depend wholly upon the quality of the teachers themselves. It depends also upon the framework within which they work, upon the interrelationships among the members of the whole school. Here, again, the hierarchical ladder system in which teachers occupy the lowest rung exercises great force. Teachers no matter what their quality cannot exercise initiative, cannot plan and carry out programs for their children with freedom unless freedom to do so is given to them both by the high official boards which determine what the teachers' jobs and the curriculum shall be and the principals in their schools who interpret these instructions handed down to them from higher officials.

The development of today's curriculum in a large city school system is a much more complicated affair than the old syllabi and courses of study. It still, and always must, contain statements regarding both skills and subject matter. But now children's "readiness" to acquire the techniques of reading, writing, and arithmetic determines, at least in a measure, when the teaching of these skills shall be begun and how fast they shall be pushed. Subject matter is now developed not exclusively by the logic of the material itself but by the interests, needs, abilities, and backgrounds of the children, all of which vary greatly with children of the same chronological age. A hard-and-fast syllabus will not fit all children in a grade even in a single school. Nor can the exclusive use of textbooks possibly keep schools up with the times.

The day has long since passed when a superintendent of a big city school system said his ideal was to look at his watch and know that 2-B children in all the schools were reading or reciting the contents of the same page of the same textbook. The ideal of today's superintendents of schools and the various high official boards is more concerned with whether children in all the schools are having genuine learning experiences in activities and subject matter which fit their maturity, their needs and abilities. The new official curriculum must be flexible. It must be a guide to teachers, stating general educational principles and the needs of children in general and particular needs in various stages of development, rather than a set of rigid instructions and subject matter to be followed for all children. The curriculum should be a framework within which the teachers exercise their judgment in planning for their children. Moreover, no curriculum statement, no matter how flexible, can be permanent. New findings in child development, new educational thinking, new teaching techniques will demand a restatement of the basic framework. Even more rapid than changes in the framework will be the changes in curriculum subject matter, which will change as rapidly as do the times. Special bulletins on new subject matter (for instance, the United Nations and atomic energy) can be issued at short intervals so that the teachers do not get bogged down in routine repetition. In short, the official curriculum given to teachers must be kept professionally up-to-date. To keep a curriculum flexible and up-to-date, to make it a guide to teachers and yet leave them freedom, is one of the major and one of the most difficult tasks of a big school system.

Our Workshop staff, who saw the process of curriculum revision in a big school system more or less at first hand, learned that this difficult task could be approached democratically. It should again be noted with appreciation that our own working relation with the Board of Education began when members of the committee working on curriculum revision asked our Bank Street psychologist to discuss with them their work on maturity levels for elementary school ages, and that later a member of our Workshop staff was asked to attend the meetings of this committee as an associate member. The new curriculum bulletins were worked on by teacher committees, school committees, district curriculum committees. Specially qualified teachers were released from their classroom to work with and for the committee. Here was a noteworthy attempt to tap the thinking of the "whole school" and get it into action.

Within the school framework teachers must be given opportunities to keep themselves up-to-date professionally. Inservice education is and always will be necessary if schools are to keep up with the times. It is hardly necessary to belabor this point, which has been stressed throughout the book. A brief summary of what we learned about inservice education will suffice. Schools and school systems have in the past met the need for inservice education largely through teacher supervision by school administrative staffs who are busy with administrative detail and through lecture courses with credits. Our experience leads us to believe that neither method covers the teachers' needs. No lecture course, no matter how relevant the content and how skillful the presentation, can take the place of work with individual teachers. The Workshop teachers themselves were unanimous and emphatic in feeling that an essential technique in inservice education is work with individual teachers.

Another essential technique in inservice education is *group discussion,* which differs sharply from the ordinary lecture. Group discussions can bring about a sharing of the problems which teachers have in common in their work and break through a sort of wary isolation in which so many teachers work; they help to extend a teacher's thinking about his own job from his own classroom to the whole school. He gets a new perspective. He thinks far more than before of what school experience his own children have had and what they are going to have after they leave him. All this makes for the development of wider interests and wider responsibilities. This development cannot be hurried. It is not a thing that can be taught directly. It develops gradually at different rates and along different lines in different groups of teachers, as we found in our later Workshops in different schools. Here a Workshop must follow the leads of the teachers. It must go slow if a particular group of teachers is resistant to taking on any new interests or professional responsibilities.

All this does not mean that there should not be group meetings at which background material is presented in an organized way. There are few teachers who do not need to know more about recent findings in child psychology in order to understand and plan for their children. Few who do not need to know a wider range of subject matter approached through relationships, not merely as a series of facts, in order to enrich their programs with children. Teachers are likely to be impatient of new background content until they see how to use it with their children. Then they demand it. And obviously all the needed background content can better be presented to a group than to an individual.

However, even at group meetings given over to a systematic presentation of some area of thinking or information, the atmosphere of a lecture course is undesirable in a Workshop. A lecturer appears as a remote "expert" with too often some suggestion of infallibility. He is there to give out; the audience is there to take in. But in a Workshop, the group—teachers and Workshop leaders—should work together. The removed, infallible expert is doomed to failure. The atmosphere, even in group meetings, should be an informal give-and-take. Some humor and laughter is an essential in inservice education technique. It is not necessary to have learning a grim performance. Learning should be fun with grownups as well as with children.

To put all this in another way, inservice education should take into account "the whole teacher." The expression "the whole child," though coined only thirty-odd years ago, has already degenerated into a cliché. The fundamentally sound idea behind this cliché—that a young human being responds as a whole or as an organism to situations—is applicable to a teacher as an adult human being. And the implication of this fundamental idea in the education of children— that all sides of a child must be developed—also applies to the professional education of teachers. All of a teacher must function if he is to perform his new job with understanding and zest, as a scientist and as an artist. We offer the expression "the whole teacher" as a sound guide in building a curriculum in teacher education, whether preservice or inservice education.

Indeed, this idea of organic interacting relationships can well be applied to "the whole school." As we have said already, if children are to have a good life in our schools all the conditioning factors within the school system have to function toward that end—the administrative system, the administrators, the teachers, the curriculum, inservice education, research. These various factors seem to be moving toward more efficient working relations, with less loss of good thinking. The whole school must function harmoniously, each member counting for what he is worth. Complexity and sheer bulk make this difficult in a big city school system. Nevertheless, if it must be done, we believe it can be done.

IT CAN BE DONE IN SCHOOLS

And so back to our first statement, that it can be done in our schools—that is, a good life can be given our children along with the acquisition of information and skills. Given a chance, children are responsive. They are eager learners when learning is adapted to their needs and interests. Given a chance, our teachers are equal to their new job both as human beings and as educational thinkers. Inservice education can help teachers to understand and enjoy their new job of creative teaching. But teachers cannot do their new job fully and adequately unless the school system in which they work also does its job. School systems as well as teachers have a new job—a job which means many modifications of their old job. This new job concerns the many factors which make it possible for teachers to do their new job—the psychological atmosphere generated by the administrative setup, the flexibility and up-to-dateness of the curriculum, the provision for adequate inservice education. A good school life for children depends upon how well school systems perform their new job. All this we learned in our Bank Street Workshops.

But there is still another and a very important factor in bringing about schools that give our children a good life. The schools we have been talking about are public schools. Perhaps it might be better to call them the public's schools, to bring home that, in the final analysis, our schools will be what the public wishes them to be. The public means parents, educators, private organizations, research workers, and everyone else—professional and lay folk. The thinking and attitudes of the larger community in the long run determine what kind of schools we have. But the larger community must wish hard enough to get into action, to think hard about what schools should give children, and work hard to get the kind of schools they really want. If responsible people wish our children to be taught by creative teachers with wide experience and background, they must insist that teacher education centers, both preservice and inservice, organize their curriculum to this end; they must insist that unnecessary handicaps be done away with, that teachers have a dignified, respected position in the school system and in the outside community. The new job of teachers involves a background knowledge of child development and a study of their particular children, an exploration of their children's neighborhood and the wider environment in which they live, an alertness in gathering source materials, an interested participation in the life problems around them—all this in addition to skilled teaching techniques. It is a difficult job under the best practical and psychological conditions. No removable handicap which makes it more difficult should be tolerated.

In our minds, the real findings of our laboratory experiment in public education is that children and teachers together can be given a good life in the public schools if all members of the school family work together toward that end. But the public must work toward that end, too. Everyone interested in children, everyone who feels that children are important for themselves and for the future of our country, has a stake in the public's schools. All these people—the public—must wish hard enough to take seriously the responsibility for seeing that our children have a good school life. If they do, it can be done.

PART IV

What Next?

19

We Have Come So Far

H OW far have we come in education? What is now happening
quite generally in our country that was happening only occasionally thirty or so years ago?

ACCEPTANCE OF CHILDREN AS INDIVIDUALS

Most of the changes that are taking place in our treatment of
children come from accepting children as people in their own right,
with needs, desires, impulses, differing from those of adults, differing, too, in the stages of development through which they pass as
they grow from birth to maturity. This acceptance of children as
children has made us much more relaxed in our general treatment of
them. We are much more relaxed in our attitude in daily routines.
We accept the individual child's rhythm and help him to maintain
it. This acceptance has come about through recognizing that, as
James L. Hymes has put it recently, there is a wide gap between what
children want and what adults want, between the way adults want to
use things and the way children want to use them, between what
children like and what adults like. We feel that compromise in such
situations where there is a genuine conflict between what children
and adults want is not only necessary but the essence of the discipline
that will develop social behavior in both children and adults. Hence
we are growing in permissiveness toward children to be, to feel, to
act like children, and at the same time we are growing also in maintaining our own rights as adults. The responsibility for maintaining
this delicate mutual relationship rests, of course, upon the adult.

A mutual result of recognizing the difference between children's and adults' needs is more effort to provide an environment which children can use in childlike ways. Children need space for their motor impulses. New schoolrooms are larger than the old ones; thirty-five square feet per child is the accepted standard for nursery school rooms. But even with better indoor facilities, children are spending more school time in the wider spaces of outdoors. Daily, groups of children with teachers can be seen on the streets going to parks for recreation, to museums, docks, wharves, railroad stations, steamships, manufacturing plants. Camping, too, is becoming a recognized part of education. Several experimental schools in New York City—among them The Little Red School House and, for a time, the City and Country School—developed country experiences as part of their regular programs. The public schools of the Parker School District in the Blue Ridge area of South Carolina send their children for two- and three-week camping experiences to Camp Parker.[72] The value of the outdoors in meeting children's needs was emphasized by U. S. Commissioner John W. Studebaker when he advised that one-fourth of the money spent for school structures be used for establishing and operating school camps.[73]

In making things right for children, there is a broadening application of the recognition of individual differences. While the first widespread efforts to meet the individual needs of children were on the intellectual plane—classifying children on the basis of intelligence and achievement, individual study plans for mastering basic skills, etc.—today we place far more emphasis upon ways of meeting all the needs of children, physical, social, emotional, as well as intellectual, not separately but in their interrelationships in the total personality structure of the individual. Resulting from the concept of interrelatedness of needs is a changed concept toward grouping children in schools with large attendance rolls. Instead of trying to follow some rigid scheme of grouping on the basis of age or

[72] Sharp, L. B., "Camping and Outdoor Education," *N. E. A. Journal,* May, 1947.

[73] Ibid.

ability of one kind or another the trend now is toward helping each child establish his own place in the group in whatever way in which he can become most effective. Instead of being segregated on the basis of this difference or that, children are brought together in all their differences to work and play together and to contribute according to their varying abilities. Thus, it is assumed, children will become used to differences, to appreciate them, and learn to live with their own strengths and limitations and those of others.

The broader interpretation of individual differences is part of a deeper understanding of children generally and, along with it, a deeper realization of how slow the growth process is, and how necessary it is to preserve both its unity and its continuity. There are three indications, in particular, that this understanding of children is beginning to have wide influence on school and welfare practices. One is the emphasis on the earliest years of life, shown in an increase in prenatal clinics, well-baby clinics, and nursery schools; and in a flood of newspaper columns, magazine articles, books, radio programs, and films on these years. Another is the trend toward having teachers stay as long as two or three years with the same group of children as they pass from one grade to another. A third is a marked change toward school promotions. Where it used to be customary to have children repeat grades if work was unsatisfactory, children sometimes remaining back year after year in a futile effort to meet grade standards, today in many school systems the idea of promotion on a given day of the school year is being replaced by the concept of measuring children's progress in terms of their own potentialities and rates of growth.

Changed attitudes toward children are resulting in changed attitudes toward evaluation. The concept of the "whole child," so often mentioned in this book, has had a powerful influence on the approach to evaluation. No longer is evaluation expressed merely in terms of subject matter mastery but at least as carefully in terms of growth in human relations, in self-control, in emotional health, and in any other aspect of total development that is important in the particular context of the child's environment. Such evaluation must rest squarely upon evidence for its validity, on records of what children do and say, seem to think and feel. It rests, too, on a co-operative basis, on a shared attempt of teachers, parents, and the children themselves to understand together the progress that is being made, the strengths and limitations marking the way. It means the abandonment of marking systems, of competitive methods, and the adoption of co-operatively accumulated qualitative statements as school records. It has resulted, too, in a changed attitude toward school reports to parents. Here, as everywhere else, there is a lessening of rigidity as acceptance of children as children becomes the rule. Sometimes, reports are sent in the form of letters to parents, trying to convey the total picture of the child's progress. Sometimes, where the situation is such that the written word might be misinterpreted, there are no reports at all but, instead, periodic conferences with the parents to talk things over. Whatever form the report takes, except in the very earliest years when a child has no interest in evaluation, children share in the evaluation process.

Two other modern trends in evaluation are the effort to find ways and means of evaluating the results of education in terms of later performance of the individual and in terms of the effect of an educational program upon the community. An example of the first is the *Eight-Year Study*[74] in which records of pupils made in four-year high school programs and subsequent four-year college programs were studied in order to compare the college performance of students attending traditional high schools with those who attended newer-type high schools. An example of evaluation in terms of the effect of the school upon the community is a study made by the University of Florida in co-operation with the Sloane Foundation (further work of the Foundation will be discussed later) in which a co-operative project of the schools of education,

[74] "An Adventure in American Education": Vol. 1, Aiken, Wilford M.: *The Story of the Eight-Year Study,* Harper, New York, 1942.

architecture, engineering, and the university demonstration school is being evaluated in terms of the improvement in housing conditions in the community as rated on a thirteen-point scale.[75] The view that education cannot be evaluated solely in terms of the individual is expressed by Dr. Paul Mort: "You can tell more about the quality of education in a school from characteristics of the community than you can from the amount and type of the training of teachers. The community is the dead give-away."

PARENTS AND TEACHERS, HOME AND SCHOOL COMING TOGETHER

The phrase "parent-teacher relations," which today has largely taken the place of the old phrase "parent education," is in itself a symbol of a changed attitude toward the role of parents in the education of children. In the past, parents were held at arm's-length by teachers willing to accede that parents could claim responsibility for children in the home but had no place in the classroom. Now the importance of parents' contribution to the general education of their children is being understood to the point where their co-operation with teachers is recognized as essential. Again, this is all part of the more profound understanding of that "whole child."

Children come to school not out of a vacuum but out of a home and a community. The first time a child steps out of his home environment into a school may well be regarded as one of the turning points of his life. Recognition of the significance of this turning point is reflected in the revolutionary change that has taken place in the way those first days are handled with young children. Not so long ago a parent left the child on his first day at school to meet the experience of strangeness with more or less fright, depending on the demeanor of the teacher and his own level of stability. Now, in good nursery schools and kindergartens and in first grades (when a child has not been to school pre-

[75] *National Education Association Journal,* January, 1947.

viously), there are conferences between parent, teacher, and child before the first day of school has come. There is an adjustment period varying in length, according to the needs of the child and the home situation, from two days to often as much as two weeks, in which time the parent is encouraged to come to school so that the child may get used to the separation experience and adjusted to the children, the teacher, and his new environment.

The school recognizes today that the child's needs cannot be conceived apart from the parent's needs; that the bond, even when an unsatisfactory one, between parent and child is very strong and cannot be disregarded by the school; that it is very important for the well-being of the child that the teacher should like the parent, that the teacher and parent get along together; that both home and school teach; that both have something to learn; that the school cannot give the child everything that he needs; that home and school must pull together. Increasing attention is being paid, in the light of the above understandings, to the importance of having the teacher know the child as a product of his home: whether he is an only child or one of several or many; his successes and failures in that home; how parents have prepared him for school; how his feelings have been handled; how his parents feel about the separation of the child from them when he goes to school; what form of discipline the home has used and is using. The different answers to these questions make the task of the school a very delicate one if the child is to be kept "all of a piece" as he moves from the home to the school atmosphere.

Realization of the need for close home and school co-operation is manifested in many ways in the practical affairs of schools. First, parents are regarded more and more as a resource in the education of children. Their confidence is considered important, so that teachers may learn from them facts about the children which are needed if the education process is to proceed intelligently. Their special skills, too, are to be utilized, as, for example, in one community where a sailor father who had traveled to the Far East gave the children many an enchanting hour as he regaled them with stories of far-off places; or another who went with teachers and children on trips in which he shared his knowledge of the rocks and the earth story.

Teachers are using many devices in explaining the school to parents. One that is gaining popularity is that of inviting parents to an evening in which they do many of the things the children do. As the adults get their hands into clay, their fingers around paint brushes, as they get down on the floor and build with blocks, as they read together some of the books the children read, participate in a dramatization, perform an experiment in science, they get a sense of the process through which their children live as they can in no other way. The direct experience of sharing in their children's school life is a powerful means of strengthening understanding and developing a partnership relation.

School administrators are beginning to realize how essential is co-operation of home and school in the whole process of education. In many places time is released for teachers to have conferences with parents. In Pasadena, for example, where this practice exists, teachers are given preconference training and help from the guidance department. In one school in this city, groups of neighbors came for a conference together and found that they could help each other in working on their problems with children. Later, at an open-house night, parents came into the classroom and discussed school plans and policies with the teachers and the older children.[76]

Mention was made earlier of masses of literature, films, and radio programs on early childhood that are developing. Educators, medical men, and psychologists are to be congratulated on the way they are subjecting themselves to the discipline of putting out material that is intelligible to laymen. Today the most profound research on childhood can be found in popular form, stripped of all scientific terminology, thus making available to all a fund of knowledge which, if

[76] Reported at meeting of Association of Early Childhood Education, Oklahoma City, Oklahoma, April 7–11, 1947.

acted upon, could have results in improved human welfare more far-reaching than can be readily imagined.

MUTUAL RESPONSIBILITIES OF SCHOOL AND COMMUNITY

The school can no more exist effectively without regard to the community than it can work effectively with children without close home-school relations. In recent years, the appreciation of the interdependence of school and community has been seen in increased responsibility both of the school toward the community and of the community toward its schools.

Responsibility of the school toward the community is indicated by emphasis on community problems in the curriculum. The broadest and most elaborate approach to the curriculum through the use of community problems has been made by the Sloane Foundation in co-operation with the American Association of Teachers Colleges.[77] Now in the tenth year of its existence, the project includes such ventures as the following:

At West Swanzen, New Hampshire, when the Cutler School burned down, the rebuilding, equipping, and decorating of the school was made a major part of the curriculum of the teachers college.

At Oak Mound, Minnesota, the citizens of the community were called in to faculty meetings to indicate the needs of the community which the school might serve. Soil conservation and farm improvement generally were indicated as the greatest needs and were, therefore, given a prominent place in the curriculum.

All the teacher training institutions in the state of Florida are engaged in working out ways in which the schools can help raise the economic level of living.

At the University of Florida (referred to earlier) housing is being made an important part of the curriculum, the work being geared to the housing needs of the community.

There are many scattered examples throughout the country in which the school is definitely taking into consideration the problems

[77] *National Education Association Journal,* January, 1947.

of the community in the development of its curriculum. At Holtville, Alabama, for example, an open country consolidated school has transformed its curriculum in attempting to meet the needs of the environment for better home making, farming, recreation, health, and cultural opportunities. Here the school is a center of education at all age levels. It has become both a day and an evening school and an all-year-round school as well. In the same state, on a county-wide basis, a similar effort has been made to meet the basic needs of the entire county. Over a period of ten years, monthly meetings, very informal, have been held in the Cherokee County courthouse at which representatives of all the community agencies—press, churches, welfare, health, farm, schools—meet to review the problems facing them and decide what share each agency, including the schools, can take in their solution. The meetings are open, and all citizens feel free to attend. So, too, are the annual picnics, usually attended by several hundred people of all ages, at which the work of the year is reviewed and new goals are set. Under the influence of such co-operative work the school has become intensely realistic in its educational approach, and the upgrading of the whole community is phenomenal.

It is often said that it is easier to attack community problems through the curriculum in the country than in the city. Certainly younger children can participate in the earthy rural problem better than in the highly complicated city problems. Certainly, too, we have more outstanding examples of a community approach to the curriculum in the country school than in the city. But there are examples, also, on a city level. One has been reported in two government bulletins, published at the beginning and at the end of a fifteen-year period, of an attempt made by the Francis Scott Key public elementary school in Baltimore to make the school serve community needs through its curriculum. It is an exciting story of a realistic attack upon the educational needs of a community of low economic level and poor living standards, in which, at the beginning of the fifteen-year period, scarcely a child ever reached high school. The reports are in the nature of before-and-after surveys and give the details of the way in which by meeting the educational needs of the children by a transformed curriculum children were kept in school longer, adults improved their own educational and vocational status, and the level of the living standard of the community was raised.

On the other side of the relationship, there has been corresponding activity on the part of communities concerned with the improvement of their schools. Such communities as Glencoe, Illinois, and Bronxville,[78] New York, have so vitally concerned themselves with their schools that they have succeeded in making their schools outstanding examples of good education. They have been able and willing to tax themselves for the support of schools far beyond generally acceptable standards and, besides, have taken a personal interest in working hand in hand with the teachers and administration of the schools in whatever concerns their welfare.

Committees of lay citizens are becoming increasingly active, determined to get at the factors operating favorably or unfavorably for the good of the school and children in school. These committees frequently begin by having experts survey the situation and make recommendations for improvement. Then they get behind legislation and work for whatever is needed to get better schools.

Taking a wider view for a moment, we realize that children cannot help but be influenced in their concepts of the world by the changing world concepts of adults. Places far off and once remote, mere places on a map, have become matters of direct experience to many adults whose lives before World War II had been bounded by their own communities. Children feel the enlarged view of adults. How this shrinkage of the world will affect the transition which takes place in children's thinking from the here-and-now to the far-away and long-ago in time and place is, as yet, a matter of conjecture. It may make the transition faster; but this we do not know. What we do know is how urgent it is that our citizens develop good

[78] In this community, the schools have been unable to counter a serious social defect, namely, restriction against minority groups.

attitudes toward the many kinds of people who inhabit the globe and from whom our children can no longer be separated.

That the schools are aware of the need is shown in the efforts made both to give a more accurate picture of life in other lands and to relate causes of the way people live to geographic and historic factors. There is not so much of wooden shoes and Dutch caps in the teaching of Holland, not so much of the merely picturesque in the teaching of any land. Instead, there is a definite trend toward basic understandings of peoples, on emphasis upon the common denominator in human relations, and on regarding differences as due to causes and as something to be enjoyed rather than ridiculed or merely tolerated.

Awareness that mere understanding is insufficient in the cultivation of human relations and that understanding must be coupled with action is shown, too, in the efforts in schools to make the classroom itself a living demonstration of fundamental democracy where each personality is respected for what he is, where barriers of race, religion, and nationality are broken down in the daily life of the classroom. In schools where children seldom have the chance to meet children of different backgrounds—this is often true in great cities where national groups cluster together in neighborhoods—exchanges of visits and co-operation in extra-school activities are encouraged in order that children may gain a wider outlook on human relations.

VITALIZING THE TEACHING PROFESSION

What is happening to teachers? Earlier in this book we spoke of the depleted ranks, the substitution of unqualified teachers to make up the appalling teacher shortage. The crisis has brought more publicity to education than it probably ever has had. Beginning with Benjamin Fine's survey of conditions, published first serially in the New York *Times* and later in book form,[79] there has been such a mass of revelations of conditions, many of them appalling, as had

[79] Fine, Benjamin, *Our Children Are Cheated*, New York, Henry Holt and Company, 1947.

never before come into the press. This, with the immediate problems confronting boards of education unable to procure teachers, has aroused the public, and there is a good beginning in organized effort to solve the problem. Seventeen states, for example, have established state councils on teacher education which through workshops, conferences, and committees, members of state and city departments and faculties of public and private colleges, are working together to find the causes of the shortage and how the situation can be improved.

The results of the deliberations of such councils and many other agencies attacking the problem point conclusively to the fact that, although salaries and living conditions play an important role in the failure of education to attract new members to the profession or hold those already in it, these are not the main causes. A study conducted by the Metropolitan Council on why college students were not entering the profession showed that not more than 50 per cent declined to go into teaching because of poor salaries.[80] The source is deeper, and the problem must be attacked at the source. The most forward thinkers in education agree that if once the true significance of teaching is grasped, its ranks will be filled by eager young people looking for a field which challenges their desire to perform constructive social service. We need to find why the challenge is lost to so many.

The effect of roused public interest in the teacher shortage is seen in the searching scrutiny given to the teachers' colleges, to the experimentation that is taking place in some of them, and to a more vital approach to the training of teachers generally. The work of the Commission on Teacher Education of the American Council has contributed substantially to the rehabilitation of teacher education. Through the assistance it gave to eighteen teachers' colleges scattered over the country for a period of five years, notable experimentation was carried on. Faculties were given opportunity to visit each other's colleges, visiting experts sat down with groups in consultation on various aspects of the curriculum, and studies of interesting try-outs

[80] Fine, op. cit.

were made and reported. Since the publication of its report, the Commission has been succeeded by the Council on Cooperation in Teacher Education. Now, teachers' college members of the Council are experimenting on their own, exchanging ideas and results of experimentation with each other. One particular piece of co-operation is a joint effort at action research whereby many studies are being attempted in the interest of finding better ways to educate teachers. Out of all this, certain clearly marked trends are evident: the application of the broader interpretation of the concept of individual differences to teacher education through guidance programs; opportunity for extending social understanding through contacts with many different people in field work experiences and travel; much experience outside the classroom with children; student teaching experiences in which the students have an opportunity to share in the solution of the problems of those schools; a rich creative life.

ADVANCING TECHNIQUES IN CO-OPERATION

In the foregoing, mention of co-operative effort has been made many times. Yet it seems important, in bringing this chapter to a close, to point up more definitely the trends toward co-operation as they exist today. Once again the concept of the "whole child" can be seen operating as groups approaching the needs of childhood from different angles find it necessary to co-operate in order to be effective. An example is seen in the rise of local community councils representing the social agencies of a community and sharing in the solution of its problems. In deliberating on the problems of children, three kinds of agencies—health, education, and welfare—stand out prominently in their imperative need for co-operation in the interest of children. This need is reflected in the recent efforts to bring together the many agencies in our Federal Government dealing with children into co-ordinated effort. It is reflected, also, on a national scale in the growing popularity of the idea that there is needed in the Federal Government a department, with cabinet representation, of health, welfare, and education.

In the scientific aspects of the problem of co-operative effort, the contributions of the social psychologists are of particular significance. In their investigations of the dynamics of groups they are throwing light on some of the most baffling problems of human relationships: what makes for group cohesion, what factors draw people together into groups, what factors affect group output, how leadership develops under differing conditions, what makes for dominance-submission relationships, how co-operation is achieved.

Here and there groups are experimenting with the findings of the social psychologists. A notable example is the Association for Supervision and Curriculum Development, which for the past three years at its annual conference has not only dealt with important topics but has also set up procedures by which the processes of group co-operation at the conferences are carefully studied and evaluated. In the field of adult education, including work with parents, much experimentation is under way which has its focus on ways of bringing groups into effective co-operative action.

Much work of this kind is needed. It is a matter for rejoicing, even though the results to date are not great, that co-operation is— perhaps out of the sheer necessities in our world situation—being brought out of the realm of wishful thinking and into that of the hard discipline of finding the techniques that will make co-operation a reality.

20

More Knowledge; More Faith in the
Potentialities of Human Beings

EDUCATION AS A CULTURAL FORCE

WE HAVE just taken a bird's-eye view of some of the educational trends in our country. Then, as school technicians, we were looking into schoolrooms to see what is happening to children; into school activities outside schoolhouses to see what is happening to teachers and administrators; into homes to see what part parents are taking in school affairs; into the community to see its relations to schools and its awareness of the need for well-trained teachers. In this bird's-eye view we found that within the field of education certain things are happening all over the country that twenty or thirty years ago we would have found only in isolated instances or not at all. These relatively new happenings show us what education in our country is moving toward and how far we have come.

Now we need a still more extended bird's-eye view. As educators we need a wider horizon than we do as technicians. We need to look at what is happening in education against the background of the culture of which we are a part and of large cultural problems and trends. We need to ask ourselves what role our profession is playing within our culture. Our public schools are not independent pellets functioning in splendid, self-sustaining isolation. They constitute a democratic institution tied in with our culture in many ways

besides their budgets. Our schools like other democratic institutions
are a cultural expression. They reflect our cultural ways of thinking,
ways of believing, ways of caring. Our schools in their aims, in their
attitudes, respond to society's aims and attitudes. That is what we
mean when we say education is a cultural expression. That is what
John Dewey meant when he wrote, "Education is a public business
with us." In the long run, society—the public—will get the kind of
schools it wants.

And what determines the kinds of schools society wants? What
makes one generation want one kind of school and another generation want a different kind? In the first part of this book we drew up
a chart of what our schools are leaving and what they are moving
toward, and in the last chapter we took a bird's-eye view of recent
changes in education. Whence came these changes? They did not
come from problems and thinking entirely within the schools themselves. They came from the impact of new situations in our country,
in the world; from the impact of new knowledge, new ideas, new
ideals in our country, in the world. All cultural changes are adapta-
tions to something new in a culture, something that has thrown out
of equilibrium a way of thinking and doing things. That something
may be a new scientific discovery, a new invention—physical or
social—a price inflation or a depression, a new war or the ending
of a war: all the things that bring new problems or make old problems take on a new emphasis or urgency. From new problems and a
people's struggle to fit them into their old cultural patterns come
new ways of living, of working, of playing, of thinking, of believing.

Cultural problems usually emerge slowly. In our day they have
come with cataclysmic speed. Our ways of thinking and feeling of
even a decade or so ago do not fit today's world. The world has a
new job. Many of us are frightened by the urgency that we feel to
find out how to tackle this new job. But old ways yield slowly to
new ways. Today the struggle between the old and the new is violent.
It must be violent when new cultural problems come upon us faster
than we can change our ways of thinking and feeling. Everyone

feels strongly, but few of us can yet think clearly in new patterns of thought. Society is divided against itself—pulling both ways, the old and the new. Our press, our radio, our government all bear evidence of the breathless urgency, the fierceness of the struggle that is going on. Our culture is suffering the pangs of giving birth to new patterns of thinking and feeling. That is what we mean when we say these are critical times. That is why the world is asking with such pressing urgency, "What should we do next?"

Where do educators, where do schools stand in these critical times? Have they a role to play in shaping our new cultural patterns of thinking and feeling? We have said that our schools in their aims and attitudes respond to society's aims and attitudes. Now we say that schools are not only a cultural expression in a democracy. We say they are also a democracy's tool for advancing cultural progress. Yet, historically, schools have tended to keep on with old patterns in attitudes, in ideas and ideals that fitted a past world rather than the world they were living in, and to leave the future to take care of itself. Their thinking and practices have responded to what the public wants albeit with a considerable lag. Schools are the last place where historic lags should be tolerated. Schools, perforce, *must* deal with the world their children are living in. They *must* think of the future world where their children will live and face society's problems and make society's decisions. They must ask, "What next?" They must, that is, if they are to become a genuine tool for cultural progress.

This role of helping to advance cultural progress takes school-men out of classrooms and makes them members of society. It gives them responsibilities for knowing what new is happening in the culture outside their immediate field of education: responsibility for having informed opinions, of having aims and ideals for our culture and the world in which our culture plays a part; responsibility for helping society itself to have informed opinions and ideals; and finally, responsibility for taking an active part in moving the culture to which they belong in the direction which they believe is progress.

This is a broad, an active role. It is a role of helping to form public opinion as well as of responding to it. It is a role of leaders, not merely of followers. To fulfill this role educators must constantly check their work in the light of the world's new knowledge. They must constantly re-evaluate their school philosophy in the light of the problems and needs of today's world. They must not only have a credo: their credo must have a social basis. And they must constantly true up what they are doing by consciously remembering the social basis of their credo.

But generalities about education as a cultural force mean little unless they are translated into specific terms. Obviously, in one brief chapter we cannot analyze the problems of the culture of the modern United States and our cultural trends; that would take more than a big book. Nor can we survey the field of education and determine whether as a cultural force it is leading or lagging; that would take more than another big book. All we shall try to do is to suggest two broad interrelated lines of thinking which if not completely new have recently been applied in new ways or gained a new emphasis—lines which we believe should be a part of today's school credo; to discuss a few concrete examples of these lines of thinking applied to education; and to suggest the need for more and harder work along these lines. In doing this we shall raise many questions that we cannot answer—which perhaps no one can answer at present. However, if they are questions that need to be answered, they should be raised.

THE QUEST FOR MORE AND MORE KNOWLEDGE

The world has always wanted knowledge. "The quest for certainty," to use John Dewey's phrase, is age-old. What is relatively new is the method by which the pursuit of knowledge has been carried on. We call it, broadly, "the scientific method." The scientific method has been accepted for some time in the pursuit of knowledge of how physical phenomena behave. In the physical sciences only laboratory findings that are based on observation, records, experimentation, and have been tested and retested under differing conditions are accepted as established knowledge. The scientific approach, until comparatively recently, was not considered feasible or even desirable in the study of human behavior and human relations. Somehow people were concerned with how human beings *ought* to behave and made little effort to find out how they *do* behave. Somehow people seemed to think they knew all about "human nature" just by living. They seemed content to formulate theories of human behavior on the basis of assumptions and opinions. The quest for certainty based on scientific investigation and experimentation did not enter the complicated realm of human behavior. How could one set up experiments with human beings? We must trust to wisdom, insight, intuition, not knowledge; to common sense, not tested facts; to diffused experience, not intensive study, to interpret human beings. So thought our forefathers.

Then, not long ago, the expression "social sciences" appeared. The very name indicates that some people, at least, believed that the scientific method can be used to solve questions of human relations. Social experiments have proved to be feasible. Social scientists have shown that human behavior can be studied through actual observations, records, and experiments just as can the behavior of physical phenomena. The study of man and society and their interactions is a realm of greater complexity than the natural realm. Experiments with human beings cannot be carried out with the same simplicity and rigor as experiments with physical phenomena. Nevertheless, if we wish trustworthy knowledge about human beings, we must carry our quest for certainty into social fields. We must study human beings—the way they behave, the way they think, the way they feel—with the objectivity of scientists. We can no longer rest back serenely on speculative, metaphysical theories or on moral assumptions or on untested opinions to guide our social behavior, to direct our social organization. Speculative theories based on assumptions are themselves products of past times, and interesting as such. But they afford us no "certainty." Certainty rests not on hunches, not on as-

sumptions. Certainty rests on scientific knowledge. We must struggle
to replace our vague hunches, our opinions, our comfortable assumptions with knowledge acquired through the slow, patient, and exacting method of science. We must work from hypotheses, to be sure.
But we must recognize them as hypotheses and proceed to test them
by critical methods. That is what the social sciences are attempting to
do. Already the old disciplines dealing with human behavior—eco-
nomics, history, anthropology—have changed radically under the
exacting method of science. New disciplines—psychology, sociology,
human geography—have developed. These new social sciences are
very, very young. They are still in the pioneer stage: they have explored only small areas of their vast field of human relations. But
the social sciences have begun exploring—and *that,* not the extent of
their explorations, is what makes them of such significance. Exploring the field of human relations is a momentous, new cultural pattern.

Bridging the Gap between Science and Its Application to Edu-
cation

Education—to return to our field—is, even now, often omitted
from a list of social sciences. Why? Perhaps because the old attitude
toward "human nature" (which you remember was assumed to be
something "you couldn't change") was more firmly entrenched in
the field of education than elsewhere. And, perhaps, old attitudes
were more firmly entrenched where children were concerned than
elsewhere. Children had been around in the world for a long time.
Everyone knew all about them, that is, how they *should* behave.
Why study how they *do* behave and what goes on inside them that
makes them behave the way they do? So the schools of the past paid
more attention to the study of subject matter and skills than they did
to the study of the young human beings they were dealing with.
Schools are no longer content to rest their thinking, their attitudes,
and their practices on theories based on speculation or inherited assumptions. Education entered upon a new era in its long history

when "experimental education" and "child study" arrived. These very terms indicate that education is developing a scientific approach to its work, that it is pressing for more and more trustworthy knowledge to guide its thinking and attitudes. Schoolmen must be scientists searching for more and more knowledge relevant to their work. That is becoming a new and tremendously significant clause in the credo of today's schools.

The bridge over the gap between science and its application to education was not built in a day, nor by any single person or single discovery. Indeed, it is still a pretty shaky bridge in many areas. And many structures which we once thought might become firm bridges have had to be redesigned or abandoned as scientists have brought in new knowledge. A brief look at the early steps in the struggle to bridge the gap between science and its application to education may perhaps show not only the difficulties inherent in the scientific study of human beings but also the difficulty of keeping the scientific approach steady under the excitement of a new discovery. Above all, such a backward look may give us some confidence that in the past thirty to forty years genuine progress has been made in understanding human behavior and human relationships and spur us on to further effort.

First, look back for a moment on some historic attitudes and beliefs concerning human beings, setting their date for yourself. You may have encountered some historic lags of these attitudes today! Consider, then, the popular saying, "You can't change human nature." The assumption behind this saying—that characteristics in human beings cannot be modified—is almost always applied to unpleasant characteristics to explain some act or attitude that society condemns. That suggests another old historic doctrine—that of "original sin." The assumption that every child is born with a heritage of evil was tied up with other assumptions: that only through external discipline and punishment can those natural evil tendencies be controlled; and that society's sole responsibility in regard to evildoers is to protect itself from them. So, logically enough, a system of laws was designed to control these evil tendencies through the severity of punishment meted out to those who did not obey the laws. One illustration—extreme but logical—will suffice to remind us how these assumptions worked out in practice: those who did not pay their debts (an offense against society) were put in prison until their debts were paid, which might mean a life sentence, since society felt no responsibility for giving these offenders opportunity for earning money. This general attitude prevailed not only in law courts and prisons but in families and schools. An absolute standard of "good" conduct was set up for children and harsh punishment was meted out for those who did not conform, under the slogans "Spare the rod and spoil the child" and "A child's will must be broken." Education as we now conceive it as providing for self-discipline and for growth of a child's social responsibility found little place in the grim days of debtors' prisons and of physically beating the evil out of children.

Still another belief, also based on an assumption, was that heredity was the controlling factor in the development of an individual. Children were not expected to "rise above the level" of their parents. Socially undesirable conduct was commonly explained by, "What can you expect? Look at his parents!" This attitude readily allied itself with another historic attitude, that one group of people were born "inferior" and so were destined by nature to serve another group of people who were born "superior" to them. And since in those grim days (are they entirely past?) educational opportunities were largely limited to the privileged, "superior" group, children did pretty well live up to society's expectations—children of the poor remained poor when they grew up and children of criminals became criminals. Thus society's attitude created what was taken to be evidence of the truth of its assumptions. A vicious circle was completed.

Then Darwin gave a jolt to the old assumptions. A scientific approach showed that environment was also a tremendous factor in the development of an individual. And as so often happens, this new idea was pressed to the extreme by its proponents. The world plunged into the controversy as to which was the dominant factor—heredity or environment. It was an "either-or" attitude, each school of thought resting its arguments on chance, fragmentary evidence in its favor, and ignoring other evidence.

Still another belief about human beings to be reckoned with was set forth by psychologists. This theory, too, was based on an assumption, not on scientifically established knowledge. An individual, so said psychologists of some forty years ago, is more or less a sum of faculties, each to be trained by itself. Our schools then based their teaching on this assumption. This was the heyday of faculty psychology and, in the schools, of separate courses of study, of subject matter for mental discipline, of "moral instruction" taught through words as a separate study.

Here, then, is a superficial glance at some theories and beliefs concerning human beings based on assumptions which have been challenged by social scientists in comparatively recent times. From their work two great interrelated concepts have emerged which would seem for practical purposes to throw much of the past into the discard. One is the organismic concept of development; the other is the modifiability of human characteristics. These two interrelated concepts did not develop suddenly. They developed from the work of many people in many fields. Psychology, biology, anthropology, physiology, sociology, all made contributions which increasingly seemed to confirm each other's findings. Schools in general were slow in applying scientific knowledge to education. Scientists themselves developed these concepts only step by step with many holdovers of past thinking based on assumptions. Here again it may be revealing to glance briefly at the early steps toward the concept of a human being as an organism responding to situations as a whole, not piece-meal, and the concept that an individual has broad potentialities for growth in many directions which may or may not develop according to opportunities given to him.

Early Steps in the Discovery of the Whole Child

Child research institutes and experimental schools began their serious study of children about the same time, rather less than forty years ago. It took some time to discover the whole child. Like America, which was not discovered entire by Columbus but bit by bit by many explorers, the child was discovered piecemeal by many explorers of a different kind. The first discovery concerned his body. The early work of most of the research institutes was largely limited to measuring children in an artificial laboratory setup. The idea that only what could be measured quantitatively and expressed numerically was reliable knowledge was a carry-over from scientific methods in the study of physical phenomena. For example: one research institute wished to get accurate measurements of physical growth. But they found that small children wiggled so incessantly that the measurements repeated from day to day showed sometimes growth, sometimes apparent shrinkage. The remedy was simple. They put the small wigglers into casts and so thwarted the wiggle. The behavior of the children—their incessant wiggling, their cries when they were forcibly kept from wiggling—did not interest these measurement-minded scientists. Nor apparently did it occur to them that the emotional experience of being confined in a cast might do something harmful to a child. Wiggling and emotion could not be accurately measured. So they must be ignored if one were to make a scientific approach. In other words, the physical development of a child was regarded as something to be studied independently, not as an interacting part of a whole child.

More or less the same attitude prevailed among scientists in their early studies of children's mental development. Extreme forms of mental retardation had, of course, long been recognized. Idiots have played a real role in history. But the "moron" arrived on the scene within the memory of many of us. The moron appeared in the educational world in the Montessori schools in Italy. He soon crossed the ocean, rapidly climbed over the Rockies, and settled from the

Atlantic to the Pacific as a member of our society. He caused considerable excitement both in scientific laboratories and in schools. If a child's mental ability could be accurately measured, we would know what to do with him. Here was something definite and comforting to hang on to. So came the era of the I.Q., then regarded as unchangeable and thus setting definite limits to the growth of an individual. Schools began segregating children of low I.Q.'s into ungraded classes which, with unconscious irony, were called "opportunity classes."

But here, again, further research greatly modified the first belief of what the I.Q. tested. The single score given as a child's Intelligence Quotient was broken down by analysis of *how* he earned his score. This analysis showed that children earned their scores not by one "mental ability" but by ability along many different lines, some of which were the result of educational and cultural opportunities. When other psychological tests designed to test various abilities were developed and a child's score in these tests was compared with his score in the I.Q. test, it appeared that a high correlation in his scores was far from inevitable. These various studies showed that the I.Q. did not measure all of a child's abilities nor did it accurately measure his native ability. Through controlled experiments it was finally established that the I.Q. of an individual could be changed to a considerable extent by changing his environment in school or family. The I.Q. was rejected as the sole measurement of a child's mental ability and became one measurement, valuable only if related to other psychological measurements and to the environment, physical, educational, and emotional, in which his mental development had taken place. This scientific knowledge advanced us one step nearer to the concept of the modifiability of "human nature" and human behavior and to the concept of the organic wholeness of a child.

The significance of the early years in total development has been emphasized by educational theorists for some time. But twentieth-century psychology has turned our attention to young children against a wider background of social thinking. With psychoanalysis another approach to the study of human beings came into our cultural thinking. Early analysts paid almost exclusive attention to the influence upon human behavior of the satisfaction or thwarting of sexual impulses. There was a kind of widespread panic when the long-tabooed subject of sex began to be talked about openly—and a special panic when Freudian analysts made sexual impulses in children play a prominent role in their emotional lives. Sex education for children became a daringly popular subject of debate—again usually treated as a separate subject in accordance with the then prevalent thinking of faculty psychology.

Psychological thinking widened. People everywhere began to talk about the new discovery of unconscious mechanisms and to look with new understanding at maladjusted adults—people who cannot adequately meet the situations life brings to them. Maladjusted adults have always been recognized and dealt with according to the social thinking of the times. When, through an array of data, the maladjustments of adulthood were frequently traced to frustration of normal needs in childhood, what happens to children when they are children took on a new and broader significance. "The emotional life of the young child" rose to popularity as a subject for lectures and discussion clubs.

There were, however, two schools of thought in violent opposition to each other about what young children needed. John Watson came forward with the theory that a baby's sound emotional development was endangered by expression of affection for him, particularly if attention was expressed by any physical contact. Frightened mothers were told to hold their babies as little as possible, not to play with them, not to kiss them. In this era, some nursery school teachers became impersonal, unresponsive creatures with masklike faces, performing the necessary physical tasks for their small charges with as little human response as possible. This extreme idea of "hands off" did not meet with general approval nor did it last long. The opposing view of a young child's needs which psychoanalysts had called to the attention of the world gained favor in educational circles but with less emphasis on sex as the primary impulse of human beings, including children. Now many analysts think of sex as only one of many equally important drives which need to be satisfied. However, analysts and psychologists alike now believe in the great importance of "security" for all children, and they further believe that security is given to babies and young children largely through expressed affection which gives them a sense of being wanted, a sense of belonging. The discovery that emotional stability or the lack of it conditions every aspect of a child's development—physical, mental, and social —has entered school thinking though techniques for giving security have not been thoroughly worked out. But, so far as we know, "security" has never been taught as a separate subject! To pay attention to the "atmosphere" of a schoolroom (in a sense other than fresh air) marks another big step toward the organismic concept and the modifiability of human beings.

The whole child was emerging under the impact of more and more knowledge. The thinking of many people, in and out of schools, about what human beings are like was changing. The concept of a human being as a sum of various faculties to be trained separately was changing to the concept of a creature of interacting faculties, the development of any one of which is not only dependent upon all the others but on a multiplicity of relationships among them.

Along with research organizations, experimental schools added their quota to knowledge of what children are like. Many early experimental schools were so full of protest against the thinking and methods of traditional schools that they rejected practically everything that was "old" just because it was old. Many of them were so eager for new social thinking in the world that, even with children, their emphasis was on "debunking" rather than on the slow building of constructive social ideas and attitudes. The founders of these early experimental schools were highly individualistic. Many approached the building up of a school from a specialized interest or belief, social or psychological. They had the zeal, the courage of pioneers. They wished to be let alone to experiment in their own way rather than to learn by sharing their experience with others. Some of the early schools overstressed certain aspects of the new psychological thinking to the neglect of other aspects. Some schools, for instance, organized their curriculum largely to allow children to "express themselves" and neglected to give the children a full rich life to express. The importance of developing the individual child created what was called the "child-centered school." In some of these schools the needs of the individual were narrowed largely to the development of his special talents and interests to the neglect of his development as a member of a group. In other schools—sometimes called "group-centered schools"—the emphasis was reversed. Living with others in a group became so stressed that the individual was rated primarily on his social adaptability without much attention to his own personality or even to his maturity. Schools with a wide variety of philosophies and practices were lumped together under the unfortunate, snobbish name of "progressive education."

As their experiments went on, these schools learned much and modified many of their early ideas. But not before they had got progressive education into disfavor in many quarters. Early faults are usually remembered more than later wisdom, and progressive education is still often derided as a "lunatic fringe" in education. On the other hand, much that these schools tried out experimentally has been generally accepted and has entered into the educational thinking of our country.

It might be well to glance at some of the discoveries made by various experimental schools and by progressive education in general. Among their real contributions was organizing a school life around children's interests in the world in which children live. They "used the environment"—the everyday world—in practical ways. They organized the curriculum around experiences for the children rather than subject matter conveyed through words. They demonstrated that children learn through play, through active investigations, active expression, and active participation rather than through passive receptivity. They threw much light on the learning process and worked out techniques for learning actively. They placed the emphasis on learning *how* to think rather than *what* to think. They learned about children from the way children behaved in an environment planned for their growth which threw much light on maturity levels. They extended education to the "preschool" level and started the nursery school movement. Unlike the research institute where the wiggling of small children was an irritating trait to be thwarted, these schools were interested in the wiggling as a need of children for motor expression and provided opportunities for motor impulses as a part of learning situations. In these schools, the child—so long split up into compartments in school thinking—finally got together and was treated as a whole child, as a human being who responded with all of himself to situations.

These schools, with their sensitivity to the influence of environment in the home, in the community, and with their experiments in a planned environment within the school, helped to show the modifiability of human characteristics and development and to dispel the old concern with the problems of nature and nurture and the relative influence of heredity and environment. They helped to change the old "either-or" attitude and to bring about the present view of men and environment as inseparable and interdependent.

In the work of researchers and schools on children and their behavior—work often done separately but fortunately now done more and more together—the keynote is *interacting relationships*. Indeed, thinking of relationships among facts rather than the mere accumulation of facts per se is what distinguishes the new from the old scientific thinking in nearly every field. For instance, what distinguishes the concept of evolution from the old type of biology, which sought primarily to classify characteristics of animals, is interacting relationships between these characteristics of animals and the environment to which they are subjected. What distinguishes modern thinking in geography and anthropology from earlier thinking in both fields is that now the interacting relationships between cultures and the earth forces in which these cultures develop are taken as basic in any interpretation of them. More and more the concept of interacting relationships is entering into interpretations of social economic phenomena. This concept of interrelationships has profoundly affected the philosophy of education. The "philosopher" no longer remains aloof from factual data. Nor does he look at such data as done up in separate compartments. The philosopher now is one with the vision to see the interacting relationships among many kinds of data.

But enough of history. More important than the steps by which we acquired knowledge about what human beings, old and young, are like, is to realize what established knowledge we now have and to strive to incorporate such established knowledge into our educational thinking and practices. Perhaps most important of all is to realize where there are still gaps in our knowledge and to press forward in any and every way that will yield us more and more knowledge.

MORE FAITH IN THE POTENTIALITIES OF HUMAN BEINGS

The scientific approach to the study of human beings seems to some people a bloodless one, mechanical, overintellectual, and remote from "real life." These people sometimes express their attitude by saying, "Human beings should not be used as guinea pigs." We think these people are confusing the study of human beings, how people actually do behave, think, and feel, with what they believe to be desirable in actual human relationships in "real life." A pure intellectual approach to life—if it could be made—*would* be inhuman, and a pure intellectual approach to the job of education which deals with human beings would be inhuman. A scientific scrutiny of human behavior and of factual material is not the total job of education. As school technicians, we must never relax our quest for more and more knowledge, yes. But the acquisition of knowledge about human beings is not the end in itself in any social science. Knowledge is the means by which we can best accomplish our ends.

As schoolmen we are more than technicians. As we said early in this chapter, schools in a democracy are a tool for cultural progress. Suzzalo said, "To an extent characteristic of no other institution save that of the state itself, the school has power to modify the social order." Power carries with it responsibility. So we, as educators, must constantly turn a critical eye on the existing social order and determine what modifications would make for its improvement. We must constantly turn a critical eye not only on the means by which we carry out our ends, but on our ends themselves. We must re-evaluate our school philosophy in the light of cultural progress, re-examine our ideals of what kind of people we wish children to become and what kind of human relationships we wish to develop in the world. These are social value judgments. Social value judgments, which essentially mean caring about what happens to human beings, not only have a place in a social science, they are the end and aim of a social science. Caring about human beings is no denial of the scientific approach to the study of what human beings are like. The end is no denial of the means. The Hippocratic oath, which expresses a social value judgment and which all medical men take, is no denial of their scientific approach to the techniques of their profession. The *social use* that medical men and schoolmen alike make of their acquired knowledge is the end, the aim of their professions. In both professions the goal, the ideal, toward which their scientific knowledge helps them to move, is *human welfare*. It is because they believe that human welfare, improvements in the social order, must be worked out on the basis of tested knowledge of what human beings are like, that social scientists pursue the quest for more and more knowledge.

If, then, the school has power to modify the social order, it follows that it has the responsibility both to think clearly and to feel deeply about what kind of social order it wishes to see develop. It is not a question of whether we attack our job of education of children with our minds *or* our feelings. Both intellectual clarity and genuine "caring about" the welfare of children are involved in the job of educa-

tion. In dealing with human beings, we need to use all of ourselves
—we need to *care* as well as to *think*. But emotion, caring about,
must not be confused with intellectual clarity. Good intentions are
admirable, but we all know they do not guarantee sound judgments
any more than knowledge guarantees good human relations. An un-
reasoning emotional approach to anything is immature. The job of
education requires both intellectual and social maturity. In no realm
of human activity is maturity so rare as in relations with the "other
fellow." In social situations we are still commonly swayed by emotion—by prejudice, by beliefs often handed down to us which we
ourselves have never examined critically, by attitudes which we accept because we like them, which is often because they work to our
own advantage. This is true not only of individuals but of nations, of
cultures. It seems to be easier for human beings to grow up intellectually than socially. If schoolmen are to be a cultural force making
for progress, they have the responsibility to grow up socially themselves.

How Big Is Your Group?

What, then, is social maturity? What are the maturity levels in
human relationships? In individuals? In nations? In cultures? Are
there any trends in our own culture and in the world which look like
progress toward social maturity and which, therefore, schoolmen
should foster? These are big questions and must be taken up one at a
time.

We begin with an individual and the way his relationships with
other human beings develop. A baby is the epitome of individualism.
His own wants are paramount to him. Or to put it another way, a
baby seeks a good life for himself and for himself alone. At the same
time, a baby is a most dependent little creature. The all-consuming
wants that dominate his approach to life have to be met by some
other fellow. At first, that may be just his mother. And at first he will
be unaware that his mother has wants of her own. Even a six-year-old
is so egocentric that in the Binet-Simon test he commonly answers

the question, "What is a mother?" by, "She is to take care of you." The interacting relationships between a mother and her baby bring about mutual dependence, different in the two members of this small group because one is mature and the other immature. The young child develops what psychologists call "identification" with his mother. His mother is a kind of extension of himself. He feels that she belongs to him and he belongs to her. The child reveals the depth of his feeling for his mother in his spontaneous play, in which he sometimes plays he is a helpless little thing who is taken care of by a mother, and sometimes he is a mother who takes care of a helpless child. This early identification of a child with the human beings who take care of him indicates a deep emotional involvement, a caring about someone besides himself. It is the beginnings of his social attitudes. That is why the attitudes toward him of the grownups upon whom he is early dependent are so important. If these early relationships, these early identifications are satisfying to him, he can later take on broader human relationships, wider identifications, and find satisfactions in being a member of bigger groups about whom he cares. Watch how this happens. If the someone he cares about also cares about him, he is likely to approach others with friendliness and with the expectation of being met by friendliness. In big words, he is building up faith in the potentialities of human relations.

As a child matures, as he moves from complete dependence out into the world, his life becomes tied in with more and more people. He becomes a member of more and more groups that he thinks of as "his." He now cares about or identifies with more individuals or groups of people. His groups are extensions of himself. He feels he belongs to them and they belong to him. And so, with increasing maturity, he wants a good life for the members of "his" group as well as for himself. His faith in the potentialities of human relations is expanding. A child's first group, which may be just himself and his mother or mother substitute, soon widens to include the other members of the family group. Gradually, he adds his neighbors, his school group, perhaps his club or his gang, perhaps his church group. Later, if he keeps on growing socially, he may care about his work group, his town or his city. Now he will not need to know all the members of his group personally to feel the tie which binds him to them. His friendliness extends to them, anyway. Still later, if he keeps on growing socially, he may develop a strong identification with his nation. Until recently, the expansion of one's group to one's nation was generally thought of as the desirable limit of social growth. National loyalty, which often meant caring for the welfare of one's own nation even at the expense of other nations, was considered desirable. Recent national and world events have quite generally suggested that an individual is a member of a still larger group. If an individual keeps on growing socially, "his" group may include the peoples of the world. He will have extended his faith in the value of friendliness and faith in the potentialities within human relations to global relations. An individual's capacity to care about more people and more kinds of people is social growth. The size of the group and the variety of groups with whom an individual can identify, can feel friendly toward, can care about, are a good measure of his social maturity. His groups extend himself. He wishes a good life for the groups of which he feels himself a member.

Becoming a member of a new or larger group does not mean a repudiation of past groups or of himself. Nor is social growth synonymous with self-sacrifice. A socially mature person is something like those dolls that have similar smaller and smaller dolls inside them and in the center, at the core, the solid doll. The core in a human being always remains the self, which as the self grows becomes wrapped around by group after group which resemble at least some part of the central self. The ability to identify with the other fellow tempers the ever-present urge for satisfactions for oneself alone and makes possible a social life which is not selfless, not based just on self-sacrifice, but a life in which the expanded self gets genuine satisfactions in a good life for others about whom one cares.

It is obvious that as individuals mature they become independent of others in many ways. Yet it is equally obvious that no individual

can live without others. Life from beginning to end is a social performance. It is being borne in upon us today that no nation can live
alone. Total independence of a nation—the old isolationist ideal—is
not possible in today's world even if it were desirable. As recognition
that our ties with other nations had become vital to our own well-
being, that we as a nation were a member of a group of nations, the
concept of "One World" developed. "One World" means more than
arranging techniques in practical situations which let us live as we
wish to live. It means identification with the other fellow nations of
the world to the point that we care what happens to them, which,
logically, should mean letting each nation live as it wishes to provided it also lets other nations live as they wish to. It means faith in
the potentialities of national relationships. With a nation as with an
individual, it is easiest to identify with others whose ways of living
and thinking are most like their own. In spite of their great variety,
Western nations have enough in common in their ways of living and
thinking to be grouped together as belonging to the Western culture.
The Western culture takes industrial and business efficiency as one
of its major goals. It values machines. It values speed. It values large-
scale operations. It values competition and the successful competitor.
People who succeed under competition in organizing or manipulating large-scale undertakings in practical ways are held in higher
esteem than the artist, the scholar, the scientist, the philosopher, the
saint. The Western culture believes, theoretically at least, in giving
equal opportunities to all human beings. Thus we have a fundamental conflict of values within our Western culture. For success in
a competitive society demands aggressiveness—let the best man win
(best, that is, in terms of Western values)—and giving equal opportunities to all human beings demands understanding what these
other people value and granting them opportunities in terms of their
own values. When the West went into the East, this conflict within
its culture was resolved by simply ignoring "giving equal opportunities" to Eastern people on the comfortable assumption that, since
they were different from Western people, they must also be inferior.

It is also true that Eastern peoples have enough in common in their ways of living and thinking to be grouped together as belonging to the Eastern culture. Historically, people of Eastern culture have not valued practical, large-scale efficiency per se to nearly the same extent as have those of Western culture. Far more than people of the Western culture, they have valued beauty, wisdom attained through meditation, tolerance for people unlike themselves. The "great men" of the East have not been those who have succeeded in manipulating practical affairs under a competitive system. The people held in highest esteem have been the great artists, philosophers, saints, seers—none of them competitors in external situations. They have not been aggressive in putting over the values of their culture upon other people (except Japan since it grafted Western efficiency on to its Oriental culture). They have not been proselyters in religion (except the Mohammedans) as have missionaries from the West. They have respected other religions and other cultures. Neither culture—East or West—has understood the values of the other culture. It was assumed that this would always be so. But the smug division of the peoples of the world into East and West, which "never can meet," is no longer realistic. Their interests *are* tied together. They *are* members of an interrelated world group. They must work together. Each must care what happens to the other. Today "One World" means even more than internationalism. It means interculturalism. The first step toward interculturalism may be intellectual understanding of other cultures and their values—in itself a difficult achievement for both cultures. But intellectual comprehension of other cultures alone does not bring about a sense of belonging to one group. Here, as in all human relations, we have to care as well as to think. We have to have faith in the value of friendliness, faith in the potentialities within human relations.

Social Maturity in Today's World

At what level of social maturity do we as individuals and as a nation stand today? In what direction are we moving? Today, a cultural trend in our country of great social, economic, and political significance, and so of significance to education, is the emerging belief that teamwork, co-operation, working with the other fellow, is the best approach to solving problems of human relations, in small groups such as living within a family of differing personalities, to solving world problems such as living in a world of differing cultures. Here we run into the most firmly rooted of all assumptions upon which human beings have based their beliefs and behavior. The assumption is that "the true, the good, and the beautiful" are absolutes. Yet, scientific anthropological studies have brought out that, though all cultures evolve concepts of the good, the true, and the beautiful, what is good, true, and beautiful for one culture may be bad, false, and ugly to another culture. This brings us face to face with what some people have regarded as a permanent dilemma of modern man. Modern man is caught in two conflicting modes of thought: the one of absolutes—truth, justice, beauty, goodness—themselves all deriving from an absolute of absolutes; the other the scientific, subjecting its conclusions to the arbitrament of hard fact to build an increasing body of tested knowledge. It is true that no satisfactory reconciliation between these two modes of thought has been worked out as yet. But is it true that no reconciliation can ever be worked out? Can one prophesy with certainty what human beings can accomplish? Do we know the potentialities of human beings clearly enough to set definite limits upon their future achievements? Awareness of a problem precedes its solution. Today there is at least more honest and courageous effort to be aware of whether, in our daily practice, we are guided by more of the absolute or more of scientifically derived values. Increasingly, people are aware that there can be no clearly defined operations in education or any other institution unless those concerned know on which of these premises they are basing their behavior. Perhaps it is failure to have come to grips with this issue that accounts for so much of the inconsistency characteristic of our social, economic, political, and educational proceedings. Perhaps, too, it accounts for much of our ineffectiveness.

This conflict in two modes of thought is particularly acute in our own country today. Perhaps because of the multiplicity of conflicting influences from which we have derived, a lack of clarity is inevitable. Certainly, however, there is more honest and courageous effort not only to examine the premises on which we base our own behavior but to press further and define the basis of the values we hold and also the basis of the values which others hold. This effort to define the basis of values might eventually lead toward some reconciliation of the two modes of thought which produce the present dilemma in which modern man is caught. There is a striking agreement in the *ultimate basis of values* as defined by those who believe values are absolutes deriving from an absolute of absolutes and by social scientists who believe their conclusions should be subjected to the arbitrament of hard fact. Both modes of thought hold that the criterion which should guide us in the determination in any situation of what is good is the effect upon the welfare of others. This—the welfare of others—variously stated in different religions, systems of ethics, social philosophies, social sciences, is their common *aim*. It is the *end* toward which all are working. The disagreements come when this common aim is interpreted in terms of action: that is, in the *means* by which each believes the ends can best be carried out.

More specifically, there are various interpretations as to who "the others" are whose welfare determines whether a social action is good or not. Often the interpretation depends upon the social maturity of those passing this value judgment. That is, "the others" to whose welfare we are sensitive are members of a group of which we feel ourselves members. It is obvious, as we have already said, that today we have levels in social maturity in individuals, institutions, nations, and cultures. We have people whose dominant identification is with a small, close, family group. To them, what is good for their own families constitutes "right." We have professional people, such as some medical men, whose dominant identification is with their professional colleagues, and what they believe is good for their own professional group constitutes right. We have people and national leaders who believe that what is good for their own nation is right. We have individuals and cultural groups who believe that what is good for the culture to which they belong is right. Any or all of these individuals or groups may profess in words that they have the "welfare of mankind" at heart. But in practice they show their social immaturity. Human beings are adepts at inventing alibis. And no alibis are commoner or more ingenious than those by which we justify putting the welfare of a group which is closer to our personal selves above the welfare of a larger or personally less well-known group of which we, intellectually and verbally, acknowledge we are members but in whose welfare our emotional involvement or identification is so slight that we can readily ignore it.

Moreover, human beings are not consistent. At one time the welfare of one group may control what they believe is right, and at another time the welfare of a different group may control their belief. This has been demonstrated recently in our own history. During the war we expanded the group with which we identified to include all nations who were our allies. Since the war we have tended to identify only with our nation, but to feel that a similar tendency in other nations is inconsistent. It is one of the commonest inconsistencies to insist upon consistency in the other fellow and fail to recognize inconsistency in ourselves! All of which is simply acknowledging well-known present human frailties and social immaturities in our social attitudes today.

The conflict in today's ideologies has been brought sharply to the fore by recent world history. An ideology is a creed, a belief of what is for the good of society. The basic aims of ideologies differ slightly. What differs radically is the kind of social order—the means—by which various ideologies believe the good of society can be achieved. People not only believe that the aims of their ideologies are absolute: they believe that their means—the methods of achieving their end— are absolute. Yet the kind of social order in which people believe *evolves* a fact which people usually fail to take into account. We have much more generally recognized that an individual in his social attitudes and behavior carries within him the imprint of his past experiences than we have that a people or a nation or a race in their social attitudes and behavior carry within them the imprint of their past experiences. And, as in all evolutionary processes, there are historical lags mixed up in the kind of social order through which people of various ideologies believe the welfare of society can be brought about.

The means, the kind of social order by which the improved welfare of human beings can be brought about, can be subjected to scientific scrutiny. It is often said that we can learn from history. History can be thought of as a rough sort of laboratory for social experiments. The knowledge yielded by these past laboratory experiments in human relations is valuable even though the conditions under which they were carried out differ in important ways from the conditions under which present-day social experiments are being carried out. Today's various ideologies which are the subject of so much emotional conflict are social experiments in human relationships on a vast scale. (They all state their *aims* in terms of human welfare.) The evaluation of the *means,* the human relationships which are set up within the various social orders, must be made in terms of the welfare of the groups living under these social orders, whether or no the groups themselves feel they are living a good life. A scientific approach to present-day ideologies and the human relationships set up within their social orders once more demands a critical eye on *all* ideologies, not just those that differ from our own. And here again in our own country we seem to be progressing—not very rapidly— but surely moving toward a more critical examination of the social and economic order we ourselves have set up and a critical judgment of how far we are fulfilling the aims which were set forth in stirring words when we came into being as a nation. We are passing slowly from contentment with mere lip service to the aims of democracy— that much-abused word of many interpretations. We are slowly turning to the examination of actual human relationships within our country's social and economic order and asking if these practices fulfill our aims, the ends which we are seeking. We are gradually recognizing that true democratic living evolves and are thinking of democracy as an evolutionary process, not as a finished order to be bragged about.

SOCIAL BASIS OF AN EDUCATIONAL CREDO

What has all this wide-ranging philosophizing about the present-day world and its difficulties, its cultures, its cultural trends, to do with education of children? Everything, to our way of thinking. Attitudes toward the problems we have posed and the questions we have raised in this chapter are the very roots of an educational credo. If these problems and questions are not faced, if no conscious attitude toward them is arrived at, an educational credo will consist only of external forms—of practices, techniques, and methodologies—without the roots from which these external forms spring and from which they derive their being. Education, like life itself, is a social performance from beginning to end. The external school, which is a superstructure, must be built on a foundation of conscious aims, of conscious attitudes toward children and society and their interacting relationships. Otherwise it cannot claim to be an educational institution. So, in concluding this book, we shall attempt the risky task of stating the social basis of an educational credo—what we conceive to be major aims, beliefs, and attitudes that are consistent with the social needs of today's children and the social needs of today's world in which these children are growing up and tomorrow's world in which they will take up their responsibilities as adults.

We believe that education is a great cultural force, and that schoolmen bear a twofold responsibility to society for furthering cultural progress:

(1) for giving the best education they can devise within the school,

(2) for supporting ideas and ideals and participating in undertakings which make for cultural progress in the larger community.

We believe that a primary aim of education is to further growth toward social maturity, within the school and in the larger outside community;

that a good life for an individual—his ability to meet life as a fully functioning human being and as a fully functioning member of society—rests primarily upon the quality of his human relations, both his practical ability to work with others and his emotional ability to care about the welfare of others;

that social growth begins through satisfying personal human relations and develops through feeling one's self a member of a larger and more varied group of people;

that a good life within a small group with close personal interrelationships like a family, and within larger groups with less personal interrelationships like the total school family, work groups like labor and management, national groups, world group of cultures, rests primarily upon the quality of the human interrelationships among the group members;

that stability in the world rests primarily upon the development of social maturity among members of the groups, small or large, both their practical ability to work with other members of the group and their emotional ability to care about the welfare of other members.

We believe that improvement in human relations among individuals or large groups lies both in deeper concern for the welfare of other people and for society at large, and in a deeper understanding of human beings, young and old;

that this deeper understanding of human beings will be furthered by a scientific approach to the study of human beings, how they behave and what needs, desires, impulses make them behave as they do;

that schoolmen should approach their work within the school with the attitude of scientists:

as technicians maintaining an objective, critical evaluation of their work through observation, records, checking of results, as learners, students of human beings, constantly pursuing the quest for more and more scientific knowledge,

as experimenters ardently yet patiently attempting to apply to education whatever knowledge about human beings, young and old, has been established by scientists;

that schoolmen should themselves strive to attain social maturity both professionally and personally;

that professionally they should approach their work within the school democratically as members of a school family with sensitive concern for the welfare of other members of the school family, with broad vision and concern for the welfare of the whole school;

that personally they should examine their own attitudes to determine to what extent they are based on prejudice, on untested assumptions, or on established knowledge;

that schoolmen should approach their work in the larger community as members of large cultural groups, and should strive to enlarge their groups:

as students of culture having informed opinions on matters of concern to their immediate community, their nation, their world,

as responsible citizens ready to support or to participate in undertakings that make for cultural progress,

as social scientists conscious of their aims and ideals for society and truing up their own thinking and attitudes and that of groups, large or small, with these basic aims for society.

We believe that the potentialities of human beings to develop as members of groups who can work together and can care about one another's welfare far exceeds their present achievements;

that faith in the potentialities of an individual is a positive factor in his development as a fully functioning individual and as a fully functioning member of groups;

that faith in the potentialities of a group is a positive factor in developing practical techniques of co-operation and social maturity in the understanding and appreciation of unlike groups.

We believe that if schoolmen have the vision to approach their work within the school and without in the world as genuine social scientists,

that if they have faith in the potentialities of human beings to develop a sense of belonging to larger and larger groups,

that if they themselves can develop genuine social maturity in their own human relationships and professional zeal to carry out their twofold responsibility to society,

that schoolmen are in a strategic position to help develop social maturity in individuals and in groups and thus to advance cultural progress in the world.

In this social basis of an educational credo, we have given our answer to the question, "What next?" both for children and for society. For the development of children and that of society stand in an interacting relationship: the society in which children grow up puts its imprint on children, and children put their imprint on society. This interacting relationship can act as a vicious circle or, at least, greatly slow down cultural growth unless the educational process is carried on simultaneously both inside and outside the school. Education, perforce, must work for the development in both children and society of those qualities which make for human welfare. It is to perform this task that we have public education in this country. It is this task that makes the public's schools of such vital significance. It is what makes it imperative for all people who have social consciences to understand in what direction our schools are moving and to help our schools to move in the directions which they believe make for cultural progress. Our very future depends upon our children and our schools.

How Our Workshop Functioned within the School System

During our first year, the principal (who really wanted us in his school) guided us through the bewildering official permissions and reports by which our small undertaking was tied to various departments and individuals higher up in the administrative system. In time we established direct relations with the District Superintendent in whose district our school lay so that increasingly it was to him we took our problems. He became our chief adviser as to next steps in our work. He also became our chief link with the still higher officials so that we came to have many direct contacts throughout the system and eventually with the Superintendent of Schools.

In addition, from the early planning stage and throughout our experiments, we had the help and advice of members of the Elementary School Curriculum Planning Committee of the New York City Board of Education, one of whom acted as our sponsor in presenting plans for our Workshop to the Board of Superintendents. One member of the Bank Street Workshop staff was asked to meet with the curriculum revision committee as associate member. This committee gave us the preliminary drafts for the pending curriculum bulletin and often asked for our comments. The person who was actually writing the curriculum came several times to our Workshop meetings to discuss her preliminary drafts with the whole Workshop group. We submitted to various members of this committee our Workshop's preliminary plans for writing of the Social Studies Curriculum for our school.

We also kept these officials in touch with our experiment by writing a long report of each year's work based on the full records we had kept, samples of which we included. A meeting with a group of higher officials was several times called by the Associate Superintendent of Elementary Schools to discuss the next step in the Workshops. Through their support, at the end of three years of our Workshop in one school, three teachers who had worked in our Workshop were released from classrooms to join our Workshop staff and our Workshop expanded to two other schools.

In one meeting at the end of five years of our Workshop, the District

Superintendent suggested that we give a course on Workshops for the district supervisors, a plan which we accepted but has not yet been carried out. In brief, in our official contacts, on every level, we found individuals ready to support the kind of experimental work in inservice education we were carrying on and ready to give careful consideration of what our next steps should be.

In our first school the principal considered the Workshop an administrative experiment as much as a Bank Street experiment. From the beginning he and the two assistant principals took a real part in the Workshop, attending our after-school Workshop meetings and joining the discussions. We gave the principal copies of the minutes of our meetings and copies of all material or suggestions that we wrote and gave to any teacher or group of teachers; also records of what we did in each class. These were records of us rather than records of teachers.

In these three years in one school with one principal, our relations with the administration developed into a wider sharing of school problems. In the getting-acquainted period, our contacts largely concerned practical matters, such as our own schedules, space for a source material library, possible removal of extra desks in a classroom, supplies, books, etc., and general policies such as possible play space outside the school yard, help from parents on trips.

But soon we were meeting with the three administrative officers to discuss school policies and attitudes, such as content of the social studies curriculum and its relation to the school neighborhood, possible improvement in assembly programs, the value of "praise cards," the possibility of reducing classroom interruptions, school jobs for the children, the placement in this school of student teachers from our own Bank Street School for Teachers and from New York University, where two of our staff were teaching. Also the Bank Street psychologist began to work with the principal on the case studies of children which the teachers wrote for him and used these case studies in her Workshop discussions of child development. Finally, in our third year, the principal asked the whole faculty to try out the tentative social studies curriculum written by the whole Workshop group. He turned his monthly conferences with teachers into curriculum discussions.

All teachers had to take some inservice course each year until they had acquired the required number of credits. Our Workshop was listed among the accredited inservice courses but was open only to teachers in our school. Many of our Workshop members did not require further credits. Each term our Workshop held 15 after-school meetings of one and a half hours, as was required for inservice courses. Also a written examination was required at the end of each semester. We tried to phrase the questions on the examination paper to give a teacher a chance to express her attitudes toward the old and the new curriculum; to show her ability to build a curriculum adapted to her particular children and their neighborhood and what curriculum materials she would use if she could; and to evaluate her curriculum in terms of her children. We gave the teachers the questions in advance and let them write their papers at home. The questions in one examination and one teacher's paper are given in Appendix 17.

Our working relations with the school administrations have varied in the three schools in which we have conducted Workshops and in one school where we have worked with three different principals; partly because of differing personalities of the principals, partly because of differing attitudes of the teachers, and partly because we came to two schools with a three-year Workshop experience in one school (see Chapter 14).

APPENDIX 2

Brief Write-Ups of Individual Children

Charles, overactive child, who cannot sit still or keep still, who is always on the go, during any working period will change his working seat two or three times, who sings or whistles or makes faces (to himself) or is constantly flying an airplane or operating a machine gun with all the accompanying sound effects—such behavior being a psychological compensation for intellectual inferiority and for an excessive power drive—has a desire to excel but cannot produce because of natural limitations—but has a very keen sense of humor and a charming personality.

Henry, motor-type child, whose major interest is in making things—but whose mother believes he should learn more arithmetic and reading. The mother's intellectual drive and unique cruelty to this boy (who has known no father) has resulted in his having an allergy to school studies—who after 5 years' exposure to New York Public Schools cannot read a 2nd reader fluently—and who suffers mental torture during the arithmetic period. Who has a violent temper and who *used* to fight at the slightest provocation.

Fred, introverted or overquiet child, who spent 4 years just sitting still
—he "sat out" all activities in my class for the first 3 or 4 months of last
term. Never talked to me or to the children. Wouldn't work at any man-
ual craft—occasionally played with clay. Was a complete non-reader,
non-number person.

Joel, self-centered child, who is one of nine children, who will work only
when he can see some personal benefit—who, because he has brought
himself up in the street under jungle rules, has gained a quiet strength
and power over other children and promptly proceeds to exploit others
in many subtle, as well as overt, ways.

Robert, a child whose parents overprotect him—whose muscular co-
ordination is very poor—who is afraid of his contemporaries—who constantly looks to the adult for protection—teacher or parent—who is so
scared of a new surrounding that it took him eight weeks to get used to
me where he could understand and follow an instruction.

Discussion of a Teacher's Presentation of a Case

The boy can't read and doesn't want to go to the library. He resents
the sixth-year children who are the librarians. He can't accept help from
children when he doesn't feel free toward them. Anything that means
books is bad to him.

The problem is to get the other children to accept him to some extent.
He does nice carpentry work. If he could make something important for
a group play, it might help. The others don't seem to have any reaction
to him at all—just ignore him. He is the captain of the athletics team.
His mother won't let him see other children. The teacher has talked with
the mother, emphasizing the importance of letting him be with other
children. He had a fight and stabbed another boy with a pencil. The
mother defends this, saying, "It was only a broken pencil—there wasn't
any point on it!" He gets into trouble when he goes to the store. The
mother thinks the neighborhood isn't nice enough for her boy, but feels
they can't move. The teacher thinks the mother hates the boy, likes the
girl better; she won't let other boys come over to see the boy, or let him
out to play with them.

It looks as though very little can be done to influence the mother, who
has an abnormal attitude toward the boy, keeping the child in jail at
home. The teacher probably can't get very far with the mother, unless
psychological help can be arranged. If this is a family that is being
helped by a good family agency, it means there is a worker in contact

with the family. The teacher could go to the worker and report conditions as she sees them and ask that the worker do something toward psychological help. The mother might accept suggestions from somebody she felt had more authority—the social worker or a nurse. The teacher is hesitant to start trying to do anything for the mother. The psychologist pointed out that the hesitancy is an indication of the extent to which the teacher has identified with the child. The teacher should therefore not have to do the next step—she has identified with the child and shouldn't have to put anything between herself and the child.

The boy's strong points are that he can make nice things, he fights well, he is the captain of the team. The teacher doesn't see how she can help him get along with the other children. She thinks he sees that all relationships must end at three o'clock, the end of the school day, and so doesn't care about building friendships with other children. The mother couldn't see that the boy did anything wrong when he stabbed the other boy.

The last two weeks, he has worked with another boy on a workbook. The teacher thinks it won't do any good even if this develops. The others disagreed, thinking that it would be a good thing even if he can't carry it over. The teacher brought a book on making things and let him keep it at his desk. The boy reads this and can make things from the blueprints. The question was asked—Are there easy things written about inventors, etc., that he could have to read? Does the mother realize how good he is with his hands? She doesn't care and she would hold it over him, might destroy this one interest he has.

What kind of things can he make? Perhaps a movable game showing how to play games. Maybe he could demonstrate how to play certain games, to the other children. The psychologist was skeptical about how long he could continue working on a single sustained project. Maybe somebody else could help him. If he could make something that the others can admire and that he can feel proud of, it might give him a place in the group. He will need a good deal of direction. He isn't capable of much self-directed work.

APPENDIX 3

Dramatic Play Suggestions

Here are some suggestions for ways of helping children expand and develop their house play, tying it in with the neighborhood.

The teacher can keep these various possibilities in the back of her mind, and bring them up in the form of questions or topics for discussion when it seems logical to do so. For instance, if she sees the children of their own accord pretending to go out and take a ride in their "car," it is a good opportunity to bring up the discussion of what a car needs to make it go, etc. If she sees the children playing that groceries are delivered, it is a good time to get them to thinking about all the other kinds of things that might be delivered to a house.

I wouldn't bring up too many of these suggestions or questions at once. The ones I am listing here should be sufficient to help the children keep a rich sort of play going for weeks. For convenience, I am grouping some of them under certain large headings:

People who can bring things to the house:

Groceryman—   (Teacher can ask children to name all the kinds of groceries they can think of; where do vegetables come from? Does everything we eat come out of the ground? Etc. A good story to read in this connection: "Silly Will," in the *Here and Now Story Book.*)

Milkman

Coal truck driver—(Do we pay for coal? Where does coal come from?)

Mailman—   (Who pays the mailman?)

Macy truck—   (What kinds of things can we buy in Macy's?)

Exterminator

Plumber

Doctor

Places where the family can go:

For a ride in their "car"   —(Do they have their coupons? Does the car have gas, water, oil, air, etc.?)

For a subway or trolley ride

Children can go off to "school"

Father can go off to work—(Good topic for discussion: What kinds of work do the children's fathers do?)

Family errands:

Go out and buy newspaper
Go out for medicine at drugstore
Go out shopping for food —(Need ration books? Why?)
Go out to ten-cent store —(What kinds of things do we buy
in the ten-cent store?)

Is everything working well in the house?

Is there a garbage can? —(What happens to garbage after the
truck takes it?)
Is the house on fire? Call
the Fire Department! —(Who pays the fireman?)
Is the telephone working?—(Where are the telephone wires in
New York City?)
Is the stove out of order?—(Everyone will have to eat in restau-
rant.)
Is there too much money
lying around? —(Take it to the bank.)

Is the family going to move?

All the furniture can be piled in a "truck" (chairs) and moved to
another house (really the same house).

Other activities that can tie in with this play:

Sewing —Curtains, doll blankets, aprons
Carpentry —Make furniture for house
Food preparation—Perhaps class could buy a bunch of carrots;
children in the playhouse could scrape them,
and all could have carrot sticks to eat.
Clay —Make dishes
Coloring —Make pictures for house
Weaving —Make rug

The house itself could easily be transformed later on into other things
such as a big boat, a grocery store, a train, a barbershop, a shoe repair
shop and shoeshine stand, etc. When this happens, might be good idea
to have it in a new corner of the room.

APPENDIX 4

How to Conduct Discussions Related to the Activity

(By the way—the word "discussion" comes from the Latin, meaning "a shaking, an examination." This gives a good clue to the purpose of a discussion. It's a kind of verbal dissection and taking of things apart to find out how they work; no different, really, from taking an alarm clock apart to figure out how the pieces are interrelated and what makes them push each other along.)

Discussions before trips:

Sometimes a trip is taken in order to find out the answers to specific questions the children have brought up (such as, "How many towers does the George Washington Bridge have anyway?"). In this case, it's a good idea to review these questions before starting out.

If the trip isn't the outcome of any particular questions, it's a good idea to talk about it first anyway, so the children have a good idea of what they are going to see. Teacher can suggest certain things children might like to be on the lookout for.

Discussions after trips:

Two kinds:

1. The "Utilitarian" Discussion.

    Why— To help the childen recall vividly the whole trip, step by step—its geographical location or direction; all the sights, sounds, smells, all the information picked up. This is to help them really digest the trip and make good use of it in their play.

    When— Usually it seems best not to discuss the trip immediately upon returning to the school, but to wait a few days until it has had a chance to sink in. Teacher can often tell when to bring it up for discussion by noticing that the children themselves are beginning to talk about it or reproduce it in their play.

            A good time to hold the discussion is just before the work period or activity period. It often provides definite stimulus for the dramatic play.

How—   Keep it fairly brief, so the children won't become restless and lose interest (about 15 minutes the maximum time).

It must be definitely guided by the teacher, who can ask leading questions such as:

> Where did we go after we crossed Broadway?
> What did it sound like?
> What did it look like?
> What did we do next?
> What was that funny thing Robert saw?
> What did we think was on that barge?

One way to get contributions from all the children in a larger group is to go right around the circle, taking turns.

2. The "Fun" Discussion.

This serves more or less the same purpose as the "utilitarian" discussion in helping the children recall vividly the sights and sounds of the trip. It makes more use of language as an art, however, and is simply a way of introducing variations and spice into the discussions. It is important to have both kinds of discussions, though not on the same day. (If possible, teacher should jot down the things the children say, and read them back to them later as a "story.")

Some suggestions:

1. Ask a child to describe something he saw on the trip without naming it, and see if the other children can guess.
2. Let children take turns acting out something seen on the trip for others to guess. (This is a particularly good device to use for children who do not speak easily or well.)
3. After trips to boats and trains, it is fun to have musical discussions. Let various children make all the sounds of trains that they can think of: bells, whistles, steam, clickety-clacks, etc., while teacher plays train music on piano.
4. Teacher can set a kind of pattern for children to fall into and carry out. For instance, if the discussion is about horses, the teacher could start out:
   > "Horses have necks just like people, only their necks . . ."
   > (Let children complete it.)
   > "Horses have legs just like people, only their legs . . ."

5. Teacher can ask children to tell how they think the river feels, what the horse is thinking, what the trains are saying, etc. Six- and seven-year-old children usually respond with enthusiasm to this idea of putting themselves in another's place and making the inanimate object do the talking.
6. Trip could be recalled entirely in terms of its sounds.
   Teacher could ask questions as:

> "What kinds of sounds did we hear out on 145th Street?"
> "Then what did we hear on the trolley?"
> "Did anybody hear anything while we were looking at the river?"

Discussions related to the activity (but not necessarily connected with trips):

Teacher can watch the children's play and note questions that come up and need clarifying. She can raise these questions and others related to them for general discussion:

> "What are all the things a boat needs?" (Get children to name all the parts they can think of—deck, propeller, etc.)
> "What does a carpenter build first? What part of house?"
> "What must be done to a train before it is ready to go?"

Teacher can sometimes stop in the middle of a story and introduce a little discussion when it seems to arise naturally, such as: "No, the story doesn't tell what was in those freight cars. What do *you* think was in them?"

APPENDIX 5

Some Techniques to Use in Taking Children on Trips

Trip Must Be Planned in Advance. Teacher must be sure she knows exactly how to get to the place where she is taking the children, and if it's a place where previous appointment is necessary, of course this must be arranged. Teacher needs to think out first all such little things as:

> Is there a good place for children to stand and see what I'm taking them to see?
>
> Are there any possible dangers which must be avoided?

Just Before the Trip. Think about the bathroom problem! Is it a time of morning when the children are likely to need to go? Be sure they have an opportunity to go before leaving the building.

Helping the Children Keep in Order out on the Sidewalk. It will be much easier for the children to walk along quietly and calmly if they have had some chance before the trip to play actively. It is almost super-human to expect them not to hop and jump around when they get out-doors, if they have been sitting quietly all of the time previously.

Might try:

Some rhythms in classroom before going,

or

A free run around in the outdoor yard just before starting off down the sidewalk.

Leaders. It usually helps the children to keep in formation if they know definitely which couple is the leader on the trip, and which couple is bringing up the rear. They like to give themselves important, responsible names. The children at the rear could be called something like "the rear guard," or the "end leaders." Each child in the line should know who his partner is, and keep the same partner throughout the trip.

"Signals." I have sometimes used a signal I called "Red Light," to get the children to stop immediately when it seemed necessary. I explained to them beforehand that I might sometimes need to ask all of them to stop very quickly for some reason, perhaps to see something or to get out of the way of something, and that they will know they are to stop at once when they hear me call, "Red Light." I have even practiced this in the classroom beforehand—having the children walk around and seeing how well they can remember to stop when they hear "Red Light." Of course, if leaders fail to follow this signal on the trip, other children can be chosen to lead for the remainder of the trip. It is a very handy signal to have when the leaders get too far ahead of the others, etc., and it is much more fun for the children to hear the teacher say, "Red Light," than it is for her simply to call out, "Stop." These young children love special "signals" and respond to them very well.

Crossing Streets. If teacher is alone on trip, it is probably best if she does not herself cross with the leaders, but stands out in the middle to help all get across, especially the rear stragglers.

The leaders can be shown a place on the sidewalk across the street where they are to walk and wait for the others. For instance, the teacher can say something like this to them before crossing: "Do you see the place where a big yellow sign hangs over the sidewalk? The leaders are to walk across and go *just that far,* and stop right under that sign."

It's a good idea to discuss the traffic lights beforehand in the classroom, to make sure children understand them, and to impress upon them the importance of watching the lights. Try to get children very conscious of the fact that the most important thing to do while crossing streets is to watch the lights.

Seeing Unexpected Things on Trips. It has frequently happened in my experience that there have been all sorts of interesting things on the way that children want to stop and see—things I had not anticipated at all. I think it is usually best to stop and see these things for a short while at least, rather than try to whisk the children away from them. It would prove almost impossible, for instance, to get a long line of children to walk briskly by a coal truck that is noisily dumping coal down a chute. Of course, they will want to take a good look at it, and it is best to accept this and let them stop and look.

The teacher can often learn in this way what kinds of things her children are really most interested in. I'll never forget taking a first grade out once to see a concrete mixer. I had thought it would fascinate them —but it turned out that most of those children were far more interested in a family of kittens discovered along the way!

Discussing the Rules with the Children. It's an extremely important matter to have the children observe the rules on a trip for safety's sake. If there is ever a trip when there is trouble with children dashing ahead, lagging behind, not following teacher's directions, etc., it should all be discussed with them very seriously upon returning, with all the dangers pointed out. Children can discuss, too, whether or not the leaders were good leaders, etc.

(Incidentally, it's a good idea to choose for leaders not always your most responsible children, but some of the more difficult ones. The opportunity and challenge to rise to leadership often do wonders for them, and they can show themselves very capable.) It's a good idea always to review briefly the "rules" and "signals" of a trip with the children before starting out.

APPENDIX 6

Neighborhood Study for First Grade

This is a plan for children who have not had many trips before. If, as kindergarten children, the class had thoroughly explored the school building, some of this could be omitted. Here I am starting from scratch, in the school building itself, gradually branching out to the immediate neighborhood and then the slightly more remote neighborhood.

I conceive of this as a project for a whole year, not necessarily broken rigidly into "units." In a neighborhood study, everything is interrelated.

I. Here is a plan for *trips,* grouped into certain divisions or areas of study which I hope you will consider only suggestive. (Trips need not be taken more than once a week.)

Our School.

Go to see nurse, custodian, kitchen (if food is prepared there).

Are there any pipes such as radiator pipes that could be traced down to the basement?

See if children can locate their room from the outside of the building.

See the big assembly room, and get the idea of how that big space is utilized upstairs as a gymnasium.

Watch coal delivery to school.

Watch milk delivery. (And this can be tied in later with more on milk.)

Our Neighborhood.

(Might take a series of walks first just to locate children's homes in the neighborhood.)

1. Various kinds of workers in the neighborhood:

Storekeepers (just walk around block with children and note all the kinds of stores).

Street cleaners (watch street repairs, if any, and street-cleaning machines, particularly the snow plows and snow-eating machines in the winter).

Postmen.

Firemen.

Policemen. (There's a police station on Amsterdam and 152nd Street.)

2. All the kinds of ways of getting places that can be seen in our neighborhood. (If possible, ride on these—if not possible, the children can go out and walk around and locate these various things.)

Busses.

Subways. (Could go down in the station and watch trains maybe, even if can't ride on them.)

Trolleys.

Cars. (At garage across street you might be able to watch some greasing, tire-changing, etc.)

Horses and wagons. (Is there a stable near?)

Boats.

Trains.

3. Food.

Start with walks just to see kinds of food in stores.

Watch delivery. (The open vegetable stands on sidewalks are numerous throughout the neighborhood and trucks can be seen there unloading in the morning.)

Go to purchase food if there is ever an opportunity for a party, or for cooking.

Might be able to watch poultry-plucking machine on Amsterdam between 142nd and 143rd Streets.

The subject of food leads very well into trains because a lot of food comes to the city in refrigerator cars that can be seen down on New York Central tracks on the Drive.)

4. Trains.

Numerous trips to Riverside Drive to see:

Kinds of trains. (Electric? Steam?)

What the trains carry.

Signals.

The whole process of putting ice in refrigerator cars. (Good vantage point to see this is down near 140th Street.)

5. Milk.

(I put this in a separate and large heading because much of the activity down on your railroad tracks has to do with unloading milk. There's a station down there where Borden and Sheffield tank cars stop. Milk cans can be seen on the platform.)

Trips to see milk cars down on the tracks.

Possibly in the spring you could even arrange a follow-up trip to the Borden Plant at 125th Street. I imagine that milk is bottled there. Teacher needs to investigate this first.

6. Boats.

Numerous trips to Riverside Drive to see:

Kinds of boats.

What kinds of things they carry.

Boat signals and river traffic rules.

Where going (to New York, away from New York, across to New Jersey, etc.).

II. How to carry on the study in the classroom after each trip.
  1. Follow up each trip with a discussion about it (usually *a few days afterwards,* not immediately).
  2. Have a daily discussion on all sorts of interesting points connected with the dramatic play and work activities. (For instance, "When Ronnie was playing with his train yesterday, he said he was putting in gasoline to make it go. How many of you know if trains need gasoline? What does need gasoline?" etc.)
  3. A "work period" each day.
  Even with limited space I think you could set up the room so as to have a variety of materials which the children are free to use during this period, such as:

Clay.
Crayons.
Paints.
Carpentry tools and wood.
Blocks.

You have only a few blocks at present, but you might fix one corner for them where two or three or even four children could play together. Blocks could be supplemented by a few orange crates, and by trucks, etc., which the children could make for themselves at the carpentry bench. There should be some toys like colored cubes or old spools, etc., so the children have something to haul in their trucks.

Also, if you could reserve one corner, screened off, for a playhouse, a few children could always play there—equip it with orange crate furniture, etc. The play that goes on won't always be house play, but can take all sorts of forms—store, boat, train, etc.

III. If the study is not actually broken up into units, what is the procedure? What happens?

As a matter of fact, the trips and the discussions that follow them will form "units" of a sort, some much longer than others. And probably most children will be interested to play and dramatize and draw snow-eating machines if the class has just been watching them and discussing them. However, I would not feel the least disturbed if some children continue to want to play trucks delivering vegetables to stores while the others are busy with the snow machines. (In fact, you can make a wonderful tie-up there—the snow plows will have to come along and clear the streets so that the trucks *can* deliver the vegetables. A neighborhood study, seen as a whole, is like this throughout. Almost everything is related.)

Since you do not have an outdoor free play period when the children can use big blocks and boxes to play and pretend in (as fireman, truck driver, boat captain, etc.), I'd be inclined to do a great deal with musical dramatizations as you did last year with your postmen games, to take the place of this kind of free play. These dramatizations can in general be based on the content of your trips and discussions, though I wouldn't feel that this must always be so. The children may work out a river-and-boat dramatization that they may want to do over and over, even when there has recently been a trip to a garage.

APPENDIX 7

Material Given to Kindergarten Teacher

How to Follow Up the Riverside Drive Trip.

Things to discuss: Get the children to recall everything they can about what they saw. They may have noticed some things we didn't! On the other hand, you can help them remember some of the things, and build discussions around them as follows:

The freight train that rumbled past below us. (What might have been in those cars? Or were they empty? Were they going into New York, or leaving New York?)

The refrigerator car standing down on the track. (What kinds of food come to the city in refrigerator cars? Meat, milk, fruits, etc.)

The man with a red flag down on the track. (Why was he there? Why did he have a red flag? What does a red flag mean?—There were probably men working on the tracks out of our sight.)

The *Gripsholm*. (What was written on it? Who came to this country on the *Gripsholm?* How did they get off the boat out there in the river? Why was that little boat pulled up the side of the *Gripsholm?*)

The ferryboat. (What are some other ways of crossing the river?)

The freight boat anchored out in the river. (How to tell a freight boat: all those derricks or booms that stick up on the decks, used for loading on the freight. What might this boat have carried? War materials for Europe? It was painted battleship-gray. Why are war boats this color?)

Things to do: When the children are playing store during the work period, some might build a train with the chairs, and play bringing meat or milk to the store from the train.

Dramatize the river scene in Rhythms. (Not all the children can do this at the same time.) You could have:

Waves in the river.

Ferryboat crossing.
Gripsholm standing still.
Train passing beside the river.
George Washington Bridge in the distance.

If you could get some flat boards, they are wonderful to use with the blocks, to push around on the floor as boats.

Read boat and train stories. (See Bibliography in the kindergarten section of our curriculum.)

APPENDIX 8

Notes Left with a First-Grade Teacher
after Bakery Trip

This is an approximate copy of rough notes left with a first-grade teacher after she asked for help on how to carry on after taking her children to a bakery.

Trips.

I found three in the neighborhood where baking is done on the premises. Try to take the children into one of these so that they can see more than they saw at Cushman's, where no baking is done:

Ross French Pastry—between 141st & 142nd Streets and Broadway.
Tasty Bake Shop   —between 145th & 146th and Amsterdam.
Triangle Bakery   —between 149th & 150th and Broadway.

Discussions.

What are all the things that are made of flour?

What else do we eat that grows out of the ground? What do we eat that grows on trees? What that comes from rivers and oceans? What that comes from animals?

What can we eat without cooking?

What else is baked in an oven besides bread and cakes?

Stories.

"Silly Will"—from *Here and Now Story Book*—L. S. Mitchell—
    E. P. Dutton & Co.
Rice to Rice Pudding—Smalley—Morrow.
The Poppy Seed Cakes—Margery Clark—Doubleday & Co., Inc.

Things to do:

Take a trip to see real baking process.
Mix up flour into paste.
Try some real cooking in school—muffins, cookies.

APPENDIX 9

Notes Left with a First-Grade Teacher
about Enriching Play

River play on the oilcloth could be helped along by some discussions that would stimulate the children to thinking a little more, such as:

What kinds of things are built *beside* the river?
What kinds of boats go *on* the river?
What is a dock like? Does a boat go inside of it?
Who could build a bridge across the river that would look like the bridge we walked over?
When a boat comes along, what happens to the bridge?
How does the boat go under it?
Who remembers what goes along beside the Hudson River? (Tracks.)
Who could build a bridge across the river that would look like the George Washington Bridge?
Who would like to build the kind of boat that goes back and forth across the river? What is it called?

When you think the children have played with that coal derrick long enough, you could place the oilcloth lengthwise down the room and give them a new perspective on it. Have it for the Hudson.

Milk.

Some questions for discussion:
Who do you think washes all the dirty milk bottles?
How does the milk get here from the country? (Take trip to Riverside Drive. Milk cans are almost always standing down on the platform there. You can read the names "Borden" and "Sheffield" on the freight cars down there.)
Who puts the milk into all those bottles and fastens the caps on?

(Even if you can't take a trip to the bottling plant the children
should know there is such a place.)

Where else do milkmen deliver milk besides to our school? (Homes,
restaurants, hotels, hospitals, army camps, etc.)

I thought the discussion this morning was fine, and the trip to find
out about the distribution of milk here in the school. Wouldn't hurt to
repeat it.

For milk play with the blocks, children could use little boxes as trucks,
and fill them with spools for milk bottles. Maybe some of the children
could bring empty spools from home.

Skags, the Milk Horse by Huber—essential story! Will lead to a great
deal of dramatic play.

APPENDIX 10

Suggestions for Post Office Play, Second Grade

Post office seems an excellent choice of unit for these children, particularly because it will be easy to visit the post office across the street.

Your plan of dividing up to construct post office, train, truck, etc.,
sounds like a very good one, too.

It is often hard to get a unit going before the children have actually
had the trip to see the post office. The trip usually provides tremendous
stimulus.

I'd be inclined to let these children do a great deal of rather informal
"playing" at first, before the unit actually gets going, in order to arouse
and hold their interest—particularly since you seem to have a number of
extremely lively little boys whose every urge is toward activity rather
than sitting still!

Here are some suggestions for "games" or activities you might try
with the children. You may be able to think up some that are more suitable than these, if these seem too elementary.

I'd try to keep them very simple, without a lot of complicated arrangements in the beginning, so that the children can go through them
quickly and get satisfaction out of the activity.

1. Trains carrying mail from one city to another. (Children may not
   yet know all the details of how letters get from the post office to

the station, but that isn't necessary in the beginning. It is one of the things they will learn as the study proceeds.)

Let four or five children line up as a "train" with arms on shoulders or any way they want to do it, and start in one corner of the room (say New York), then go around to the other corner (say Chicago or any city they want to choose). Different groups of children can take turns being trains. Perhaps there could even be two trains at once, one going in each direction—but work out a plan of different "tracks" so they won't collide.

Perhaps children can bring from home real letters (or just the envelopes) to use in play of this sort. A big collection of actual letters would make the play seem very real—also some magazines, since they are delivered in the mail, too.

2. Airplanes carrying mail. (Surely the children know about air-mail letters.) Your little boys, I should think, would love to swoop around as airplanes from one "city" to another. You can encourage the class to be quite critical about these airpalnes, so that the play doesn't just consist of rushing about.

Have them watch and pick out the airplane that flies well and lands like a real one, etc.

3. Trucks or postmen collecting mail from the boxes on the sidewalk. (Probably this is something most of the children have seen. You could stand up several children at various points around the room to be mailboxes. Other children could pretend to mail letters in them, then let one or two children as postmen go around to each box in turn to collect the letters.)

(All of this sounds extremely simple. I imagine the children will think of details they'd like to add.)

4. Lots of crayoning and painting and clay work. (Just leave the children free to draw postmen or model them, etc. Some children may like to color and cut out "stamps.")

APPENDIX II

How to Start Creative Language

(Copy of material left with kindergarten teacher at her request.)

Best creative language comes when children are telling how a thing *looked, felt, tasted, smelled,* etc. (Their sense impressions are very vivid to them.)

Suggest to the children that they make a story which you will write down. Give them a way to start, such as:

"If you were the *Gripsholm,* children, what would you see while you were out there in the river?"

Follow along with other questions:

"How would the water feel against your sides? . . . What would you be thinking out there, while you were anchored in the river? What would you be doing all day long? All night long?"

Or you might make a spring story, getting the children to think of all the things that *come in the spring,* such as:

New grass and leaves.
Spring clothes.
Sunshine.
Trips to the river.
Etc.

And then all the things that *go away in the spring,* such as:

Snow and cold.
Winter coats and galoshes.
Etc.

It's hard to do "stories" such as this with the whole big group, and hard to find time to work with individuals. You might sit down with a small group of children during a work period.

APPENDIX 12

First-Grade Charts

We went out in the yard
We saw the flag on the roof
We saw five floors
We saw Roy fix the windows
We saw the painter paint the garage across the street

We went for a walk in the school
We saw the nurse and the doctor
We saw Mr. Linski
We walked up the great big steps
We saw the big office
We saw big children at work

We went for a walk
We saw a trailer
We saw a milk truck
We saw a bus
We saw a moving van
We saw a florist
We saw a taxi

R R R R R R R
Round and Round and Round it **went**
We saw a concrete mixing truck

We went down to the cellar
We saw the furnaces
We saw the ashcans
We saw little hand wagons
We pushed the wagons
We saw the elevator
We saw coal

We saw a coal truck
We saw a coal man

The coal went sssss
br br br br br br br

I like to see the coal truck
When it backs up
We like to watch
The coal slide down the chute
It makes such a clatter
Bump, bump, bump, bump

Cold, cold, cold
Steam, steam, steam
Hats, sweaters, ear muffs
Mittens, coats and mackinaws
Cold, cold, cold

We went to the Hudson River
We saw boats
Tugs, tanker, ferryboats
Motor, and a barge
Next week we will go to the Harlem River

We went to the Harlem River
A policeman helped us cross the street
We rode on a trolleycar
The dimes went ding ding ding ding

We saw coal barges and tugs
We saw captains of the tugs and barges
The tug captain was in the pilothouse
We saw steam shovels and coal conveyors

We saw train barges
We saw a man fixing the bridgekeeper's house
We saw a coal truck

A Tugboat

I want to pull a coal barge
I want to pull train barges
I want to pull a sand barge

I want to pull a steamer
I want to pull, pull, pull

We saw a derrick
It picked the coal off the barge
Off went the coal

This is a tugboat
This tug pulls a coal barge
This is the smoke.
    (Child's picture. The above is his story about it.)

I pull the train barges
I pull the coal barges
Puff, Puff, Puff
I am a little tug

We have new goldfish
We found them in our room
They swim and swim and swim
Sometimes they sleep
One is named Jim
One is Judy

Walking to School

Vincent and his mommie
    went crunch, crunch, crunch in the white snow
Georgie went slip, slip, slippety on the ice
The children's feet went crunch, crunch, crunch, slippety slip

We went to the garage
The garage is across the street
We saw gasoline pumps
We saw the air pump
We saw oil pumps
The man put air into the tires of his car
S S S S S

It is cold, cold, cold
It is freezing—Oo   Oo   Oo

We put a pan of water outside
The water turned to ice
It is cold, cold, cold   Oo,   Oo,   Oo

Next Tuesday we will go to the firehouse
We will go to Engine Co. No. 69
We want to see engines,
    firemen, the pole, trucks,
    and the chief's car

The Firehouse

We walked and walked and walked
We walked ten blocks
We came to the firehouse
The fireman opened the doors
We went into the firehouse

We saw three fire trucks
We saw one red car
It was the chief's car
One truck was the hook and ladder
Two trucks were called fire engines
We saw the fire tools
We saw the hats and coats
We rang the bell on the truck

The firemen go to school
They learn to put out fires
They use hose, hatchets, and nets
They use hook and ladders and guns
They put water on the fire
The engine goes ooh ooh
The bell goes dong dong

We saw water, sand, and gravel and cement
We saw a concrete mixer
It went round and round and round
We saw a tractor
The tractor went put, put, put
The electric drill went br . . .

We walked to Riverside Drive
We saw boats on the Hudson River
We saw motorboats
We saw a tugboat pulling a barge
We saw two ferryboats
We saw an oil tanker
Sea gulls were flying over the river

The Hudson River

Tugboats pulling barges
Ferryboats going back and forth
Motorboats going faster
Oil tanker anchored
Sea gulls flying high and low

Sea gulls flying high and low
Battleships, aircraft carriers anchored in the water
P.T. boats and motorboats
    sailing faster and faster
pr pr prrrrrr
Ferryboats sailing back and forth

APPENDIX 13

Suggestions for Simple "Weather" Experiments

What happens to things in hot and in cold weather?

On a cold day ask the children if their shoes feel loose on their feet, when they first come in. Later on in the day, when feet have warmed up, ask how the shoes feel.

Here's a real experiment to show expansion of heat, if you can get the materials. I quote from *Experimental Practice in the City and Country School,* edited by Caroline Pratt: "Mr. —— used an iron ball and ring. He showed the class that the ball exactly fitted in the ring. Then he warmed the ball, and the children saw that it would not go through the ring. When he heated the ring, however, the ball passed through."

Things to do with snow.

Bring some in and watch it melt.

Catch flakes on dark clothing and notice the lovely crystal shapes. Look at them through magnifying glass.

(What else melts besides snow? Try some crayons on radiator.)

Rain and water.

What happens to the water in the street after it has stopped raining? Take a trip to street to see water rushing into sewer.

Fill a jar with water and put it out to freeze.

Experiments to show that water evaporates, and that therefore there is water in the air.

Put some water in a saucer. Keep it in room several days and note that it disappears.

Put some water on floor, in two places, one where sun shines and one where it is shady. Note that they both dry up like water on street after rain, but the water in the sunny spot goes faster.

Fill a shiny metal cup or drinking glass with colored ice water. Moisture soon forms on the outside of the cup. Where did it come from? Does the cup leak? No, because the water on the outside is not colored. The water comes from the air. Cool air can hold less moisture than warm air. The air next to the cup was cooled and the moisture gathered on the cup. *Water gets into the air not only because of evaporation from rain, etc., but because plants give off water.*

Cut a small hole and slit in a piece of cardboard. Fit the cardboard around the stem of a small potted geranium plant. Around the stem of the plant and over the slit in the cardboard, paste gummed paper tape or adhesive tape. Over the cardboard invert a large glass jar. If the preparations are carefully carried out, no air or water vapor can enter the jar unless it is carried in by the plant. In a day or two the inside of the jar will be covered with drops of water which have been given off into the air by the growing plant.

References.

Bulletin of the Association for Childhood Education: *Science and the Young Child.*

Craig: *Science for the Elementary School Teacher*—Ginn and Co.

Landreth: *Education of the Young Child*—John Wiley and Sons, Inc.

Pratt: *Experimental Practice in the City and Country School*—Greenberg Press.

APPENDIX 14

Workshop Meeting: Using New York as a Laboratory.

NEW YORK CITY:

Two chief points—

1. Each year, children need to learn about New York in more mature terms. Program is either *direct* study of New York or *back and forth* from past and faraway to New York. Not merely to know about their "home town." The only situation for *firsthand observation—laboratory method.* Actual relations with long-ago and faraway and children's lives; *or* comparison of ways of living and working.
2. In new curriculum history, geography, and civics are combined as social studies. (Read official bulletin, p. 14.) Called "Human Geography" in Grades 3 and 4. Curriculum in first and second grades is human geography on a younger level; 5–6 is human geography with "social values." (What people care about; ideals in how people treat one another. Human geography puts the *why* behind the *how* people work. Teacher needs to know everything!)
3. Source library that we are building up is rich in detailed work patterns of New York.

HUMAN GEOGRAPHY OF NEW YORK CITY. People—earth forces.

What has earth (earth forces) in New York City done to people? What have people done to the earth? Answers to both in terms of *how* we *work*—and work in terms of how New Yorkers have met their physical needs—food, clothes, shelter, and roads. Not that beliefs and ideals are unaffected by earth forces. "Hell" is thought of as hot in hot countries; cold in cold countries! Also we need to know cultural level —particularly science level of culture. Remember the city is not a parasite. Gives as well as takes. Will talk about this later.

ROADS: Manhattan is an *island* surrounded by three waterways, as no one can doubt since the recent tugboat strike. A dramatic exhibit of our dependence upon river roads. Leftover influences of our old "water culture" shown on *island streets*.

(1) Early separate settlements—streets were laid down at right angles to coast. Later a grid of streets running length of island with right-angle river-to-river streets was laid down over parts in between settlements. (Look at this early Vielè map, which shows original earth characteristics with grid of streets added.) Streets were numbered in Greenwich Village and also on later grid. The two Fourth Streets met at an angle. This made Fourth Street in Greenwich Village a curve; so now Fourth Street crosses Twelfth Street!

(2) *Grid:* laid down as long rectangle—long side running from river to river. This decreased up and downtown streets and increased cross-town streets. Response to a "river culture." Enlarged present traffic problem threefold over what it would have been if grid had been square. Necessitated building streets running length of island (subways, elevated, raised highways).

(3) Irregular streets like *Broadway* follow Indian trail around hills.

(4) *Canal Street*—Canal built by Dutch to drain old marsh. (Look at pictures in source library: few skyscrapers around Canal Street—quicksand of old marsh makes construction expensive.)

Harbor—tip of island best for early trade, hence location New Amsterdam. (Not for Indians, who needed high land for protection from attacks and had village north of marsh.)

Piers—The piers now go right around Manhattan—the city owns the piers and rents them. There are at least twelve different authorities in connection with our harbor. As good source material, the chairman showed a small pamphlet giving the duties of these authorities.

The real Harlem River is just a small stream which runs into the shallow, narrow strait that we call the Harlem River. Since the Harlem is not deep enough for big steamers, it is used by the barges which bring up coal, gravel, sand, etc., which unload on the banks of the Harlem where there is space for storage. Because of the coal yards, some electric plants are located in that area.

The tides go up the Hudson as far as Albany. There are no waterfalls between here and there. Albany has an elevation of less than twenty feet. This fooled Henry Hudson. The Hudson River when it reaches

Manhattan is not actually a river—geologically it is a fiord. The actual river ends at Haverstraw, where the river deposits most of the load of soil it is carrying. Geology is important to river work. Little silt is deposited in the Hudson after it passes Haverstraw, which means little dredging is necessary to keep a deep channel. Moreover, the deep Ambrose Channel in the Upper and Lower Bays is really the old Hudson flowing between high cliffs of the old fiord. This area sank long, long ago and with it sank the old Hudson and fiord walls. The land once came to an abrupt edge over which the Hudson dashed in a waterfall. There is still an abrupt edge, now deep under water. It is a continuation of the same abrupt edge which makes the geological change from the Piedmont to the Atlantic Plain over which the rivers fall and which has consequently been called the Fall Line. New York would have been one of the Fall Line cities if the waterfall had remained above sea level. The tides that sweep in from the ocean scour this old river channel and keep it deep for our big boats.

New York is a port for the entire country as well as for us locally. So the Federal Government keeps our channels dredged where necessary and makes harbor maps for the pilots.

The tides hit the tip of Manhattan, divide, and go around the island. At the tip of Manhattan, tugboats struggle hard when the tide is running strong. I doubt if Indian canoes could have made it. In early exploration days, the Delaware River was called the South River, and the Hudson the North River. We still call the Hudson the North River though of course it is west of New York. And we call the water east of Manhattan the East River though it is not a river at all—it is a part of Long Island Sound. These confusing names all have an interesting historic basis. How many of you have noticed that the signs along the Henry Hudson Parkway show the Half Moon on them?

FOOD: Our *city markets* are near waterfront—piers or railroad. All along the waterfront are the warehouses and refrigerator plants. Near 130th Street is a large refrigerator plant. One of the best times to visit it is on cold days when children are warmly dressed, although it is more dramatic to go on a warm day.

No food grown on Manhattan. Fish only raw product which New York workers themselves get directly from source. *Fish market*—fish brought from Long Island settlements and resold and carried back to same settlements. *Downtown* vegetable and fruit markets are a historic lag—retained by vested interests—some have moved—Brooklyn now gets its supply direct and not through Manhattan. Markets related to weather (heat) and peak load of electricity. Jobbers an important part of transactions on piers.

City Markets—should visit nearest one. Stores and pushcarts are city patterns.

Relation to Roads

Freight on West Side. Can see products of West coming in.
Refrigerator cars; warehouses; A & P "climate room" for bananas.
Boats from all South America and Europe.
Vegetables and fruit now coming by airplane.
Science experiments back of all these work patterns.

No time left for *shelter* in relation to our local earth conditions. Or for *city housekeeping*—utilities, etc. Or for *what city sends to other people.*

We'll discuss those things another time.

Discussion: Rest of time, you should talk about how you can use New York as a laboratory for your children—kindergarten through 6th grade. Has anything I have said suggested some application you could make to your curriculum?

APPENDIX 15

Suggestions for Discussion with Children on Roads. (Includes railroads, water roads, airways.)

First Discussion.

1. Begin by finding out what children know of subject from own experiences. Accept personal stories (not too long!). Bring discussion back to subject when children digress.
2. Add any dramatic or significant experience of your own.
3. Ask children if they would like to keep a record of what they knew before starting a unit as well as what they learned. Jot down key remarks by the children. Brief verbatim reports tell us more about the children than generalized memories. Also good material for making stories and reading charts.

4. At end suggest definite observations for children to make in neighborhood (on way to school) which can be the content of the second discussion. These two discussions should bring out:

Notable interests of the children.
Notable gaps in their information.
With older children, notable similarities and differences in immediate neighborhood's use of roads and any faraway and
long-ago environment which may be subject of their unit.

*Samples of Type Questions: Kindergarten, Grades 1 and 2 First Dis-
cussions.*

What did you see coming to school this morning? What did it sound
like? How did it go?

These children live largely in the here-and-now world, which they take
in directly through their muscles and five senses. The younger the child
the more need to let him supplement words by dramatic action. Follow
up any leads through block play, drawing, dramatic play, or dance or
songs. Expressive "outgo" is a genuine part of children's learning. Suggest they look for new moving things. Make your own remarks in terms
of action and how things look and sound and smell.

Kindergarten: Emphasize variety of *moving things*—delivery wagons,
vans, trucks, taxis, fire engines, horses and wagons, airplanes, etc. From
your notes tell story of *things on our street,* using some key remarks of
the children. Tell story in images and action rather than intellectual information. Go on to people who use the street—children, fathers, mothers, postmen, policemen, firemen, storekeepers, etc. Tell story of *workers
on our street.* Add any relevant drawings children make. Take trip
around block to gather source material.

Grade 1: Same approach, but carry discussion further to *function* of
the moving things. Where was coal truck going? Do we use coal in our
school? In your home? etc. Trip to cellar. Any other truck (milk, vegetable, etc.) can be used to prepare for neighborhood trip. From your
notes make simple reading charts.

Observations (after your suggestion) may well include water hydrants
and lead to firemen or water in house—its use, etc. Suggest drawing what
they have seen. Children keep individual books of their drawings with
reading charts. Select from all their remarks any that you want to follow
up in detail.

Grade 2: Same approach with more detail and questions which lead children to wonder *where things come from* and *how they got to our street,* school, stores, homes, etc.—that is, by trains, boats, trucks, airplanes. Trip to Hudson. Bridge over, tunnel under, boats on Hudson.

Samples of Type Questions: Grades 3, 4, 5, and 6 First Discussions.

Grades 3 and 4: Interests of these children are widening from the here-and-now to the faßaway and long-ago. Still necessary, however, to make some direct connection between their familiar world and the intriguing unknown world. Still need personal experience approach and lead out. Many possible avenues out. Emphasis on where things come from leads to what New York workers do for us and what faraway workers do. There are the beginnings of:

Natural resources.

Interrelated pattern of city and country.

Under the streets. (Is fascinating to their age. Ask if they have ever seen a street dug up. What did they see? [Pipes.] What was inside those pipes that we use in our houses? [Water, gas, electricity, telephone wires.] Also subways. These are products of workers in city but all materials brought by some road from far away. Roads are a part of units on food and clothes as well.)

City workers (paid by city or federal), street cleaners, postmen, policemen, firemen, etc., all part of our road pattern. All rich leads.

Construction of streets, of tunnels under river. Ask for observations of what happens on Hudson; call it a water road. Boats a great interest at this age. Establish use of Hudson as a road and apply to river roads in geography and history. In both grades utilize personal experiences of Puerto Rican children and children from South. Roads and transportation in *war,* including airplane, transports, etc. All this can lead to *science experimentation.* Also dramatic possibilities in these leads.

Grades 5 and 6: Begin with personal experiences and tie up with likenesses or differences in any *history* or *geography.* Constantly check on children's images. Images should permeate their writing as well as painting. Important to stress *likenesses* as well as *differences* in various cultures. (Dutch wooden shoes, for instance, not as important as use of bicycles—prewar.) Tie up roads (airways as well as land and water roads) with earth conditions. Develop relief maps and science experiments to illuminate content. Quick dramatic episodes, writing as if they lived in distant lands and past cultures.

APPENDIX 16

Workshop Meeting: Maps as Tool for Thinking

What is a map? It records something—anything—in terms of *its space relations* on the surface of the earth. The thing recorded may concern a characteristic of the earth itself or of human beings who live there. What is a *good* map? A map is not just good or bad—it is good *for* something. Always think if the map you are using is good for *your* purpose.

Today I want to talk about maps as tools for thinking out relationships, and what relationships children of different ages can use for *their* purposes. As we discuss follow the sequence of experiences in space orientation from kindergarten through 6th grade that is suggested on our social studies chart. (Note: chart on pp. 194–195.)

When do children begin to recognize space relations? Very early. Probably a baby's first measurement in space is the length of his arm— what he can and cannot reach. A two-year-old knows *where* his food, his dishes, his clothes, his toys, etc., are kept. This *orientation* in space is the beginning, the foundation of later *map thinking*. We should foster its growth, in situations which have meaning for the child— but not abstractly, not unless he can use this thinking in some way.

Kindergarten, Grades 1 and 2.

1. How far are kindergarten children oriented in space? Completely oriented within their room—but not in school building. (Chance for trips within school building.) Vaguely oriented on familiar streets. Orientation in wider and wider reaches of neighborhood grows normally. Seven-year-olds "know their way around" in quite wide area. Know where river, subway, stores, other children's homes, etc., are. They should be helped to clarify space relations through school experiences, but only in *situation which they can use for their own purposes.*

2. *What are these situations?* What does the child *do* with these experiences? Chief use in kindergarten and first grade is in play. Orientation *does* help constructive play that is based on neighborhood experiences. First-graders will actually and spontaneously construct a very rough map in blocks (if they have enough of them) as a basis for playing back work they have seen on trips or in independent experiences, such as homes, school building and

buying at grocery store, street with traffic and stores, river and docks and boats with coal, etc., perhaps farmers across river raising food and sending it across in ferries to city markets. *Space relations help such play.* Such a map is *functional*. It is not a demonstration map: it is a tool through which children clarify the relationships in their experiences. Let's call it a *tool map*. The play on such a map is really human geography—people using the earth. It can be very rough and serve its purpose. Farmers can be simply "far away," or "across the river." These children really understand little beyond the *here-and-now*. Farmers are still vague to them. In large groups such as ours, we may need to supply *symbols* which all the children understand. For instance, a strip of blue oilcloth laid on the floor for rivers which the children know. In painting, first maps are just oriented pictures. Look at these three maps made by first-grade children in one class at intervals during one year. They illustrate strikingly what relationships were clear and what not clear to these children, and how trips to rivers and the top of a high building from which the Bay could be seen clarified the relationships. The first map shows Hudson and East River; boats on both rivers, bridges on land *not* spanning rivers. Second map shows an outline of land symbolizing island—water *not* close to land; and bridges on horizon arching over water *not* touching land; only land shown is the island—no land on other side of water for bridge to come down on. Third map shows island, land across both rivers, with bridges spanning them.

Grades 3 and 4 (also 5 and 6).

1. In these ages children begin to use vicarious experiences. They learn about faraway or long-ago people, how they used the earth (which is really what work is, in its simplified form). Indians in Manhattan should still be primarily a play experience in which children live the lives of Indians, feel like them, take on the Indian ways of finding and preparing their food, making their clothes, building their houses, getting around on land and water.

Easier for children not to jump from both here and now at one time. The direct method of firsthand observation should be kept as far as possible to make the long-ago on Manhattan *real* to them. Places Indians used, etc. In same way firsthand observation should be used to make far away real. Things coming from far away, etc. If Indians on Great Plains are in curriculum, it is still an experience in human geography. The earth forces the Plains Indians used dominated their lives. (Earth forces, of course, include grass and buffaloes. Earth forces are anything people found, did not make.)

2. Immature third-graders should use their maps for play. Rough-modeled maps are best as first maps; then painted maps. Accept them if they show the fundamental relationships no matter how inaccurate as to shape and size. For instance, if their map shows Manhattan as an island, Hudson, Harlem, and East Rivers connected with bays and so with ocean; United States if barrier mountains in East and West with huge, flattish valley between into which rivers (rain) flow from East and West mountains into Mississippi and so down into Gulf of Mexico. Graphic relief maps have realistic symbols of water and land forms, as in this map of North America which I painted. On such a map you can play the game of a thunderstorm in various parts of United States and have children trace with finger where the water would run. Such a game gives the sense of drainage—explains rivers and making of soil.

Grades 4, 5, 6.

When to use the globe? All two-dimensional maps lie. Different projections contain different lies. Choose the projection in which the lie is least important for situation you are studying. (Discussion of the lies in Mercator projection, where pole is the same size as equator. The teachers measure South America and Greenland on globe and then on Mercator.) Have children check all flat maps with globe. Study of globe should be combined with science—gravity, whirling of earth, seasons, axis pointed toward North Star—all relevant and should be done in one of three upper grades. Magnets can be played with before children can understand them. Every map records certain facts—it is a demonstration map. Maps used to be used primarily to show *location* and *shapes of political areas*. All right when children are old enough to have political boundaries mean something. Maps can be used to clarify relationships on a much younger level. For instance, children can work out for themselves the relationships of rivers and the location of our chief cities when water roads were our chief method of transportation.

APPENDIX 17

Examination Questions

1. Discuss how you have used the environment of New York with your class through trips, discussions, and activities in social studies area— geography, history, civics, current events.
2. What trips listed on the mimeographed copy of trips for your school seem to you valuable for your class? Feasible?
3. What units have you had this term? How are they related to curriculum areas?

Answers to be written out of class and put in Bank Street box in office before end of term.

Examination Paper by a Teacher of First Grade

1. Class social studies program centered around home, school, and neighborhood. First trips in neighborhood were taken to find homes of children. During these trips the children were interested in stores, delivery trucks, and transportation facilities that are part of the neighborhood. When the children played "house" in their play corner they usually found it necessary to extend their activities outside of the home. They went to the park to give babies an airing. Children were sent to school and to the store for food. The moving van moved furniture on moving day. They telephoned the stores, coal company, doctor. Father and mother rode to work on the subway. The family went on trips in their auto. A stop was made at the gasoline station. The superintendent cleaned the houses and took care of the furnace. Carpenter was called in to repair the house.

We took a trip to the bakeshop to buy a cake for a Halloween party. The saleswoman told us about the delivery of cake and bread to the various branch stores. The following week we visited a bakeshop that baked on the premise. Because of lack of help we were permitted only to look in from the outside. We bought a loaf of bread. The proprietress gave us some wheat flour, wheat grain, and a growing wheat plant. The children discussed the process of baking—making flour—distribution of flour and bread. They spoke about other foods that need baking or are baked, e.g., potatoes, apples, pudding, pies, etc. In their play corner they pretended to go through the baking process by mixing flour and water.

They discussed necessity of including cereals and bread in their daily diet.

Children visited the five-and-ten to buy candy and decorations for party. They bought paint at a hardware store. They became interested in a scissors-grinding truck. We watched for the truck whenever we walked along Broadway. Children wrote a story about the scissors-grinder and his work. Children were interested in a butcher truck. They asked the delivery man questions about the meat.

We visited Riverside Drive Park to see trains that bring food to the city. We saw the boats on the river that are used for war purposes.

We made quite a study of the school. We observed the milk truck bring cans of milk to cafeteria. We saw how coal was delivered to school. We visited nurse's office, principal's office, stockroom, bookroom, library, cafeteria in morning when class 5–1–4 was starting the distribution of milk to classrooms. The children visited boiler room four times because they were interested in furnaces, shoveling of coal, and delivery of coal. Saw doors to cellar on 145th Street.

As a result of the school trips, the class had discussions, dramatic play, rhythmic dramatic play. They played nurse—they shoveled coal in their rhythmic play. They played delivery of coal—shoveling of coal into furnace of school and home, etc. Because of the interest in coal we took a trolley trip to bridge at 145th Street over Harlem River. They saw coal barges, tugboats, trains, coal trucks, derricks. As a result of this trip they made a rather crude derrick, coal truck, barge. They used a blue oilcloth for Harlem River. Of course, there was much discussion about trolley ride, direction, derricks, trains. Children were excited when they saw a coal truck at our school street belonging to the same company as the truck that they had noticed being loaded along the river.

We observed new curb being made along street on our street. Children examined tools in toolbox on street. They observed men using tools. They asked men questions about their work—why a string was used (make a straight line)—why iron was used at edge of curb. They observed electric drill. There was no keeping them away from classroom window while electric drill was used. One Friday afternoon a steam-shovel was scooping up the chopped-up concrete in front of the school. We watched the derrick from the window. Then we went outside to watch the worker in the cab, and the scoop loading the truck. The children played derrick, discussed the use of the tools, and had fine rhythms as a result of this activity. We will continue observing the repairing of the street when the men resume work after the snow is cleared.

We walked along our school street to watch the snow plows. The children are interested in the clearing of snow. They know that there is a shortage of workers because of the war.

Now they are interested in distribution of milk. We took a trip to see all the stores that sell milk and milk products. We looked for milk trucks. We interviewed the monitor who delivers milk to our classroom and asked him to explain his job to us. We asked the worker in the cafeteria how much milk was delivered to school for school cafeteria. We know that milk for the cafeteria is delivered in cans because we observed a milk truck bringing milk to school. The custodian's assistant told us how and when the bottles of milk are delivered to school. We hope to observe milk trains and platforms at Riverside Drive. We hope to take a trip to Sheffield's in our neighborhood, if possible. The children are showing an interest in trains as a result of the discussion on milk delivery. Riverside Drive will prove of great interest in the study of trains.

2. Trips valuable and feasible:

>School (all trips listed)
>Short walks to see where children's houses are located
>Riverside Park
>Hudson River, 145th Street
>Harlem River, 145th Street Bridge
>Traffic on Broadway
>Trolleys and busses
>Subways and subway station at 145th Street
>Railroad along shore of Hudson
>Stores (all stores listed)
>Construction and repair in community
>Public library
>Pushcart market, 145th Street to 140th Street—Eighth Avenue
>George Washington Bridge

3. Units—I called my unit by a broad term, "home-school-neighborhood."

How related to curriculum area

Health Education

>Values of milk, bread, cereals, fruits, vegetables.

>Rhythms—were based on trips and experiences—e.g., shoveling coal, using pickax, mixing dough for bread, trains, snowballs, etc.

Reading

Charts—experience charts based on trips and class discussions (children increased reading vocabulary).

Language

Children told sounds they heard on trips, e.g., sound a coal truck makes, electric drill, shoemaker store, coal furnace, scissors-grinder truck, coal sliding down chute, derricks, steam-shovels, boat whistles, trolleycar—coins dropping into coin machine on trolleycar, wind, automobiles on snow, milk bottles.

Children wrote class stories on trips. Discussion after trip and before work periods. Dramatization—dramatic play.

Literature

Stories read to class, e.g.

"Biting Marion" from *Streets*—Co-operative School Pamphlet—John Day.

"Silly Will" from *Here and Now Story Book*—L. S. Mitchell —E. P. Dutton, Inc.

"Poppy Seed Cakes"—Margery Clark—Doubleday & Co., Inc.

Arts

Painting—drawing—clay

Almost every child has painted or drawn pictures of experiences and trips. We have pictures of school, boiler room, coal trucks, boats, shoemaker, scissors-grinder, milk wagons, trains, moving van, derricks, barges, workers repairing street.

Carpentry—coal truck—constructing milk wagon.

Clay—modeled clay coal.

Science

Planted wheat grain.

Mixed flour and water. What foods does mother bake?

Learned direction when taking trip over Harlem River—crosstown trolley travels east and west. Sun rises in east (shines in room in morning).

Watched repairing of street.

Learned contents of concrete.

Made crude toy derrick for play.

Saw and studied bridge over Harlem River.

Where do snow and rain go? Sewers—evaporation.

Penmanship

Wrote outstanding words in unit:
BAKE, MILK, TRUCK, COAL, SCHOOL, BOAT, SCOOP, etc.
Some children wrote simple stories.

Numbers

Measured quart—how many glasses in a quart.
Read names of streets—number of staircase in school (e.g., stair 6)
Read thermometer (warmer—colder)
Count materials—measure materials.
Compare sizes, e.g., tugboat—barge.

APPENDIX 18

Outline of Work on Units

Fourth Grade: Op D Class (Disturbed Children)

Week of February 23: Unit on Roads
Questions: Why does Hudson River have only one bridge while East River and Harlem have many?
Why was it called "Hudson River"?
Map Work: Establish directions on map.
Put in bridges, tunnels.
Clay maps in pan.
Paint large map on beaverboard.

Week of February 28: Unit (continued)
Lighthouses.
Locating school.
Placing rivers on map.
Clay map in pan with water.
Read "Boris" to class.

Week of March 6: Unit (continued)
What comes on ships to New York?
Why must all things come here?

Means of approach to Manhattan
  Tunnels
  Bridges
  Highways
  Airports
  Rivers, harbor
Manhattan in early days. How Manhattan looked to Henry Hudson.

Week of March 13: Unit (continued)
  Rehearsal for Assembly.
  Work on booklets.

Week of March 20: Unit on New York City
  Booklets: Research on pictures drawn.
           Reports on booklets.

Week of March 27: Unit on New York City Long Ago
  Reports of committees
  Research
  Read to class from history book and from *Wooden Shoes in America.*

Week of April 3: Unit (continued)
  Indians in Manhattan: Read from *Age of Discovery.*
  Dutch in New York: Read from *Wooden Shoes in America.*
  Discussion on both.
  Chart of vocabulary.
  Continue listing "What I Learned about New York" after discussions.

Week of April 17: Unit on New York, Old and New
  Indian life in Manhattan.
  Henry Hudson
  Dutch in Manhattan: Read from *Wooden Shoes in America.*

Teacher's Log on Work on Units

February 16

Wednesday, during the conference period, one girl reported that someone threw a snowball at her but it was dirty and hard. I asked what made the ball that way. Answers were the obvious ones. I then asked what had happened to the snow. Someone said it melted.

  T.: "How did it melt?"
  C.: "The sun."
  T.: "Where did it go?"

C.: "Down the sewer."

T.: "Where is that?"

C.: "Under the ground." (I then established the fact that we refer to our streets as the pavements, because the ground is paved.)

T.: "How do you know or how can you tell where the sewer is?"

C.: "By the open irons at street corner." (He then drew the grating upon the board.)

T.: "What is the hole you see through the grating?"

C.: "The pipe that is the sewer."

T.: "How big do you think that pipe is?" (Several guesses as to the size were then made.)

T.: "Where does that pipe go to?"

C.: "To the river."

T.: "Which river?"

C.: "Hudson River."

T.: "How about on the next block, the next block, etc.?"

C.: "It all goes to the Hudson River."

T.: "Suppose we lived far away from the Hudson River, then what would happen to the sewer pipes?"

C.: "We don't know."

T.: "We also don't know the exact size of the pipes. That's two things we don't know. What else is the sewer used for?"

C.: "Water from our kitchens and bathrooms goes down the sewer."

T.: "How does it get there?"

C.: "In pipes."

T.: "Don't you think we ought to find out more about that too? How can we find out?"

C.: "Let's ask the 'super.' Ask the street cleaner. Look in books."

T.: "Where can we get the books?"

C.: "In the library."

T.: "Who will volunteer to find out?" (Several raised hands.)

T.: "Let us keep a record of the discussion we had. Where shall we write about it?"

C.: "In the diary."

We then wrote a composite digest of the discussion and the decision.

At one time during the discussion of sewers, I asked: "What would happen if we lived in a city that had no river?" One boy said: "I guess they would build a large hole in the ground and let the soft earth suck it in."

When I dismissed the class at 3 o' clock, one boy pointed to the drainpipe enclosure in the outside yard. That I thought was significant. Apparently the discussion interested him.

February 18

Turned my room into a graphic picture of Manhattan Island. Two rows of seats covered up with wrapping paper to represent Manhattan—aisle on the right being the Hudson River, aisles on the left being the East River and the Harlem. Upon children's suggestions we placed several books and boxes on top of desks to represent buildings on Manhattan. We also put a pointer across aisle of Hudson for the George Washington Bridge. The entire class became boats—ferry, battleships, P.T., submarine, etc. All took a trip around Manhattan Island and many volunteers went to blackboard and drew Manhattan Island as we saw it. I then gave these children large pieces of wrapping paper and they drew and painted Manhattan Island with waters around it. Those who didn't paint did something in clay.

February 23

Established directions—north, south, east, and west—on maps made by children. During the morning discussion a child wanted to know why the Hudson River was thus named. I asked for volunteers to bring in that information. Several volunteered to go to the public library. I asked what book in the room might have that information. Someone answered, "the history book." But being non-readers or poor readers and that particular book being very much over their heads, I knew I would have to read it to them.

February 24

One child did find out that Henry Hudson discovered the river and thought he was a Dutchman. We then had a discussion on the whys and wherefores of Henry Hudson, with most of the information supplied by me. I also read to them several extracts from the history text, which is most inadequate. That brought us to the discussion of the maps as drawn by the children last week. We discovered that very few maps showed "the entrance" to the Hudson River—that Henry Hudson could not enter if he were to follow some of the maps. We established the concept of a harbor. The children fixed their maps to show New York Harbor.

February 25

I hung up a political map of New York City and we traced the harbor. I then asked, "How does a captain of a boat know which part of the harbor is safe?" After many guesses, which included the answer "By means of a compass," someone finally said, "A lighthouse." Most of the children did not know what or how it worked. Several volunteered to go to the library and bring in something about a lighthouse.

Someone suggested we build up New York City out of clay. I suggested we make a large map on beaverboard. Two boys made one today and one boy made the Empire State Building and another the Statue of Liberty. So we are started on a clay city.

One girl, Anne, found a short poem, "The City," in a copy of *Story Parade* which she asked to read to the class. She studied it before nine and read it during the discussion period.

One boy, Robert, who is very interested in drawing, came in with several sketches of New York made at home.

One boy told me he went to Riverside Drive to look at the George Washington Bridge and made a sketch in the room of what he saw the day before.

Read story of "Boris" to the class.

February 28

We discussed the lighthouse in the Hudson River.

February 29

Several children said they went to see it during the weekend.

March 1

We continued to work on the clay (map). Several boats have been made and placed. Found a WPA story (or rather, a child found it in library corner) on Monday. A real thriller about a barge in the East River. Am reading it to class. Went to school library Monday and several children found pictures of lighthouses.

March 2

Continued building up Manhattan on map. Now have a variety of boats—tugs, cruisers, aircraft carriers, etc. Also some known skyscrapers. Some interesting paintings were made with city as the theme. Entire class stood around the map and we criticized some of the boats made— some were removed by suggestion of children as not fitting in. Others were planned. A suggestion was made that we write names, places, and things on the map. I appointed a committee, with help of class (first committee appointed in unit), the best printer to print signs for map and paste them on. The committee met in the afternoon and searched for spelling of words needed in geography textbook. The chairman of the committee made a list of names needed and the children started.

March 3

We already have Hudson River, East River, George Washington Bridge. The child doing the printing is a very poor reader but is doing this job beautifully and enthusiastically.

Today we got sidetracked from Manhattan to the war, and the entire period was spent on war. We learned the meaning of two new words: "neutral" (someone reported on Turkey) and "radar" (from picture *Destination Tokyo*). The discussions of previous days on New York Harbor was a great help in clarifying Tokyo Harbor and the protection of it by mines and submarine nets. We used the map to show how the harbor was entered by the U. S. submarine when it followed the Jap ship and why it had to follow the Jap ship.

Week of March 6

Spending the time preparing for Assembly program. All the children who worked on the large map (clay city) will tell just what their contributions were. We started booklets, individually, on New York City. I find that when a non-reader or a poor reader draws a picture (for a booklet) first, his desire to find information about that picture results in his doing research unsolicited. Also I discovered that they have picked up a great deal of information via the morning discussions.

Week of March 13

Some children who had been to the movies during the weekend reported that they saw a lighthouse which had a revolving light on top. Others saw the Empire State Building and the Chrysler Building. I taught the class "Sidewalks of New York," to be sung at the end of the program in Assembly.

Spent most of the week practicing the Assembly program. The children did well.

Week of March 20

Current events occupied the attention of the class mainly, this week the eruption of Mt. Vesuvius providing main topic of conversation and subject in drawing.

On unit we started *New York of Long Ago,* decided to form committees on research. Asked what they would like to know about old New York—and questions such as the following were asked:

How did the Indians live?
Where are the Indians now?
What happened to them in the interim, 1609 to now?
How did the Dutch live?
What kind of houses, clothing, language did they have?
Where are these Dutch people now?
We formed three committees:
  1. Indians
  2. Dutch
  3. New Yorkers today

Someone suggested we build up old Manhattan similar to the one we made on present New York. We are now engaged in doing that. One boy drew and painted a large picture of the *Half Moon.*

We summarized "What I Learned about New York City" in the diaries. We also made up a vocabulary list, both on chart and in diaries and both to be illustrated—former by pictures from magazines and papers and the latter by own drawings.

Week of March 27

Listed facts learned about New York. Class gave me the facts, which I wrote on the blackboard and class copied into diaries.

Monday morning the discussion centered around Henry Hudson, the Indians, and trading. I read to them extracts from history book on that topic. Then a child wanted to know what happened to all those Indians that lived here. I explained the westward push—and the wars and the intermarriage which accounted for some of the decimation. Omitted the fact that the Indian was largely decimated by the white men's (or Europeans, as I call them, by design) diseases, which they contracted after the latter's appearance.

Tuesday morning the discussion centered around the war and the Russian victories. One child wanted to know whether we would own Germany after Hitler is defeated. I threw the question out: "What do you think we ought to do with Germany and the German people after victory?" The answers were most interesting.

Carl: "After the war, put all the Germans on WPA!" (This tops them all.)
Nelson: "Kill as many Germans as they killed Americans."
Richard: "Make them work for Russians and for us for nothing."
Billy: "No, that's no good, that's slavery."

Child: "Kill all the Germans except those in concentration camps. Take those out and let them be boss."

Child: "Divide Germany and give Russia one-half and keep one-half for U. S."

On unit: Discussed the reasons for Dutch settling on New York (Manhattan). I asked what reason people have for leaving one country and settling in another, or why some of their parents left Puerto Rico and settled in New York. Answer was: "To find a job." I told them that was the same reason the Dutch came here—in other words, "trade." I then asked what other reasons people have for leaving country and coming to the U. S. Answer: "Freedom." We then discussed the refugees from Hitler, Europe, etc.

Week of April 3

Monday: Indian discussion today was on how Indians made fires and how it was used. To illustrate how friction causes heat, I had them rub their palms together and feel the heat created. I also had them rub the sides of their pencils against the desk and then feel how warm the rubbed spot got. One child drew on the blackboard the fire stick used by the Boy Scouts.

Tuesday: A Bank Street member visited for a couple of hours during Arts and Crafts. The children responded very warmly to her. They readily explained all the things they were working on. Some were painting Indian scenes on large wrapping paper. Some were sewing on aprons, some were making clay things for the map, and one boy, the most mature boy in the room, was making a doll out of the inside of a toilet paper roll. Everybody was very busy and very happy.

Wednesday: In the afternoon the Bank Street member gave a demonstration lesson with class from 3 to 4 P.M. She brought along an intriguing drum, fascinating Indian feathers, an interesting animal skin, and Indian corn which was later distributed among the children. She did some scenes from Indian life to which the children responded very enthusiastically. They were most co-operative. Even Jimmy.

To prepare them, I had to read to them from various books on Indian life.

Thursday: The next day I had to continue the dramatics—by request —and we did one or two more scenes. I don't think mine were as good as the ones the Bank Street member did. I guess I'm not as adept in the technique as she is.

APPENDIX 19

The Americas

Note: A sixth-grade teacher's outline for the year's work in social studies based on the Workshop curriculum but bearing in mind the children's experience with the old curriculum in the preceding year.

Last term the children studied the United States by sections as well as American history through the Revolutionary War. The children have no idea of the relationship between geography and history, i.e., the relationship that exists between where man lives and how he lives. I thought some time could be profitably spent this year in our social studies work if we highlighted this relationship as an approach in studying our ties with the American nations and our connections with the rest of the world.

This approach would give the children an understanding of:

1. The genesis of the American countries.
2. Geographic factors and controls as such.
3. The relationship between surface, climate, natural resources on the one hand and people, their occupations, customs, religion, history, etc., on the other hand.

The children would appreciate the interrelationships of the Americas with one another by understanding:

1. Similarities and differences in surface, climate, natural resources.
2. Their parallel history—indigenous people, discovery, exploration, colonization, independence movements, and development as independent nations.
3. Their present stage of development—culture, economy, and politics.

As the work progresses the connections of the Americas with the Old World—Europe, Asia, Africa—would be developed and the present relationships studied.

The general plan as seen at this stage would be a statement of the problem: What the connection is between where people live and how they live. The child will be brought to understand the problem through:

1. Discussion.
2. Reading.
3. Dramatization.
4. Review of material studied—e.g., deserts, arctic regions, industrial East, agricultural South, etc.

In order to solve our problem we must answer the following two questions:

1. What must we know about the place?
   a. Surface—mountains, rivers, lakes.
   b. Climate—rainfall, temperature, altitude, winds, ocean currents, distance from equator.
   c. Natural resources—soil, minerals, wild life, forests, water power, etc.

2. What must we know about the people?

   a. Who lived here?
   b. Where did they live?
   c. What of their food, homes, clothing, customs, education, religion, government, transportation?

We can best find the answers by dividing the job among us in the following manner and having the following groups (committees):

Map Committee
   1. North America.
   2. South America.

The job of the Map Committee will be to find all we can about the geographic factors in the Americas. They will illustrate their findings by:

1. Making three-dimensional physical maps of North America and South America.
2. Writing reports on various regions.
3. Painting pictures of various regions.
4. Making more detailed (smaller) models of various regions.
5. Demonstrating (perhaps experimentally) the properties of such factors as climate (rain, winds, temperature, altitude), fertile soil, land formation, river formation.

Natural Resources Committee

The job of this group will be to find what the natural resources of the Americas are and what part they play in the lives of the people. They will:

1. Indicate resources on large outline map of the Americas.
2. Prepare reports.
3. Prepare diagrammatic material showing source, development, uses, etc.
4. Paint scenes connected with natural resources.
5. Construct models, diagrams.
6. Demonstrate properties, uses, ways of extraction of various resources (science).

People Committee

The job of this group will be to study the people who lived here before the coming of the Europeans. They will attempt to study the cultures of these people, compare them with one another (especially the previously studied North American Indians) and with the Europeans.

They will carry on the following activities:

1. Write reports.
2. Paint.
3. Construct people (models), scenes, masks.
4. Dramatize aspects of their culture.

The successful carrying through of this phase of our work will lead us in succession to:

1. A study of the exploration period in the Americas (a review of North America).
2. A study of the colonization period (a review of North America).
3. A study of the various independence movements (a review of United States).
4. A study of the postcolonization period (18th and 19th centuries).
5. A study of the present century with special emphasis on the part the Americas play in world affairs.

These aspects of the work will, on completion, give us an understanding of the Americas living together and in the world. All the work will be oriented toward understanding the implications of a "better world."

Living together in peace.
Global concepts.

Modern developments in science.
Human relationships—art, customs, government.
United Nations.

APPENDIX 20

Earth Forces in China
How They Conditioned the Life of People

Notes used by leader of discussion.
1. Begin with studying Thorne-Thomsen's map of Eurasia.
   a. China was cut off from Europe by difficult lands to cross. Only difficult camel trails. (Describe how they look from air.) China developed her own culture apart from European Mediterranean.
   b. Make group deduce how mountain erosion built northern and southern plains with little intercommunication.
2. Northern plain.
   a. Would northern plain have good soil? Why not farms there? What besides soil do we need for farms? How did mountains affect climate? Get answers from map. Discover the shut-in lakes on map—means salt lakes. Why dry land in high plateaus? Deserts. Other plains have no trees. Where do rivers from northern plains empty? Any good for trade? Why not? Now Soviet Russia is developing some trade and also some farmland.
   b. Only grass on most of northern plain. If mankind originated there, probably had different climate. Pulse of Asia; Ellsworth. Dinosaur egg with baby inside found in northern Asiatic plain. May have been before rise of present mountains. Northern horse originated there. Also northern camel.
   c. How could men live there? Nomads. Followed horses, camels, yak in search of grass. Horses led them to Europe in dry years. Tribal invasions brought Dark Ages to Europe. Were absorbed by time of Renaissance. What material for houses is there on northern plain?
3. Southern plain.
   a. Look for three fertile valleys. How do you know an old river, senile river? Fills up bed. Builds delta. Causes floods. Yangtze

Kiang and Hwang Ho like our Mississippi. A land of canals.
Yangtze deep.

4. Farm hill land terraced—held soil. Farmlands average 3,500 people
per square mile. Just getting around to terracing in United States.
Poor transportation and poor communication kept China from becoming united. Consequently modern China is trying for roads and
literacy, that is, schools. Get a Chinese to tell how they are spreading
reading.

5. Ancestor worship also kept China from changing its work patterns.

6. Likenesses and differences. Chinese read from right to left—less
important than that they read! Women wear trousers, men skirts.
So do we now. Skirt has been an emblem of not working. Fundamental likenesses more important to stress than superficial differences.

7. Moving industries west in war.

8. Sun Yat-sen.

Record of discussion at meeting.

Bank Street Workshop leader had been asked by the group of teachers to talk about China. She brought to the school a large graphic
relief map of Eurasia and other graphic relief maps.

Leader: "Our real purpose is to teach children how to *think,* how to
see relationships in different kinds of materials. If you have no images
of a country then it is possible to make up for it with a good map.
Basic work of the country goes back in large measure to the land. It is
through using the resources of their land that people meet their basic
needs. Cultural level, the inventions by which they use the land, you
have to give to the children. Research is only of value if you answer a
'why'?"

Teacher: "Why did China choose rice?"

Leader: "The environment gave China rice; it is the great native grain.
China grows the soya bean in vast amounts in the colder north."

Leader described the terraces of China, how every inch of land with
good soil is cultivated. She suggested that if we had tried this method
we might have avoided our own problem of erosion in the South. The
United States Government is now teaching the South about the value
of terraces. For thousands of years Java has been cultivated with very

little erosion because they know how to use the land. She mentioned that the life of a Georgia farm was once only about eight years because of the improper use of the land. The farming parts of China are not eroded at all. In China there are 3,500 people to a square mile of farmland. They don't have many animals. Land is too valuable for grazing. They do have some chickens. In China the pattern is small crowded farms, then flood, then famine.

Leader wondered how much of this material about China could be told to the children of our school. *One teacher* thought her group couldn't take it. *Another teacher* thought perhaps hers could.

Another teacher gave a brief report on what she had told her children—they understood the world famine.

Leader then discussed the great Chinese rivers; suggested the rivers be labeled "river roads," emphasized that China was a land of canals; that this fact is seldom mentioned. In the Soviet Union they have planned canals. They have created a dramatic situation by literally taking boats right over the Ural Mountains. The Chinese had their industries on the coast; moved them to the hills during the war. Thinks the industries will never be moved back, though the cities may be. China has opened a vast, new industrial area.

In doing China with children show them that they couldn't have a united country without means of communication, roads and canals. There also has to be a common language, which China lacks. China also needs modern means of communication, radio, etc. Roads, communication, schools—you need these for a unified country.

The group asked why all the continents take on a triangular shape. *Leader* explained the quadrilateral theory, not completely accepted by scientists, as to why the great continents tend to be triangular.

The *leader* asked if what she was telling the group meant anything to them in terms of teaching techniques. The group said it did.

The group was asked to suggest what it would like to do next.

APPENDIX 21

Notes Kept by Bank Street Member Working in the Sixth Grade on "Consumers" and "Mary's Coat."

October 3

This room has a lively atmosphere, plenty of maps on the wall (commercial, not made by the children), newspaper clippings, a shelf of books and pamphlets. The tone of the group is excellent. The children seem to talk freely with each other. Mrs. F.'s manner is polite, not personal, and I saw no signs on this day as well as on any of my subsequent visits of harsh or regimented discipline.

I was not able to see signs of any work on their study of "Consumers" and didn't ask about it at this time.

October 17

This time there was a spirited discussion, with the election the important piece of news. There had been plans for a straw vote which was taken and an active pro-Roosevelt sentiment expressed. The children then reported on their work in the unit. They have a Junior Consumer Club and on this day a report was given on shoes. It was stilted, largely copied material in which neither the reporter nor the children seemed to have much interest. When the teacher called for personal experiences in buying and wearing shoes, there was real interest and a good deal of adequate discussion. I talked with Mrs. F., who feels the difficulty of so intellectual a unit for the children. Suggested the possibility of tracing back some product to its source, preferably clothes because of New York City being the center of manufacture and their interest in the clothes they wear. Suggested that a possible activity of renovating or salvaging might be used.

I brought Mrs. F. the names of several books on consumer education for children, *Johnny Get Your Money's Worth,* by Ruth Brindze (Vanguard Press), *Behind the Show Window,* by Jeanette Eaton (Harcourt, Brace, Inc.), and I also brought in one from our library for her to use.

Mrs. F. has also told me that she is due to give an Assembly program on the fourteenth of November and in the afternoon meeting confessed to me that she feels troubled since she is aware of the inappropriateness of the topic, "Consumer Education," for such a program.

October 24

I came into the room after a very poor Assembly program had been given by another group, and the children were conscious that the program was not only uninteresting to them but disapproved of by the adults, so there was an outburst of discussion as to what they could do to make theirs a good one.

I then suggested a possible starting point for an Assembly program, gave them a little bit of an idea of how to work out a parody form by giving them a couple of verses for a starter, i.e., "This is the coat that Mary wore, it looks fine and grand as it stands in the store." There was a lively interest in such a program but with some hesitation from the children and Mrs. F. as to whether they could put it through. One youngster questioned the relevancy of this subject matter to their unit, "Consumer Education." Several others talked him down with very adequate ideas as to how they could include the consumer angle in this "play." Feeling so accepted in this discussion, I suggested that Mrs. F. let the children start rehearsing that very Monday, and much to my surprise, she was very eager to go on, so there was a jolly beginning rehearsal as much a surprise to Mrs. F. as to me, I'm sure. She very quickly got on to what I was trying to do with the youngsters and, although grateful for the start, was not at all sure that she would be able to carry on. However, we left it that she would try to get what she could from the children in the way of verses and that they would dramatize as much as they could until the following Tuesday.

October 31

A most gratifying time with Mrs. F. and her children. They have written verses sufficient to take us all the way back to the sheep in the production of clothes and are still full of ideas as to the form that the whole thing should take. We had a real rehearsal this morning. Some of the children gave their parts with tremendous charm and intelligence.

November 6

I came in for an afternoon of special rehearsal in which some fine points as to entrances and exits, timing, etc., were brought out. The children have begun on sheep's masks, a lorgnette, the railroadmen's caps, all sorts of odds and ends to vivify the performance. I brought in a book of simple tunes, suggesting that they make their own verses for some parts of the play for which we could find no ready-made ones and showed them again how easy it was by offering one.

Later in the afternoon I talked with Mrs. F. alone about the possibility of a backdrop. She was hesitant but I assured her that even a simple, crude thing would give the children the confidence they need and give them a sense of finish to their performance.

November 14

The play was given this morning and received with acclaim by children and adults alike. In these few days they had made a tremendous mural with four panels showing the four parts of their little play. The painting was simple, even quite young for sixth grade, but tremendously childlike and charming. Their acting was as free and happy as any I've seen. Their love for the whole job was evidenced to me in the last little finishing touch of special programs cut in the form of a child's coat and carefully printed for the principals.

After the play I talked with Mrs. F., not the children, about how they could go on with their unit from here. She has in mind a poster campaign for the whole school. She'll need help with the art side of this, but it is an excellent next step.

November 28

Didn't visit the group but when I met several of the children in the office, they told me with tremendous pride that they had been asked to repeat their performance for the fifth-grade Assembly.

Mrs. F. talked with me in the group meeting after the discussion of "rewards" by the Bank Street psychologist. She told me that she felt the play was the most rewarding experience she and the children had ever had together. (See Chapter 7.)

January 2

The follow-up of the play with a poster campaign on "Consumer Education" bogged down somewhat, but several visits were made to the group to help them arrive at possible slogans for posters, to plan composition, pictures, bright colors, etc., and to discuss the materials necessary.

The few times I visited the class later in the month there seemed to be some real activity on the art side. The posters were being drawn on the blackboards with some nice humor evident in some of them.

We also arranged a trip to a dress factory, and the most satisfying aspect for the children that came up in our discussion was the accuracy of the processes that they had presented in their play. They had brought back some new exciting information, namely, the ideas of mass production and the speed with which workers have to work in a factory, but what they lingered over were comparisons with their own presentation of the making of a garment and what they saw in the factory.

Excerpts from text of play written by sixth-grade children.

THE STORY OF MARY'S COAT

Narrator:
> Here is the coat that Mary wore,
> Looks pretty fine as it stands in the store.
> Examine it thoroughly,
> Study with care.

Mrs. Smith (examining coat with lorgnette):
> Will it take snow and rain?
> Will it stand wear and tear?
> Will this coat be warm
> When the wind blows?
> Is it fast color or will it fade?
> Does it come in another shade?

Narrator:
> Here's Mrs. Smith, Mary's mother.
> She went downtown to the store
> And bought the coat that Mary wore.
> She'll keep it brushed and pressed and neat,
> And Mary will wear it proudly
> Up and down 145th Street.

II.

Narrator:
> Now let us take you back of the scenes.
> Let's look at this coat and what it means,
> What went into it and how it was made
> By tailors and fitters who knew their trade.

> Here are the workers, busy as bees,
> Cutting and sewing and pressing with ease.
> Making the coat that Mary wore,
> The one that she bought in Mr. Jones' store.

Cutter:
> I am the cutter who cuts all day long.
> My hands must be steady,
> My scissors are strong.
> Then Mary's coat will fit her just right.
> And it won't be too loose,
> And it won't be too tight.

Tailor:
> I am the tailor who works the machine,
> My hands must always be very, very clean.
> My seams must be straight,
> My hems must be neat,
> Then Mary's coat cannot be beat.

Presser:
> I am the presser who presses and presses
> Coats and suits and even dresses.
> Mary's coat took lots of care
> Before it was ready for her to wear.

All three workers:
> Now it's all ready to be sent to the store,
> To be the coat that Mary wore.

III.

Narrator:
> Now we're going back again
> To see from where the material came.
> Did it come by boat?
> Did it come by train?
> The answer to you we'll soon make plain.
> Here is the train that brought the things
> All the way to the factory door,
> That made the coat that Mary wore,
> The one that she bought in Mr. Jones' store.

IV.

Narrator:
> Back, back again we are going

To where the wool is slowly growing
Upon the backs of all the sheep
While they're awake (all sheep: Ba-a-a-a-a)
And while they sleep.
The wool for the coat that Mary wore,
The one that she bought in Mr. Jones' store.

Shearer:
   I am a shearer, I am, I am.
   They usually call me Silent Sam.
   But today I'll be glad to tell you the tale
   Of Mary's coat that she bought at a sale.

Narrator:
   Here are the sheep that gave the warm wool.
      (All sheep Ba-a-a-a up and down scale.)
   The shearer will fill many bags full;
   The sheep are sheared in the early spring.
   The men all shear till the dinner bells ring.
   The wool is sorted and packed in bags.
   Some have tickets and some have tags.
   The bags are loaded from truck to train.
   From Texas ranches to as far as Maine.

   To the factory now the wool will go,
   Where it will be cleaned as white as snow.
   Then dyed and woven it will be,
   For Mary's cloth coat, as you will see.
   Now here is the coat that Mary bought.
   To buy a good coat she had to be taught
   About materials of every kind,
   Buttons and coats that are interlined,
   Hems that are straight—thread that is strong,
   Colors that surely will last very long.
   These things you, too, can learn if you try,
   Then you will know just how to buy,
   And you too will be a wise consumer,
   So your pocketbook will be in good humor.

APPENDIX 22

Sixth Grade Play about "Atomic Energy" with Preliminary Notes

February 25

This teacher's group is approaching the study of Europe through the idea of postwar reconstruction as well as the present-day contributions from many lands. I suggested to the teacher that he let his children read from the stories of children in Europe during the war and brought in that set of stories called "Youth Replies: I can," which he expects to use with the children. I promised also to find for him a large outline map of Europe on which he would like to do topographic relief and natural resources, taking Europe as one large land mass rather than in terms of political divisions.

March 4

On my second visit the children reported on music in Europe in the nineteenth century, as well as science in the twentieth century. In this group the children are functioning on an intellectual level so far in advance of their age levels that one can hardly think of them as sixth-grade children. Of course this is not true of all the children, but there are enough of them in the group to make possible a social studies program with the sky the limit. Alice started by reporting on the Russian composers in prerevolutionary Russia, and from there on the contributions of European music and science were set forth and discussed with understanding and adroitness by the children. When Jimmy told about the development of science as a world-wide rather than a national undertaking, I asked the children whether they had talked about the present-day revolution in world science, and of course they responded with an interested and very factual discussion of the invention of the atom bomb. What I would like to see a group like this do is to develop their intellectual curiosity toward Europe as a geographical entity, and I suggested to the teacher the possibility of studying the invention of the atom bomb as a co-operative international effort, with the possibility of a dramatic presentation later in the year.

The following are samples of materials which were written by the children during the process of planning their play. The play changed a great deal during the practicing and was never written down until the final performance, when stenographic notes were taken.

The Atomic Energy

The scientists worked and bled,
Not even a word was said,
You know that a scientist was very smart
To crack the atom apart.

Props:

Scene I: Radio, Wool, Table, Skates.
Scene II: Newsstands, Newspapers, Rope, Shoeshine Box, Pocketbook, Magazines, Clips (for magazines).
Scene III: Clip Board, Bedsprings, Box, Sign, Briefcase, Smocks.
Scene IV: Typewriter Paper, Amplifier, Buzzer.
Scene V: Cord (electric).

Plot for the Atomic Bomb Play

Scene I:

Scene I takes place in the home of an aged couple.
The radio is turned on. Classical music is heard.
Teen-aged granddaughter comes in. She turns dial.
Famous singer is heard. Granddaughter swoons.
Program is interrupted by newsflash.
The flash turns out to be a speech from the President about the atomic bomb.
Startled family listens.

Scene II:

Scene II takes place in the same home, but this time a large family is sitting around.
Conversation is based on the atomic bomb.

Scene III:

Scene III setting is much simpler, so that it can be changed very easily.
Time, about a week later. Discussion is still about the atomic bomb.
Oldest grandson walks in. Everyone clatters around to ask where he has been.
He says he was working on the atomic bomb.
He tells them about how it took co-operation, and the peacetime uses.

Scene IV:

Scene IV takes place in Lise Meitner's laboratory.

Scene IV

L.M.: Switch the instruments off, Doctor Hahn.

O.H.: Switch off, Doctor Meitner. Take out the trays of U-235.

L.M.: All right, Doctor. I'll take a sample in the test tube. Wait a minute! This is strange! It's the wrong color. It's as if it wasn't U any more.

O.H.: Hmmmm, you're right. It doesn't seem to be. Wait, let's see if tray number two is the same. Yes, it is.

L.M.: And so is tray number three. Something must have gone wrong, unless—unless we've hit on something. Let's make the same operation over again.

O.H.: Yes, I'll start the instrument. Put new trays in.

L.M.: Switch on.

O.H.: Switch on.

L.M.: Switch off. Look! These trays! The same thing has happened again. We ought to have these analyzed.

O.H.: I'll buzz for Fortnich, the chemist.
     (BUZZ)

L.M.: Here he comes.

F.: Yes.

L.M.: Doctor Fortnich, we would like you to test these samples of U-235.

F.: All right. I'll have them for you in a couple of hours.

O.H.: Couldn't you rush it? We may have hit on something very important.

F.: All right, in that case I'll have it for you in a minute. (Leaves.)

L.M. and O.H.: Good.

F.: (Returns) Well, I've got it. Mostly U-235 with traces of barium and krypton th—

O.H.: Barium and krypton!

L.M.: They shouldn't be there; in fact, they weren't there when we started.

F.: Well, they're there now.

O.H.: Where did they come from? Do you think, Lise, that—

L.M.: We must have—

W.: Doctor Meitner!

L.M.: Please, I'm very busy.

W.: But it's important.

L.M.: What is it?

W.: The S.S. guards have come to your home and office. They were looking for you. I've brought your most important papers.

L.M.: Thank you, I wonder why they're looking for me. I've noticed they haven't been giving me my materials and instruments lately.

O.H.: It must be because you're Jewish.

W.: Look! The S.S.! You must get away. I'll help you pack.

L.M.: All right.

O.H.: I'll stall them. Here are our papers. You must carry on our work. (BUMP BUMP)

O.H.: Yes?

S.S.: (Appear at door.)

O.H.: Come in.

S.S.: Heil Hitler! Where is Lise Meitner?

O.H.: Oh, it's three o'clock. She's out to lunch. Any message?

S.S.: Yes, tell her to report to district three police station. Good day. (Rips name card of Lise Meitner off door.)

Scene V:

Physics laboratory at Columbia University. News of atomic fission is discussed. Professor Einstein attends conference and is persuaded to go to the President and ask for the money to develop the atomic bomb project.

APPENDIX 23

Samples of Children's Papers: Fifth Grade

Land

Jane wrote: "If we didn't have any land we wouldn't exist or even be born or if we were, we'd be falling through clear space. We need land to walk on, grow things on, make shelter on, or if we didn't have it we'd starve or perish to death."

All the class decided some kind of land was necessary for everybody and always had been. They said people couldn't live in a land where it was too cold or where it was so dry that nothing would grow. They thought one thing that had made the United States great was that we have so much land that is good for growing things that we need.

Farms

Bill wrote: "We need farms because they give us food. They give us, milk, meat, vegetables, and fruit. We could not eat without farms. Farming is a hard working job. Farmers have many acres of land. There are many people in the United States that have to be fed. I couldn't drink milk, vegetables, meat, and fruit for my meals if we didn't have farms."

The class decided that farms must have good soil and enough rain to make things grow. If there isn't enough rain, sometimes people build dams and irrigate the dry land. The Indians raised a few things to eat but most of them ate wild animals and wild fruit and vegetables. Explorers carried much of their food with them. They drove pigs on the trail when they marched. White people brought cows, horses, pigs, and chickens to our country. The Indians had none of these animals.

Roads

Alice wrote: "If we didn't have roads we could not eat. Farms are in the country and we need Roads so the trucks can bring vegetables, fruit, and meat. The cows give you and I milk and if we did not have roads we could not drink milk."

The class thought the United States had many good roads. They named roads for trucks and automobiles, water roads for boats, railroads for trains, and air roads for airplanes.

Water

The class said we use water in many ways. We drink water, we wash in water, we have water roads for boats, we use water in industries.

Air

The class said there was air everywhere on earth, not just in our country.

Trees and Wood

Jack wrote: "If there were no wood I wouldn't be writing now with a pencil and wouldn't be sitting in my seat. The floors we are standing on would not be here."

The class said that there were many trees in our country when white people first came here. They said the explorers found many forests. Settlers cut down many trees.

Coal

Anne and Paul wrote that we would freeze and die without coal.

The class said Indians did not use coal. They used wood for fire. The class said we had lots of coal in the United States.

Oil

Susan and Lynne wrote about oil that we use in cooking. Lynne also wrote that we needed oil for cars. David wrote that gas is used for cars, planes, and trains.

The class decided that gasoline is made from oil that comes out of the ground and that we have much oil in the United States. The Indians and explorers did not use oil.

Metals

Margo wrote: "If we didn't have metals we wouldn't have machines and if we didn't have machines we wouldn't get oil out of the ground."

The class decided that most of the things we use such as their desks and their clothes are made by machines. They said the Indians did not use metals. They made their tools out of stone and wood. The explorers brought some machines like guns. They had tools made out of metal. Farmers today use machines on their farms. Automobiles, engines, and planes are machines. The class thought we had many machines in the United States today. That was one reason why we were a powerful country and won the war.

Bridges

Gerry and Ellen wrote about bridges.

The class said our big bridges like the George Washington are made out of metal. They can cross big rivers. The Indians used logs made out of trees to cross little rivers.

Science

Mary wrote: "In Bablo [Balboa] days they had science too. But they had not as much science as they had now. Science is a very interesting study. If they were no science nobody will know nothing about the moon and the atom Bomb and plane and car and train and about the sun too."

APPENDIX 24

Sixth-Grade Play: A Visit to Mexico

The following play was worked out by the children without any written dialogue. After its successful performance the children were asked to write about their play. One of the boys brought this, saying that he wanted to remember the play later on so he wrote it out. Of course it is not accurate, but it gives the sense extremely well. Only portions of the play are given here.

Cast: Editor   Secretary
       Reporter (Ralph)   Photographer
       Office boy   Reporter (Rudolph)

Scene I:

(Scene opens. We find editor walking into his office reading a newspaper. He sits down at his desk and starts to open his morning mail. Reporter [Rudolph] comes in.)

Editor: Hello, Talts. The arrangements to be present at the San Francisco conference are ready. You are to leave at once.

Reporter: I'll do my best and I'll be back in a few days.

Editor: Tell Kingsley and White to come into my office as soon as they arrive. I'm going to call up the Pan American Airlines and see if I can get two tickets to Mexico.

(We now switch you to the secretary's office.)

Reporter: Hot dog! Where do we go this time? Germany, Belgium, or maybe the South Pacific?

Editor: You go to ahhh . . .

(Office boy comes in.)

Office boy: Pardon me, boss, here's your tickets to Mexico.

Photographer: Who's going to Mexico?

Editor: You are.

Reporter and photographer together: Mexico!!

Photographer: What do you think this is, boss, a vacation?

Reporter: After I've been sleeping in foxholes, eating in foxholes and once a shell burst fifty yards away from me and now, to Mexico!

Photographer: Boss, why do *we* have to go to Mexico?

Editor: I want you to go down there and write a story on how to have a Good Neighbor Policy.

Reporter: Well, boss, I guess you talked me into it. When do we leave?

Editor: In two hours.

Photographer: Two hours! What do you think we are? I have to say good-by to my folks, pack my clothes, why I even have to have my hair done.

Reporter: So do I. . . . I mean I have to say good-by to my folks too.

Scene II:

(Airport in Mexico City.)

Man: Hello, Mrs. Tomlin. I haven't seen you in ages. Where have you been keeping yourself?

Lady: Oh, I've been working for the Red Cross. Do you know when the next plane will arrive?

Man: Let's ask the lady at the information desk.

(Enter two men.)

Happy: What are you doing in these parts?

Dingle: Oh, I got me a big job now as the Mayor's chauffeur. Fifteen pesos a day.

Pedro: Are you sure not a week?

Dingle: A day.

Happy: Whom are you waiting for?

Dingle: Some reporters from New York. Probably some stuffed shirts.

Loud-speaker: Plane coming in on Runway 7-A. Clear the field.

(Plane lands.)

(Hostesses check the passengers off the plane. The airport starts to get deserted.)

Reporter: I knew there would be no guide waiting for us. That's what you get for being a nice guy.

(Happy comes up and offers his assistance. As he is about to take them away, Dingle runs up.)

Dingle: Are you the two reporters from New York?

Reporter: Yes.

(He explains that he is their guide. He takes their bags and tells them that he is taking them to the finest hotel in Mexico City. He then tells them what they would do throughout the next day.)

Scene III:

(Marketplace in Mexico City.)

(Scene opens. We find sellers opening their shops and displaying their ware. Sleepers come in and start to go to sleep. Tortilla sellers and flower girls and buyers come on. Tortilla sellers and flower girls begin to sing. Sleepers awakened by the music begin to dance. Reporter, photographer, and guide come in.)

Photographer: What a beautiful scene. (She walks off to the side and starts to take pictures.)

(Guide tells about a city with 365 churches for each day of the year.)

Photographer: Would you ask those tortilla sellers and flower girls if I could take their picture?

(Guide talks to them. They line up for the picture. The photographer is about to take the picture when a burro and its owner blocks her view. After much trouble the picture is taken.)

Scene IV:

(Scene opens in editor's office.)

Secretary: Boss, here's a telegram from Kingsley and White.

(Editor takes the letter. Reads it.)

Editor: They say they'll be home today. They may come any min—

Reporter: Hi, boss.

Editor: Hello, Kingsley.

(Reporter tells about the things he saw and heard of. Editor tells him he would rather read it in the paper than listen to it now.)

Editor: And as a reward I'm going to send you to the front lines in Europe.

Reporter: We don't want to go to Europe. We want to go back to Mexico, the land of color and music.

Editor: What's the use?

APPENDIX 25

Notes on a Workshop Meeting with Science Resource Leader

The science resource leader was the *leader* of this discussion. He opened by saying that he had looked over the social studies curriculum, especially the science section, which he felt was quite good. He asked if they could tell him what it was that made elementary grade teachers shy away from science teaching. The consensus of opinion was that it was due to lack of confidence which stemmed from two causes: teachers do not rehearse experiments ahead of time, and they think the children expect them to know all the answers. *A teacher* commented, "Should it be an experiment that you are presenting? Isn't the 'let's find out' idea more important than the 'here's the way it happens' idea?"

The leader took as an approach to a scientific problem the question, "Why do Arabs wear white woolen robes in the desert?" How can we use this question both for social studies and for science? What has white got to do with it? What has woolen got to do with it? How do we find out that white repels the sun's rays? We can take two thermometers and protect one with a white paper and one with a black and compare the temperature readings.

He then pointed out that the range of temperature in the desert is much greater than in other places and asked for reasons. A teacher replied that the air in the desert was very dry. He asked, "How does proximity to ocean or other large body of water make the temperature more even?" The reply was that water gains and loses heat at a slower rate than earth. *The leader* asked, "How can we show this in the classroom?" *A teacher* said that with a pot of water and a pot of earth and two thermometers this could be demonstrated. Another said that the experiment would be completed by letting both pots cool again after they had gained heat by being placed on the radiators.

A teacher asked, "How can you get across the idea of directions?" If you have a window in your room that gets the sun, you can set up a board with a pencil set perpendicularly in it so that it will cast a shadow. Appoint a monitor to make a mark each hour where the shadow falls on the board. This, then, marks the movement of the sun from east to west, and thus those points are established and from them you can place north and south. To impress directions on the children put emphasis on such names as *West* Street, *South* Ferry.

The science specialist said that he noticed that music was a strong part of this syllabus. He took a tuning fork and struck it and placed it on the table and the note was heard; however, when it was struck and held in the air, no sound could be heard. Why was this? The sound waves were dissipated in the second case but reflected in strength from the table, which acts as a sounding board. That is why stringed instruments need a box as well as strings. A light ball suspended by the side of a tuning fork will bounce back and forth when the fork is vibrated, showing the presence of the sound waves even though they cannot be heard.

A teacher gave the example of the dog teams that Steffanson would have tied outside his snow house. The sound of their fighting could not be heard if a man were sitting with his head up inside the house, but if he lay with his ear to the ground the sound came through perfectly clearly to him.

A teacher spoke of the play telephones which are made of two Dixie cups and a length of string as an example of the transmission of sound vibrations. *The science specialist* pointed out that it works better with waxed cord—that it can easily be demonstrated that the sound waves are being transmitted by the cord, for if you pinch it the sound is stopped.

APPENDIX 26

Annual Report of Bank Street Public School Workshop, 1948–49. (Excerpts.)

The program of the Workshops can be presented in a few major categories, although it is obvious that these areas are by no means separate in function:

I. Staff and Organization
II. Services to Individual Teachers in Classrooms
III. General School Services
IV. Workshop Courses
V. Research Program
VI. Curriculum Research
VII. Broader Aspects of Program
VIII. Planning for Next Year

The present setup of the Bank Street Workshop continues in somewhat the same pattern as that of last year. We have continued in P.S. I, III, and IV, Manhattan, as fully as staff permits, and as the demand for our services persists. . . .

One departure from past policy has been to make it possible for teachers not attending Workshop courses to receive classroom help and to admit to the courses some people who are not having contact with our worker in their classrooms. We feel this a good procedure at this time, particularly in School I. Some teachers here have begun to feel familiar and secure in the discussion of the new program in education but still want help in the implementation of their curriculum needs; conversely, other teachers have wished to continue Workshop courses, sometimes for the practical purposes of increment credit, which these courses carry, but did not feel the need for guidance in curriculum enrichment in their classrooms. . . .

We have continued to offer teachers any services for which they have expressed a need. We feel this to be a sound approach, even with teachers who have worked with us for some time, because their acceptance and use of our contribution is a developmental process, growing in depth of understanding as well as in practical application. Teachers progress from using us merely as the source for a story, or group reading mechanics, or setting up of a unit, to developing with us a total experience and planning for the outcomes in learning. . . .

We have been co-operating with the district co-ordinator of the science program, and working with him and one of our assistant principals. We have helped to develop science curriculums for the fourth and fifth grades which have received widespread approval. We feel that we had a special contribution here in helping teachers to see the possibilities of a science program growing out of the total experience, as well as becoming one of the enriching factors in it. . . .

Our assistance has been asked in all the schools on requisitions of materials and books. In addition to the special materials and books that have been made available to the Bank Street Workshop through special grants of funds by the Elementary Division, we have worked on general supply and book lists. . . .

It is interesting to note that as one works with these teachers over a long period, progress goes somewhat from the immediate, practically applicable techniques toward theoretical understanding and personal experimentation. Of course, this is not the straight line to growth and each year we are attempting to respond and relate to these growth periods. But as we function with groups for longer periods, we find teachers with deeper readiness for self-activity, so that our program becomes a Workshop in the best use of the term. . . .

In all the schools there has been the beginning of thinking toward curriculum concept, growing out of and closely related to the field of child development. Wherever possible the child development series in the Workshop sessions has been followed by visual aids materials to demonstrate new curriculum concepts, and then rounded out by discussion of curriculum problems in specifics. . . .

Members of the staff are called upon to participate in innumerable group meetings as specific as parent groups in some schools and as broad as nation-wide conferences in other cases. One member of our staff has been called upon several times this year to discuss the question of the contribution of the experimental private school to public education. Others have served on panels to discuss the ways in which we adapt the new program to the realities of the public school classroom. We have presented our program to university classes. We have been asked to serve on various Board of Education committees such as Curriculum Revision. We have met with other groups experimenting in the schools, notably the people carrying out an experiment on new techniques in block building. . . .

We feel in thinking toward next year that we have reached this point (that of not conducting a Workshop) in our work with School I. This school has provided three of this year's Workshop staff, it has become deeply conscious of the dynamics of the interrelatedness of child needs and curriculum development, its administrative staff is tremendously interested and involved in providing creative supervision and in helping teachers in the implementation of the new program. The Bank Street Workshop group is far too realistic to consider all of this development as direct outgrowth of its program, but it would be false modesty not to feel that considerable drive in these directions was provided by its approach. We feel that at this time the Bank Street group might make better use of its services if it were to spread to another school. It is the hope that in the relationship with School I the Bank Street Workshop will remain extremely active in an advisory role and stand ready to help whenever called upon. It is also hoped that whatever research work is current in School I will proceed there. . . .

We have an ever-growing need for broadening the base of our contribution and would hope to amplify the research, the writing, and the participation in broader educational groups as a goal for next year. We also see the need for taking our contribution up to supervisory levels. . . .

The year has been a fruitful one in the consolidation of past service and the development of new ones. It is unrealistic, however, to think of the situation without its problems and even pitfalls, but the schools in which we work may be described as open and letting in the light, and in deep need of further development. Even if every teacher in each of these schools were completely accepting of our offering, we would still need to work desperately hard to bring to classroom practice a profundity of approach that makes of teaching the creative, dynamic performance that is theoretically accepted in the new education. That must remain the major goal and larger scope of our program.

APPENDIX 27

Sample Schedules of Workshop Sessions

School II

1. February 8 — Registration and Planning.

2. February 15 —⎤
3. March 1 — ⎬ Anecdotal Records—their making, their uses,
4. March 8 — ⎦ and their value.

5. March 15 —⎤ Film: *Near Home.*
6. March 22 — ⎪
7. March 29 — ⎬ Curriculum Analysis and Adaptation. (Sessions
8. April 5 — ⎦ divided according to grade levels.)
9. April 12 — Visual Instruction in the Classroom. (Specialist from Board of Education.)

10. April 26 — Science in the Classroom. (Specialist from Board of Education.)

11. May 3 —⎤
12. May 10 — ⎬ Map Thinking and Map Making. (Geography
13. May 17 — ⎦ specialist.)

14. May 21 — Trip Around Manhattan.
15. May 31 — Review and Examination.

School III

1. February 10 — Registration and Planning.

2. February 17 —⎤
3. February 24 — ⎪
4. March 3 — ⎬ The New Teacher in the New Program.
5. March 10 — ⎦

6. March 17 — Play Materials and Activities:
                    (a) Film: *Understanding Children's Play.*
7. March 24 —   (b) Informal Dramatics: Use of Puppets and
                         Dramatic Play.
8. March 31 —   (c) Activity Program in Action. Film: *Meet-
                         ing the Emotional Needs of Children.*
9. April   7 —   (d) (1) Assembly Programs (3rd—6th-
                              year teachers).
                         (2) Ways of Dramatizing (Kinder-
                              garten—2nd-year teachers).
10. April 28 — Mechanics of Organizing a Work Period.
11. May   5 — Social Studies Curriculum.
                    (1) Kindergarten—Second-Year Teachers.
                    (2) Third- and Fourth-Year Teachers.
                    (3) Fifth- and Sixth-Year Teachers.
12. May   12 — Arithmetic Thinking. (Board of Education Spe-
                    cialist.)
13. May   19 — Science in the Classroom. (Board of Education
                    Specialist.)
14. May   26 —
      or 21   Trip Around Manhattan.
15. June   2 — Review and Examination.

A Note About the Author

From her appointment in 1906 as first Dean of Women and first woman on the faculty at the University of California and throughout her thirty-four years as Chairman of the Bureau of Educational Experiments (now known as The Bank Street Schools), Lucy Sprague Mitchell has left her mark as an initiator and leader in many phases of the educational field: her work with children, teachers, and her many books and publications.

In her first experiences as a teacher of children, she worked with three educational pioneers: Caroline Pratt, founder of the City and Country School; Elizabeth Irwin, founder of the Little Red School House; and Harriet Johnson, first director of the Bank Street Nursery School. She has taught all elementary school ages and has been teacher or educational adviser in fourteen experimental schools. She is currently Chairman of the Bank Street program, a plan dedicated to the teaching of teachers and the establishment of school workshops in private experimental schools. It is Mrs. Mitchell's belief that this work is a major contribution to the advancement of public as well as private education.

In 1912 she married Wesley Clair Mitchell, the economist, and they made their home in New York City. With four children of her own, Mrs. Mitchell had to make the most of spare moments: much of the famous Here and Now Story Book *was written on top of a Fifth Avenue bus.*

Her other books include Our Growing World Series; North America; Horses, Now and Long Ago; Young Geographers, *and she is co-author of* Manhattan, Now and Long Ago; Skyscrapers; My Country 'Tis of Thee *and* The People of the United States.